T0166465

THE PLAYWRIGHT'S
VOICE

Other TCG Books by David Savran:

Breaking the Rules: The Wooster Group

In Their Own Words: Contemporary American Playwrights
Includes interviews with: Lee Breuer, Christopher Durang,
Richard Foreman, Maria Irene Fornes, Charles Fuller, John Guare,
Joan Holden, David Henry Hwang, David Mamet, Emily Mann,
Richard Nelson, Marsha Norman, David Rabe, Wallace Shawn,
Stephen Sondheim, Megan Terry, Luis Valdez, Michael Weller,
August Wilson and Lanford Wilson.

THE PLAYWRIGHT'S
VOICE

AMERICAN DRAMATISTS ON MEMORY, WRITING AND THE POLITICS OF CULTURE

DAVID SAVRAN

Theatre Communications Group

The Playwright's Voice: American Dramatists on Memory, Writing and the Politics of Culture is published by Theatre Communications Group, Inc., 355 Lexington Ave., New York, NY 10017–0217.

Condensed versions of interviews with Tony Kushner, Paula Vogel and Mac Wellman appeared in *American Theatre* magazine.

Due to space constraints, credits for author photographs and page xi epigraphs can be found on page 359.

This publication is made possible in part with public funds from the New York State Council on the Arts, a State Agency.

TCG books are exclusively distributed to the book trade by Consortium Book Sales and Distribution, 1045 Westgate Dr., St. Paul, MN 55114.

LIBRARY OF CONGRESS CATALOGING-IN-PUBLICATION DATA

The playwright's voice : American dramatists on memory, writing, and the politics of culture / edited by David Savran. — 1st ed.
p. cm.
ISBN 1–55936–163–8 (pbk. : alk. paper)
1. Dramatists, American—20th century Interviews. 2. American drama—20th century—History and criticism—Theory, etc. 3. Culture—Political aspects—United States. 4. Autobiographical memory in literature. 5. Playwriting. I. Savran, David, 1950– .
PS352.P575   1999
812'.5409—dc21   99–18985
CIP

Book design and composition by Lisa Govan
Cover design by Carin Goldberg

First Edition, May 1999

To Loraine and Jack Savran,

Who fostered my love for theatre

And took me to see my first "adults only" movie,

Who's Afraid of Virginia Woolf?

Contents

Acknowledgments

First and foremost, I want to thank all the playwrights for their extraordinary generosity of spirit, for the clarity and force of their ideas and for their willingness to engage with me on a number of complex and contentious issues. These conversations proved illuminating and provocative in often unexpected ways, and have helped me to understand the contradictions at play in American theatre and culture at a critical—and, it seems to me, rather perilous—historical juncture.

Second, my heartfelt appreciation to Benjamin Gerdes, who devoted himself brilliantly to the difficult task of transcribing the tapes while retaining a powerful sense of the speaking voice. His hard work, care and dedication helped to turn the completion of this project into a genuine pleasure. And his thoughtful feedback on both the interviews and introductions was invaluable.

Third, I want to thank the many people with whom I have discussed this project and who have, in very different ways, facilitated its completion: Mark Cohen, Bonnie Metzgar, Terry Nemeth, Gwendolyn Parker, Steven Samuels, Ronn Smith, Sylvia Stein; the students in my contemporary drama classes at Brown University; and Samantha Rachel Rabetz for her fine editing of the manuscript.

Finally, my great thanks to the two people without whom this book would not exist: Paula Vogel, with whom over the past twenty-five years I have enjoyed a peerless conversation—one to which this volume will, I hope, make a small contribution. And to Scott Teagarden, whose remarkable insights into theatre, writing and culture are everywhere woven into this text.

WARDEN: You're taking nothing with you but the clothes on your back.
CHAPLAIN: I'm taking much more than that.
WARDEN: Aw. Maybe I'd better have you frisked on the way out.
CHAPLAIN: You could strip me naked and I'd still have these.
WARDEN: These what?
CHAPLAIN: Memories—shadows—ghosts!

—**Tennessee Williams,**
Not about Nightingales (1938)

Like performance, memory operates as both quotation and invention, an improvisation on borrowed themes, with claims on the future as well as the past.

—**Joseph Roach,**
Cities of the Dead: Circum-Atlantic Performance (1996)

The Haunted Stage

In the final moments of Paula Vogel's *How I Learned to Drive*, Li'l Bit sits down at the wheel of her car, sees the spirit of her Uncle Peck in her rearview mirror, and smiles. No matter where she goes, the reflection suggests he will follow. For in that moment the play brilliantly—and literally—illuminates a ghostly presence that will always comfort and unsettle her. Yet *How I Learned to Drive* is hardly unique in its habit of raising the dead. As the twentieth century comes to an end, American plays are suddenly full of ghosts, ghosts that are absolutely central both to the plays' themes and to their emotional impact. From the spirit of Uncle Peck to the surprisingly gentle apparition of Ethel Rosenberg in Tony Kushner's *Angels in America*, from the ghost of a forsaken lover in Philip Kan Gotanda's *Ballad of Yachiyo* to the specter of a black Abraham Lincoln (called The Foundling Father) in Suzan-Lori Parks's *The America Play*, the American theatre is truly a haunted stage.

Why, I wonder, is it haunted? What is it haunted by? Why have these emanations from a different time and a different place mysteriously taken up residence in America's theatres?

The haunting of American stages is undoubtedly a complicated phenomenon with as many causes as there are ghosts. And there is no question but that today's theatre is by no means unique in its fascination with things mysterious and unexplained. For the occult has become extremely popular during the nervous nineties. Stephen King remains a synonym for best-seller, *The X-Files* racks up Emmy awards, while the latest incarnations of *Alien* or *Halloween* (along with their barely distinguishable kin) fill the local multiplexes. Trying to understand the renewed popularity of various occult genres, one must bear in mind that they do far more than arouse terror. For the occult is also an ironically comforting experience insofar as it is always about mastering the unknown, controlling the uncontrollable, attaching a shape and an identity to formless and nameless fears. And it is little wonder that the first hour of an occult movie is always far more frightening than the second, and the vague intimations of an alien presence on a spaceship far more unsettling than the slime-dripping monster that belatedly rears its ugly head. For horror cannot be vanquished until it is seen and comprehended. Unseen, it is uncontrollable. The final victory over an occult terror signals therefore not only the hero's but also our own vicarious (and temporary) mastery of terror.

At the same time, however, the occult does more than assuage our own personal fears. It also operates on a broader cultural level, as a way of dealing with certain anxieties that we, as a nation, harbor. And in attempting to understand why the nineties have borne witness to a resurgence of the occult, I am tempted to read our monsters allegorically, as the materialization of new anxieties. In the wake of the Cold War, the geopolitical equilibrium of forty-five years has given way to a more unpredictable world order that has seen a proliferation of limited and local wars, and increasing alarms about the spread of chemical, biological and nuclear weapons. Confronting these developments, we Americans, in seeing the alien queen or Godzilla killed off, can imagine our triumph, however provisionally, over our own alleged enemies—be they Saddam Hussein, Fidel Castro or the next dictator du jour.

The recent occult revival may also represent the flip side of a new wave of spirituality that is linked to the New Age movement. For the past ten years have seen the burgeoning of a multibillion-dollar industry of services and products that betray what trend spotters call a spiritual renaissance, as manifested by a rekindled interest in Asian philosophies and religions, meditation, alternative medicine, twelve-step programs and various religious fundamentalisms. During a period of doubt and insecurity, when there seems to be such a hunger on the part of so many to believe, the new spirituality confirms the existence of a benevolent higher power, while its complement, the occult, imagines that power to be more terrible than benign. The appearance of ghosts, angels and monsters in a wide range of cultural productions thus functions ironically to confirm that there is an order to the universe and a meaning to life and death. It suggests there are patterns and moments of clarity in human history. It proves there's someone out there who cares.

While this renewed popularity of both the occult and the spiritual is useful in explaining a surge in population of theatrical ghosts, spirits function rather differently on stage and on screen. For while there are undeniable similarities between theatre and film, the two occupy very different cultural niches. Tony Kushner and Wes Craven may use the same devices but the different media guarantee that these devices will produce different meanings and effects. It is important therefore to consider the relative cultural positions of theatre, on the one hand, and film and television, on the other.

Perhaps the most obvious distinction between theatre and mass culture is the former's considerably higher admission price. A ticket to Broadway or a regional theatre can cost up to ten times the price of a movie ticket or four times that of a month of cable TV. Surveys, not surprisingly, have shown that most regular theatregoers have far more disposable income than the average moviegoer. Theatre's costliness means that it remains a more specialized art form and its audiences (like those for many independent films) are often well-educated and highly professionalized spectators. They pride themselves on their taste for work that is by and large more aesthetically adventurous, confrontational and politically liberal than Hollywood's product. They go to the theatre, in other words, because it is more likely to tackle serious social issues in serious ways. (The exceptions to this pattern are the megamusicals and dance spectaculars which, delivering a sumptuously wrapped package, appeal to a wider audience than most so-called straight theatre and provide, essentially, a more classy—and live—version of mass culture.)

Popular movies like *Titanic* (as well as more modest efforts like *Forrest Gump*), although relying on tried-and-true formulas and old-fashioned plots, have come in recent years increasingly to depend on special effects. Computer-generated images and sounds allow filmmakers to guarantee that their product will be bigger, shinier—and, most important, newer—than anything that has come before. Theatre, in contrast, remains curiously wedded to the past. Not only is it one of the oldest performing arts, but its legacy seems far grander than its somewhat precarious present state. Most regional theatre companies anchor their seasons on the classics—from Shakespeare to Tennessee Williams, Ibsen to Rodgers and Hammerstein—while Broadway has been deluged over the past decade by so many revivals that the Tony Awards have had to invent new categories for them. At the same time, the

American theatre has not become, as most opera has, merely a museum in which the classics are annually trotted out in fancy dress.

The lifeblood of theatre remains new plays, plays that give relatively knowledgeable audiences an opportunity to see debated, and to debate themselves, important social issues. The vitality of social drama does not mean that Brecht's activist (and revolutionary) theatre is alive and well and living in America. But it does mean that theatre remains a forum for the examination of often difficult and contentious issues. For example, racist institutions, sexual violence, homophobia and even the workings of capitalism are interrogated more openly and vigorously in theatre (and in independent film) than in mass culture.

At least since the 1930s, with the Federal Theatre Project and the Group Theatre, and continuing with the development of Off-Off-Broadway in the 1960s, the stage has been defined as a critical and oppositional force in American culture. And the most honored and well-known playwrights—from Williams, Miller and Albee to Kushner and Vogel—have invariably acquired their renown in part by challenging received opinions. The relatively oppositional positioning of theatre, moreover, together with its status as a public forum, has enabled a number of playwrights to become forceful public advocates and intellectuals, penning opinion columns and op-ed pieces and speaking out against various attempts to curtail civil liberties and freedom of speech. Given this history, it is little wonder that conservatives in Congress have targeted the National Endowment for the Arts for extinction and that theatre artists in particular, especially the so-called NEA Four (Holly Hughes who is interviewed in this volume, Karen Finley, John Fleck and Tim Miller), have been caricatured as the wanton and indecent destroyers of what pass, in some quarters at least, for traditional American values. And while Congress has yet to extinguish adventurous and daring art in this country, the decline in public funding (combined with the clamor of the Christian Coalition and other right-wing activists) has intimidated some theatre companies into designing more conservative seasons.

Given theatre's historically oppositional footing, it is unlikely, it seems to me, that ghosts and the occult function on the stage simply to comfort the spectator and reinforce the status quo. (Even in mass culture, this process of reassurance is complex and uneven insofar as no occult film is ever able to put completely to rest all the demons it has raised.) But before analyzing exactly what ghosts enable a playwright to do, I want to consider theatre as a unique medium, since it is quite literally haunted in a way that film and television can never be.

For theatre is distinguished from mass culture by more than its penchant for social criticism. It is also the most literary of the performing arts and plays have long (and somewhat misleadingly) been considered a branch of literature. Despite the high profiles of certain directors and designers, playwrights and their plays are usually taken to be the generative forces behind most all theatrical productions. Performances may be evanescent, but the playwright's written word is imagined as a kind of time capsule, a tomb in which are interred both his or her own ideas, predilections and emotions and the remains of a vanished time and culture. (It is little wonder that the citizens of the fictional Grover's Corners include a copy of *Our Town* in the cornerstone of their new bank.)

If the playtext is indeed a kind of memorial, then theatrical performance must be akin to awakening the dead. For both performing and reading are ways of remembering; they jog the memory and help restore what has been lost. But if performance is an act of remembering, it must also remember what in effect was never there. For in bringing a written text to life, performance always reveals that the text is incomplete, that it is composed of what are, in effect, dead words. Yet as a form of resuscitation, it must revivify this incompletely realized artifact in relation to the desires, fantasies and beliefs of the playwright—which can be endlessly hypothesized but never fully known—and to those of the living actors, designers and director.

Performance based on a written text thus always (and uneasily) occupies two historical moments: the moments in which it was written and in which it is performed. Negotiating between past and present, theatre is always about not the coincidence but the gap between written text and performance, writer and director, character and actor. Theatre, in short, is always about the impossibility of representing what was never fully there in the first place. For performance is always in thrall to a written text that is not quite alive, yet not quite dead. Film may be haunted by the absent actor whose luminous reincarnation fills the screen, but theatre is haunted by the absent playwright whose text functions as a kind of ghost, mediating between death and life.

Given the status of the dramatic text as a memorial, an incomplete project, a ghost, it is little wonder that the theatre, from Greek and Renaissance tragedy to Japanese Nō, has long been linked to the occult and populated by ghosts. Actors are alive on the stage before us, but they are of necessity only standing in for those imaginary beings who, like the ghost of King Hamlet, vanish before we can touch them. As Mac Wellman's *Crowbar* so powerfully suggests, every performance, like every theatre building, is haunted by what has come before, by the ghosts of characters and actors who have trod the boards. Entering a suburban multiplex, we are swept into the future, dazzled by technology, computer animation or, at the least, the play of light on a brilliantly blank screen. But entering a theatre, either a Broadway house or a repertory theatre whose walls are invariably dotted with photographs and posters from previous productions, we walk into a past that is haunted by the spirits of dedicated, hardworking and sometimes inspired artists. And despite recent advances in sound and lighting technologies, theatre remains curiously antitechnological, a place for those who do and those who act—in the broadest sense—a site for remaking and reimagining the self. For if film is about technology and plotting, then theatre is about character, about the richness of a human subject about whom one fact is indisputable: he or she at some point is going to die. And in commemorating this mortality, each theatrical performance also silently acknowledges its own evanescence, the fact that it is a unique and fleeting occasion that can never be repeated. Like Hamlet, it always dies at the end of the last act.

At the close of the twentieth century, as the American theatre has tried to carve out a space for itself distinct from film and television, it has become the place where we meet both our own past and that of our culture. For it is my contention that ghosts are so important on our stages because they are a point of intersection between memory and history. Memory, on the one hand, is usually understood to be spontaneous, a part of lived experience. Connecting us with the past, it fills us out. It gives us identity. It is alive, immediate and concrete. It is communicated through the body, through gesture, words and rituals. Memory is in our blood, in our genes. History, on the other hand, is assumed to come to us from outside. It is constructed through cultural narratives we read or watch or listen to. Even our own memories become history only when, in effect, they are no longer ours, when we meet them again in someone else's stories. For no matter how vibrant or how densely populated by the sweating, teeming masses, history always has something vaguely abstract about it.

The theatrical ghost is a figure uniquely positioned in relation to both memory and history. As a token of memory, the ghost is intensely personalized, emanating from and materializing characters' fears and desires (and playing off of our own as well). For like Uncle Peck or Yachiyo, the ghost returns almost ritualistically to tell characters (and audiences) what they know but would rather forget. It is thus a concrete manifestation of fears and desires that, because they have never been resolved, literally haunt a character. For the ghost traditionally is a tortured soul who has not yet found peace but who walks the earth seeking satisfaction. The ghost, in short, is unfulfilled and only appears to those figures who are themselves unfulfilled. For the ghost is always the token of an intensely personal loss, a loss so great or so painful that one is loath to acknowledge it. And coming to peace with the ghost means coming to terms with this loss in such a way that it is transformed, as if by sorcery, into a kind of profit. Thus, *How I Learned to Drive* is about learning that what has been lost can never be struck from one's memory, that L'il Bit must live always with the unexpectedly comforting reflection of Uncle Peck in her rearview mirror. It demonstrates that Peck, like all ghosts, is also her own reflection, a figure who has taken root inside her and yet stands apart, watching her from a distance.

If history is understood as a chronicle of struggles among nations, peoples and classes, then the theatrical ghost is also a historical figure. For it is the product not only of personal memory, but also of an interplay of social, political and economic forces. The ghost may not be that of a celebrated public figure, but it nonetheless serves as a representative and reminder of the skirmishes that constitute history, skirmishes, for example, between parents and their rebellious offspring or between Hasidic Jews and Afro-Caribbeans in Crown Heights.

Insofar as each skirmish has a winner and a loser, then the ghost must be seen as a casualty of history. For it is usually numbered among the losers. It may not imagine itself a victim but its refusal to die, to disappear, leads one to suspect that it has in some way been wronged or oppressed. Thus, for example, the spectral figures of Yachiyo and The Foundling Father are the spirits whom the victors would rather forget. *Ballad of Yachiyo* resurrects a young woman who has committed suicide to illustrate the tragic effects of the sexual double standard in a small Japanese-American community. And *The America Play* calls up a black Abraham Lincoln stranded in The Great Hole of History to represent the legacy of slavery that continues to haunt American society. Both these oppressed spirits roam the earth because they cannot be consigned neatly to the past. Rather, they are the sign of the interpenetration of the present by the past, of the fact that we still live with the demons, spirits and ghosts of those persons and oppressive social institutions we thought we had put behind us.

Located on the threshold between two worlds, the ghost is a token of the fact that society lives in all of us and that we are both its reflections and its makers. It thereby ends up, perhaps surprisingly, breaking down the distinction between memory and history. Or more precisely, it represents the occasion for the transformation of memory into history, the individual into the collective and the particular into the universal. It demonstrates that what is memory for some is history for others. For as we watch other people remembering, the struggles in which they participate and the society in which they are forced to play their parts are illuminated and clarified. We see their defeats reimagined, if not exactly as victories, then at least as spurs to rethink and reclaim their losses. We see memory itself become a kind of phantom, the illusion produced by individual consciousness in thrall to History.

Living as we do in a uniquely forgetful culture that regards last month's headlines as dusty chronicles, the theatre provides a way of *re-membering*, of literally piecing together what has been lost. For the American theatre is haunted in so many ways: by its own glorious past, by the culture of which it is a part, by the written texts of vanished playwrights and by characters who are in turn stricken with memory. It is haunted by the fact that it is no longer a central feature of American culture. As so many plays by the playwrights in this volume suggest, the theatre at the end of the twentieth century is also haunted by the idea of America, by the ideal of a nation founded on the glorious principles of freedom and equality. It is haunted by the sixties, the last truly progressive and utopian era—one through which most of the playwrights lived and whose dreams continue to inspirit them. Yet a mere glance at the recent history of this nation reveals that these utopian promises have consistently and brutally been betrayed. For America itself is haunted quite specifically by the disillusionment and the losses of the past twenty-five years: by the growing disparity between rich and poor, black and white; by the backlash against feminism and affirmative action; by the increasing power of social and fiscal conservatives; and by the gradual whittling away of possibilities for and incitements to change. Taking up these betrayals, theatre (as *Angels in America* so vividly demonstrates) analyzes them even as it works to keep alive the utopian dream. It is, in a sense, haunted by an America that has yet to be born.

Despite their utopian character, the ghosts that drift across our stages are in the end only ghosts, that is, a sign of the increasing inaccessibility of a living past. As history has in recent years been displaced more and more by nostalgia—a whiff of the past from which social struggles have been conveniently excised—we can now imagine and experience history only as an intervention or invasion from without, as a ghost which suddenly materializes to confront a frightened and amnesiac population. As if to acknowledge and treat this amnesia, the theatre has for some become a space in which to remember what we have forgotten, and most important, to remember together. For theatre is a communal art form. It transforms an "I" into a "we," individual spectators into a group that assembles almost ritualistically to commune, to share fears and desires and to work out its anxieties. Unlike the movies, which for most people represent an intensely privatized and individualized experience, the theatre creates, as if by magic, a temporary community out of the multitude assembled to watch the ghosts tread the boards. And might it not be precisely the communal nature of theatre that will guarantee its survival even in an era when it is swamped by mass culture?

Most of the playwrights I interviewed thirteen years ago for *In Their Own Words* were pessimistic (to say the least) about the future of the American theatre. Yet several pointed out that the American theatre in fact consists of many different theatres, each with its own past and prospective future. And in the time since that volume was published, these theatres have yet to expire. Even the combined fury of Jesse Helms and Godzilla has been unable to stamp them out. Rather, Broadway, Off-Broadway, touring companies, regional theatres and even small experimental collectives seem to be experiencing something of a renaissance (and I point out this good fortune with a certain trepidation, knowing that it may not last). The causes of this renaissance are legion and have as much to do with the revitalization of cities, a drop in the urban crime rate and the precipitous rise of the stock market as with a reinvigoration of playwriting. But this volume unequivocally attests to the fact that a new generation of writers has appeared that has absorbed the innovations of the experimental theatre of the sixties and seventies. It is no longer obsessed with proving its contempt for the allegedly deadening effects of domestic realism, but instead moves easily (and without guilt) between realism and various highly theatricalized and/or presentational styles. At the same time, this generation, reared on movies and television, has breathed new life into theatre by at once borrowing and keeping its distance from mass culture. Taking identity politics for granted, it deals with questions of sexuality, race and gender with a frankness and combativeness that were unimaginable forty years ago. American theatre has been further reinvigorated by playwrights like Edward Albee, Terrence McNally and Ntozake Shange who may have come of age in the sixties or seventies, but whose playwriting has continued to move in original and unforeseen directions. For all the playwrights in this book are American originals who have produced bodies of work that play memory off of history, calling up ghosts in order to reread the past, to make it mean differently—and so to reimagine the future. They prove that the theatre may be haunted by its past, but that it is by no means dead. They prove that America may not have fulfilled its promises to all of its citizens, but that the idea of America— as a utopian nation—remains irresistible.

March 1999
Lincoln, Rhode Island

Edward Albee

The details of Edward Albee's youth are so well known they hardly bear reinteration. Named for his adoptive grandfather (owner of the Keith-Albee vaudeville circuit theatres), reared in luxury, kicked out of prestigious schools, he achieved instant success with the 1960 Off-Broadway production of *The Zoo Story*. Two years later, on the occasion of his Broadway debut, he suddenly found himself the most controversial playwright in America with *Who's Afraid of Virginia Woolf?*, acclaimed by some critics and theatregoers as "exhilarating" and "shattering" and reviled by others as an obscene, "sick play." Nevertheless, the unexpected success of this three-and-a-half-hour drama permanently changed the face of Broadway.

To this day, Albee remains a fiercely independent and uncompromising writer. A three-time Pulitzer Prize-winning playwright, he is heir to several traditions: the American naturalism of O'Neill and Williams, European existentialism and the self-reflexive modernism of Joyce, Eliot and Beckett. Albee's plays are anything but derivative, however, and from his earliest one-acts, he has honed a spare, precise and acerbic style that subjects human relationships to intensive scrutiny. For his plays take the stuff of naturalism—its focus on the nuclear family and bourgeois self-deception—in order to deconstruct it, to fragment and interrogate it and so defamiliarize that which is usually taken for granted. Albee's plays, in short, are about disorientation, about the incongruities between and among character, setting and action. Turning the living room into a kind of theatre, he examines the roles people take up and the games they play both to confront and to shield themselves from their fears and desires. Invigorating Broadway with the dynamism and danger of the experimental theatre, Albee—a self-styled "demonic social critic"—has endeavored to use the stage to make "statement[s] about the condition of 'man'" and "the nature of the art form with which he is working."

As a maker of statements, however, Albee remains more the speculative than the polemical writer for whom "entertainment means engagement," yet whose radicalism is arguably more formal than explicitly political. For he remains more metaphysician than moralist, and his plays are notable in part for their high seriousness—even at their most bitterly and incisively comic. Nonetheless, his work is dedicated to interrogating both the social and the theatrical by launching "an attack on the *un*conscious" in the belief that this offensive will produce social change. Perhaps the most radical examples of Albee's methods are the interlocking one-acts, *Box* and *Quotations from Chairman Mao-Tse Tung* (both 1968) which remain among the most serenely audacious plays ever performed on Broadway. The former (part of which is reprised at the end of *Mao*) is a play without characters, a post-apocalyptic threnody in which a woman's solitary voice mourns a vanished world. With a large, empty cube for a set, the voice laments the passing of an order that produced rationality, progress, art and geometry. Testing the limits of beauty, it puts memory, loss and pain at the service of art: "When art hurts. That is what to remember." Using the theatre as the vehicle for a kind of unpleasure, it examines the disparity between art's aesthetic power and its political impotence (although clearly a product of the social upheavals and the avant-gardism of the late sixties, its timeliness has not faded). *Mao*, meanwhile, sets four characters who deliver three interwoven monologues on the deck of an ocean liner that sits within the cube. Yet the play itself is also framed insofar as it both follows and precedes a performance of *Box*. Calling into question the basis for naturalistic drama— the congruence between container and the thing contained, between environment and character—the interwoven plays interrogate the relationship between the aesthetic and the social, forcing the audience to assume a far more actively interpretative role than it is accustomed to.

Although most of Albee's plays are less radical in their methods, his defamiliarizations of American naturalism and the well-made play are peopled by characters who, if not exactly ghosts, nevertheless disrupt the production of identity in provocative ways. Even *Virginia Woolf*, arguably Albee's most traditional play, is a struggle for control of the contradictory narratives that produce identity. Who, finally, are the real George and Martha? Or the real America whose first presidential couple they commemorate? In *The Lady from Dubuque* (1979), the house of a woman dying of cancer is invaded by the eponymous lady who claims to be her mother. Incredulous and exasperated, the dying woman's husband quietly asks the lady, "Who *are* you? *Really?*," to which the latter responds with the play's most important and baffling question: "Who are *you*? *Really?*" For although the lady is a stranger, an angel of death, a mother, a figure who brings both comfort and discomfort, the play refuses to identify her and she becomes the sign of the provisional and experimental nature of all identities. *Tiny Alice* (1964) is set in a great mansion whose library contains a huge model of the mansion, a model so real that it renders the mansion a mere "replica" of the model. This vertiginous space is presided over by Miss Alice, who, despite her almost limitless wealth and power, is herself only a "surrogate" for a greater Miss Alice, who is herself only a "surrogate" for a greater Miss Alice—and so on.

Among Albee's recent works, the one that most clearly foregrounds this seemingly infinite chain of ghost-like doubles is *Three Tall Women* (1991). This most "objective" of autobiographical plays fragments a woman much like his adoptive mother into three characters of different ages: ninety-two, fifty-two and twenty-six. Not until the second act, however—after the eldest suffers a stroke and is herself split into two— does it become clear that these figures describe the same woman at different stages in her life. As the characters provoke and unnerve each other, Albee cunningly dramatizes the process of reflection, the fact that one experiences one's self as both subject and object, as the one who knows (or never quite knows) and the one who is known (or never quite known). As the characters variously remember and look forward to a future that has already happened, they remind us that "you *can* think about yourself in the third person without being crazy." At the same time, the characters' fears that their material goods might be stolen points to the always precarious and vulnerable nature both of their possessions and of this self-as-third-person. For living under a regime of private property, the self, like the things around it, is always defined by the possibility of its being purloined. One is always threatened by the knowledge that one can never be fully self-possessed.

In dramatizing the impossibility of self-possession, *Three Tall Women* also performs the passage of time, turning the theatre into a site of memory. Visualizing temporality, it turns temporal difference into spatial difference. Although one may live both literally and figuratively beside one's self, the play shows that there is "*another* kind of joy" that issues from that dual positioning. For the play's second act introduces another figure, The Boy, who never speaks and is clearly a stand-in for the author. His silent presence suggests that being beside one's self, looking forward and looking back, living the time of the "now" and the "always," also happens to describe the position of the writer. For in dramatizing the relationship between mother and son, the play simultaneously enacts the relationship between writing and performance, the fact that these acts are no more coincidental than the three tall women. In his introduction to the play, Albee reflects on the process of composition itself, acknowledging that writers "have the schizophrenic ability to both participate in their lives and, at the same time, observe themselves participating in their lives." Acting as surrogates for the dramatic text, the three tall women represent a visualization of the process of writing. And the play that bears their name, by bringing together writing, performance and memory, does what theatre has always done best. It performs a kind of exorcism: "I know that I 'got her out of my system' by writing this play, but then again I get *all* the characters in *all* of my plays out of my system by writing about them." Getting a character out of one's system means putting her up on the stage. Which means that writing for the theatre is finally a question of lost and found. Only by finding a character, pinning her down, is the author able to let her go.

July 27, 1998—Edward Albee's house, Montauk, New York

EA: I was confused a little bit by your introduction, which starts out as being about literal ghost stories. And I don't think either Paula [Vogel]'s Uncle Peck or Tony [Kushner]'s Ethel Rosenberg is a ghost. I think your idea of the ghost of American failures, of the American past, is much more interesting. I don't think there are many literal ghosts in American drama. The classic example of course is *Our Town*, where we have the dead talking, and it's moving and wonderful. Have I ever written a ghost in a play? Ghosts of what people could have been and things like that, but I don't think there are many ghosts.

DS: But it seems to me you have a number of characters who straddle the line between the living and the dead. What about the lady from Dubuque, for example?
She's not a ghost. She's a substitution.

When we talk about ghost stories, we usually think of something mysterious and indistinct . . .
I think of spooks.

When in fact the lady from Dubuque is an incredibly precisely defined figure.
And in *Angels in America*, she's not a ghost, she's really there. That's what's so nice about Tony's use of her. She's not dead, she's literally there, out of her time period. She's in nobody's memory. She's real.

Except that she seems to be called up by Roy Cohn and his guilty conscience.
Then how can anybody else see her? I don't think it's the use of a ghost. People can't bring ghosts alive for other people, only for themselves. Your major concern is much more interesting, I just worry for you on that example.

The only issue I question seriously in your introduction and really have a lot of trouble with is this deconstructionist theory of yours, that a play does not exist completely as literature, it exists only in performance. We have to argue this out before we go any further. A string quartet does not exist only when people hear it, anybody who knows how to read music can hear a complete and accurate performance of the string quartet by reading it. Anybody who knows how to read a play can see and hear a complete and accurate performance of the play.

But plays and music are not notated in the same way. Musical notation can be more precise.
I don't think there is any difference in that one area. Performance styles change in string quartets. You have the Russian romantic style, then you have the Emerson String Quartet, which is severe. Styles change as much as performances change. The only difference is that nobody goes around rewriting Beethoven, and people feel they have a right to rewrite playwrights. That is a corruption. I don't think plays are made any better by performance. If the play's any good, most performances aren't as good as the play. If the play is lousy, performance can make it seem better. I have violent disagreement with this theory of yours that a play is dead and must be brought to life. It permits all sorts of excess and corruption, and it's intellectually invalid.

I know this is something you've always been very insistent upon. And I must confess that when I read your plays I get a very exact, perhaps uniquely exact, sense of what is happening.
I'll tell you why. Because unlike many playwrights who rewrite like mad, Tony [Kushner] for example, when I write a play, I write one draft of it because as I'm writing it, I see it and I hear it as a performed piece on stage. I know exactly what it looks like, I know exactly what it sounds like, and I have some accuracy about what the play does to me as an audience. And I'm very precise in putting down all of that, as precise as a composer. I work very much like a composer. The play I put down on paper is the play I'd like to see reproduced by the "musicians," if you will.

What you notate are the effects.
My notation indicates the nature of the characters by how they respond specifically to things.

Motivation is never really spelled out.
I think it is. Everybody has a choice about how they respond to something. The character could not respond to a specific event in a way other than the way he does or he would not be that character. This is not true of all playwrights. You go back to Jean-Claude Van Itallie in 1959, 1960, when he was writing plays with Joe Chaikin's actors. This improvisatory technique of building a play communally has been going on, not since the Greeks, but at least since Shakespeare's time. There's

nothing new in it. There are plays that are written completely and there are plays that need a little fussing around with. I don't change anything in my plays except to cut a little bit if I'm being too verbal.

So then what we see is a first draft?
No, we see a final draft. I don't do a first draft, I write the play.

Which is precisely the way that Mozart composed.
Beethoven did, too, a lot of composers worked that way. If that sentence looks about three words too long, sure, I'll cut those words to make its musical rhythms proper. But I don't evolve a play with actors or directors. A lot of perfectly good playwrights do. I don't work that way, maybe that's why I take objection. What you say is not true of all plays and all playwrights. I don't think playwrights who work the way I do should be subjected to the kind of thing you recommend.

Although I've had these ideas for a long time, they have been strengthened by recent conversations with Paula [Vogel]. She, for example, does talk about production as a kind of collaboration.
There are a lot of people who feel that way, but there are a lot of us who don't. Beckett did not feel it was a collaborative effort. Harold Pinter does not see it as a collaborative effort. I don't. Tennessee [Williams] didn't really, but was forced by Kazan and others to make commercial changes in his plays, and also he got to the point where anything anybody told him would impel him to make changes. Playwrights I find more interesting don't make collaborative changes. Brecht, his changes were made by political necessity. If the party line swerved, he'd change his text. Or if the play needed a different approach in Hanover than in Berlin. But those were entirely different models. Ionesco did not rewrite. Genet did not rewrite. A lot of the writers I respect. I don't think Pirandello worked a lot with actors, either.

So many of the playwrights you mention are specifically concerned with interrogating performance, theatricality, the assumption of roles, the dynamics of self-presentation—Genet, Beckett and you, too. I find that all your plays, in one way or another, are about playing.
But all those playwrights wrote literature, you see.

That's also what makes theatre unique, the way it occupies both of these categories. It is both literature and a performing art.
It's interesting that a play can have this double access to people. Through reading and performance. I will defend to my dying day my theory that

an important play is rarely improved by performance. It's thirty-some years, in the case of *A Delicate Balance*, between the original production and the last one on Broadway a few years ago, and I had to change two lines. The play had not dated in any way. I just changed, "Our dear Republicans, as dull as ever," to "Our dear Republicans, as brutal as ever." I put a line in to the effect that they don't sell topless bathing suits anymore. If plays have sufficient validity and three-dimensionality to begin with, I don't think they need to be updated or made more accessible to an audience.

That's due to the particular kind of writing you do.
Which is also the kind of writing most of the playwrights I admire do. End of that discussion, you know my point. One of the troubles with our theatre is the compromise being made for audiences all the time. Our regional theatres, for example, are reaching for a wider audience and as a result not doing difficult, important plays anymore. The triumph of the middlebrow is happening in our theatre, in Britain, too, for heaven's sake. *Oklahoma!* at the National Theatre.

I was reading the collection of interviews with you . . .
Endless and boring and repetitive.

. . . and back in 1962 you were talking about this, the timidity of the commercial theatre.
It's gotten worse. It's all economics, as we know, making a buck. It has nothing to do with what people used to think of as the function of art. Populist America—all the arts must be aimed at the heartland because that is the nature of America. That merely makes people write simple tunes rather than dodecaphonic music, and simple ideas, nothing really complex, nothing terribly disturbing, which is the opposite of the function of art.

How much of an impact do you think television and film have on this situation?
I don't think that the kind of audience that went to theatre back in the fifties, when I started, is so different from today's. They went to the movies, now they stay home and watch television. Television is worse than movies, despite its extraordinary potential to be educational and informational. The way it's usually used it's a mind-deadener. It's the same with serious dance, serious music, serious poetry, serious drama— they're all minority participations. And they shouldn't be required to be anything else, because it corrupts them. I would love to reach an audience of millions all the time, but I would want to do it on my own terms, and nobody wants to give me that opportunity.

You strike me as virtually unique among major playwrights in having written so little for film.
I've written nothing for film.

Though two plays of yours have been filmed.
A Delicate Balance is the play word for word, with a minute cut out of it. And *Virginia Woolf*, to the extent they could remember their lines, is my text also, aside from those two glorious sentences which I've discussed before—and which I didn't write: "Hey, let's go to the roadhouse," and "Hey, let's come back from the house." Yes, that's lovely. I don't want to become a screenplay writer because I would probably not be able to do what I wanted.

One thing I'm curious about, getting back to the subject of ghosts . . .
I do think that *Our Town* had an enormous influence on me, as I hope it had on everybody. I cry even as I think about that play

I love teaching that play.
Everybody thinks, "Oh, what a cute little play." It is a savage, existentialist play. It is so terrible and so beautiful. There's a moment in *The Skin of Our Teeth* where I cry every time I think about it, too. I probably mentioned that somewhere—I mentioned everything somewhere. It's the moment in the great storm, when Mrs. Antrobus calls to her son for the first time by the right name, and calls out Cain. It's a breathtaking moment. Thornton was so good when he was good.

You're right that you don't have any literal ghosts in your plays, but you do have characters that have doubles of each other, or surrogates, as you say in *Tiny Alice*. In *Three Tall Women*, A, B and C are triples of each other. But even that scheme is complicated by the fact that there are two A's in the second act, there's an A who's walking around and an A who's comatose. There's a proliferation of doubles although they're not ghostly in the conventional sense.
There are refractions and resonances and reflections, sure.

But there is also something profoundly material about them.
Because they're not ghosts.

The same thing is true with Miss Alice, who is one of a series of surrogates.
Yes, of course, of the real Miss Alice who lives in the model.

I can't help but notice how crucial this figuration is in so many of your plays.
It has been; I just don't think it has anything to do with ghosts unless you redefine ghosts.

What I am trying to do is expand the category. And you're helping me do so. How do you start a play?
I discover that I'm thinking about a play, I think about it for a long time, it comes more into focus, ultimately I start writing it down, and find out more and more as I go on. I reveal to myself the play I have been writing without knowing it. Moving from the unconscious to the conscious.

You've talked about writing as a form of self-discovery.
I don't know whether it's self-discovery; I don't know that I learn anything about me, I learn about what's going on in my head. I make a distinction there because while there are some writers who write extensively about themselves, I don't think I do. I write about people who have affected me over the years. I don't think it's exactly self-discovery, it's discovery of what I'm about, which is being a writer, the ideas going on in my head. I don't modify them.

Could it also be that through the act of writing you find out what is inside you, that which has made you you. I'm thinking specifically of *Three Tall Women*, which you describe as autobiographical.
Biographical—I'm not there. I make the assumption that the stuff comes out because I've come to a lot of conclusions and I want to express them. I try very hard not to think about the metaphorical, allegorical, symbolist, political, social—any implications while I'm writing it. I only concern myself with the absolute three-dimensional reality of the piece. That's why I insist that absolutely all of my plays are naturalistic.

I wonder if one reason why you haven't written for film and television is because all of your writing is essentially about theatre.
Theatre's more about listening, while film is more about looking. When I saw the film, *Titanic*, I hated it a lot because the dialogue was appallingly bad, hideously, really. I was flying over to London the other week and it was on. I didn't put the sound on. It's a much better film if you don't listen to it. Very, very skillful. Beautifully done film, I admired it not having to hear it. But plays—I've said this somewhere and you've probably got it down—you can take a blind person to a play and they can understand it completely. You can take a deaf person to a movie and, unless it's a serious European film, they can understand it. That's one of the reasons I get so tired of technical innovations being considered so valuable and so important in theatre. My favorite thing to tell my playwriting students is that, at least in theory, any play that can't be done with a couple of chairs and a lightbulb has something wrong with

it. In effect that's true, it's about people in relationship with each other, and what they say to each other and what they do not say to each other and, of course, what they do to each other. Drama is much more involved with ideas and words than film or television.

Although you're usually very specific about the kind of setting you want, so many of your plays could also be performed in an empty space.
As long as they don't use the wrong space. There was a production of *Who's Afraid of Virginia Woolf?*, an American production [Saratoga International Theatre Institute] that was first done in Saratoga Springs and then went to Tokyo—which I thought was a much better place for it—in which the two couples were wearing dinner clothes, the set was all black glass and chrome, lights came up from the floor, the painting over the mantel—the representation of Martha's mind—was a moving painting. It was so wrong. A lot of wrong stuff happens, of course, when directors are showing off how clever they are. Sure, a lot of my plays could be done with no set, but they must not be done with symbolic sets. If it's a naturalistic play, it must not be a symbolic set . . . unless. I love Brechtian simplification, I think it's wonderful. The first time I saw the Berliner Ensemble—I saw *Galileo* in Berlin in '59—I was startled. My God, that scene in Galileo's study. Three walls, an ornate desk, a chair—that was it, along with a model of the known universe hanging up above like a chandelier. That was all that was required. I believed everything. Formalization and stylization go back to the Greek days, but sometimes people get clever.

It seems to me part of what you're doing is turning the living room into a theatre, particularly in comparison with your predecessors, Miller and Williams. Your characters are involved so consciously in role-playing. . . .
I think I've just found a better way to describe what I do, antimatter turning into matter. Unconscious to conscious.

And of course antimatter cannot be seen or even conceived of . . .
. . . until it's turned into matter, yes.

Getting back to this question of doubles, as I was watching *Tiny Alice* in Hartford [Hartford Stage Company], it occurred to me that it's really a play about pronouns. Then when I was reading *Three Tall Women*, I realized that that, too, is a play about pronouns. The first scene of *Tiny Alice* is all about the difference between "I" and "we," the one and the many. It seems to me that Miss Alice's conundrum can be identified as a problem of pronouns. Moving between a first-person and third-person singular pronoun, she is both "I" and "she."

Yes, as Alice herself says, "I . . . she," as Miss Alice, but Alice herself doesn't establish that.

While in *Three Tall Women*, the movement is between first-person and second-person singular pronouns, "I" and "you." This questioning of identity, of who's who, goes on in so many of your plays.
My new play, *The Play about the Baby*, continues the exploration begun in *The Lady from Dubuque*, about reality being determined by our deserving it and by our need for it.

So you mean we produce our own realities?
We always end up with the reality we need to have, the one that is fitting for us. In *The Lady from Dubuque*, that was Jo's mother because Jo needed her to be the mother and she became the mother. No reality there, but we accepted it as an intellectual conceit. It became real because it was what should be.

Do you detect a change in attitude from your early plays toward the manufacture of reality? I'm thinking specifically of the way that *Virginia Woolf* seems so obsessed with getting rid of illusion, and showing that marriage must be based on truth.
That would be quite a contradiction, with *Tiny Alice* only a year or two away. I think I just go back and forth. I can't think about myself in those terms. I read these long fictional pieces that people write about my work, sometimes it's very interesting, sometimes it isn't. I have great difficulty thinking of myself and my work in those removes. Because I use the unconscious—so much more than many other writers—in formulating the reality in my work. It's not mystical, but it's almost a mist to me.

The antimatter.
And I guess I take it on faith, when I finish the piece, that's what I intended to do. Which is why I can't make value judgments as to why one play is better than another.

I know that music is very important to you. Do you ever associate a certain piece of music with something you're writing?
I've said this before: I think every writer should begin the day by listening to a Bach fugue, it clears the mind absolutely beautifully. No, I try to stay far away from music when I'm writing, I don't want anybody else's music getting in the way of the music I'm writing. I know my classical music probably as well as any amateur does, any nonprofessional musician. I know an awful lot more about it than a lot of people, because I wanted to be a composer when I was a kid.

And this is why a play of yours is almost an opera without music.
I'm aware of music when I'm writing, and if you really wanted to scan my sentences, my paragraphs, you could conduct them.

Which is one reason why you refer to Tobias's long speech as an aria.
There is a specific, beautiful rhythm. I don't write in blank verse you understand, as Eliot did. Maybe I've learned a lot from Eliot, even plays I don't like, *Murder in the Cathedral*, which I think is a terrible bore. The two that I do like, *The Family Reunion* and *The Cocktail Party*, I remember seeing in my teens. I think you can conduct my plays. Directors discover this, that towards the end of rehearsal, they can stay way in the back so nobody can see them, close their eyes and conduct the speeches. I can tell, when I've directed a play of my own or anybody else's, if it's holding up or not, because of the rhythms. It's interesting that you can have something so formal as conductible rhythms in something so naturalistic as a play. You find it in Harold [Pinter] of course, and you find it in David Mamet, too. They're aware of that ear quality, the formalization.

I was interested to read about your early theatregoing experiences.
Jumbo and all that.

Yes, because your writing is so full of movement and color.
But then I started going to see straight plays, including *Hellzapoppin—*that wasn't a straight play, but it was wonderful. I was in London the other week and saw *The Iceman Cometh*. Don't. I remember it much better than it is now. God, there's a lot of clunky writing in that play, it's endless. But it was very powerful. I sat there, originally, way back in the balcony with my jaws open in awe as I watched, as I listened to that play. What was it, '48? Oh sure, my family sent me to musicals all the time. Yes, very interesting. Nothing changes.

You also talk about *Suddenly Last Summer*.
That was important, as was my first Chekhov. *Suddenly Last Summer*, probably more so than the monologue in *The Iceman Cometh*, gave me the freedom to write Jerry's long speech in *The Zoo Story*. Watching *The Iceman Cometh*, the idea that pipe dreams are essential, probably influenced *Virginia Woolf*, a play almost as long.

I'm curious about your relationship with Williams because, like you, he really expanded the horizons of American realism.
Yes, certainly he did. They really criticized him when he wrote *Camino Real*, didn't they? And that was a very interesting play.

It seems with Williams, as with you, that there is always a kind of naturalistic core.
Oh yes, everything in the theatre must be naturalistic no matter what the degree of stylization is. If it's not based on three-dimensional reality, it can be in serious trouble.

That three-dimensional reality is something based on characters, though, isn't it?
Yes, of course. Some people are surprised that all of Beckett's plays are completely naturalistic. I've directed enough of them to know this. These aren't symbolic characters, these are real people. There's Winnie, buried up to her waist in the first act, literally buried up to her real waist in a literal sand dune—real person, literal sand dune. Act two, she's buried up to her neck, which is why there's no act three. I directed that play as an absolutely naturalistic piece.

One thing that Beckett does, and that I think you're doing, is working from this naturalistic core, but also introducing a real—I'm tempted to say violent—disjunction between what's happening to the characters and the setting in which they're placed. *Box* and *Quotations from Chairman Mao-Tse Tung* are probably the clearest examples.
That's literally on the back deck of an ocean liner. I got that from Claudel, whom nobody does anymore. Wasn't *Partage de midi* set on the back of an ocean liner? My new play is a little bit different in that I want it to be set in a sort of no-man's-land. I want it to be such a performance piece that it's like it's set in a vaudeville theatre.

During the sixties and seventies in New York, did you see much experimental work? I mean, you were involved in so many different kinds of theatre. But I'm thinking specifically of Richard Foreman, Robert Wilson, Richard Schechner?
Yes, I've familiarized myself with all this, and as long as it's not partial theatre, it's admirable. So much of it has turned out to be doing something new and different without continuing to fill it out, and that's been a problem with a lot of the work. You have to familiarize yourself with other work, learn from other people's failures, successes. If you're sitting in a room somewhere, not aware of what's going on in the world, you're going to reinvent the typewriter. There's no point.

Getting back to the question of these doubled figures, and whether you'd call them ghosts, I find it interesting that so many of them are women, the three tall women, Miss Alice, the lady from Dubuque.
I don't know what that means.

It's often been noted that some of your women characters are very strong or aggressive.

Women think my female characters are much more accurate than men do. I've never had any trouble having my female characters understood by women.

I can't help feeling as though, in some respects, you're putting heterosexuality under a microscope.
I don't think of either heterosexuality or homosexuality as being subjects, I think of people, in and outside of their culture.

Why is it that virtually all the relationships in your plays are heterosexual relationships?
Probably because the majority of relationships in the world are heterosexual. Maybe I'm trying to reach more people. I'm certainly not trying to hide anything. Nor do I see any reason why a playwright who's gay should write about gay subjects. If we can ever get rid of that thing where a playwright who's gay is referred to as a gay playwright. Nobody refers to Arthur Miller as a straight playwright. It's so preposterous. I don't think I'm shying away. There have been gay characters in my plays, from time to time. Benjamin and Daniel in *Finding the Sun*. Gay characters turn up in my plays, I imagine they're about as frequent as they are in real life.

But I've been thinking about the history of gay theatre—whatever that means—and the extraordinary changes over the past thirty years. I know that in one interview you referred to *The Boys in the Band* as simply a bad play.
It's a very bad play, a loathsome play, sets back the gay movement thirty years, the self-loathing on the part of all those characters. I wouldn't co-produce it, they wanted me to, I wouldn't have anything to do with it. Not because it was about gay people, but because it was so self-loathing and reaffirmed the attitude of smug superiority on the part of straight audiences. "Look at these sick fags." I loathed the play for that reason, because I thought it was desperately unfair and dangerous.

But it seems to me that since *Angels in America* . . .
There was a world before *Angels in America*—I keep trying to remember this. We go back quite a number of years, we have to go back to dear Lillian Hellman. And ten years before Tony [Kushner] wrote *Angels*, we had a plethora of gay plays.

Torch Song Trilogy.
And the two that are better than that, Kramer's play *The Normal Heart*, he wrote two of them, and the other fellow, Hoffman's play, *As Is*. Better plays, I think, than *Torch Song*. Not much new there.

What I'm thinking about specifically is the emergence of what Tony and a number of other people call the new queer theatre.
Define it.

It seems to me that the gay theatre, as it emerged in the sixties and seventies, was very much focused on a specific minority of people: self-defined gay men. Whereas the new queer theatre is intent on interrogating sexuality in much wider terms, all forms of sexuality.
Then it ceases being gay theatre. Good. I'm opposed to ghettoization.

This is why, it seems to me, this new queer theatre in some ways looks back to you much more than to writers like Mart Crowley or Harvey Fierstein. This is what I meant about putting heterosexuality under a microscope.
Yes, but it's not because it's heterosexuality but because that's the way that the great majority of people live their lives, as heterosexual people.

So it's human relationships.
Yes, alright, sure.

In many interviews you've described yourself as a social critic.
I think all art that is any good is holding a mirror up to people, saying, "This is who you are, this is how you behave. If you don't like it, why don't you change?" It doesn't have to be directly politically activist. For example, we vote the way we do because of who we've allowed ourselves to become. So by examining the way people have become, I'm examining why people vote the way they do, why they think the way they do. It's moving from the macrocosm to the microcosm.

How?
I think people could change the way they think politically and socially if they would really examine the way they live their lives. These are individual people who represent a whole way of life and thinking and being. And I'm still stuck with the majority who are the people that I was adopted into, these WASP, upper-middle-class bigots who are horrible people.

Which is why your plays are so concerned with shaking up that order and getting people to reexamine what they believe.
Yes, I've written plays with blacks in them, haven't had many Asians yet—but you write basically what you know, from where you come. You have to. Any play, any work of art, should be socially useful if it can help you to reexamine your values and understand why you behave the way you do. Otherwise it's just decorative.

So that even a play like *Three Tall Women*, which seems less explicitly political than some of your other plays, is . . .

. . . an examination of what we let ourselves become, as a result of outside forces and our own weaknesses and failures. That's what it's about.

Consequences.

What happens because of what we do and what we do not do. The sad thing about that play is that the girl has to watch, she can't do anything about it.

She doesn't see it, she can't really understand.

Of course not, nobody's allowed to see themselves. That's why she says at the end of the play, "I deny you."

It's that denial that allows her to become B.

C, who's innocent, doesn't know any of this stuff. The other thing, if I ever make a film of that play, I can't have B and C in the second act played by the same actors who play the parts in act one. It would only work in the theatre, it doesn't work in film. I've been thinking about that a lot. I don't know if it'll ever be a film anyway. I'm happy with it as it is.

What prose fiction do you particularly like?

As my mind gets slipperier and slipperier, I find I prefer shorter books to longer ones. I like short stories a great deal. I probably read more nonfiction these days. I read a lot, I'm always reading. I'm reading a wonderful book now. Thomas Bernhardt, the Austrian writer, wrote a book of 104 short pieces. Very interesting, marvelous, fascinating. I also read a book about a woman who turns into a pig.

What's that called?

I think it's called *A Woman Who Turns into a Pig*. I picked it up in London.

Do you think of writing your plays as producing a kind of autobiography?

An autobiography of my mind, sure, but not necessarily of me. The way my mind examines things and thinks about things. I guess I'm convinced all of my plays occur because I want to examine something. I pay very little attention to what it is I'm examining while I'm writing—I don't want to discover the meaning or the symbolism or any of those things. So it's an autobiography of how I think creatively, which may not be the same as how I think about other things.

So it is a documentation of your consciousness?
Well, the unconscious—very important there. That's where creativity exists, in the unconscious. Technique and control in the conscious mind. Why do I always write characters who are more interesting than I am? Or are they? I mean I don't find myself a particularly dramatic person, but my plays are dramatic. I would rather go away than yell.

Although you're rather famous for having a wicked way with words, like some of your characters.
I don't shout much.

I suppose it is an autobiography of the way my mind works. And I suppose it works the way it does because of the way I grew up, my environment and my reaction to it. One thing that is very important: I let a play be exactly what it wants to be. How it wants to be, the degree of stylization. I allow it to determine that. Form and content codetermine each other, I don't try to impose my ideas on my ideas. That's the best way to put it. I don't try to censor or control what is going on in my mind creatively. I write to discover what that is. So far it's been some pretty dramatic stuff.

The more I think about your metaphor, the more fascinating I find it: antimatter becoming matter. Antimatter doesn't exist in a sense, until it's transformed, like the unconscious.
Which occupies ninety percent of the brain's time. The thinking time.

In the introduction to *Three Tall Women*, you write about that play as being about your mother. I'm trying to remember the phrase you use: "To get her out of your system."
I haven't thought about her since then.

Is it some sort of exorcism?
I suppose it must be an exorcism, but I was not bothered by it for twenty years before I wrote the play, I was just doing a dutiful son thing to this unpleasant, not very nice woman. I like the irony that she disliked me, she disliked my work, and then she became the subject of my play. It was not cathartic in any way. I suppose it exorcised, since I don't think about it now—that's what exorcism is, isn't it? But I don't think she was a demon.

But the play's also a crucial one in determining your relationship to the theatre, and what theatre can do.
I am the container for the thing contained. I write because I'm a writer. I get ideas for plays because I'm a playwright. It's simple. Some people get ideas for novels, I don't. My mind works like a playwright. It wasn't

a choice that I made, I was slow in coming to it. Stuff going on in my head is becoming a play and eventually it becomes enough of a play that I need to start writing it down. Then I start translating into conscious terms what has already been existing. It is a form of translation.

I realize for you that the play you've written is a finished product. But you've been privileged to work with some great directors and actors: Alan Schneider, John Gielgud, Irene Worth. What generally has made for a good production of your work? An intelligent, sensitive, experienced hand, whose interest is fundamentally in displaying the play as it wants to be, rather than imposing. I find those the most interesting to deal with, which is why I direct so much of my own work, because I don't impose. I like to direct the world premieres or the first performances of my work.

Did you learn from Alan Schneider? Alan, as well as a bunch of other directors that I watched, taught me a lot about the craft of directing. I direct my own plays because I know what they look and sound like. I can be more accurate than anyone else can be. Is it collaborative with the director? It's collaborative as long as they do what the playwright is after.

So the collaboration depends on their being outstandingly good readers. Absolutely, and on their understanding the psyche, the environment— understanding the piece. That's why Alan was better with some of my plays than with others.

Have you ever seen a production of one of your plays that was quite different from what you'd envisioned but that you found surprisingly illuminating? I have to go back to what I said before: I've never seen a production of a play of mine that's made the play seem better than I thought it was. I've seen a lot that have made it worse. A specific revelation? I can't say so. They may have found things that no one else had thought about, but they were already there. That's the difference between a good production and a bad production. A good production finds all sorts of things embedded in the text, but a bad production distorts by imposing outside stuff. It's that simple.

Of course in finding these things that are in the text, a good production will find things in the text that you are not aware of. Ah, consciously aware of. They couldn't have found them, if they are valid, unless I put them in there. Consciously or not. Antimatter/matter again.

I'm intrigued by your understanding of the doubleness of language. At one point you described it as "both a disguise and a nakedness."
Well people use language to define things and to avoid defining them, don't they? It's escape and engagement, you just have to keep your ears open and listen.

And both happen simultaneously.
Depending on the characters, yes. Which I suppose is why I write more complex characters than simple ones. People who are capable of that duality. But Brother Julian, no duality there at all.

That means that words can—and often are—used as weapons.
Sure, the pen and the sword. Well, all you can write in a play is what people do or do not do, say or do not say, and the resonances of that, that's all you can write. You don't need to have all this terrible exposition, description, he thought, she thought, that you have in novels.

One important thing you did early in your career was to get rid of the well-made play and so much of that old-fashioned machinery.
I'm writing one now that goes back and uses every bit of it.

Of course *Virginia Woolf* uses it.
That's a very naturalistic play. The entire play takes place in the time of the performance. That's the only one except for the one-act plays. *Zoo Story* does, obviously, *Sandbox* does, *American Dream* does, but the longer ones, no, they're different time periods, locations, but not *Virginia Woolf*.

And that technique requires a more retrospective kind of play. So much of *Virginia Woolf* is comprised of the characters looking back, telling stories, making up competing versions of reality, which is something your characters do all the time, making up competing, often contradictory, versions of reality.
Wait until you see the new play, *The Play about the Baby*. Filled with it.

Even in *Three Tall Women*, where you have only one real character, each one has different . . .
No, in the first act there are three separate people. I tried something in *The Play about the Baby*. There are two acts, but the second act begins with the last five minutes of act one. Played exactly the same way, identically.

At one point, in a very early interview, you described yourself as an eclectic playwright.
People go to see other people's plays and say to me, "Oh, deeply influenced by you." I go see them, I can't find it. I guess there is a style I write in that overlays all of it. I try not to think about it, because that would make me self-conscious about writing, and writing has got to be innocent. If you think about yourself while you're writing, you can't write. The plays fairly give the illusion of being written in different styles, different removes from reality. I move around dramatically. I hope I'm eclectic because it means I've learned from other people, other styles. It doesn't mean imitative, it means using whatever methods are most effective for what you're after. That's my understanding of it, what I meant by eclectic. Not derivative. I'm naturally derivative, everybody is.

We see what works.
And we're sure of it.

So often as I was reading each of your plays, I thought, "This is a really central text, this is the one that I'm going to have to focus on in my introduction." I find that a fascinating phenomenon, that you're able to write in a number of different, I don't think "styles" is accurate, but you write a number of different kinds of plays and each is absolutely central to your basic concerns.
I would hope so.

What do you think of Tennessee Williams's late plays? They're not generally held in very high regard.
I'm sad about some of them, because I think that if Tennessee had been in full command of his creative faculties, they would be, some of them, quite extraordinary. But he wasn't, and they aren't.

Do you know *In the Bar of a Tokyo Hotel*?
Yes. I've seen that produced twice, in the most horrible kind of stylized productions—what Tennessee wanted, with that particular way of speaking. Terribly wrong. But he's incapable of not having interesting ideas, he just wasn't in command. They had to take Shaw's plays away from him in his nineties because he was simplifying them so he could understand them. I wish Tennessee had been in better control.

I realize you've already spoken about the state of the American theatre, and I know you've been involved with nurturing young writers in a number of ways.
It's very simple. If you're a playwright, you like to go to plays. And you would like to go to more plays that you're happier being at, and so if

you could encourage more people, you think there's a chance you might end up seeing more plays you like.

Do you think that the American theatre is ever going to recover, to become a popular theatre?
Back to the nonexistent great days, you mean? There never were great days. There will be wonderful playwrights and commercial hacks. And there will be experimental playwrights and nonexperimental ones. Ones with interesting, complex minds and others without them. It's going to go on.

When I began, there wasn't a regional theatre, no theoretical home for the noncommercial play. That was Off-Off-Broadway. I don't know where they're going to be done now, with the regional theatres falling by the wayside. It probably will impel more and more playwrights not to try anything noncommercial, unfortunately. That's dangerous. There will always be some that do what they have to. They end up being the most interesting ones.

Then most of them will have their work done in tiny theatres, and a few will break through.
Will break through to a larger audience without demeaning their own talent.

By writing plays that have to be plays, as opposed to movies.
Exactly. I can't imagine any good play being as effective as a movie. I think it has something to do with that old theory of mine that all film is fantasy experience and safe, because we know it has not happened. While a play is happening as we experience it. Our suspension of disbelief is complete and it is a real experience. Something can happen.

Anything can happen.
Yes, and a film has already happened.

But also already not happened.
That's right. I think that's the fundamental difference, and why theatre is not popular with many people who want their theatrical experiences to be escapist, rather than engaging.

So it's so crucial that theatre hold onto that engagement.
It would be nothing without it. It would be nighttime TV.

So this is something that's built into the medium itself.

It's got to be built into the individual writer, too. I think half the writers who don't sell out just don't know how, wouldn't be very good at it. I speak to myself sometimes, "Edward, why don't you write a real commercial play?" I wouldn't know how to do it. How do you start? You start by lying, you start faking, then you get embarrassed.

Which is why there will never be _Virginia Woolf II_.
Exactly. Though some people misunderstood _Marriage Play_ as being that.

Jon Robin Baitz

Growing up in Los Angeles, Brazil, South Africa, Amsterdam and London, Jon Robin Baitz had a peripatetic and lonely childhood. And although raised in comparative luxury (his father worked for a large multinational corporation), he had the opportunity to observe firsthand both the subtle and not so subtle exploitation of the Third World by the First. Living for six years in South Africa and attending high school there, he found that being immersed in the "day-to-day evil" of apartheid made him feel both "increasingly comfortable" and "increasingly anguished." Returning with his family in 1978 to Los Angeles, Baitz attempted to confront and interrogate America's complex relations with the rest of the world. For Baitz, of all the playwrights in this book, is the most explicitly a postcolonial writer. His plays are peopled by characters on the move—diplomats, expatriates, corporate executives, along with their various dependents—who work for a government or corporation they distrust and know will turn against them when they are no longer of use. Being always in transit, they are a kind of displaced persons, always temporary about themselves, always feeling comfortable and guilty, self-assured and vulnerable.

At the same time, Baitz's characters—almost all of them white and members of the upper classes—imagine themselves the stars of what is unmistakably a new global drama. For the world through which they pass is not the old colonial system in which foreign armies forcefully subdued local populations. In Baitz's theatre (as in the world), that system has been supplanted by a neocolonial order in which corporations and representatives of Western governments have learned how to exert more subtle and insidious control over the Third World. Thus the West, for example, by making loans through the International Monetary Fund, has facilitated a salutary modernization of production in parts of the Third World, while producing some rather unpleasant side effects, that is, tacitly encouraging the expansion of child labor practices and shoring up highly stratified class systems. By so strengthening the power of multinational corporations and Western-style elites, neocolonialism reinforces the subjugation of the Third World to the First, in effect repackaging colonialism with a smile.

In all of Baitz's plays, in particular *The End of the Day* (1992) and *A Fair Country* (1996), this new world order serves as a backdrop for an investigation of the way the boundaries between the personal and the political have broken down. For deception is the rule in the new global order as one constantly hoodwinks one's enemies, friends, family and—most ominously—one's self. So a corporate executive like Kenneth Hoyle in *Three Hotels* (1992) markets powdered milk formula to the Third World despite knowing that his business practices represent a kind of "manufactured thuggishness." But Hoyle, who has developed both extremely paternalistic attitudes and elaborate mechanisms of justification and denial, is by no means a villain. On the contrary, he is obsessed with providing for his family, consumed with guilt and is eager (yet frightened) to quit the company. His wife, Barbara, another casualty of his business practices, acts out her own ambivalence in a speech to company wives that effectively destroys her husband's career. This short work contains what could be considered the recipe for most all of Baitz's plays. Take an omniscient corporation, an all-too-easily exploitable Third World, a brutal but well-meaning husband, an unfulfilled and resistant wife, a victimized (and, in this case, dead) child. Throw in a dash of betrayal and a handful of guilt. Mix them all together and you get a dish in which everything has been transformed: masters turn out to be more obsequious than their servants, the best intentions produce the worst results, confession leads to disaster.

What makes Baitz's writing so provocative, however, are less his variations on this recipe than his use of exact and exacting dramatic forms. *Three Hotels*, for example, consists of a monologue for Barbara bracketed by two for Kenneth, each set in a different hotel room. Barbara's serves as a pivot, not only revealing the many truths, both public and private, that Kenneth would prefer to repress, but also reiterating the very words of the speech that destroys him. The monologue form also becomes an index of the emotional separation between husband and wife and the fact that they have no real way of connecting. Yet at the same time, the play clearly shows that these two almost self-destructively well-intentioned people are equally mortgaged to the same system of loss and betrayal. There can be no real winners in this new world order (at least among the upwardly mobile functionaries that fill Baitz's plays) because every choice turns out to be the wrong choice. How can you know what to do when you don't even know what you are really selling? Well being or misery? Aid or destruction? Or for whom, in the end, you are working? Self, family, company, government, world? How can you ever hope to answer these questions when moral principles have become completely relative and mutable, sold to the highest bidder? For finally *Three Hotels*, like all of Baitz's plays, suggests—scandalously—that within the postcolonial order, absolutes and certainties disappear. The selves that populate this world no longer know who they are. They have become collections of contradictions and clichés, promises and betrayals. These ghostly selves, condemned forever to roam the earth, are haunted by loss—and not only the loss of once-stable geopolitical orders or systems of belief. For Kenneth and Barbara are also in mourning for their son, Brandon, killed on a Copacabana beach for his shiny diver's watch. For both husband and wife, Brandon is the sign of their sundered connection and a reminder of passing time, irrevocability and eternity. He—implicitly equated to the dead children of African mothers—is the wrong that can never be righted, the ghost forever haunting the disconsolate.

As a postcolonial writer living in a nation that remains profoundly ambivalent about its imperial mission, Baitz is dedicated less to answering the questions that arise about America's role on the world stage than trying to ask them in the right way. For like the high school student silently bearing witness to the "grim drama" of apartheid, he has fashioned for himself the part of somewhat dispassionate, almost noncommittal spectator. And while all his plays are based upon realistic observation, they also take a certain delight in keeping an aesthetic distance—shuffling the sequence of events and making an almost cinematic use of montage (it is little wonder that he so artfully adapted *The Substance of Fire* [1990] for the big screen). For his scene breaks disjoin not only time and space, but also cause and effect. They represent a way of questioning the laws that would assure us that a particular moral

June 12, 1998—Jon Robin Baitz's office, New York City

DS: How did you get interested in theatre?
JRB: In my early twenties, I was at loose ends and living in Los Angeles, but not feeling at home there. Through friendships with mostly older people who were involved in the now-defunct Padua Hills Playwrights Festival, I started going to a lot of plays. Theatre seemed like the perfect, easy avocation for an outsider to jump-start his interest in the world or at least mesh his internal monologue with the one he was hearing outside all the time. You didn't need to be trained, it seemed to be made up of malcontents and underachievers like me, and I started scribbling. I was a parrot, I would go watch a play and then I would come home and write. At the time there was a big, lively, vital Equity waiver theatre scene in Los Angeles. You could go six, seven nights a week and see interesting theatre.

Did you go to the theatre at all when you were a kid?
No, but life was theatre. I left L.A. when I was seven and we were in Brazil for a few years, where there were all kinds of theatrical combinations of foreignness, outsiderness, strange otherness. Then South Africa, which exponentially multiplied the strangeness I felt in Brazil. So I had an odd sense of being foreign which I think is very useful for being a playwright.

How is it useful?
If the rules of the place aren't immediately available for scrutiny, if the codes of behavior and the laws are foreign, and if you're sort of bewildered, it provides that inevitable prerequisite for being a writer, which is to pull you away a little bit. It gives you just an unasked-for, inadvertent, little push back. You start watching very carefully—and a lot earlier—to figure it all out. I think I might have become a writer had I never left the States, but not the same kind.

What playwrights do you feel influenced by? Because in some ways I think of you—and I mean this in a good way—as a very literary writer.

After he saw my first play, the first production of *The Film Society*, Peter Sellars said to me that I reminded him quaintly of Sir Arthur Wing Pinero. Then he told me I had to develop a thick skin, which I guess I've done. I am sort of a sponge, though. Maybe because in some ways I had grown up like a little, English schoolboy. I was initially attracted to Hare, Stoppard and Brenton more than to Mamet, Shepard, etc. And I don't know why that is. My first associations with the theatre were not even connected with the Padua Hills Playwrights Festival, which was fairly far out there. It was started by Sam Shepard, Murray Mednick, Maria Irene Fornes and John O'Keefe, and even in their presence as teachers, even though I didn't write like any of them, I was still writing a kind of play that depended heavily on language, and on formality, even though they're not exactly formal plays.

Your work seems quite a distance from the Off-Off-Broadway experimental tradition. And I wonder about your relationship to Arthur Miller, because like his, all of your plays wrestle with serious moral issues.

In my case, that comes out of a sense of not measuring up. I can't speak for Mr. Miller, but I find moralizing frankly suspect. I try to break it down. I grew up in a culture, an upper-middle-class world where things are either good or bad, and South Africa contributed to that. I was indoctrinated into thinking, "This is a good thing, this is a bad thing." So that's the monologue in my head—that sort of constant judging, murmuring voice—and it's not a useful thing. So I don't feel that I'm as hip to the combination of those judgments as Miller is. I'm more bewildered. If I write about morality, it's from the standpoint of the unreliable narrator.

It seems to me that all of your plays are about questioning any moralizing project. For there is no morally unimpeachable position. Whatever choice a character makes turns out to be the wrong choice. I'm thinking in particular of *A Fair Country*.

I think action is dangerous and inaction is even more damning and dangerous. You're always being tested, and I don't think it's a healthy way to live. But the only way out of it is to try to write yourself out. Contorting the contortionists. Harry Burgess does a particularly horrible thing, but there's a little sliver of rationalization and justification, first having to do with, "I have to get my family out of this place. It's terrible." But then comes the awful fact of his prospering in the short term from his decision. So there might be a little ambition there. I guess I sometimes think ambition underlies everything, that it's all about getting ahead. I'm not cynical about it, I'm just really curious about how that works.

I'm fascinated right now by people's third acts. I'm fascinated by someone like Harry Burgess and where he is now. I feel like we're in America's third act right now. I've been thinking a lot lately—and this is a total sidebar—about the trajectory of Jerry Brown from a Kennedy-like scion of a dynasty to a man reaching out for a kind of spiritual component, away from the money, away from the establishment, and becoming the mayor of a very diverse little town—Oakland. I find that fascinating, and probably filled with a kind of guilt. So all these things are kind of gin-soaked in guilt. I haven't written children very well because they're usually so innocent.

Are you thinking of Gil as an example of an innocent child?
He's fairly innocent, he's trying to do too many things, to protect too many interests, and none of them are really his. Ultimately he over-extends himself emotionally.

I was amused by the comment that Nathan Lane made in *New York* magazine that when he first read *The Film Society*, he imagined the writer to be a fifty-year-old college professor. Because you're writing is rather different from that of the other playwrights in this book insofar as it is so much about relationships between unmistakably parental figures. Characters under thirty are either absent from your plays or not the center of dramatic interest.
They're usually powerless against the reckless forces of their elders. There aren't that many young people in my plays, and this geriatric problem is slightly alarming to me. I'm very slow to address it because I'm just now figuring out the first part of my life and trying to write it. In the first part of your life, you feel powerless. You watch these older preachers make terrible mistakes and decisions and understand what might motivate them, but that doesn't make them less frightening. The children are typically invisible. In *Three Hotels*, there's a dead child. And, through a number of corrupting acts, his parents are implicated in his death. In *The Substance of Fire*, the children are forced into a kind of endgame with their father, who acts out of an almost complete absence of parental judiciousness. I guess the reason for the absence or near absence of children is an inherent sense of just how little a child can do, how powerless one feels as a kid. But in *The Film Society*, I was thinking of the one child at that school who was worth it, who was worth Jonathan Balton's making a stand-up choice for. I kept trying to think of what I see as a worthwhile choice. And even in *Mizlansky/Zilinsky or Schmucks* [1998], Paul Trecker falls squarely into the role of the enslaved child, though he certainly loves Mizlansky.

In reading your work, I started to feel that you're the only real postcolonial playwright in this book.

Who are other postcolonial playwrights?

I think of Wole Soyinka, Derek Walcott, Caryl Churchill. If they're not from the Third World, they're probably British. Like their work, yours is concerned with questions of exile and displacement.

So is the work of Alan Bennett, even though he's almost exquisitely English, if there's such a thing, with plays like *Single Spies*, *A Question of Attribution* and the play about Guy Burgess with Alan Bates and Maggie Smith. Also *Talking Heads*, the monologues, about being exiled. Go on.

Thinking of you as a postcolonial writer means first of all that you're interested in questions of imperialism, in the broadest sense. *Three Hotels* is so obviously about economic imperialism. But it's more accurately a kind of neoimperialism—raids by multinational corporations have come to substitute for foreign armies. Also, as you were talking, it occurred to me that in describing the relationship between parents and children you are also describing the relationship between the First World and the Third.

Thinking about the way that children are treated and thinking about the way baby formula is marketed in the Third World, you begin to locate yourself somewhere on this axis, on this map. Again, guilt-soaked writing. My father was vice president of, what I thought at the time was, an enormous, faceless, bureaucratic, monolithic, selling machine. And so intrusive and so insistent and so damning. And we were part of this weird culture, that to some extent consisted of diplomats and other mercantile people. There's something about selling stuff. There's something that's very dangerous when your culture is completely consumed by this lassitude and you're the purveyor of it in another country. Maybe lassitude is not the right word, but this system doesn't get examined. And it pained me, in some ways, to be part of that. It pained me then, it pains me now. Someone once wrote something about me after my second play, and it's remained true. He said that I examine the way systems operate. It sounded so clinical at the time, and so dispassionate, but it's a better explanation than any I've been able to come up with.

And crucially, it's a system that must be understood both politically and economically in global terms.

It may be positioned in global terms, but I have no ideology, I don't even have a dialectic. I just sort of lurch forward with this very middle-class notion of right and wrong. It just so happens that the components that make up this notion include a childhood spent as the son of an executive for a huge multinational living in some very dramatic places. Had that not happened, I might have grown up to be a TV writer or something. It's an accident. The intelligent observations and all the claims are so easy to make. But what really sticks is memory—if they come out of memory. What really sticks is the image of the country club, with iced tea, and the almost sexual aspect of all of that, the loneliness.

Your own memory?
Yes. I've come to terms with not being as smart as I'd like to be. But I'm sensitive to other people's discomfort, to what's in the air around me, I'm sensitive to mood and language. And I'm curious about how expensive one's lifestyle is. I guess maybe those make up an inadvertent post-colonial concern. Exile is everywhere in those plays. And it continues—*Mizlansky/Zilinsky* is filled with shipwrecked people who've been passed up.

So exile is the state in which all your characters live?
Totally.

Which is why hotels are so important. The hotels through which you pass.
I say, "Anything's possible."

And questions of memory seem to come up particularly when you're in transit. Which is why, it seems to me, that the main characters in your plays have to be older—so they can remember, so they can have all these memories, so they can be haunted by the past and by decisions made and unmade.
I pick that strategy. I think that's why I've been thinking lately about regret and third acts. I often think I'm going to write about Harry Burgess's last days in Venice, California. In my dad's eyes, I feel like I've seen a whole film going on for years. In my mom's face, I definitely see a big movie playing itself out. A little Hitchcock and a little Fellini and a little Douglas Sirk. I guess that my sensitivity to reading the film in their eyes and on their faces makes for writing older characters. They're filled with regret.

I go through this thing where I just feel so old. I feel so preposterously old. I always had it, even as a little boy. I was tentative about games, "Why are they throwing me a ball? I don't understand. . . ." Now, I've reached a place where the physical world is finally wonderful to me. Which I think is childlike in a way. I love the beach and I finally love the sensual world. Now I'm trying, as an experiment, to write a play which is filled with young people rather than old. Because there is also a great anger at the admission of defeat and the cynicism of growing old. I've started to feel a teenager's rage in writing now.

So you're describing a kind of personal regression, which also happens in some of your plays, in *The End of the Day*, for example. And even *Three Hotels*, insofar as it's about remembering and going back. That seems to me to be the purest of your plays. Definitely. It's not my favorite play—I don't have a favorite—but it came out whole, unadulterated. What exactly do you mean?

First, the structure of it is so lyrical and neat, with its three self-contained, yet interwoven scenes. But I'm particularly interested by your use of language in it. In the first scene, Kenneth is using a completely corporate, official language. He speaks in complete sentences and is very much in control. Then in the second scene, Barbara seems to find it frankly very difficult to articulate. She seems afraid to speak at the same time that she's compelled to speak. For to be able to speak, she has to get at something that is largely inaccessible to her. Then it's a surprise when it rushes out. And she's recreating a very fuzzy, ghastly event. And she has unsuccessfully tamped down the death of Brandon. When that monologue begins, she's just talked about it for the very first time, and she isn't alive yet, she's still sort of half-dead. We're watching someone tell herself a story in order to come back to life.

And as she comes back to life, she dies again—at least to Kenneth. I find the last scene so powerful because he is haunted by her absence, and by his mother's absence, and by Brandon's. All three of these people are dead to him. And then as this happens, as he confronts their loss, he too becomes unable to speak. It's almost too much. The battle in doing that play is to find a way to make it fluid, but also difficult, dangerous and hard to get through. The third scene has no cover at all, and he tries here and there to do a little shtick and stops himself cold. He's just all denuded, drained out, unadulterated.

And in good Freudian fashion, in finally confronting his losses, he almost becomes those very people whom he has lost. He tries to become two things, he's a chameleon. He's a sensitive man, I think, and it's tragic when you see people become tougher than the world they're scared of. I have a hard time talking about some of these plays because they become little monoliths in my head. And the purity of writing them is diluted by the experience of getting them up. That's one part of the theatre that I can't figure out my place in. This might just do me in. I feel very protective of *Three Hotels*, and—are you allowed to say this about yourself?—it was a really important play for me to write. It was a hard play to write. I struggled for years before writing it, even though it came out whole. It jumped around in my head, but then there's this thing called a production. And it's about actors and how it's received in the world. I know this sounds like a totally crazy run-on sentence, but what I'm trying to get at is that my own feelings about the play start to commingle with the way it's received. I have a hard time reclaiming it and making it private again, so it just seems like an empty shell: "Been there, done that." The experience is drained out. So I think there's something not useful about affirming or interpreting the play, because all I can do is summarize. That's how distanced I am from it. Really terrible.

That's also the situation of your characters when confronting their own lives.
Yes, exactly.

Since you brought up the subject of production, what makes for a good production of one of your plays?
Two things. There's a particular kind of actor that has an affinity for all the contradictions in my writing. There's also a kind of director that is able to balance the action with all the ambivalence and paralysis. The production of *Mizlansky/Zilinsky*, I thought, fulfilled some really deep, deep fixation. I was hypnotized. I could have watched it night after night after night—unlike any other play I've written. It was almost fetishlike. It had to do with temperature, memory.

Some people do Shepard plays really beautifully, they're born to Shepard. Ron Rifkin's melancholy and his way of straddling two worlds suits my work, Dan Sullivan's almost microscopic constructions, and Joe Mantello's sensitivity to temperature and tone. Actually, I don't know how to answer this question. I don't know what makes a good production, some sort of sympathy with the plight. But why would they do the play if they weren't sympathetic? You have to be able to hold a bunch of opposing ideas in your head at the same time, and suppress some of them and the impulses that come out of them.

I was thinking about the importance of civility for all your characters, the way Graydon [in *The End of the Day*] insists, "Civility is a jewel." Isn't this in part about working out a particular kind of relationship between text and subtext? Your characters so often do not allow themselves to think and feel, and they try to hold so much down. It's a kind of denial that colors everything they do.
That's true of all of them, with the possible exception of *Mizlansky/Zilinsky*, which is about an explosion of rage and outraged behavior. But yes, I think manners are everything. I'm not good at having access to the real stuff, that interplay between text and subtext. Some writers can do that, and directors more so than writers. Most of the writers I know are autodidacts, to varying degrees. I write very automatically. I'll be in

a situation and it'll stay with me in a horrible way, and that's what gets me writing. The play I'm writing now comes out of a trip back to South Africa last summer, when I sat on a veranda in Johannesburg with a bunch of American and English journalists and found them completely contemptible. They were sort of performing for me, performing stories about how dangerous South Africa had become, and how dangerous their jobs were, and how great it is to disseminate the news, what a cool, hip position that is to be in. And it was a revolting afternoon, with barbed-wire, razor-wire fencing. So we are revenge artists now—I think I'm in phase two.

So your earlier writing is more about distance than your new work?
Yes, I'm able to write more about my here and now and what life feels like now rather than about and through memory. Somehow that after-noon in Johannesburg with the journalists seemed emblematic of white colonial assumptions, which I even see carried over here. It's terrible to talk about something you're working on, but I have to. I thought, I could be listening to this conversation, or be part of this conversation, just as easily in Brentwood or Pacific Palisades. Or, this could be L.A. and these guys could be talking about O.J. Simpson and their fear of riots in East L.A. So maybe I'm a little removed or I've pulled back, ever so slightly, from writing about the ghosts of dead kids.

But on the other hand, the force of that experience must have had something to do with your memories.
I hadn't been back in twenty years, and I was a visitor, and was feeling very proprietary about my tragic South Africa. And exhilarated by the change. So I found the kind of cool machismo of the journalists, of both sexes, repulsive. And useful in a really sick way, the unearned detach-ment and cruelty. And then I realized I had been there before them. Most of them had not been in South Africa very long. It also made me realize how much I resent the entities and the institutions which pro-vide us with what we know, and how we know it.

Like the media.
Yes, the monoliths that are not unlike the company in *Three Hotels*. I do this thing, I keep writing about how easy it is for an individual—if there is such a thing now—to be silenced and join some bigger entity. Also, phase two—I'm a little bit older than when I wrote *Three Hotels*. A play that doesn't work terribly well, but that I feel very close to is *The End of the Day*. I feel like I'm sort of being pulled towards the tone of that play, and that's closer to *Mizlansky*, a sort of funny fury, funny rage.

Closer to satire.

Yes, which is always the death knell.

Why?

Anybody can satirize anything, it's the easiest thing in the world.

I want to get back to the question of displacement and exile and how this relates to an idea of America. Your characters are always reinventing themselves and sometimes shuttling back between the Old World and New World, between London and California. And America becomes a place for revitalization.

Here you can start from scratch. One of the great things about this country is that it's made up of people who remake themselves again and again. The part of South Africa I was in was very English, very colonial, and that template is so much about, "What's my class, what's my rank, what class are you in?" Not just race, we're talking about social standing. That's such a weirdly English formula. We have less of that. Money seems to be the great equalizer. There's a kind of energy here, and I guess I'm still a foreigner after all.

Your work is also less focused on political struggle than a lot of American playwriting.

I don't even know what that is anymore.

At the same time, I was wondering if being a gay man has something to do with that sense of disorientation and displacement in your writing.

It has, but it's changed now. Now there are so many kinds of gay men. I think it has more to do with growing up gay and foreign, a recipe for displacement, not feeling you're part of any group. Now most of American culture is about being gay, and if it's not about being gay it's a rip-off of gay iconography, of gay lifestyles. But I'm still left feeling like a visitor. If I had been a little, straight, American jock, a surfer in Durban, no doubt things would have come back differently. But my brother is a jock, and a composer, and his music is all about a kind of marriage between First and Third Worlds.

I was also really interested in gender roles, in *A Fair Country*, for example, and the very difficult position of women who have so many responsibilities and expectations placed upon them. It seems to me that your work shows the impossibility of that position. That's one reason Patrice goes crazy.

There's a kind of helplessness that comes from being saddled with those expectations you're talking about, when you have to sublimate. These women are not living up to their promise. They've surrendered. They're disappointed and lonely. It was very difficult watching my mother trying to cope with being a good wife, doing the right thing, serving the right stuff and being sort of uniformed. When in fact she was a comedienne in disguise, deeply subversive, funny and suspicious of the establishment. But she didn't have the wherewithal to express that, except in asides to her children, and maybe to my dad. But there was great anxiety about being judged and failing, and I don't know too many people like that now. I think that's sort of changing a little bit. It's like Eric Fischl paintings—those mothers.

Of course diplomacy and the business of diplomacy are masculine domains. And consciously or unconsciously, your work explores the homoerotic energy in that sphere. *Mizlansky* is about the secret language of guys, and speakerphones. But what's that really about? Do you know the code? Do you know the password? And then finally that becomes about how far will you go in denying who you are and selling what you believe, what little you've got. It's not that serious—it's a serious play, but it's comic. I really am interested in secret language. The secret language of acceptance. I make it sound planned out, but these are the little connections. I love listening to overheard dialogue and taped stuff. Watergate was entirely responsible for my wanting to be a playwright. I can locate it all in the transcripts of those guys going, "Let's call Dean and, you know . . ." And the great black poetry of everything implied, inferred and oblique on the Watergate tapes. I don't know why it speaks so ringingly to me. And *Mizlansky* is all about that. My friends who first produced it started doing radio plays in L.A. and were going to do it for the radio and that made me go back to it, because they called up said they thought it would be like those tapes.

In your recent conversation with David Hare in the *New York Times*, you talk about the oppositional position of theatre in U.S. culture. Certainly, it seems to me, it has been at least since the 1930s. Can theatre maintain the oppositional political stance that goes with that position? How?
Obviously, theatre's been on the run lately. I think it's important that it not become too comfortable, too subscriber-friendly, too rich, too eager to please. I think theatre has to be in the hands of, married to, cherished by young people. Otherwise, it's just affirmation, it's just High Holy Days. I don't know what's happening with that. Theatre's marginalized in American life now in such an alarming way. The only exciting thing I see is really great writing, and I admire almost all my peers enormously. I don't particularly respect most of the institutions that produce our work. Which sounds like biting the hand a little bit, but it's where I am. I see a sort of determinism at work, especially in New York. I hope some of the

younger institutions start to thrive and bubble. But I can't honestly say that I see a theatre that's a local, continual, ongoing, opposing presence.

Do you think this has something to do just with the contradictory position of theatre in this country? On one hand, people go to the theatre because it's not TV or movies, because it's different, more challenging. But on the other hand, theatres also feel they've got to expand their subscriber base.

They need to expand in order to continue to attract not just playwrights, but all artists. It's this awful catch-22. But maybe it's just a holding pattern, this sort of smog thing. I feel bad about saying this. It's not that I don't respect the institutions, or the people who built them. Gordon Davidson, Dan Sullivan, André Bishop—they were the heroes who made it possible for all of us to work the way we work. It doesn't feel the same, though. I've watched it change since my first produced play in 1985. From 1985 to 1998, I watched a great bewildering attrition, and what I call "the last audience," these generally willing, older folk. The frustrating thing in the conversation with David Hare was he couldn't explain why the young people weren't coming back. I had no idea why. On the other hand, I've been reading plays by young playwrights lately and seeing big signs. There's a big young theatre scene in Seattle that's really interesting. I've heard about it in Minneapolis, though I haven't seen it. But in Seattle, maybe it'll be like grunge rock and just mushroom. It's disconcerting to me to be a part of something that feels like it's fading, and it wasn't when I started not that long ago. Until recently, actors could make an okay living going around and doing plays. There was a circuit of the Old Globe, the Taper, Seattle Rep, the Guthrie and New York, and it ain't there now. It gets harder to cast plays. Now I have this tiny mini-theory that at the end of the century the theatre we do here in New York is more about exhilarating acting than anything else. That's the sound of one hand clapping.

Haven't there been cycles over the past forty years? The sixties, for example, was a decade of playwrights, and the seventies was a decade of directors. I'm not sure what the nineties are about, despite the fact that there are some great writers out there.

There are, I think it's a matter of weathering just how unimportant we all are right now.

What about Hollywood? Obviously, that's a crucial element in this whole system. *Mizlansky* **is in part about Hollywood,** *The Substance of Fire* **has been made into a film, and, from looking at your index cards on the walls, I suspect you're doing a film of** *A Fair Country.*

That's right, it just finished.

How do you see one, the general relationship between theatre and Hollywood, and two, your aesthetic investment in film?

I hope I can straddle both. It gets very hard. I find myself spending more time doing film work right now. I just finished *A Fair Country* and handed it in to Paramount, waiting to hear back. I finished an adaptation of a Robert Penn Warren novel a few months ago, and that took a couple years. I am waiting to find out what will happen with that. I'm going to write a movie with Robert Altman in the fall. I'm going to write a TV pilot. What I worry about is that the plays I want to write will become postponed until they become distant memories, and then, unwritten plays. That's a test of character, that's all it is. It's so simple, either you have the wherewithal to use that as a means to an end or you don't. I'm very clear about all that work. I have a date on which it stops and I'm a playwright again. I don't know how long you can do that, though. I'm starting to feel slightly torn and a little tattered by it. At a certain point you have to look at precautionary tales and see all the unfulfilled talent, and then it becomes about your commitment to something. Which ends up starting a whole new cycle of resentment and recrimination. If I think of the theatre as some sort of ghastly religion and a playwright as one of its acolytes, its priests, I start to resent that monologue. So I'm just ambivalently trudging ahead, but very excited about the new playwriting I'm doing.

I'm not a good screenwriter. I write dialogue, but I have no idea about forward motion, I need a lot of help. It's such a great thing to do—screenwriting—there's such grace in it. It's so much about mathematics and architecture. The really, really good ones who don't want to direct but just want to be screenwriters are so rare. Once in a blue moon, the work is extraordinary. I watch a movie like *Bulworth* and I think it's magnificent. It's really brave and dangerous, and it will probably be remembered as an incredibly important and ironic victory over the system. So I talk myself into thinking it's worthwhile and I can do worthwhile things. The television thing is not conventional television. It's not my love, though. My love is the theatre, but I just can't do it all the time anymore. I can't afford to, don't think it'll feed me. The movies are the great form of our time. They're a big, big draw. They're magnetic. I'm really not interested in the establishment. My hope is that independent film will start slightly to replace my feelings about being a playwright. But I never expect to be a completely full-fledged member of the screenwriting world. The danger is just this hole of unwritten good plays, or bad plays for that matter, because someone's paying you to adapt a Somerset Maugham novella. That's the end of the world, that really is.

I was astonished by the film of *The Substance of Fire* because it's so radically different from the play.
You can't tell the play's story again, it would have been death up there, it would have been like watching cardboard. That story was so much about what was missing in that play—its structure was about intermission, in a weird kind of way. It's a challenge to reinvent it, for the film is not the same story as the play. I hope there's an audience, and there actually was not an audience for *The Substance of Fire* as a film. Quite literally, nobody went to see it. The studio that released it actually didn't know at a certain time it was playing. They had to be told that it was still in a theatre, and they professed great surprise. A lot of the film's reinvention was at the insistence of Dan Sullivan. I think if I'd been on my own, I wouldn't have been as bold about it, because it's such a director's medium. He took the lead, and we worked together on *A Fair Country*, too. It's an old story: the problem of Hollywood. There's no new plot. The only thing you can do is push yourself and apply the same standards. *The Substance of Fire* is special because we raised the money and did it ourselves, and it was very much like doing a play. Nobody got in our way.

So playwriting for you is still a much more personal medium.
It's my fixation, my fetish. If I have any place in the world as a writer, it's as a playwright, I think. Not as a screenwriter. Larry Kramer told me that I'd never be remembered for my screenplays. But I might possibly, possibly be remembered for a play or two.

At the beginning of this interview you talked about writing yourself out. As I was listening to you talk about writing, and your relationship with your parents, I heard how personal your writing is and, in a sense, autobiographical. Even if you're not necessarily narrating things that really happened, so much comes out of your experience.
Right, and I think when I said phase two I was talking about trying that with a different lens, maybe a longer lens.

When you say, "To write yourself out," what does that mean exactly?
What context did I use it in? That I had written myself out by writing these stories of dislocation and exile? I think that's what I meant.

Does it work for you in perhaps a psychoanalytical way?
Yes, but it's not necessarily available to me once I've done it. It doesn't necessarily culminate in, "Now I know." It doesn't work that way. I'm interested in this set of little problems and triangulating myself on that now. That's it. Psychoanalysis, in contrast, at least when it's successful,

leads to a kind of reconciliation or at least an acceptance of chronologies or of one's inability to make a chronology, and motives, and one's narrative in some way. Playwriting doesn't really help you with your narrative. I'm always struck by the great thing Robert Stone said in an interview, which was that he had a schizophrenic mother, so as a child, life didn't provide him with a sufficient narrative. And he writes to give himself one. I had a bifurcated childhood. Maybe I write to . . . I was going to say, I write to . . . it's not psychoanalysis, though, it's not like life, so it's . . . could I be more inarticulate about this? I couldn't possibly.

Philip Kan Gotanda

On the way to becoming a playwright, Philip Kan Gotanda has discarded several different professions the way a snake casts off its skin. He started college planning to become a radical psychotherapist, got involved in the Asian American Political Alliance, went to Japan to study ceramics, spent two years as a rock songwriter and singer and finished law school before writing his first play, *The Avocado Kid or Zen in the Art of Guacamole* (1979). Moreover, as he acknowledges, his playwriting grew out of his interest in songwriting and his frustration with the confines of rock and roll. Since then, as he has written a body of diverse and provocative plays, he has also dedicated himself to directing independent films. In becoming an artist, however, Gotanda has less abandoned these other professions than absorbed them into his vocation as playwright. For all his plays bear the imprint of his interests in psychological process, in the politics of Asian-American identities, in the energy of turning unformed material into an object of beauty, in the musical qualities of the dramatic scene and in the presentation of criminal evidence. And like him, his protagonists are by and large characters who enjoy trying on different roles and identities, discovering what fits and what doesn't, what is to be salvaged from the past and what rejected.

All of Gotanda's work extends and challenges the borders of realism. While his dialogue tends to be flatly realistic, most of his plays are constructed of short scenes whose juxtaposition is anything but realistic. Frequently setting word and image at odds with each other, his plastic stage can be seen, as he acknowledges, in relation to several different traditions: American modernist and postmodernist theatre, from O'Neill to Shepard; film and television montage, from Eisenstein to MTV; and both traditional and experimental Japanese theatre forms, from Nō to Butoh. "Reinvent[ing] traditional Japanese art forms from a Japanese-American perspective," Gotanda draws on these different traditions in order to break down the distinction between reality and fantasy. For it is sometimes impossible to tell in his plays if an event is really happening or if a character is only imagining it. And while this is most evident in *Day Standing on Its Head* (1994), all of his plays disturb the relation between the objective and subjective as if to demonstrate both the untenability of the distinction and the crucial importance of fantasy in structuring desires and identities.

Inspired in part by Magritte, in part by German Expressionism, *Day Standing on Its Head* is a dream of sorts in which the protagonist Harry remembers and/or invents traumatic incidents, loves and betrayals; in which characters change identities unpredictably; and in which sex and politics, the past and present, become profoundly intertwined. *Yankee Dawg You Die* (1987), the story of two Japanese-American actors condemned to an eternity of playing stereotypes, provocatively calls into question the distinction between their off-stage selves and the roles they are called upon to play. It thereby both critically interrogates Hollywood's representations of East Asians and points out the impossibility of not, to some degree, internalizing these stereotypes. *Fish Head Soup* (1987), taking the family as the primary site for the production of identity, plays with the conventions of family drama and the difficulty of knowing reality from appearance. Pivoting on a fantasy of "the perfect Japanese-American family," it suggests that the people you know most intimately are in fact the most mysterious. Is Papa catatonic or just maddeningly headstrong? Is his younger son, Mat, a filmmaker, actor, porn star or ghost? Or all four?

Despite their diversity, all of Gotanda's plays foreground a series of related questions: What makes a self? With what is it constructed? Why doesn't it cohere as it is supposed to? For Harry's plaint from *Day Standing on Its Head* echoes silently through all Gotanda's work: "What's happening to me? I'm lost, lost. . . . I'm nothing. . . . I no longer exist." Gotanda's protagonists attempt to deal with this identity crisis by attending to history, in other words, by attempting to come to terms with the past, with their memories, their cultural heritage and their families. For most of his plays are retrospective and dramatize both the need and the fear of confronting the past. This becomes clear *in Day Standing on Its Head*, which takes the spectator inside Harry's head as he remembers what did and did not happen, and manages, if not exactly to exorcize his demons, at least to mitigate their rage. Or in *Ballad of Yachiyo* (1995), which calls up the spirit of Gotanda's aunt, Yachiyo, to examine the fatal consequences of the sexual double standard in the Japanese community on Kauai. Or in *Fish Head Soup* in which "everyone," sharing a "pot of soup," becomes an emblem for a family's confrontation with its ghosts: "When it's good and the family is all sitting around eating together—Mama, Papa, the kids—a man can never feel alone. You can feel your entire family there. Even the dead ones." For memory, family and ritual serve in Gotanda's plays not only to connect one to the past but also to give one an identity, to help one recover that lost self.

Yet the past for Gotanda is not a forgotten paradise. On the contrary, it represents, as *Yachiyo* makes clear, a heritage that is in some ways as oppressive as it is liberating. For Gotanda is no knee-jerk cultural nationalist. And his plays are dedicated not to taking refuge in the past but to learning to live with contradiction. This contradiction is inextricably linked to Gotanda's own position as a highly professionalized sansei (third-generation Japanese-American), working to carve out a hyphenated identity in a nation in which the pressure to assimilate remains unabated, while the lines of identity politics are becoming all the more sharply drawn. Or as he puts it, "Asian-Americans are just like everybody else, but Asian-Americanness can never be separated from who they are." For as this interview makes clear, Gotanda is intent both on staking out and calling into question the uniqueness and singularity of Asian-American identity.

This contradictory project is played out most explicitly in *Day Standing on Its Head*, in which Harry relives his days as an activist to confront both his own betrayal of his associates and theirs of him. Pulverizing the category "Asian-American," the play suggests that there is no politically or morally pure position. At the same time, the play testifies to an important historical shift that, as Gotanda notes, the L.A. uprising made tragically clear, and that serves as both the context for his recent plays and is their focal point: "This model that had grown out of the sixties and seventies, this *politics of the Third World* that I had been weaned on, was gone. I'd been in denial, thinking that no matter how Asians are being treated, out in the streets we're still all in this together: black, brown, yellow. And what I witnessed was that it had fallen apart. It didn't work anymore."

November 10, 1997—Hotel Metro, New York City

DS: How did you get interested in theatre?
PKG: Pretty much by accident. I was working as a musician and couldn't make a living at it, having a hard time after my second year of college. I was playing at a club in North Beach in San Francisco that was sandwiched between two strip clubs. I used to write my own songs and sing them myself, and no one was listening. They were drinking and whatnot, and it was only when the stripper came in and started dancing to my music that they actually began to pay attention to it. Then I thought, "There's got to be a better way to make a living than this." So I went to law school, and since I couldn't really perform, I decided to try writing a musical, although I hadn't liked musicals until then. I had no interest in theatre, had never studied it, had seen very few plays, and almost no musicals. But I thought I might expand on the songwriting format. So when I was in lecture hall, with legal aides doing my work, I wrote a musical based on a fairy tale. That, in fact, was a good choice, because fairy tales have a really nice structure. As soon as I got my degree, the East West Players in L.A., run by the actor Mako, wanted to do it. So I went down to L.A., did the musical, played in the band, and that was my first experience with theatre.

I thought it was interesting, but not an epiphany or anything. And I thought I'd write another one, and I wrote it, and I wrote another, and another, with less and less music, until finally I was writing straight plays with no music. I've been doing it now for sixteen years, and it's been a nice living. It's never been an overwhelming sort of passionate thing, but I love what I'm doing and I truly enjoy being in theatre. I think my first two loves were music and film, but theatre's something I can't give up. And maybe it's something I've learned, and my body has grown accustomed to, and it's become a new sort of muscle, and a part of my mind that I never would have used.

When you were a kid, did you go to the theatre at all?
Absolutely not. It wasn't a part of my world. My father was a doctor and my mother was a schoolteacher. I grew up in a Japanese-American com-

munity in Stockton [California], and it just wasn't part of our world. The closest thing might have been some traveling Japanese theatre troupes that went through, but my parents were American-born, and it was never part of my background. So in essence, I grew up on television and film and comic books. I don't have a strong background in literature.

So the fluidity of your plays, the way you use time and space, comes partly from film?
Right. One of the things I've felt over the years is that you are a product of your time and personal background, and you shouldn't be embarrassed by it. But I think some of my plays initially were a little too musically informed, and a little too cinematic. I didn't try to find a theatrical way of telling the story. But over the years I've been able to develop a way of telling a story that is comfortable coming out of my body and has a cinematic quality. My intention is not to duplicate film on stage, but to create a way of telling the story that encompasses my own historical aesthetic. *Ballad of Yachiyo* is written and presented in a theatrical manner, with cinematic, rhythmic and musical aspects to it. The whole point was to find my own way of telling the story in theatrical terms. That's been my journey, and it's been very much informed by film, television and music.

When you did start writing for the theatre, and I assume, seeing more theatre, what work did you find interesting? In the introduction to your plays, Michael Omi mentions Sam Shepard . . .
. . . who, I think, influences a lot of writers in my generation. He was the first I came across whose work made sense to me—I got it. Before that, I don't think I could read plays and "get them." They were just plays on paper that should be on stage that I couldn't connect with. Something about his work—I was able to feel it as theatre: "Maybe this is what I should feel when I read a piece that I can imagine visually." Something about his rhymes, the way he tells the story, fits my body, fits my psychological architecture, whatever that is. There have been a few other things I've really responded to. In San Francisco, I watched a piece by a puppeteer named Winston Tong who was doing some extraordinary stuff. He had these dolls that he would seat on stage and move, and carry on an unspoken dialogue with. Something happened on stage that I can't explain, but I felt, "This is so compelling, and so potent, and I've never felt or seen anything like this before." The other time was first seeing Sankai Juku. This was when they first came to America—now they're almost a cliché. But the first time I saw them, I thought, "This aesthetic comes from a totally different world." And yet as it ripped apart the things I'd always thought theatre should be, it was planting

something new. Then there were some other folks, although I don't know if they've influenced me so much as I admire them. There was a group called Culture Clash, three Latino guys in San Francisco who got started with Luis Valdez, and they do very political comedy sketches. They're truly one of the first Latino groups that was able to work beyond the boundaries of politically correct theatre, of acceptable politically and culturally specific work. Anna Deavere Smith—I really respect her work—and Tony Kushner.

When you mentioned Shepard, I was reminded how in your work you consciously play with the theatre, with the idea of performance, most obviously in *Yankee Dawg You Die*, but also *in Fish Head Soup*, because Mat is an actor/director. I was also thinking about the kind of language that Shepard uses—flat and colloquial, but at the same time there's something crackling about it. I've been struck by a similar quality in your language. Were you conscious of these things in Shepard?

Later I became more conscious of trying to figure out why his writing made sense to me, but at the time I tried not to question it. I read so much stuff that didn't do anything for me, that I could not respond to in a physical way. I really use my body to respond to things, to make choices about my work and what I write about. I don't know whether with Shepard it was because his work came from a particular era, or that he played in rock and roll bands, or that I grew up on that kind of music, but there was a rhythm to the way he told stories—maybe the performative aspect of it—that I could get. And I started by writing songs, which is a different way of thinking about form. A lot of my songs are based on an old blues structure, which is what a lot of rock and roll songs are based on. Also, the very particular way he was talking about America. He comments on it through dreams, through long, extended monologues that, in their rambling, sort of unstructured way—although they're highly structured—allowed me to understand what he was saying about America in a way I wasn't able to do with other writers.

Your work, too, is so much about American mythologies—what America means, what hopes and dreams have gone into the making of America. As well as all the disappointments.

A lot of my work has to do simply with finding my place in this country, in this world, in this time. Trying to get to the purest form of what that state and that place really is. *Ballad of Yachiyo* captures what I call a melancholic transcendence. Or a beautiful sadness. But melancholic transcendence describes a kind of writing in which mood and tone and a state of being are as important as the linear narrative—they're very much part of the journey. In that mood and tone there is a way of feeling the world, and that is part of telling of the story. My stories are informed by my own personal background, politics, personal interests. But I'd also like to think they reach back a little beyond that, whether it's genetic or passed down through some special space of a dream. That's all part of what I'm trying to capture as perfectly as possible: this entire state of my being and past beings, and funnel that into my work. The work is an attempt to find where and what that moment is that captures everything perfectly. Of course it never can.

So this is why you talked about your body in describing your way of responding to and writing theatre. Because this is a process that goes through your body.

It's of the body. What I've discovered over the years is that I'm not good at doing television or film when I'm hired to write. I can do it, but it doesn't feel comfortable. I have to listen to my body. The more I listen, the more I can hear. If I stray from it, I'm less likely to hear it, and less aware that I'm not hearing it. I'm in a place right now in my life where that's the most important thing: not to write anything but what my body gives me. That's why some of my plays took years to write. Twelve years for *Yachiyo*, thirteen for *Fish Head Soup*, ten for *The Wash* [1987]. I wrote a new play called *Sisters Matsumoto* [1998], which I've been thinking about for ten years. I just allow them to accumulate in my body. I know it's one story, and I think about it over the years, I dream about it, and I'm slowly creating it, giving it more and more life. At a certain moment it'll just jump out. When people commission me, I never know what the play's going to be. I'll say, "It'll be this or this, or it may be totally different. If you can accept that, then let's go ahead. But don't expect me to write what we agreed upon, because it probably won't be that." It's a little trouble in terms of my film work. But I've come to understand how I write and how I create, and I allow my body, as it were, to create what is, in a sense, a personal voice, a voice that is me again.

I'm so interested to hear you talk about your writing in terms of finding your voice and what you call melancholic transcendence, because I kept feeling in *Ballad of Yachiyo* that it's almost as though you're finding your voice in her. She's the ghost that's haunting the play and when she comes back at the end, she is literally a ghost. And although the puppets you use are reminiscent of Bunraku puppets, I kept thinking about Nō. Because Nō is always about the appearance of a ghost who tells his or her story, and having told it, having undergone a kind of purgation, or transcendence, can go back.

I hadn't thought about it at the time, but there is the idea of a ghost having her tale told and then being able to go on. In fact, my wife mentioned that, in essence, the writing of this play has given Yachiyo the life she never had. I want her to be remembered, to be known to have had an emotional life, and have it played out in a public way. To give her a beginning, a middle and an end. A person who is in my blood. The idea was to allow me to complete her story, as if it had been fully for myself.

I don't know whether you're familiar with Freud's essay on mourning and melancholia. But according to Freud, identity is established through loss. And there are basically two ways in which that is done. One is through mourning, by which one internalizes something or someone that has been lost and it becomes part of the self, part of one's identity. Mourning is a conscious process, as opposed to melancholia, which is unconscious. The melancholic doesn't even realize he or she has lost something or someone, but that process of internalization goes on nonetheless. So I'm really interested when you say that reconstructing *Yachiyo* is not only compensation for her loss. It's also about your own self-construction, your own body. You're mourning her through your body.

Very much. One thing I've tried to do over the years is to become less and less conscious of what I'm doing, if that makes sense. To get out of my way. And that comes partially from simply accepting and being comfortable with myself, allowing whatever comes out to *be*, without thinking about how it is going to be seen or judged in a different cultural and political time. To become more unknowing of what I'm doing. I hadn't thought about it until just now, but when I was young I was very interested in religion. In fact, when I got out of high school, I wanted to live in a monastery for a whole summer before I went to college. And I know my working has a lot to do sometimes with what is almost a form of meditation. You get out of the way of yourself, things that are unimportant just float through and pass by, and you can observe the world in a pure way.

When you're writing, do you use any specific techniques to get into a meditative state, or to let your unconscious do more of the work?

I always write first thing in the morning. As soon as I get up, I have coffee, I don't talk to anyone, I don't see the news, I don't read the newspaper. And I work for as long as I can. It may be for half an hour, it may be for twelve hours. By the afternoon, usually I can't write, but if I take a nap and wake up, then I've found that state again, and I can write. It's not a sleepy state, I'm wide awake, my mind just seems clearer of the pressure after a nap. Recently, I had this real nice writing mode I got into for just about a month, and I was able to write continuously. This had never happened to me before. It usually happens in little moments, and normally you have to work really hard to get the stuff out. I wrote in blocks of time. I would work for six hours, sleep for four hours, work for six hours, and whenever I was hungry, I ate. My wife's really a very cool person. She said, "Do whatever you have to do, and I'll leave you alone." Because I said, "This is really pleasurable. This may never happen again, so while I'm experiencing it, let me just go on this ride." And at the time, I was able always to be in that state. And I was able to write a new play very quickly, a new screenplay. But this was my own screenplay. I also wander around San Francisco to various coffeehouses because I find that I work really well in them, and I have favorite ones all over the city. If I can't write for a while in one, then I move to another one, then to another one, and sometimes I move back to my office in my house. Sometimes I drive and sit in my car at Golden Gate Park. Laptops can go anywhere.

How do you start to work on a play? Do you get an idea of what it's about, characters, lines of dialogue?

Usually it's a story. An event that just sticks in my mind and stays with me. I'm always interested in things, events, moments. After it sticks with me long enough, I begin to think of it as a possibility for a play and then, again, I just think about it over and over. Then I usually try to write the play, but I can't do it. I'll come up with a couple scenes, then I'll put it away and go back to old work. I keep coming up with little drafts and sketches and go back to them over and over. *Yachiyo* was very much like that. In particular, I couldn't find her voice, and I would go back to it and back to it. The periods in between got longer and longer. I almost thought I'd given up on it, until my wife got sick and had to go into the hospital. For some reason, being in the hospital with my wife and staying in her room overnight allowed me to start to write the play again. I don't know why. She was fine, she just had to have an operation. For whatever reason, in her room through a day and a night and a day and a night, I just wrote, and I came up with a draft.

In the brief interview in *American Theatre* published with *Ballad of Yachiyo* [June 1996], you discuss having seen David Hockney photographs and how they clicked for you formally and freed you up.

I received an award a few years ago at the Mark Taper Forum along with Hockney and Kathy Bates and a few other folks. I was remembering he takes photographs and puts them together in photo collages. And I was really having difficulty with this play, so I began to put it on cards and put it up in a linear fashion, and then I moved the cards around to see if it allowed me to see the play with a fresh eye. It didn't eventually work, but it became part of the piece and I've always liked it, even though it only occurs in one portion of the play.

I also felt you playing with form in a similar way in *Fish Head Soup*. At the end of the second act, Mat has a fantasy of the perfect Japanese-American family. And that's so interesting to me because this maker of fantasy in the play is himself a playwright of sorts. He is for his family both lost and found, dead and not-dead, simultaneously. And that, of course, is precisely the status of a ghost.

I never thought of him as a ghost, but everyone kept asking me, "Is he a ghost, is he alive or dead?" I don't know. I have so many ghosts in my works.

I often think of a ghost as being connected to personal memory in the sense that one brings up or brings back a ghost in the way you've brought back *Yachiyo*. But a ghost is also connected to history, to the past, to a different place and culture. It's as though the ghost is the way in which the personal and the historical come together.

It's almost as if it's a form, an archetype, that allows one, by focusing on it, to gain passage through it. It's a structured form that, as you said, allows the personal and the historical to be found in a state that is contained and knowable and allows one to float in time. To float in time and to meld together all those elements. I guess it's true, because I do like to move in time. One should be able to move all through time, through history, to be free to go to all those places.

It's as if the ghost authorizes you to do that.

An agreed-upon form that allows other folks—and you—to understand what you're doing.

I've noticed that your plays are so concerned with history. One is always so conscious, with your Japanese-American characters, whether they're nisei (second-generation Japanese-American) or sansei, for example. Also, I notice in so many of your plays, the primary relationships are intergenerational ones—parents and children, or parents and a surrogate child—which strikes me as somewhat unusual. I wonder if you've thought about that.

No, I haven't. I did notice there was a progression of plays that dealt with a father figure that initially talked some, and then he talked less. In *Nisei Fisherman* [1982], he talked a lot, then in *The Wash*, he talked and grunted a bit, and by the time you got to *Fish Head Soup*, he was catatonic. And I thought, "Now that's interesting." I'm not too sure why I deal with stories that involve intergenerational relationships.

One of my thoughts is that it's through intergenerational relationships that the past is transmitted from one generation to the next. And those relationships make for a particular kind of history for you, one defined by family and connected back to Japan.

It seems as if I'm always trying to remember, to trace my historical and cultural lineage from its origins to where I am now in order to explain where I'm going to go. My grandparents were immigrants. I wonder if it's an immigrant thing with a specific twist to it in that my parents, because they were interned in camps, put a certain spin on the journey of the immigrant in America. This was an event that happened to all of them, and it created a sort of mass psychology that became normal, but in some ways was pathological. I wrote about this once in one of my plays, *American Tattoo* [1983], about having a hand reaching into one's skull and creating a psychic scar. It's comparable to being punished, beaten, put in a room by your parents. And on some level you say, "I must be bad. I don't remember doing anything, being bad, but it's my parents house." Then you're let out of the room and told to go back and be part of the household again, but you always carry with you this idea that you must have done something wrong. As a consequence, my parents and family were trying to forget a certain part of their story. By and large, Japanese-Americans did not talk about that event for the longest time. They longed to forget it, to put it behind them, in a way that I think has to do with a very Japanese way of doing things—you just go on with life. But for me it meant having a secret. This event made one very tentative about one's place in America. It isn't quite a distress, it's almost more of a fear that if you do the wrong thing—which was an actual fact for my mother and father—the outside world might turn on you. And the outside world for them was the white world. My parents said that you can have white friends, but know that they may turn on you at any moment.

So I'm always trying to figure out my place in the world. When I was growing up, the history books, the stories I was told, the information passed on in the media and television didn't include me—and this was common for a lot of people. I'm not complaining. As a consequence, I've tried to find out how we existed in the past, and how I'm existing now. Coupled with my parents' not wanting to tell stories about the past, it's always been a journey for me, trying to figure out where I belong and what is my historical and cultural lineage. To understand who and what I am and my place in the world.

Has Japanese theatre at all helped you with that? I'm thinking of the use of the puppets in *Yachiyo* that are reminiscent of Bunraku.
Early in my career, I was always saying, "No, what I'm doing is very specifically American," because there's always the concern that people are looking at my work as Japanese. Now I'm more loose about that. You can see it in whatever way you want to. It simply is what it is. My degree was in Japanese art. My intention was always not to duplicate Japanese theatre in any way, but rather, knowing the spirit of it, to take

forms and use them for myself, in my own way, with my own aesthetic. So the puppets were inspired by Winston Tong, they didn't come from the Bunraku. From there, we were able to get Bruce Schwartz on board, who is an extraordinary person who works with puppets. He came out of retirement to help us, to build things and to train the people who manipulated them. I think he, in fact, knew Winston Tong.

Though I use a language that at times includes Japanese words, my works are sometimes judged as being irresponsible Japanese theatre. But that is inaccurate. For me, it is simply a way of creating a fiction that let's us know that sometimes people are speaking Japanese and sometimes English. It allows people to know that this is America, but that at times the language is from the Meiji era because that's when my grandparents came over. So I had to create my own way, an American way, a way to tell all those things and let people know about these other influences, and yet it had to be an American form—so it really is an invention. A lot of Japanese folks look at my work from time to time, and some are polite and some are not polite in saying, "I don't understand why you use Japanese language like this." Or, "You use forms and they're inaccurate." Or, "This is not how a Japanese person would think." I try to say that's not the intention, they're not Japanese. In the case of *Yachiyo*, they're second-generation, born in Hawaii, influenced by their liminality. They've moved out of the particular place and time, and now they're experiencing all these other influences around them, and changing. I knew my uncles and my aunts from that particular era and they were the folks you see on stage. In answer to the criticism that this is not how a young Japanese woman would approach the world or think and feel, I say, "My characters are not young Japanese women." Yachiyo was born and raised in Kauai, and is in a liminal situation, in a place that is both of her mores but also changing. And that allows her to experience and be influenced by and to influence a lot of other things that are happening around her. Kauai had Filipino, Portuguese, Chinese, Korean and Japanese—all these elements going on that influenced who they were. Japanese was only part.

I was also interested in the way Willie's involvement with the union gives you a way of presenting the economic exploitation of these Asian workers.
Initially that played a much bigger part. But through the drafts, the personal life story came to the foreground, and a lot of the strike material receded into the background. There were some very major strikes going on, and the one I refer to tangentially is the first interethnic strike in the 1920s when the Filipinos and Japanese actually got together, which was a big turning point.

What makes for a good production of your plays? What do you look for?

My brief response is that I look for the tongue that allows for the tongue of my story. But to answer more fully, I've set out to do two things. Because of my material, I worked initially with smaller ethnic theatres around the country. And they were the ones that were willing to do my work when no one else had any interest, except for a few regional theatres. Over the years, I've seen that my works have become of interest to most of the large regional theatres in major metropolitan areas. I try now to work with both kinds in every town. In L.A., I work with the East West Players, and also with the Taper and Southcoast Rep. In San Francisco, I work with the Asian American Theatre Company and also Berkeley Rep and some of the other theatres. That's the long way of saying my expectations are different in what I consider a successful production. What I want in a smaller, ethnic-specific theatre obviously won't have very many bells and whistles. It's like working with your family. Everyone knows everyone, there's a shorthand. You're able to reach a level of specificity in the telling of the story, and a layered way of telling the story that perhaps is deeper than you could someplace else where you didn't have people who understood everything you'd gone through historically and politically.

Whereas at Berkeley Rep, they allow me to put forth the best possible production that I can in terms of designers, actors, everything. I can draw actors from all over the country, Asian-Americans who are best suited to play the roles. So I am able to show to the world a form of theatre that has not often been seen, a way of telling a story that has not been validated. That's very important to me, too, to see the work that money and time can provide by bringing together all the best artists from all over the country. At Berkeley Rep, Sharon Ott is informed about my work. [Sharon Ott is currently Artistic Director of Seattle Repertory Theatre.] We spend a long time discussing the nature of it, how it should be presented, and what I ask of someone who is not of that world. To Sharon's credit, she has spent a great deal of time trying to understand my world by living within it. As a consequence, I trust her directing even though her own historical background, her personal life, her timeline hasn't intersected with my own in terms of geography and culture. So I want to work with Berkeley Rep and with the Asian American Theatre Company. It's one way of allowing both groups to know each other, and perhaps to survive, and also to understand the benefits of having both of them around. They accomplish different things and serve different purposes, and it's to their mutual benefit, artistically and economically, that both survive.

One thing that I think is very important about your work is the relationship between what's spoken and what remains unspoken. Because in most of your plays, there are characters who are repressing a lot. Does that relationship between spoken and unspoken change between Berkeley Rep and East West Players?

Yes, it does. Can a person not of a specific culture write about it, direct it and bring to it what it needs for a truthful telling? It does make a difference when Sharon Ott directs, and it has to, because she's lived a different life. That does not mean that she can't bring to it many things that are special or authentic. But Sharon, and Oskar Eustis also, have spent a lot of time being with me and living in that world. So they understand it in more than a book-learned way. But even then, it's important that the cast understands the difference between normal conversation and how characters deal with each other in an unspoken way. There are degrees to which one directs a line at someone else, whether it's right in their face or more oblique. A line can be spoken in many different ways. Since I work repeatedly with many of my actors, they know my world, and it helps them in being able to tell the story. I worked with a very large regional theatre doing *The Wash* which depends so much, if not on the page, at least in its presentation, on indirection, subtext and what's not spoken. Unless you know that and understand that, you're not presenting the play I've written. In one of the critiques of the play, people were saying that the characters spend too much time not getting to the issue, and that I should have them say at the top what they only get around to saying in a later scene. Because this is a subtle distinction, I might think, Maybe it does need to be more direct. But I began to realize that I have to protect my material. You have to make people aware how your material is specific and unique, what makes it special. And to do your work, they have to be able to present it on its own aesthetic, literary, dramatic and culturally specific terms. Because otherwise the material's not special anymore in terms of what it should convey. It's not authentic. I think that's the key. The world is no longer authentic. It's really up to me to keep it more authentic. So if a theatre doesn't have a feel for the work, and I sense that they're just dropping me in to fill their quota—I mean it's a practical time, people need to get their funding and make sure they look good on paper—then I won't do it, even if they're well intentioned. And/or I will be as truthful as possible and say, "These are the things I need. Can you understand what I'm saying?" Because unless we're speaking about the same thing, it's really no benefit to either of us. My hope is that I'll be transformed in some way by a new institution and that they and their constituency, their audiences, will also be transformed by the work.

Is it fair to say that this transformation is at the heart of the politics of your work?
I'm saying transform, but that's a big, powerful word. There are also very small things that a play can do. But I think it's important that the voices be authentic, which doesn't necessarily mean naturalistic, but that they come from that world. And if that's done, it can't but in some way change the people watching the play and listening to it. That's as much as I can ask a play to do. To make an audience feel something about the world, to be moved, as it were, by the world, and have their bodies and their minds shifted a bit. If you can get that, that's great.

I feel that in some of your plays you are trying to intervene in gender politics, to point out the patriarchal nature of Japanese-American culture. In *Yachiyo* and *The Wash*, for example. How consciously do you set out to do that?
I am very conscious of it, conscious of the roles of men and women in the community in which I grew up. So I do, in a sense, look for a story, pick a story, invent a story that in some way embodies those issues. But the issue cannot be bigger than the play. Then it's no longer a dramatic piece, it's a dissertation. I've been careful about trying to pick issues that feel very real, and not to comment on them in a politically correct way, but rather to tell a story with a truthful, authentic voice. In doing that, I've always tried to give all my characters what I'd like to think of as their dignity. There's never anyone who's the villain or the bad person. You see that the world is shifting around these characters, and some can change and some can't. It's a consequence of the passage of time, and history moving on.

That's an interesting point you make about not writing villains, because in *Yachiyo*, Hiro could so easily be a villain. And yet he's not at all.
Everyone's a little guilty, everyone's a little not guilty. Everyone shares, to some degree, in the destiny of the work and the story. That's how I experience life.

This closely knit network of guilt, of destiny, makes me think of the importance and centrality of the family unit in your work. Even *Yankee Dawg* is a kind of father/son play. And the family so frequently has a utopian dimension to it, because within the family there are certain wonderful possibilities that can be, if not exactly realized, at least imagined. There's a chance for joy and fulfillment within the family, even if it's just a fantasy, like Mat's fantasy of the perfect Japanese-American family. And I was thinking about that utopian idea of the family and its connection to food— that's so important in your work. Food provides nourishment, cooking is a way of caring for someone. And fishing, in particular, seems a way of connecting people to the earth, to the waters. And fishing is done primarily by men.

Food is both something I was drawn to unconsciously, but also became aware of consciously. In relation to the family, food is emblematic of almost everything nonverbal that my dramatic world is about. Films are doing that a lot lately. Modern Chinese films are all about food. In a family that has a history and a tradition that has not yet been destroyed, food says everything. What you eat, how it's gotten, how it's presented, who eats what, in what order it is eaten—everything. The whole world—history and technology—are in that one thing. You don't have to beat people over the head with it either. Even though in theatre it's hard sometimes to present real food on stage night after night, food and the act of eating are very, very important. Because as a symbol they can tell you so much.

And of course eating is pleasurable. It's an important pleasure, like sex. Although I think there's actually more food in your plays than there is sex.
They're both universal so most people can identify with them.

I know you've made a couple of films now. How do you see the relationship between your theatre and independent film work?
They just seem to fit naturally into my life now. I don't know if it's because over the past five years I've begun to do both, or to do a specific type of film. They're all made by myself and my friends. That's different from the work I've done in Hollywood, where I have, however, been writing the projects I wanted to write. But it just wasn't satisfying. And I've found doing my own films—the first one was thirteen minutes, the second was half an hour—is tremendously satisfying. They've all been shown at Sundance and other important festivals. One was presented on Public Television. I approach them in the same way as my theatre, in that I present exactly what I want to present, a story that comes out of my body, even if it seems at the time that no one's going to want to look at it. The most recent one is called *Drinking Tea* [1997], and it's basically about an older man who's dying of something, of cancer, and has a younger wife. He suddenly moves out of the house and moves in with an older woman who's kind of a spinster. And the older woman is also dying, and he takes care of her until she dies, as if he's trying to find out something about his own impending death. Then after she dies, he moves back home and asks his wife to take care of him until he dies. And she, of course, refuses, having been put through this shame. But through his insistence, they work out a kind of understanding whereby she agrees to take care of him. And she never forgives him, but she takes care of him until he dies. And that's the end of the story. I was supposed to do something a little more upbeat. But this story is

based on my uncle, and I thought, I love this. My body feels it and I can see it in my head. I know how it's told. And it's done just fine. It's gotten me into a director's lab and a writer's lab at Sundance.

Theatre and film are very different in terms of how you do them, how you write them, the process. But they don't come from two different worlds. While I was here in New York I had the actors in my cast read my next film, and as soon as I go back I'm going to start working on this film, which is going to be feature length, done for almost no money, basically with friends. I've tried to work with the same actors over and over. There's an understanding, that I will give them substantive roles, in theatre and in my films, if they in turn will make themselves available to me. One of my actors, an older actor, Sab Shimono, makes a very good living doing TV and film, but he'll pass on that and come out here and do an Off-Broadway play because he really likes the material. I then will feature him in my half-hour film playing a central role, which he otherwise never gets to do. It's a very full, complicated role. That's about the only way you can make this thing work and get the actors you want for both film and theatre. If you don't have this kind of artful sharing, it's very hard to pull off these things, because it's about money and time. Almost all of the cast are people with whom I've worked over the years and developed a relationship. They feel all of the same world. They fit comfortably together.

So you're talking about a kind of alternative family that you've constructed with your collaborators.
That's one of the few ways to do the things I'm doing.

I wonder how your work in film intersects with your plays, especially *Yankee Dawg*, because your plays are filled with the images that Hollywood and mass culture produce of Asian-Americans, and Japanese-Americans specifically. For these stereotypes have a tremendous amount of power. It seems to me that part of your project is not so much to get rid of all these images, but to offer different ones. And to write wonderful parts for Asian-American actors.
Some of my earlier works are a little more explicit in their social commentary. Certainly in *Yankee Dawg* I was looking at the representation of Asian-Americans in Hollywood and the media. But now my work has more to do with authenticity, presenting characters in an authentic light. I don't want to keep saying the same thing over and over. I've commented on certain things in my plays—internalized racism, the camps, stereotypes. But you're always evolving personally. As I said earlier, my work has to do now with trying to find my place in the world, in a world that basically has no limitations in space and time. Through

my work I can explore all my influences and see whom and what I'm made of.

So all of your work is autobiographical in a sense.
It's also invented. At the same time that I'm in the process of trying to understand and discover, I'm inventing myself. It's a dance in which you have to be aware of everything that's going on around you. It's a dance—you're discovering yourself and inventing yourself as you move along. There is a tension between inventing and discovering, not knowing and living in the moment. As you get older and accept yourself, you learn to navigate, and this balance of controlled tension allows you to live in a state of heightened odds.

When you talk about your work in terms of the balance between culturally specific theatres like East West Players and larger ones like The Public Theater or Berkeley Rep, it makes me think that your strategies provide a possible model for a resurgence of theatre in this country. Moving back and forth between different communities, different venues, seems to me a way of keeping theatre vital and relevant to people's lives.
I do know, for example, that Sharon Ott and I have had to work through certain situations in terms of race and culture in America. Our relationship has always been strong artistically, but the world around you changes. Because the times are highly racialized, it became difficult at one point for us to work together. Even though we wanted to tell the same story, how we looked at the story was totally different. We weren't seeing the same thing. This is something of a commentary on America right now: an event will happen, and depending on your racial, cultural, ethnic or gender background, you may see something totally different and truly not understand what the other person is seeing. So Sharon and I had to find vocabularies that were close enough so that we were describing the same event, the same issues. Although there's a lot upon which we don't agree right now, it was worth it to continue to work together. The advantages were more important than the disadvantages. And we would continue to work together knowing that there is an unavoidable tension at certain times. But you have to figure out how to work through that. My hope has always been, and Sharon's too, that this serves to make the material deeper and more capable of conveying issues of the time.

It seems to me that foremost among these issues is the participation in an antiracist struggle, which I think is one of the unspoken—and in *Yankee Dawg*, not so unspoken—subjects of your work.

That's such a complicated issue and it seems at times as if there's no resolution. The most I can hope for is that we are talking about the same thing, that we create a language and vocabulary that allows us to communicate, though we sit on opposite sides of an abyss.

And theatre is crucial in allowing that kind of communication to take place, that dialogue.
Anna Deavere Smith or Tony Kushner or Culture Clash are all doing that in this world called theatre where everyone can look and focus on it. You're able to feel and experience and know all these things that are happening in a larger context—and in the real world beyond the theatre. That's why I love their work so much.

Holly Hughes

In 1990, Holly Hughes was accidentally catapulted to notoriety. One of four performance artists de-funded by the National Endowment for the Arts for the allegedly indecent content of her work, she (along with Karen Finley, John Fleck and Tim Miller) suddenly found herself the target of all those who felt that the government had no business funding the arts—even in the embarrassingly paltry way it had during the 1980s. She has since become a crusader for an uncensored art that is dedicated to asking vexatious political and sexual questions in a complex and provocative way. From her early anarchic satires of detective fiction, *The Well of Horniness* (1988) and *The Lady Dick* (1985), to her more recent solo reflections on identity and loss, Hughes has been instrumental in reinventing lesbian theatre. A charismatic performer, Hughes always offers herself up as exhibit A in her solo work, questioning her feelings, her desires, her history, in a public forum. As she explains it, her work is "about making myths, poetry and comedy out of personal experience." It is an interrogation, in particular, of her identity as woman and lesbian, an enactment of "the push-pull of being an outsider—the romantic idea of being an outlaw versus the reality of feeling like you're exiled in your own culture and within your own family."

Growing up, like most lesbians and gay men, in a heterosexual family, Hughes examines both the exoticism and banality of her own stigmatized identity. At the same time, her focus on inheritance allows her to confront her simultaneous rejection and internalization not only of the middle-class values to which her parents so desperately clung, but also their very persons and identities. "I simply can't imagine," she writes, "becoming something other than my parents."

World without End (1989) stages that unimaginability, playing out Hughes's conflicted relationship with a figure whose desire she both copies and refuses. "Living in the mess" her mother made, she knows that her mother's unquiet spirit is "still calling" her. "I'm completely grown-up, and she is dead." Because Hughes remains haunted by her, she works feverishly to understand her "mother's invented French," a secret language of feminine desire. And she learns to speak this language only, in effect, by becoming her mother, by momentarily taking up her mother's identity. The piece dramatizes the contradiction that, in order to desire, Hughes must become both herself and her mother, both lesbian and heterosexual. Possessing and being possessed, she summons up her mother's ghost to ask a series of questions "about what it mean[s] to be a lesbian, what it mean[s] to be white." The act of passionate recollection becomes the dramatic mission of the piece: "I wrapped my arms around my mother's body, and my questions and I jumped into the flames. *World without End* is the record of how we burned."

As a lesbian writer and performer, Hughes uses performance as a privileged medium for examining the ways by which identities—both her own and others'—are produced. All of her solo work explores, discovers and stages the elusive presence of a ghost, an other (like her mother), who has taken up residence within the self—a set of disordered impulses and desires that always seems to come from elsewhere to disrupt the subject's best-laid plans. Simultaneously, it attempts to remember a lost, forgotten tongue, like her mother's French, that can be used to articulate lesbian desire. For as Hughes knows all too well, there is not exactly a long, rich, proud tradition of lesbian representation on stage (or in literature, for that matter). So Hughes must, in effect, start from scratch, or rather, from the secret, half-remembered tongues that she has inherited from her culture and her family. Calling attention to the indispensibility of narrative for the construction of the self, she delights in using the stage to construct herself, however provisionally, as woman and lesbian. She does so, like most performance artists, by producing deeply self-reflexive pieces, by imagining the self to be a kind of theatre in which one can try on a number of different roles. Her work thereby dramatizes the necessarily performative nature of identity, that identity—sexual and otherwise—is an activity that is socially constructed and learned. In enacting the disjunction between private and public selves, it uses a frankly presentational form that is designed to cast the audience as a collective witness. Standing, as she puts it, in the beams of "light shining out of [the audience's] eyes," she transforms the spectator into an active, if silent, accessory to the production of her various selves.

During the "gay nineties," as "out" lesbians and gay men in America have become increasingly prominent both on stage and off, they have created a new, queer theatre that challenges the slightly old-fashioned dramatic styles and stereotypes of predecessors like Jane Chambers, Mart Crowley or Harvey Fierstein. If the latter, during the sixties and seventies, attempted to empower a discrete and newly visible homosexual minority, the new, queer theatre (of Hughes, Tony Kushner, Paula Vogel and others) is intent on questioning the stability of any and all sexual identities. Thus, *World without End* is not afraid to reveal the heterosexual woman that lurks somewhere within Holly Hughes. At the same time, frankly reacting against the separatist lesbian-feminism of the seventies, the piece is more concerned with that which defies representation than with trying to carve out a space for an unblemished "woman-identified woman." For Hughes understands the extraordinary potential of live performance not only to allow a performer (and her audience) to imagine the unimaginable, but also to provide a space and occasion for a new community to coalesce. Through performance, Hughes is thus hammering out what could be called a politics of skepticism (or, if you prefer, a deconstructive politics) that leads her less to fashion an escape from a homophobic and misogynist culture than to try to use the contradictions already at play within that culture to mock and undermine its power. Like those queer theorists who take delight in reading Freud against the grain, Hughes attempts not to prove that perverts are normal, but to demonstrate that there is no such thing as normality because all desire is perverted. Simultaneously, her work tacitly acknowledges the fact that performing—understood as the act of staging the ghosts that haunt the self—is, by custom and definition, a rather queer occupation.

Since having been targeted by the NEA, Hughes's work has become more confrontational and polemical. *Clit Notes* (1994) is in part about the de-funding, and in part about her identity, not only as lesbian but as poster child for indecent art: "I've become a symbol. I've been buried under meanings other people have attached to me." But by recollecting her past, by scraping away the layers of meaning with

August 16, 1997—The apartment of Esther Newton (Holly's partner), New York City

DS: I realize, Holly, that you are unique in this book because you have an art/ performance background rather than a theatrical one. And I know you've written about this, but can you explain what drew you to theatre, to performance?

HH: When I started out, my training—such as it was—was as a painter. And I was a really terrible painter, but I wasn't going to let that stop me. It hasn't stopped a lot of other people, as far as I can see. It was a good excuse to wear the kind of clothing I liked. So I came to New York to be a feminist artist. I don't know if anyone reading the book will remember feminism—it was a kind of seventies thing, it's kind of gone the way of polyester, but I got involved with this New York Feminist Art Institute. It was a collective, but by the time I got there all the members of the collective had stopped speaking to each other. But I was in New York. I didn't imagine making theatre at all. I was really looking for…I was looking for girls, let's face it. Looking for babes. I had no lesbian skills. I got in through the back door, in all senses of the word. And it was harder to be a lesbian in real life than it was, say, in a Mickey Spillane novel. There, you could just look cross-eyed at a girl and she was yours. I didn't play softball, I was carnivorous, all I had going for me were a couple of cats. But I saw a sign. I literally saw this sign: "Double X-Rated Christmas Party for Women." It was at Club 57 in St. Mark's Place in the basement of a Catholic church. I think the priest must have been drunk or so busy buggering the altar boys that he had no idea what was going on there. Eric Bogosian was performing there, Ann Magnuson—all sorts of people who have either become famous or died. I went to this party and I just walked inside another world. It was a collective, using the word collective in the loosest sense, because mostly they were refugees from other collectives, women who wanted to be in theatre, and some of them, like Lois Weaver and Peggy Shaw, Split Britches, had been performing with other theatre companies and in Europe, and wanted to get a space for women to perform in the States.

When was this?

'82. And then in '83 they . . . we got a space on 11th Street. This tiny, narrow railroad apartment—two people were a crowd. And we couldn't decide whether it was going to be a theatre or a social club. If you wanted to make theatre, you did. Various outsider communities might be organized around sports activities or culture or political activities, but this was making community through making theatre. It was really a contrast with other feminist spaces. It wasn't separatist, men could come, in fact, there was a guy who was a professional Santa who used to hang out there in costume all the time. You could smoke, drink, you were encouraged to be outrageous and sexual. It was the heyday of Andrea Dworkin-style feminism, and this was a refuge from that. Ideas like butch/femme didn't have to be reclaimed because they weren't thrown away. There was this wonderful sense of anarchy. I was in conversation once with a woman who claimed she was a producer of videos. It was probably my first and last conversation about money. And I blew it! She wanted to do a lesbian-erotic video. And I said, "Oh, of course." I heard myself sort of positioning myself as a pornographer, because although I had thought about writing porn, I hadn't actually written any. I said, "Of course I could write a screenplay for you." And the result was *The Well of Horniness*. But she said she couldn't sell it to 42nd Street because men would not beat off to this. So it was very painful when I was accused of being a pornographer years later, because it brought back that early failure. It's not that I haven't tried, you know, it's just much more difficult than I thought. So theatre became a way to meet girls. It became an intersection for art, sex and politics.

Back in the late seventies, early eighties, did you see much performance?

I was going to galleries, and I did see some early Laurie Anderson. I saw Stuart Sherman. A friend I'd gone to school with in Michigan worked as an intern with Pat Olesko, so I saw some of her stuff, which I thought was great. I saw Spalding Gray. I still didn't think that was what I was going to do. It seemed like, "Oh, this is really simple. Anybody could do that." Just like I wrote porn and did so well with that. I got involved at WOW and it was kind of overwhelming. I got sucked into this. It was not just for dancing, it was a lifestyle. So then I started seeing work in the East Village, at the Pyramid Club, 8 B.C., the Limbo Lounge.

John Jesurun?

I saw his series, *Chang in a Void Moon*, which I loved so much. I saw early Karen Finley, Ethyl Eichelberger and a lot of other people who either became famous or died. You could see four or five performances a night.

You might not be able to hear them. They might not turn the music off. The only run of *The Well of Horniness* in the city was literally a run. I did shows at three different clubs in one night. I remember one time they were stealing the props off the stage as we were performing. At another place they didn't turn off the dance music, and ten minutes of that can seem like a European experimental theatre endurance race. I really loved what drag theatre was doing, how outrageous it was. The most legitimate theatre I went to see was the Ridiculous [Theatrical Company].

I think Ethyl Eichelberger, in particular, was a genius, one of the greatest performers I've ever seen. But I hadn't realized how important gay male drag was to your work. I was inspired by the silliness, and how manic it was, just wallowing in pop culture and high culture, and rolling it all into one big thing. I didn't see a lot of feminist theatre, but my experience with cultural feminism was that we were supposed to be more nurturing and more natural. It was a kind of bleed with the moon aesthetic. When I first came to the city, I actually was in a performance piece at AIR Gallery, which was a women's cooperative gallery, in which I played a vagina. And I got to say, "10,000 years of the patriarchy," and went, "Wooooo." We were banging against the gallery walls. We played music of the matriarchy with instruments like little shells we got from Pier 1 Imports. I felt really distanced from that. In the same way that before I came out, I was a born-again Christian. Which was actually very good training for being a lesbian of the seventies—you were sitting around in circles and singing folksongs, talking about love and trust, but with a lot of anger. Very passive-aggressive. And I had the same feeling about being a born-again Christian that I did about what we now call cultural feminism, in that I tried desperately to believe in Jesus. I had friends who had epiphanies and that sounded so great. I felt the same sense of being an outsider around cultural feminism. I was an antiporn feminist until I realized if I carried through with it, I wasn't going to have sex anymore. So I thought I'd rather have sex than be a good feminist. I wanted women to have as much fun as I saw these guys having on the bar of the Pyramid. I wanted us to be bigger and louder and sillier and I was really inspired by gay male aesthetics.

It seems to me that your reaction against cultural feminism has been very important in defining your work. You so very pointedly flirt with and enjoy many of the conventions, the attitudes and the activities that were demonized by cultural feminism. But even formally, the way in *The Well of Horniness* and *The Lady Dick* you use detective fiction—which is probably the quintessential masculine genre—and turn it around and make it mean something quite different.

Part of the idea behind cultural feminism was that you could drop out of the patriarchal culture and invent another one, "A thousand points of light"—no, wait, that wasn't a feminist who said that. But it was separatist. That was your way of dealing with a hideously misogynist culture. Now there's been a big shift in feminist politics towards engagement. Women aren't essentially better than men, that's not the problem. So a lot of my work has been fueled by wanting to represent my experience, lesbian desire, in a more complicated way than it sometimes is in the heat of political debates. If you're from a minority community and are continually demonized, erased and distorted, you first have to assert that gay is good or black is beautiful. But there's such a temptation to create a counter-propaganda that flattens and distorts the complexity of the experience. So I've wanted—and I've certainly irritated a lot of feminists with my work—to talk about the contradictions. In the seventies, there were whole categories of human experience that were seen as essentially male. Finances, money—I didn't have any so it wasn't a problem. Well, it was a problem. But sex was an inherently male category that women supposedly weren't interested in it. Coming out was such a disappointment because I was interested in having sex with women, and then I found out that lesbians weren't doing that anymore, but were opening food co-ops and doing useful work. But I felt like that was just another layer of silence around women's sexual desire.

Because desire was associated with a certain masculinized culture.
For a lot of women, the only kind of sexual power was the power to say no. The concept of female sexual agency is pretty recent and could only have happened after *Roe v. Wade* and birth control.

A lot of the performance you found interesting in the early eighties was solo performance, and yet your first pieces are plays. It took you a while to get to solo performance.
I didn't immediately imagine that's what I was going to do. Partially because I was still primarily interested in meeting girls, and a good way to meet them was to cast them in your show. The first solo I wrote evolved without my intending it to be a solo piece. I was writing about my mother's death—*World without End*. And I suddenly thought, This is a solo piece I could perform. This coincided with the escalation of attacks on arts funding and shrinking economics in theatre. There are a lot of people who would like to work in larger group situations, but all they can get produced is solo work. And at the same time there was a renewed interest in memoir, autobiography and first-person narrative. So it was an exciting moment.

Apart from performance, what theatre did you see, even when you were a kid, that had an impact on you. You write about shows like *Bye Bye Birdie* and *The Sound of Music*.

I did have thespian leanings as a child, and actually I was in a play called *Headin' for a Weddin'*, a hillbilly farce, when I was in the seventh grade. It was completely white-trash stereotype and my stage business, such as it was, was sort of scratching and picking lice. But I completely loved theatre, and I actually did my first solos at that age. I wrote these telephone monologues in which I was a woman in a dowdy outfit getting rejected by a man—and people thought they were hilarious. I don't know where this character came from. I performed them at school assemblies, then I started getting asked to do them at birthday parties and stuff. I wish I had a document of those pieces, but I have an idea that it was about learning to perform female humiliation and being rejected and being unattractive—and that was really hilarious. In fact, I was this painfully shy, gawky weirdo—and I remember this pain—but these performances didn't remove the stigma of being a weirdo, in fact it made it worse. I felt that if I could perform rejection so well then I wouldn't be rejected. But I was. Then in high school there were only musicals and I couldn't sing and so I dealt with that by feeling superior, although I did see stuff like *The Pajama Game*.

As a gay person, you look back and read for signs of your identity and how you were trying to discover yourself. And as an artist, looking back at a completely antiartistic, anti-intellectual milieu, I found all these coded images of gay life and gay sensibilities most prevalently on *Hollywood Squares*.

Paul Lynde.

I would be sitting at a little TV table eating my grilled Velveeta sandwich, and the question put to Paul Lynde would be, "Why do motorcyclists wear so much black leather?" And he'd say, "Because chiffon rips so easily." Or, "What did Archimedes discover in the bathtub?" And he'd say, "Things look bigger underwater." These are words to live by. Actually, when I was in high school, my mother brought Paul Lynde to Saginaw. This was another pivotal moment—I'm going to have to write about this. She was part of some women golfers' association and poor Paul was reduced to like doing things like *The Fourposter* in nearby Flint, Michigan. So they lured him to the country club in Saginaw where a bunch of women with Dairy Queen-style hair could see him. I remember watching him—and it's the seventies—walk into the room, he's got on this denim leisure suit, and like pounds, kilos, of gold chains, like he just escaped from the living fag stereotype museum. Just the nel-liest of the nellie. I didn't even know that I subscribed to that museum's newsletter, but I totally recognized him. At the same time that he's mincing across the indoor/outdoor, all these women are fainting into their chicken salad, "Oh! So handsome! He is so masculine!" His complete performance in Saginaw was getting up to the microphone and saying, "I get really good vibes from being here in Saginaw." And then he had to sit down and watch a one-woman show—maybe this was the first solo piece I ever saw—a one-woman *Man of La Mancha*.

That really happened?!
You can't make that shit up. Yes, he watched the one-woman *Man of La Mancha* with the help of about three dozen Bloody Marys. These ladies were just creaming over Paul Lynde, these ladies I was being groomed to become, junior leaguers, golfers, ladies who shopped in this small town. I couldn't figure it out. Is it because straight women really want somebody who's nellie? Or maybe because his fame eclipses his problems with a traditionally masculine presentation? I just remember thinking, This is my people. Take me Paul, wherever you go, I shall go.

That kind of outrageous puncturing of middle-class life I found on television. I remember somebody said, "I really love that Phyllis Diller." And I know that supposedly she's another example of self-effacing humor. But I read her as a woman who's completely making fun of domesticity, who hated her husband—who was another failure at being a man, she had to cut the meat for him—and was always making fun of housework. The message I got was that this stuff is ridiculous. I just loved how big, loud and inappropriate these people were.

That's fascinating because I find your work is about questioning domesticity and other bourgeois rituals as much as it is about challenging gendered norms. Even then you were drawn to these people who were attacking middle-class niceties.
I don't think I was aware of it then, but I found something really stultifying about Midwestern, middle-class life.

And domesticity.
And my mother spending all of her creative energy worrying about whether the brown spots on the lawn next door would pull down the property values. There's a great line in Claire Chafee's play *Why We Have a Body*, where she talks about women's minds shrinking down to one sentence: "Where did I put my pocketbook?" So much energy put into repression and sublimation, although I could never figure out what you were supposed to sublimate all of your libidinal energies into. I guess the lawn, back to the lawn. Getting out ring around the collar.

And my mother was really nuts. I think early on I got the message from this woman, who was really sexual—and inappropriately sexual—that sexuality was a form of power. She wanted to be an artist but could never commit to doing anything, and was really struggling because she was really sexual, passionate, smart and completely terrified—she couldn't imagine life outside of a small, middle-class town.

My mother's instructions around sex were so revealing of where she was at. I remember her urging me to stay a virgin, but it wasn't because of Jesus, it was because the more men you slept with, the pickier you got. The best man in bed—I'm sure she didn't use that term—might not be the best meal ticket. And saying that you had to choose between wanting to have sex and wanting to have a job. Having to earn a living was unthinkable. The mother didn't have to work. The mother had nothing to do with her time. She didn't houseclean because we felt that's what black people were for.

So, there was a linkage between sexual freedom and financial independence that sort of constellated around my mother. Sex, art and class. My mother was really interested in folk art. She didn't get original folk art, but reproductions. And so much of our energy went into hating people who might be considered folk. That whole middle-class romanticization of poverty and the other—while you're making sure there's a firewall between you and them. I did find middle-class conventions really stultifying. Of course, now in retrospect, I see that response was part of a cultural moment, of feminism, of the civil rights movement, of the antiwar movement. But also I feel lucky in many ways that I had a middle-class experience. I went to a good school, had decent dental care, health care, I really benefited from the system that I kind of despised. Which gives me more sympathy for my mother's quandary: How could she live if she pursued what she was passionate about?

Your work is so precisely about playing out that contradictory relationship to your mother and the culture she represents, which is why, I think, it has such complexity and nuance. I suppose I see your solo work as a kind of exorcism—perhaps that's too strong a word—an attempt to come to terms, to understand all the important things you got from your mother, and all the things you had to reject.

I'm just amazed at how present my early childhood is for me, how much time I spend playing out dramas that initially were staged over the cookie jar when I was three years old. When you're talking to your partner and she turns into your mother—or you turn into your mother—you learn how you get out of that cycle, and also how you fit in. What's your responsibility towards the past, towards the "sins of the fathers"? My mother came from this army family whose obituaries bragged about how many Indians they'd killed. There were a lot of amazing Navajo artifacts in the house I grew up in.

You can find your place in relationship to the past and to the future by making art out of it. And of course, I already hear the voices saying, "It's just therapy!" There is an element of exorcism, but there's also a way of writing or creating a piece in which the creative process will take you places you couldn't imagine. You'll find something you didn't know when you started. It's a way of thinking through experience. Being an artist means that this reimagining of relationship isn't finished. I look back at *World without End* and I understand that relationship in a different way than I did then. But I have a record of who I was at that moment in relationship to my mother, and to larger questions that were raised by her death. I was just at the Association for Theatre in Higher Education conference, and a solo artist was talking about reviving a piece she'd done about ten years ago. And she said, "I'd have to go back and rewrite it." I like the idea of owning an artifact as a memento of a specific time in your life. It's historical. It doesn't mean your insights aren't evolving. So, *World without End* is a snapshot of where I was at a certain point, and of a level of resolution with Mom, sex, men, women, whiteness, etc. If I were to take those same elements today, it would take me to a different place.

It's interesting to hear the language you use to describe your way of working, because I've come to realize that one thing most of the playwrights in this book have in common is that their work is about ghosts. *World without End* is about how you're haunted by your mother, and you perform the act of being possessed. You talk about sitting with your lover and all of a sudden she becomes your mother. Your work is so much about changing identity, trying on different identities. I see that as a kind of possession, never knowing what or who is going to come into your head. Do you think about your work in those terms?

The haunting, yes. I feel that early childhood dramas continue to get played out. Something frustrating about becoming a healthy functioning adult is that you feel like you're still acting out the two-year-old role in relationship to mommy, begging for the cookie.

I would like to return to *World without End* in the future to talk about whiteness. When students—or maybe most people—are grappling with questions of racism, the first idea they get is that something horrible happened in the past, but I didn't do it and I'm not responsible. First of all, racism is not safely contained in the past. And yet even for more sophisticated people who see racial injustice happening today, well-meaning white people: what's their relationship to it? Part of it has to do with the way I profit in this culture from being white. With ancestors who've fought to maintain the distinction between whiteness and otherness. What does it mean that I am able to become the big weirdo and cultural subversive? A place was made for me because I am white, because at least half of my family was upper- to middle-class. What relationship does that have to what I am now? I turn to art to try to work out that relationship. What is the role of that history? We had a Navajo rug that I grew up with and my mother was always saying, "You can't tramp dirt over that thing, it's worth a couple thousand dollars." That was her idea of something of value. When my mother died, my father decided to donate it to a museum, and it was worth a half a million dollars. This amazing fight then ensued over who wanted tax deductions and their name on the plaque. This was such an upsetting and disturbing moment, because I thought someone in my family, probably my grandfather, killed off the culture, or the cultural independence, of the people who made this. We don't know the name of the artist who made it, but we have a list of people who vacuumed it, or hired black people to vacuum it. It seemed the perfect symbol of my relationship to the past, and how we'd forgotten our quite hideous role. This was booty. And I don't know very much about the culture, except that my family tried to wipe it out.

Another important theme of this book is history, and the role history plays in playwrights' writing, which is precisely what you're talking about. I suppose that your solo work is in large part about your relationship to different histories. But history is most accessible through memory.

I'm working on this new piece—which I really have to book a date for or I'll never finish. Without adult supervision, I never finish anything. But it starts with the idea that the first thing I tried to write as a kid was a history of my hometown because there wasn't one. A day of feeling there's no history. How did we get here and why? It constellated around the fact that no one seemed to have a satisfying explanation of where the name of my hometown, Saginaw, came from. I started to think as a kid that there's no history, or there's an unspoken history but it's covered up. So that leads into my solo work in that I wasn't interested in facts. If I wanted a history of my hometown, I needed to invent it. That interplay between invention and the facts is what we call history.

That interplay is also very much about the unpredictable relationship of the self to the culture of which it's a part.

And wanting to place yourself on unshiftable terrain. Because then there's the level of personal history. My father was one of those middle-class 1950s dads whose huge presence was mostly as an absence. He was always working. There were all sorts of things we couldn't do or couldn't eat because, "Your dad likes that," or, "Your dad hates this." But who was this person? I talk in this new piece about how he was like an animal that crawled out of the woods and would eat what we set out for him, and then would just crawl back in. We didn't know where he came from, what he did, what he was. He seemed completely alien. My father had a working-class history that had to be completely covered up in our family because he was marrying up and reinventing himself as a middle-class person. But this feeling was unspoken. And I've also been haunted by images and feelings of incest. In this new piece I'm trying to write about the fact that my father and my sister had an incestuous relationship. It's difficult to talk about because I don't want to name the relationship that way, and my sister's still alive. Images of it come to me in a little burst of seeing through the cracks in the door at night, or just of sex. But what was really pivotal was my incredible envy of her relationship with him, and being haunted by the feeling that my father had rejected me.

Something I've been trying to work out is that I'm attracted to women who are masculine. I'm very interested in masculinity when it's embodied by women. What does this have to do with my relationship to my father and his absences? And I can already hear the voices turning lesbian sexuality into pathology but, in fact, whose erotics aren't made up of these little scars and push-pulls? And what is masculinity? It's a thing that possesses bodies, but doesn't have a body of its own.

It's a performance.
And what is the performance about? I rejected the traditional formation of the masculine being performed erotically by people with permanent penises. These are the things I'm trying to weave together in this new piece.

I wasn't aware of this when I started, but now I think about the way that solo-autobiographical work relates to the tradition of witnessing and testifying that's been so much a part of social change movements. Whether in the black church, or in second-wave feminism—consciousness raising. People today have some vague sense of what it was, but they didn't participate in it and don't know how powerful it is to sit around in a room and uncover narratives that aren't being talked about. There was a burst of women talking about what their lives were really like. There's a real connection to that in my work. A lot of solo performance work is being done by people who come out of these marginalized groups, outsider groups, and want to disrupt the official narrative that's either erased or distorted them. It very much relates to an

American political tradition in which first-person narrative is so important. There's a memoir boom now, and a backlash against it that's like the backlash against solo work. You have stories of people surviving incest, and of lots of gay people coming of age and erupting out of the silence that assumes we're all heterosexual. You have really interesting and powerful narratives coming out of disease, AIDS, cancer—Susan Miller's amazing *My Left Breast*—and lots of stories.

American culture has really worked to police the border between the high and the low art forms, between politics and art. Tony Kushner, Adrienne Rich and maybe Anna Deavere Smith are celebrated as artists who are also political—see, you have to be tremendously gifted to pull this off. They are great artists despite the fact that they deal with politics—because there's a sense that art becomes polluted by politics. So that's part of the backlash against autobiography, because it's breaking the silence. There's been an obsession with "the real" and "the true" on TV, on *Oprah*, an explosion of confessions, "My mother's a slut" kinds of stories. And certainly in American theatre, a lot of celebrated work has been thinly veiled autobiography—Tennessee Williams, Eugene O'Neill, Sam Shepard. Whereas a lot of autobiographical work is fictionalized. In Mary Gordon's book about looking for her father who died when she was nine, she discovers that he had invented a life that was completely different from what she experienced. So a lot of the book is about imagining who he was. I find that my work is at that juncture where high art and low art meet.

Hearing you talk about the pleasure of self-invention makes me think that your work differs from a lot of the memoirs-cum-fictional narratives. I don't want to sound too literary, too much like a theorist, but your work is not about finding your essential self, but about trying on different identities and different selves, and recognizing they are fictions and that, in fact, identity is always a fiction.
It's a fiction but it's also real! [laughs]

In that it produces very real effects. On you and the people around you.
And one of the ways I talk about my work—I've been teaching a lot about developing autobiographical material for performance—is by saying that everything is true and some of it even happened. Trying to highlight the tension between the stuff of identity and self being both invented and absolutely necessary. As a feminist, I'm a social constructionist, but I don't experience my lesbian identity as something that's been constructed. It feels like who I am. But even as I start to look at that, who I am starts to fracture and fragment and become different

kinds of answers. At the risk of sounding really simplistic, one place to start grappling with issues of diversity is to take a moment and realize the incredible diversity and complexity of experience that exists within you—maybe that's an antidote to reducing people to stereotypes. And a lot of my work is about recuperating stereotypes, taking back images, like butch-femme, that have been stigmatized and rejected, often by the left and by feminists. Female sexuality is dangerous and bloody and scary and insatiable.

Esther [Newton] and I were just in Michigan teaching the first Introduction to Gay and Lesbian Studies class that they [Kalamazoo College] had, and we spent some time making lists of stereotypes people had of gay people. Of course they often overlapped with people in the arts—but that's another story. Some think that stereotypes are all bad, but in fact, up on the board we'll have male effeminacy, masculinity in women, cat lovers. There's something true about these stereotypes. These stereotypes are often representative of real people, but they've too often become images that have been used to hurt us. How do we deal with that? Often middle-class white people want to get rid of all stereotypes, which means getting rid of drag queens and butches and people who are not assimilated and lady golfers. As a writer, how do you negotiate between the dominant culture's use of these stereotypes and your real relationship to them?

Because stereotypes in a way are "true lies." You're right—they have been used to stigmatize and destroy people, but we can't think without them. In *Dress Suits to Hire* [1987], Little Peter is a very important character for Michigan and Deeluxe— the figure they can't do without. He's a necessary lie. Which points out to me the fact that phallic sexuality generally is a necessary lie, which of course flies in the face of lesbian-feminist attempts in the seventies to get rid of the phallus.

I remember discussions with women in the seventies and even the eighties about whether penetration was okay or not okay. "Could we be more hands on, please?" *Dress Suits* was fueled by the idea that you can't escape the culture, even though these women are living by themselves. Although it was never clear whether Deeluxe was alive or dead. It's so hard to tell with so many people if they're alive or dead. But certain by-products of the patriarchy, like the concept of masculinity and femininity, haunt us. You can't shut them out. Like living in a sandstorm, the sand just comes in through these invisible cracks. One way that feminists tried to deal with gender oppression was trying to get rid of gender. But in fact, gender's part of the way we understand experience. Maybe we can come up with new meanings and new genders, maybe we can change its meaning. But I don't know if we can get away from it.

And Little Peter was part of it. I didn't think about this until recently, but Little Peter lived in Deeluxe's hand, and Deeluxe was played by Peggy Shaw, a butch lesbian who later did this amazing piece, *You're Just Like My Father*, talking about her butch sexuality living in her hands. And I think that's true, that's where butch sexuality lives. I remember having coffee with my partner and looking at her hands, and that was so important. What were her hands like, how did she use them? And Peggy, in *You're Just Like My Father*, spends a lot of time talking about her hands and that's where her sexuality is, and it was something that was completely unconscious. Ten years ago, there wasn't the cultural space for Peggy to have talked about having her desire live in her hands. To have it be that uncoded. Not that I don't like coding— I love coding, coding can be fabulous.

As I was reading through your book, I saw that the pieces are in chronological order, and when I got to *The Lady Dick*, and one speech of Garnet McClit, I suddenly and very clearly heard the voice of your solo performance for the first time.
That's interesting.

And I was thinking about the fact that *The Well of Horniness* and *The Lady Dick* are both essentially mysteries. It's almost as though the Holly Hughes solo performance persona is also a kind of detective, trying to find something, to get someplace. The process of searching is a kind of engine, in formal terms, that drives your solo work. Of course, your pieces also encourage the audience to take on the role of detective. You don't make a lot of connections for us. We also play the detective, putting the pieces together, trying to figure out whodunit.
I was fascinated by the character of the detective. Of course Garnet's voice is my voice, although in a butch wrapper. There's something tied to the erotics of the film noir that could easily translate into a butch-femme erotic system. And reading my mother's mystery novels, there were lesbians all over the place, there were always perverts. They were all about perversion and shadows. And I think in some ways that my work is about searching for female bodies. Where's the dead body? It could be anyone of us. We could be dead and not know it.

But also searching for the murderer. Who is it who has—or who doesn't have—those criminal fantasies?
Right, the romance of the criminal, the love of crime. Those forties and fifties' noirs were really heavily about masculinity and femininity, and the crime was always about sex. And the clothes were so fabulous. So in a way you don't want to solve it.

How do you work on a new piece, how do you develop it?
Different ways. Parts of *Clit Notes* I did as improvisations and I booked
nights at Dixon Place. I get blocked a lot, and so I'm always trying to
find some way to throw myself slightly off-balance so that the words
will come out. Parts were stories I kind of improv-ed in front of live
audiences. Images will come to me and I never know where they're
going to go, so it's like putting together different pieces. I work with
Dan Hurlin a lot and I show my work to a few other people. It's useful
to hear it out loud, but it's also good to hear what people are responding to, and what they're not responding to. Pieces tend to get stuck
when about two-thirds of the stuff is done and I can't figure it out.
World without End was really stuck and I realized what I needed when I
was doing a reading in Buffalo, New York, and these men came up to
me because they thought I was a hooker. Which was fine, but I wanted
to talk about pleasure and danger, the story of my relationship with my
mother, and how you negotiate that relationship as a lesbian. How do
you find pleasure in a world that's so dangerous for women? I hadn't yet
found the danger. I needed to reveal some of the rocks. So I'll set little
deadlines for myself and do readings, and then I really need feedback.
This process sort of shatters the idea that it's a solo piece. I learned form
Peggy Shaw that if somebody finds some things really irritating, you
should expand them. That's usually where the richest stuff is. Particularly if someone says, "You should never say . . ." or "Women never
feel . . ." Because I am a pervert, I go to those moments and try to make
them the heart of the show.

So a piece can start with almost anything, whatever happens to be there.
Yeah.

**Do you do much actual writing, sitting down at your computer and writing some-
thing out?**
Yes, I do, and then changing it because of the necessities of performance. How do you make this more active?

**So, the performance itself is the most important criterion because you don't really
know about something until you show it to people.**
Yes. I feel it's a costume that I put on, in a sense. And it changes the way
you move and maybe you have to let it out here and there, or maybe it
needs more feathers, or fewer feathers. Well, no, I would always think
it needed more feathers, more sequins. I don't feel a piece is finished
until I've performed it. Various times I've thought, I'm really a writer,
that's where my strengths are. I should just write it and let other people

perform it. And it isn't that there aren't people who could probably perform it better, but performing has somehow become part of the writing.

Have you ever seen anybody else perform a piece of yours?
I've seen several productions of *The Well of Horniness*. A few years ago there was a student production of *World without End* at NYU in which they turned it into a five-person piece. Somebody was probably performing the porcupine, and it was a dance-theatre piece. I taught as an adjunct at NYU for several years and I was in the lobby. I heard students talking about it, and somebody said, "I heard this is really good." And another said, "But it's three dollars." I feel like it's great if people want to do my work, including the solo stuff. And I mean really—do whatever they want with it. One line I draw in the sand is wanting women to do it. There's so much great drag literature out there, there's so much that could be converted into drag so easily that I kind of insisted—I am not interested in policing what the term "woman" means. You know who you are! Women should make it their own.

As actors should do with any play.
Yes. I recently did a piece when I was in Kalamazoo that was very exciting, and I want to do more of these workshops with personal narrative out of which people usually evolve short solo pieces. I took a theme, which was family portraits, which I thought was appropriate for middle-class students in the midwest, and made an ensemble piece out of these personal narratives. It was interesting to work in a completely different way. It's exciting to stumble upon a different way of working, weaving these different voices together around a theme. Since I don't really do plot, I don't understand it. I think a plot has yet to emerge from my life. A plot is just an invention. It hasn't been the story of my life, which has been more like theme shows or a maze or something like that. Color schemes have organized my life, food groups.

But when you say "maze," you're using a spatial metaphor and so many of your pieces use spatial metaphors. Looking at a question in spatial or geographical terms. I love the story in the introduction to *Clit Notes* about the Mystery Spot.
I actually turned that into a performance piece. I think the journey, the trip metaphor is a useful metaphor for how I live my life and how I do my work. I think of things in terms of space, of creating rooms for something to happen, where you have the room to explore something. I notice it very concretely on the subway when a certain kind of man occupies space very differently than women or, oftentimes, other people who are marginalized.

Marginalization is a spatial metaphor, too.
It's imaginary geography, but also real. It becomes real when a black person walks into a white neighborhood and gets killed. He's crossed out of the margins that he's allowed to operate in. I feel that that is an important metaphor.

Do you think this use of metaphor comes from the fact that you started as a visual artist?
Probably. When I was making this piece in Kalamazoo, the way I thought about it was not so much that I was writing it, but sculpting it. I don't know what I could do to take that somewhere, but I keep describing pieces in terms of texture, or hot and cool, rather than traditional literary terms. It's just a different language for talking about the same thing.

Like your mother's invented French.
Yes.

As you know, and might want to forget at this point, you are rather famously one of the NEA Four. Since that happened in 1990, have things gotten worse?
Much worse.

How do you see the crisis in funding for the arts both in terms of the NEA and more broadly?
It is a crisis, and I think a lot of people don't realize that the NEA no longer funds individual artists. There's no support for the sort of edgy, multicultural, weird stuff, which the NEA didn't fund enough of, in my opinion. And it gets related to other problems. You can talk about affirmative action, or the demonizing of tenured radicals, or the rampant anti-intellectualism which is part and parcel of the whole Republican Revolution. Because critical thinking can smash these easy answers that are the foundation of the "Just Say No" approach, all the simple answers they throw out there for complicated social problems. So, I think the NEA is really on the ropes, and it's part of a much larger problem. One thing that I really faced—and that was devastating to me when I was trying to organize and speak out about this—was that people on the left, people who ostensibly were my allies, did not want to make a case for art that was controversial, particularly art that talked about the body. If you read the stuff that comes out of People for the American Way, they make bland appeals to the symphony, the ballet, fingerpainting for underprivileged children—all of which is well and good, and I think should be part of the cultural smorgasbord. But they

don't talk about the work that was actually under attack. It's left up to the right to define the work. And they were getting a lot out of the NEA by explicitly attacking work that dealt with the body, and particularly the body that's othered because of HIV, race, sexuality, and work that was controversial because of its location in the cultural arena.

I happen to really love Annie Sprinkle's work and think it's very interesting. But I can't tell you how many meetings I would go to where we would get stuck on arguing whether Annie Sprinkle was an artist or not. And so a larger strategy about how to fight the right never evolved. Now you have people like Alec Baldwin and other Hollywood liberals who talk explicitly about me and Mapplethorpe and others as mistakes: "There have been some mistakes, but we've corrected them." A few people, like Carol Vance, have done some interesting work about this, but people who have a platform and are intent on saving the NEA do not talk about work that's edgy, in your face and controversial, and that deals with the body and sex.

I don't want this to sound too pessimistic, but do you see this as symptomatic of the virtual disappearance of oppositional political culture in the arts under Clinton?
I think that's part of it. That disappearance and also the growing corporatization of the arts. It's valuable, I think, to have work that isn't funded by Disney, and isn't about Disney, to have an alternative culture. And it's also the result of a puritanical streak in American culture that goes across the political spectrum from Jesse Helms to the left, where people on the left have felt that sexuality isn't an area of political concern like class or race. I would go to town halls in downtown Manhattan, at Judson Church, for example, with the downtown dance community. You think these people are really on the edge, talking about a movement research journal that dealt with artists and sexuality and gender. But the arguments coming out of those people in '91 or '92—it could have been a P.T.A. in Terre Haute: "This is disgusting. . . ." There were a lot of recycled arguments that drag is misogynist. Or, "Why were we doing this? Why weren't we being good children?" There was a huge rush in the early nineties by artists who weren't dealing with the body to distance themselves from that. It's certainly a tough sell, but I think that we lost because a case was not made. We let the right define the discourse so that controversial meant bad.

Certainly we got a little attention, I got a few gigs, but I think something bigger, more profound, that effects more people, was lost. A lot of the artists who were attacked are dead or are not really making performance work anymore. If you're out there like Karen Finley, you're naked in a number of senses. Karen's really limited her performances since then, like many other artists. It's had a chilling effect. We're in a lull as you mentioned, partially because of Clinton, and because the left hasn't figured out how to stay active with somebody in office who calls himself a Democrat. You can't underestimate how the growing power of multinational corporations has eroded so many things and cut into the time we have to consider these things. The corporations own all the newspapers, all the media, so they frame the discourse. The idea out there is that the best art is the art that sells to the most people. If so, then Sylvester Stallone is the best living American actor and Neil Diamond is our greatest musical star. And the left seems really becalmed or stuck. There's lots of talk about building coalitions and getting beyond identity politics, but that does not deal with the conditions that caused identity politics to occur in the first place. It's great to say we're going to have coalition-based politics, but it really means that you can't just say to gay people, "Shut up about being queer." You really have to commit to dealing with race and other issues. I don't know, it's very confusing and it feels like a dead time. I'm sure it's not a dead time. The one sign of hope is the UPS strike. When this book comes out we'll know how that has played out.

Considering these circumstances, how do you feel about performance as a form of political action? Do you feel it's politically effective?
I think it is, to a certain extent, but it's really shifting in a lot of different ways. The forces that are coming to bear on the performance world right now—and I don't know how it's going to turn out—are the funding crunch and the corporate culture's raids on edgy, marginal cultures that can be put on HBO or be a crossover hit. This isn't to denounce those people as necessarily sellouts. But the loss of spaces and loss of funding as ticket prices go up affect who can see the work. At the same time, when I first started doing the work, there wasn't that much lesbian culture to be seen. Now you can stay home and watch *Ellen*. I was actually surprised at how good the first *Ellen* episode was. I mean, okay, she doesn't want to be called a lesbian, but it was smart, and it was one of the first instances of gay culture visible to the mainstream. And it was from a queer perspective, it wasn't trying to address straight people. It was representing homophobia. All of those things are going to have an impact on the world that I was functioning in, and I don't know what that effect's going to be.

It doesn't seem to be good news in American theatre. I'm so continually aware of the economics and class politics of theatre. The tickets for two of the shows that I saw since returning from Kalamazoo, Paula Vogel's *How I Learned to Drive* and *Gross Indecency* [by Moisés

Kaufman], which I absolutely loved, are forty-five dollars, which excludes a huge number of people. I know at the same time, the people in the show are not getting rich. Maybe Mary-Louise Parker's already rich which is why she could do it. But those economic considerations really box American theatre into a very narrow space, to return to the spatial metaphor. What can the subscribers stand and what will they go for? For a long time performance has been an alternative to that, and part of it has been because of ticket prices, but the prices keep steadily rising. I don't know what's going to happen. I'm not optimistic about alternative culture. Maybe stuff is going to happen through the Internet, but it's not going to be theatre. Now it's lots of conspiracy theories and virtual sex. Which is better than what happens in most of the big world out there. It's entertaining, at least. What do you think? I feel very pessimistic.

I, too, feel very pessimistic. But I feel a little bit more hopeful about mass culture. The wave of lesbian films over the past few years, and lesbian chic. That's a really interesting phenomenon and I don't know where it's going to go. But I also think it's important that people like you or Split Britches, who are playing a very different role, find ways of supporting yourselves. There are so few oppositional voices.
Oppositional is good. Alternative is a word that's been co-opted, like "alternative rock," which isn't alternative. You can listen to the music that ten million people listen to or the music that five million people listen to.

I do think that the biggest problem facing any of us interested in progressive art is trying to hold onto some sort of oppositional culture, to be able to articulate something radically different.
Yes, and to find the spaces where those voices can be heard again.

Tony Kushner

When Bill Kushner diligently guided his fourteen-year-old son Tony through Wagner's twenty-hour *Ring* cycle, he little suspected his prodigious offspring would end up some two decades later writing the theatrical epic of the 1990s.

For *Angels in America: A Gay Fantasia on National Themes* (1992) has changed the face and scale of the American theatre. Having amassed the Pulitzer Prize for Drama, two Best Play Tony Awards and a spate of other prestigious awards, it has proven, against all odds, that a play can tackle the most controversial and difficult subjects—politics, sex, disease, death and religion—and still find a large and diverse audience. This achievement is even more remarkable when one considers that all five of its leading male characters are gay. Bringing together Jews and Mormons, African and European Americans, neoconservatives and leftists, closeted gay men and exemplars of the new queer politics, *Angels* is indeed a gay fantasia, writing a history of America in the age of Reagan and the age of AIDS.

Tony Kushner, a self-described "red-diaper baby," was raised in Lake Charles, Louisiana, the son of professional musicians. The Kushner's rambling house on the edge of a swamp teemed with pets and resounded with music. Young Tony developed an appreciation of opera and the Wagnerian scale of events from his father (*Moby-Dick* remains Tony's favorite novel), while from his mother Sylvia's involvement in amateur theatrics he learned to appreciate the emotional power of theatre. (He still vividly remembers her performance as Linda Loman in *Death of a Salesman*—and the tremendous identification he felt with her.) But at age six, when he developed a crush on Jerry, his Hebrew school teacher, he knew he was not like the other boys. Growing up, as he puts it, "very, very closeted," he was intrigued by the sense of disguise theatre could offer. And because he had decided "at a very early age" that he would *become* heterosexual, he avoided the theatre in town, where he knew he would find other gay men.

In the mid-1970s, he moved to New York to attend Columbia, where he studied medieval art, literature and philosophy, and read the works of Karl Marx for the first time. Still fascinated with theatre, however, he explored the groundbreaking experimental work of directors like Richard Foreman, Elizabeth LeCompte, JoAnne Akalaitis and Charles Ludlam, immersed himself in the classical and modernist theatre traditions and got involved in radical student politics. It was not until after he graduated from Columbia, however, that he began to come out. And much like Joe Pitt in *Angels, Part One: Millennium Approaches*, he called his mother from a pay phone in the East Village to tell her he was gay.

Angels in America pays energetic tribute to these diverse experiences and inspirations. Drawing on Brecht's political theatre, on the innovations of the theatrical avant-garde, and on the solidly American narrative tradition that stretches back to Eugene O'Neill and Tennessee Williams, it invents a kind of camp epic theatre—or in Kushner's phrase, a "Theatre of the Fabulous." Spanning the earth and reaching into the heavens, interweaving multiple plots, mixing metaphysics and drag, fictional and historical characters, revengeful ghosts and Reagan's smarmy henchmen, *Angels* demonstrates that reality and fantasy are far more difficult to distinguish than one might think. It also verifies, as political activists have insisted since the 1960s, that the personal is indeed the political: exploring the sometimes tortuous connections between a personal identity (sexual, racial, religious or gendered) and a political position, it dramatizes the seeming impossibility of maintaining one's private good in a world scourged by public greed, disease and hatred.

Yet *Angels in America* is not only a play about loss. For it consistently attests to the possibility not only of progress but also of radical— almost unimaginable—transfiguration. Its title and preoccupation with this utopian potential, inscribed in even the most appalling moments of history, are derived from an extraordinary mediator—the German-Jewish philosopher, Walter Benjamin. In Benjamin's attempt to sketch out a theory of history in "Theses on the Philosophy of History," written in 1940 as he was attempting to flee the Nazis, this most melancholy of Marxists uses Paul Klee's painting, *Angelus Novus*, to envision an allegory of progress in which the angel of history, his wings outspread, is poised between past and future. Caught between the past, the history of the world, which keeps piling wreckage at his feet, and a storm blowing from Paradise, the angel "would like to stay, awaken the dead and make whole what has been smashed." But the storm "has got caught in his wings" and propels him blindly and irresistibly into an unknown future.

For Kushner, the angel of history serves as a constant reminder both of catastrophe (AIDS, racism, misogyny and homophobia, to name only the most obvious) and of the perpetual possibility of change, the expectation that, as Benjamin puts it, the tragic continuum of history will be blasted open. And the concept of utopia to which he is linked ensures that the vehicle of enlightenment and hope in *Angels*—the prophet who announces the new age—will be the character who must endure the most pain: Prior Walter, a man born too soon and too late, suffering AIDS and the desertion of his lover. Moreover, in Kushner's reinterpretation of American history, this utopia is inextricably linked both to the extraordinary idealism that has long driven American politics and to the ever-deepening structural inequalities that continue to betray and mock that idealism.

It is hardly coincidental that *Angels in America* should have captured the imagination of theatregoers at a decisive moment in history, at the end of the Cold War, as the United States was attempting to renegotiate its role as the number one player in the imperialist sweepstakes. More brazenly than any other recent play, *Angels*—not unlike Wagner's *Ring*—takes on questions of national mission and identity. It also attempts to interrogate the various mythologies—from Mormonism to multiculturalism to neoconservatism—that have been fashioned to consolidate an American identity.

At the same time, the play is intent on emphasizing the crucial importance of the sexual and racial margins in defining this elusive identity. In this sense, it is clearly linked to the strategies of the activist movement, Queer Nation, whose founding in 1990 only narrowly postdated the writing of the play. This offshoot of the AIDS activist group ACT UP agitated for a broader and more radical social and cultural agenda. As Queer Nation did, *Angels in America* aims to subvert the distinction between the personal and the political, to refuse to be closeted, to undermine the category of the normal and to question the fixedness and stability of every sexual identity. Reimagining America, giving it a camp inflection, *Angels* announces: "We're here. We're queer. We're fabulous. Get used to it!"

January 11, 1994—Tony Kushner's apartment, New York City

DS: How did you first get interested in theatre?

TK: My mother was a professional bassoonist, but when we moved down to Louisiana she didn't have enough playing opportunities, so she channeled her creative energies into being an amateur actress. She was the local tragedienne and played Linda Loman and Anne Frank's mother. She also played Anna O in *A Far Country*, her first play, and I had vivid homoerotic dreams about her being carried around by this hot young man who played Sigmund Freud—you can make all sorts of things about that!—and I have very strong memories of her power and the effect she had on people. I remember her very much in *Death of a Salesman*, everybody weeping at the end of the play. She was really very, very good in those parts. So I think it had something to do with being a mother-defined gay man [laughs] and an identification with her participation. And then there were other obvious things. I grew up very, very closeted and I'm sure that the disguise of theatre, the doubleness and all that slightly tawdry stuff, interested me. I acted a little bit when I was a kid but because most of the people who hung around the theatre in town were gay men, I was afraid of getting caught up in that. I had decided at a very early age that I would become heterosexual. So I became a debater instead. And then when I got to New York, I started seeing every play.

When was that?

1974. I arrived at a pretty great time. Broadway had not died completely. So you could still see some interesting Broadway-type shows: *The Royal Family*, *Absurd Person Singular*, things that were sort of trashy but really well done, with actors like Rosemary Harris and Larry Blyden. Musicals were already dead, but there was something that resembled excitement: *Equus*, *Amadeus* and all that shit, which I knew wasn't good but at least had energy. And at the same time there was all this stuff going on downtown. I saw the last two performances of Richard Schechner's *Mother Courage* and then I watched as the Performance Group disintegrated and became the Wooster Group. I saw Spalding

Gray's first performance pieces and *Three Places in Rhode Island*, Lee Breuer's *Animations* and JoAnne Akalaitis's *Dressed Like an Egg*. And I saw one piece by Foreman, I think it was *Rhoda in Potatoland*, but I didn't understand it. It was the first piece of experimental theatre I'd ever seen and I was horrified and fascinated. My first real experience with Foreman was his *Threepenny Opera*, which I saw about ninety-five times and which is one of my great theatre experiences. When I was in college, I was beginning to read Marx. As a freshman, I had read Ernst Fischer's *Necessity of Art* and was very upset and freaked out by it. The notion of the social responsibility of artists was very exciting and upsetting for me.

Why upsetting?

I arrived from Louisiana with fairly standard liberal politics. I was ardently Zionist and where I grew up, the enemy was still classic American anti-Semitism. It was a big shock to discover all these people on the left at Columbia who were critical of Israel. My father is very intelligent in politics but very much a child of the Krushchev era, the great disillusionment with Stalinism. I guess I just believed that Marxism was essentially totalitarianism and I could hear in Fischer, and then in Arnold Hauser, a notion of responsibility that is antithetical to the individualist ideology that I hadn't yet started to question.

And there were two things that changed my understanding of theatre. One was reading Brecht. I saw *Threepenny Opera* in '76 and thought it was the most exciting theatre I'd ever seen. It seemed to me to combine the extraordinary visual sense that I had seen downtown with a narrative theatre tradition that I felt more comfortable with. And there was also the amazing experience of the performance. When Brecht is done well, it is both a sensual delight and extremely unpleasant. And Foreman got that as almost nothing else I've ever seen. It was excoriating and you left singing the songs. So I read the "Short Organum" and *Mother Courage*—which I still think is the greatest play ever written—and began to get a sense of a politically engaged theatre. When I first came to Columbia I was very involved in trying to get amnesty for draft evaders, and I did a library sit-in in '75, which was a big experience for me. It was the first successful political action I'd ever been involved in. And I met all these people from the Weather Underground who were still hanging out in Morningside Heights, and got very deeply into the mythology of radical politics. And in Brecht, I think I understood Marx for the first time. I understood materialism, the idea of the impact of the means of production, which in Brecht is an issue of theatrical production. I started to understand the way that labor is disappeared into the commodity form, the black magic of capitalism: the real forces operating in the world, the forces of the economy and commodity production that are underneath the apparent order of things.

Because of Brecht I started to think of a career in the theatre. It seemed the kind of thing one could do and still retain some dignity as a person engaged in society. I didn't think that you could just be a theatre artist. That's when I first read Benjamin's *Understanding Brecht* and decided I wanted to do theatre. Before that I was going to become a medieval studies professor.

Why?

I loved the Middle Ages and I think there's something very appealing about its art, literature and architecture, but I was slowly getting convinced that it was of no relevance to anything.

What about the Middle Ages? The connection between art and religion?

I have a fantastical, spiritual side. And when I got to Columbia, I was very impressionable. The first class I took was a course in expository writing taught by a graduate assistant who was getting her Ph.D. in Anglo-Saxon literature. So we did *Beowulf.* I found the magic and the darkness of it very appealing and I was very, very moved by—and I still am—being able to read something nine hundred years old, or two thousand years old in the case of the Greeks, and to realize that it isn't in any way primitive. And you also realize—although I don't believe in universal human truths—that there are certain human concerns that go as far back as Euripides or Aeschylus.

And of course Medieval art and culture predates the development of bourgeois individualism. . . .

Exactly.

Which you go to great pains to critique.

And it's extraordinary to see that great richness can come from societies that aren't individuated in that way. The anonymity of the art is terrifying to a modern person. It's not until very late, really until the beginning of the Renaissance, that you start to have artists identifying themselves. You realize these human beings had a profoundly different sense of the social.

At the same time, I started to get very excited about Shakespeare and Ben Jonson. I directed Jonson's *Bartholomew Fair* as my first production at Columbia, and it was horrible.

It's a very difficult play.

Yes, I know. I didn't start easy—thirty-six parts. I couldn't even find thirty-six actors. One of them didn't speak English and we had to teach him syllabically. And you can't understand most of it anyways because of the references to things that have long since disappeared. But I had fun doing it and decided at that point—although I'd tried writing a couple of things—that I would become a director, because I didn't think that I'd ever write anything of significance. I was also attempting to follow in the footsteps of people I really admired, like Foreman, Akalaitis and Liz LeCompte. I thought that the best thing to do was to write the text as a director. And so I spent two years answering switchboards at a hotel and two years teaching at a school for gifted children in Louisiana. I directed several things there to get over my fear of directing, *The Tempest*, *A Midsummer Night's Dream*, and I did my first take at *The Baden-Baden Play for Learning*, which I'm beginning to think is, next to *Mother Courage*, the best thing Brecht ever wrote. And then I applied to NYU graduate school in directing because I wanted to work with Carl Weber because he had worked with Brecht—and he looked like Brecht. And at my second attempt—George Wolfe and I just discovered that we were rejected by him in the same year—I got in.

You mention *Bartholomew Fair*, with its multiple plot lines, like your own work, and you also speak of the American narrative tradition with which your writing certainly is engaged.

I think it's completely of that tradition.

What impact have Miller, Williams and O'Neill had on your writing?

Miller, none. I do actually admire *Death of a Salesman*. I think it really is kind of powerful. And I can see how, in its time, it had an immense impact. And it's still hard to watch without sobbing at the end. But some of it is a cheat. It's melodramatic and it has that awful, fifties kind of Herman Wouk-ish sexual morality that's disgusting and irritating. And unfortunately, Miller went around talking about what a tragedy it is, the little man and all that. But it really isn't, it's incredibly pathetic, or bathetic. I sneered at O'Neill for a long time but I'm beginning to realize that two or three of his plays—not just *Long Day's Journey into Night*—are amazing. I went back and reread *Long Day's Journey* and found it so complicated and theatrical—it's about theatre in ways that the tradition doesn't allow for. I've always loved Williams. The first time I read *Streetcar*, I was annihilated. I read as much Williams as I could get my hands on until the late plays started getting embarrassingly bad, although there are some that are much more interesting than I realized. But I loved *Night of the Iguana*. And I've always thought *Orpheus Descending* is a fascinating play, much more fascinating than the Broadway production directed by that Tory weasel, Peter Hall, which I thought was just awful. I'm really influenced by Williams but I'm awestruck by O'Neill. I don't feel that he's much of an influence because he's from a very different tradition with a very different sensibility.

On the other hand, I'm always struck by the utopian longings in *Long Day's Journey*, Edmund's dreams of the sea which, I think, tie into your work.
But O'Neill's utopian longings are inseparable from death. He's a Catholic who doesn't believe in redemption, but in death instead. I was so struck by that in *Moon for the Misbegotten*: the only thing that you've got to look forward to is to rest in peace. Josie's wishing Jamie a quiet time in the grave. It's horrendously bleak and very Irish, isn't it? It's also very New England, the fog people. I don't feel that I'm a fog person. I think I'm a lot more sappy than him. Even Williams, eating the unwashed grape "as blue as my first lover's eyes," that whole vision that Blanche has of dying at sea has more space and possibility and hope than O'Neill. I've become very influenced by John Guare whom I think is a very important writer. I have to admit to not being nuts about *Six Degrees of Separation*, which I am confused by, but I think *Landscape of the Body*, the Lydie Breeze plays, *House of Blue Leaves* are amazing. Like Williams, he's figured out a way for Americans to do a kind of stage poetry. He's discovered a lyrical voice that doesn't sound horrendously twee and forced and phony. There are astonishingly beautiful things scattered throughout his work.

As I was watching *Perestroika* [*Angels, Part Two*], I also thought about Robert Wilson.
Hollow grandiosity. [laughs]

But the opening tableau, the spectacle, the angel.
I saw *Einstein on the Beach* at the Met in '76 and was maddened and deeply impressed by it. I'm very ambivalent about Wilson. The best I've ever seen him do—the piece I loved the most—was *Hamletmachine*. I was horrified by what I saw of *Civil Wars*. It really seemed like Nuremberg time—done for Reagan's Hitler Olympics. And what he does to history—and I'm not alone in making this criticism. This notion of Ulysses S. Grant and Clytemnestra and owls and kachina dancers—excuse me, but what is this? What's going on here?

So you see a complete dehistoricization?

Absolutely. And to what end? What are we saying about history? Because these figures are not neutral, they're not decorative. You do see ghosts of ideas floating through, but it just feels profoundly aestheticist in the worst, creepiest way, something with fascist potential. Also, the loudest voice is the voice of capital: this costs so much money, and you've spent so much money, and it's so expensive. There's a really unholy synthesis going on of what is supposed to be resistant, critical and marginal, marrying big money and big corporate support. He's an amazing artist, but it disturbs me. I've always felt much more drawn to Foreman and early Akalaitis. JoAnn did some very interesting things with *Dead End Kids*. And with Foreman, even if you're completely awash in some phenomenological sea, you absolutely believe there's a stern, terrifying moral center, and so much blood and heart in it. What I like about Wilson, and I felt this watching *Hamletmachine*, is: this is such tough theatre, this is hard work. I was always afraid of making the audience work.

Your work does bring together so many of these things: Brecht, the American narrative tradition, downtown theatre, Caryl Churchill. . . .

I left out Maria Irene Fornes. She's very, very important to me. I got to watch her go from really experimental stuff like *The Diary of Evelyn Brown*, a pioneer woman who lived on the plains and made endless, tedious lists of what she did during the day. And Fornes just staged them. It was monumentally boring and extraordinary. Every once in a while, this pioneer woman would do a little clog dance. You saw the monumental tediousness of women's work, and that it was, at the same time, exalted, thrilling and mesmerizing. And then she moved into plays like *Conduct of Life* and *Mud*. I think she's a great writer and the extent to which she's not appreciated here or in England is an incredible crime and an act of racism. And she's the only master playwright who's actually trained another generation, so many wonderful writers like José Rivera, and Mickie Cruz and Eduardo Machado. And she's a great director. And then Churchill is like . . . God. The greatest living English-langauge playwright and, in my opinion, the most important English-language playwright since Williams. There's nothing like *Fen* or *Top Girls*. She came to see *Angels* at the National Theatre and I felt hideously embarrassed. Suddenly it sounded like this huge Caryl Churchill rip-off. She's a very big and obvious influence. One of the things that I'm happy about with *Perestroika* is that it's bigger and messier. I found a voice and it doesn't sound as much influenced by Churchill as *Millennium*. The important thing about the British socialist writers, even the ones that I find irritating, is that that style comes out of the Berliner Ensemble touring through Britain. They have a strong Marxist tradition they're not at war with and they've found a way—Bond, of course, did it first—to write Marxist, socialist theatre that has a connection with English-language antecedants. So it was very important for me to read Brenton, Churchill, Hare and Edgar. During the late seventies, when there was nothing coming out of this country, they seemed to be writing all the good plays.

Whenever I teach *Angels in America*, I start by noting how important it is that it *queers* America, the idea of America. As the subtitle makes plain, this is a play that deals with national themes and identities, and recognizes that gay men have been at the center of that. Although Queer Nation had not yet been formed when you started working on the play, I still see the play connected to its politics. How do you see *Angels* in relation to the development of queer politics?

I'm in my late thirties now and of the generation that made ACT UP and then Queer Nation, a generation stuck between the people that made the sixties and their children. I see traces of the Stonewall generation, of Larry Kramer and, even to a certain extent, Harvey Fierstein, but also the generation of Greg Araki and David Drake, that totally Queer Nation–Boy Bar kind of thing. (I have problems with both of them. I didn't like *The Living End* at all.) But I feel that I'm part of a group of people, Holly Hughes, David Greenspan. . . .

Paula Vogel.

And Paula. I told Don Shewey in the *Voice* that I think of it as a change from the Theatre of the Ridiculous to the Theatre of the Fabulous. The Queer Nation chant: "We're here. We're queer. We're fabulous. Get used to it," uses fabulous in two senses. First, there's fabulous as opposed to ridiculous. It's amazing in *The Beautiful Room is Empty* when Edmund White writes about Stonewall being a ridiculous thing for these people. That's the essence of the ridiculous. It's a political gesture, what Wayne Koestenbaum calls "retaliatory self-invention," a gesture of defiance. And the drag gesture is still not completely capable of taking itself seriously. I don't want to talk in a judgmental way, but there's still a very heavy weight of self-loathing, I think, that's caught up in it. You couldn't say that Charles Ludlam was self-loathing. But there is a sense in which the masochism—I'm sounding like Louis [from *Angels*] now—and the flashes of really intense misogyny (when another victim of oppression is sneered at and despised because of her weakness) come from the fact that one hates one's own weakness. There's a certain embracing of weakness and powerlessness in the whole Ridiculous. . . .

John Waters, too, is such a good example of that.

Yes. And there's also an incompatibility with direct political discourse. How can you be that kind of queer and talk politics? And of course what AIDS forced on the community was the absolute necessity of doing that, of not becoming a drab, old lefty, or old, new lefty, of maintaining a queer identity and still being able to talk seriously about treatment protocols and oppression. So there's fabulous in the sense of an evolutionary advance over the notion of being ridiculous, and fabulous also in the sense of being fabled, having a history. That's very important, that we now have a consciousness about where we come from in a way that John Vacarro and Charles Ludlam, when they were making it, pre-Stonewall, didn't have. Think back to Jack Smith, that whole tradition of which he was the most gorgeous and accomplished incarnation. Ludlam died before ACT UP started. Had he lived, there's no question but that he would have had no problem with it. I knew nothing about his theoretical writings when he was alive, I just knew he was the funniest man I'd ever seen. But he was working through a very strong politics and theory of the theatre, and I'm sure the times would have made many amazing changes in his art. So I feel we're another step along the road now. It's incumbent upon us to examine history and be aware of history, of where we've come from and what has given us the freedom to talk the way we do now. We're the generation that grew up when homophobia wasn't axiomatic and universal, and when the closet wasn't nailed shut and had to be kicked open.

The progress narrative you're constructing here makes me think that _Perestroika_'s idea of history is not only rooted in dialectical materialism but also in your belief in the possibility of progress and enlightenment.

As Walter Benjamin wrote, you have to be constantly looking back at the rubble of history. The most dangerous thing is to become set upon by some notion of the future that isn't rooted in the bleakest, most terrifying idea of what's piled up behind you. Scattered through my plays is stuff from Tennessee Williams, Robert Patrick, all the gay writers that came before. When I started _Angels_, I started it, following Brecht, who always did this, as an answer: you find a play that makes you mad— either you love that it makes you mad or you think it's abominable—and needs to be responded to. I had seen _As Is_ which I really hated (I hated the production even more than the play). I had seen so much bad gay theatre that all seemed so horrendously domestic. And it's even in _Torch Song_, although I really love _Torch Song_, which, obviously, is an important antecedent. When Arnold, who desires to be straight, turns to his mother and says, "I only want what you had," there's something that's really getting missed here. When I started coming out of the closet in the early eighties, and was going to the Coalition for Lesbian and Gay Rights meetings, it was so bourgeois and completely devoid of any kind of left political critique. There was no sense of community with any other oppressed groups, just "let's get the gay rights bill passed in New York and have brunches and go to the gym." It was astonishing to discover that only ten years before there had been the Gay Activist Alliance and the Lavender Left and hippie, gay people, and I thought, "What happened? Where did they go?" And of course they went with the sixties. But ACT UP changed all of that. Now it's hard for people to remember that there was a time before ACT UP, and that it burst violently and rapidly on the scene.

It seems to me that this development of queer politics has in part prepared for the success of *Angels in America*.

Absolutely. It kicked down the last door. The notion of acting up, much more than outing, is what really blew out liberal gay politics. I mean, you depend upon the work that's done by the slightly assimilationist but hard-working, libertarian, civil rights groups, like the NAACP, but then at some point you need the Panthers. You need a group that says, "Enough of this shit. This is going too slow. And if we don't see some big changes now, we're going to cause trouble. We really are here. Get used to it." Up until that point, the American majority—if there is such a thing—fantasizes that the noise will just go away, that it's a trend. The way the play talks, and its complete lack of apology for that kind of fagginess, is something that would not have made sense before.

Unlike *Torch Song*, in which Arnold just wants to be normal, *Angels in America*, along with queer theory and politics, calls into question the category of the normal.

Right.

This is what I mean by queering America: there is no such thing in this text as a natural sexuality.

When I met you at TCG and was so stupid about Eve Sedgwick's *Between Men*, you suggested I go back and look at it again. And I did. And then *Epistemology of the Closet* came out and what she's saying is true for all oppressed groups in this country. This project of pushing the margin to the center is really the defining project, not just for her, but for bell hooks and Cornel West and so many feminist writers. Creating the fiction of the white, normal, straight male center has been the defining project of American history. I'm working on a play about slavery, and reading eighteenth century texts and it has been the central preoccupation in American politics for the entire time during which this land has been trying to make itself into a country. The founding fathers weren't getting up and arguing about making homosexuality legal, but it's been an ongoing issue. And in this century, as you point out in your book [*Communists, Cowboys and Queers*, University of Minnesota Press, 1992], it's been an obsession during various times of crisis. It always seems to me to be the case that in the concerns of any group called a minority and called oppressed can be found the biggest problems and the central identity issues that the country is facing. Also, because of Brecht, when I was writing *Bright Room* [*A Bright Room Called Day*, 1987] and reading the history of the collapse of the Weimar Republic, I realized that the key is the solidarity of the oppressed for the oppressed—being able to see the connecting lines—which is one of the things that AIDS has done, because it's made disenfranchizement incredibly clear across color lines and gender lines.

Which is why the play also goes in a sense beyond the identity politics of the 1970s. Or rather, it's interrogating identity politics and attempting to valorize coalition politics.
I think that's a good way to put it. There's still a lot to be explored in identity politics and for me one of the big questions in *Perestroika* is: what exactly does a community mean, and what kind of threat does somebody like Roy Cohn pose to the notion of identity politics?

One scene that I found very interesting in regard to that is the one in which Louis confronts Joe about his legal briefs and broaches the idea of lesbians and gays as a class.
There's an amazing term in constitutional law: suspect class. It isn't a community of like-minded people with similar material interests, as in the working class, but rather a group that has been formed, to a certain degree, by hostility from without. From the point of view of the Constitution, the forces that shape the group into a class are suspect rather than the people in the class. I find that a fascinating idea. In America, you can always talk about social justice but never economic justice. There is no such thing—supposedly—as economic class in this country. So there's a community that seems to be incredibly clear at times and then at other moments, depending on which way the light is striking, disappears completely.

You were talking before about Brecht and the importance of a materialist analysis. In your work, however, there's a much more indirect relationship between culture and the workings of capitalism.
We're in a different time. And, of course, the clearer Brecht gets, the more trouble he gets into. The closer he is to Trotsky and the further

away he is from Lenin, the better he is. There's also a question in Brecht of historical agency and subjectivity: are we the subjects of history or are we completely subject to history? Do we make it or are we made by it? That's not certainty. And with *Arturo Ui*, it's a miracle that in the middle of it he could see it all happening so clearly. But finally it's unsatisfying because Hitler was in many cases supported by the proletariat, so something else was going on. And now we're in a period of such profound confusion, it's certainly impossible to be a Marxist now. It's almost impossible even to be a socialist.

Why do you think it's impossible to be a Marxist now?
I don't want to start sounding like the more right-wing perestroikans from Russia, but I do think that we really have to ask questions about the notion of violent revolution as the locomotive of history. And that is in Marx. Of course being a Marxist is an odd idea to start with. . . . Was Luxemburg a Marxist or a communist or a socialist or was she a . . . Luxemburgan? And you read people like Luxemburg and Benjamin and the weirdos and rejects, and those are the people who speak now, even Trotsky in his exile days. Although there are things in Marx that are still of incalculable value.

It seems to me that it's useful to distinguish between Marxism as a political program and Marxism as a mode of analysis. Isn't the latter indispensible?
Yes, if you mean dialectical materialism. I think that rigorous, classical dialectical materialism is probably of great value. But any method of analysis that becomes Jesuitical is problematic. And consider that some of the most powerful political movements of the twentieth century have been led by people who were not materialists. Martin Luther King, Jr. was not a materialist. He was a Baptist minister. Liberation theology is in some ways a materialist interpretation of the Gospels, but in other ways it's founded on notions of sacrifice, for instance, that are profoundly lacking in Marx. It's difficult to separate out the political Marx from the theoretical Marx. In the parts of *Capital* that I've read and in some of the early Marx, he talks about things that are not purely materialist forces. He actually uses words like magic, spirit and soul in *The Economic and Philosophic Manuscripts*. So a Marxist-Leninism that rejects the spiritual world is something we have to be very skeptical about. Take Yugoslavia. There must be a way of analyzing what's happening in the Balkans in a historical materialist fashion. But I also can't help but think—and maybe it's just because I'm sloppy—that there's something else going on. You start to think in a kind of New Age-y way about energies in the world. Brecht did, and you can see that in his poetry.

There's injustice everywhere and no rebellion. I think Adorno was really wrong: after Auschwitz we need poetry all the more because you can't talk about these things except by recourse to forms of expression that are profoundly unscientific.

That really ties in with Benjamin and the conjunction between the political and religious, Marxism and Judaism. His politicization of Messianic time as Utopia is absolutely crucial to your project.
And his sense of utopianism is also so profoundly apocalyptic: a teleology, but not a guarantee. Or a guarantee that Utopia will be as fraught and as infected with history. It's not pie in the sky at all.

I keep thinking of that line from the *Angelus Novus*: "Where we perceive a chain of events, [the angel] sees one single catastrophe which keeps piling wreckage upon wreckage and hurls it in front of his feet." The scene in heaven in *Perestroika* really took my breath away, seeing the wreckage behind the scrim.
And there's a whole scene that we didn't perform because it just didn't play: they're listening on an ancient radio to the first report of the disaster at Chernobyl. And these are very Benjaminian, Rilkean angels. I think that is also a very American trope. In *The American Religion*, Harold Bloom keeps referring to this country as the evening land, where the promise of Utopia is so impossibly remote that it brings one almost to grieving and despair. Seeing what heaven looks like from the depths of hell. It's the most excruciating pain, and even as one is murdering and rampaging and slashing and burning to achieve Utopia, one is aware that the possibility of attaining Utopia is being irreparably damaged. People in this country knew somewhere what they were doing, but as we moved into this century, we began to develop a mechanism for repressing that knowledge. There's a sense of progress, but at tremendous cost. What will never be.

And it's Prior who carries the burden of that in *Angels*.
Yes.

And of course embedded even in his name is the sense that he's out of step with time, both too soon and belated, connected to the past and future, to ancestors and what's to come.
He's also connected to Walter Benjamin. I've written about my friend Kimberly [Flynn] who is a profound influence on me. And she and I were talking about this utopian thing that we share—she's the person who introduced me to that side of Walter Benjamin. The line that he wrote that's most important to her—and is so true—is, "Even the dead

will not be safe if the enemy wins." She said jokingly that at times she felt such an extraordinary kinship with him that she thought she was Walter Benjamin reincarnated. And so at one point in the conversation, when I was coming up with names for my characters, I said, "I had to look up something in Benjamin—not you, but the prior Walter." That's where the name came from. I had been looking for one of those WASP names that nobody gets called anymore.

Despite all these utopian longings, at the center of both *Bright Room* and *Angels* are characters, Agnes and Louis, [respectively,] who are, in one way or another, liberals. I realize that *Angels* is not about Louis, but structurally he is at the center; he's the one who ties all the characters together. Not that his viewpoint is the prevailing one.
Right.

So in both plays you've foregrounded well-intentioned liberals whose actions are at an extraordinary remove from their intentions. And of course we know from Brecht, among others, that ethics are always defined by action. Why did you put these characters at the center?
I've never thought of Louis and Agnes as a pair but they really are. I think they're very American. American radicalism has always been anarchic as opposed to socialist. The socialist tradition in this country is so despised and has been blamed so much on immigrants. It's been constructed as a Jewish, alien thing, which is not the way socialism is perceived anywhere else in the world, where there is a native sense of communitas that we don't share. What we have is a native tradition of anarchism. And that's such a fraught, problematic tradition because Ronald Reagan is as much the true heir as Abbie Hoffman. Abbie Hoffman was an anarcho-communist and Ronald Reagan is an ego-anarchist. But they're both anarchists. And anarchism is a tradition I have a lot of trouble with. The strain in the American character that I feel the most affection for and that I feel has the most potential for growth is American liberalism, which is incredibly short of what it needs to be and incredibly limited and exclusionary and predicated on all sorts of racist, sexist, homophobic and classist prerogatives. And yet, as Louis asks, "Why has democracy succeeded in America?" And why does it have this potential, as I believe it does? I really believe that there is the potential for radical democracy in this country, one of the few places on earth where I see it as a strong possibility. It doesn't seem to be happening in Russia. There is a tradition of liberalism, of a kind of social justice, fair play and tolerance—and each of these things is problematic and can certainly be played upon in the most horrid ways. Reagan kept the most hair-raising anarchistic aspects of his agenda hid-

den and presented himself as a good old-fashioned liberal who kept invoking FDR. It may just be sentimentalism on my part because I am the child of liberal-pinko parents, but I do believe in it—as much as I often find it despicable. It's sort of like the Democratic National Convention every four years: it's horrendous and you can feel it sucking all the energy from progressive movements in this country, with everybody pinning their hopes on this sleazy bunch of guys. But you do have Jesse Jackson getting up and calling the Virgin Mary a single mother, and on an emotional level, and I hope also on a more practical level, I do believe that these are the people in whom to have hope. I mean, I don't want to get paternalistic about it either. And Agnes is, as her name says, an egg. She is unformed, while Louis is a much more . . . the characters are very different. But I feel that these are the people whom the left either can hook onto and mobilize, or not. I feel that in Germany in the late twenties, these were the groups of people who came out and voted Communist in that one election before Hindenburg blew it for everybody. Their genuine good nature, their fear, lack of insight and weakness were played upon, and the left did not find a way to speak to them. Louis is a gay version of those whom ACT UP could have enrolled and then radicalized. And I do feel that ACT UP did that. Now we'll see how lasting it is.

Although none of the characters is involved with mass movement politics.
But the play is set—and I think this is very important—when there's no such thing in the United States for generally progressive people. For someone like Belize, there isn't anything. The Rainbow Coalition has started to waffle and fall apart. And there is nothing in the gay community. There's the Gay Pride parade and GMHC [Gay Men's Health Crisis] and going up every year and getting humiliated at the City Council in Newark. '84–'85 was a horrible, horrible time. It really seemed like the maniacs had won for good. What Martin says in *Millennium* now seems like a joke that we can all snigger at, but at the time, I just wrote what I thought was most accurate. The Republicans had lost the Senate but would eventually get that back because the South would go Republican. There would never be a Democratic president again because Mondale was the best answer we could make to Ronald Reagan, the most popular president we've ever had. So none of these people had anything they could hook into, which is the history of the left. When the moment comes, when the break happens and history can be made, do we step in and make it or do we flubber and fail? As much as I am horrified by what Clinton does—and we could have had someone better—we didn't completely blow it this time.

I'm interested in father-son relationships in the play—the way that Roy is set up as the son of a bad father, Joseph McCarthy, and how he, in turn, is a bad father to Joe. And the scene between Roy and Joe is juxtaposed against the S/M scene between Louis and the Man in the Park. But isn't that S/M dynamic really crucial for mapping so many of the relationships in the play? Both Louis and Harper seem amazingly masochistic, in very different ways.

I hope that the two scenes speak to each other in the right balance. I don't know if you've read Dale Peck's book, *Martin and John*. It's extraordinary. He's one of the few gay writers I've read who really deals with the issue of the father in gay life, as opposed to the mother. A lot of what he does is to play variations on father-son relationships, the father as a sexualized identity. There are things that I wanted to tackle with that, though. I want to explore S/M more because I feel that it's an enormously pervasive dynamic, that it's inextricably wound up with issues of patriarchy and that there are ways in which it plays through every aspect of life. I think it's something that needs to be understood, thought about and spoken about more openly.

I agree, that's why I've been writing about the relationship between masculinity and masochism in our culture.

We, subjects of capitalist societies, have to talk about the ways in which we are constructed to eroticize and cathect pain, as well as the way pain is transformed into pleasure, and self-destruction into self-creation. What price must we finally pay for that? I'm glad you're writing about it. Until now, there's been a kind of dumb liberation politics—all forms of sexual practice are off-limits for analysis and GSMA [Gay S/M Alliance] is fine, we just leave it in the bedroom. But of course it's not just the kind of S/M that's acted out that needs to concern us. I think that sexuality should still be subject to analysis, including the question of why we're gay instead of straight, which I think has nothing to do with the hypothalmus or interstitial brain cells, but has to do with trauma.

But isn't all sexuality rooted in trauma?

We're just good Freudians. Yes, it's all trauma and loss and the question is, are there specific forms of trauma? I believe that there is an etiology of sexuality that's traceable if anybody wants to spend the money on an analyst. Oedipus is still legitimate grounds for exploration and inquiry. And I think that the notion of the cultural formation of personalities is of tremendous importance. In another sense, I really feel that it was incredibly important that Roy's generation of gay men have that kind of deeply patriarchal, gender-enforced notion of the seduction of youth, the ephebe and the elder man. Unbelievably, we still see that popping up in the plays of certain people whose names I won't mention. All the older gay man wants is the younger gay man. That comes down from the Greeks, homosexuality being a form of tutelage, of transmission, of dominance and submission. It felt to me that that would absolutely be part of Roy's repressed, ardent desire for Joe. And then what you see replicated in the blessing scene is a form of love which has to flow through inherited structures of hierarchical power. These are some of the oldest questions with which we've been torturing ourselves: what is the relationship between sexuality and power? And is sexuality merely an expression of power? And is there even such a thing as a sexuality? Do we all want to end up like John Stoltenberg married to Andrea Dworkin? Is male sexuality always aggressive? What do we make of the Phallus? And then, what's to be made of notions like the lesbian Phallus? And how do we escape it? Any inquiry into that speaks to the larger questions which for me are really the most exciting, interesting and difficult ones: if we buy into the notion of the construction of these forms of behavior, and the construction of personalities that engage in these behaviors, do we believe in the deconstruction of these forms? What is that deconstruction? There's the issue of reforming the per-sonality to become a socialist subject, starting with the trash that capi-talism has made of us. And people who are formed in the image of the individual ego . . . how do we remake that ego in a way that isn't itself masochistic? Is there a form of unmaking that isn't destructive?

This is why I'm so fascinated by Brecht's *lehrstücke* plays. The *Baden-Baden* play: by what process, that isn't submission, does the indi-vidual ego become part of a collective? All that Brecht can arrive at is death and submission. It's that very experimental form he was working in before he had to leave Germany and decided to become Brecht the genius writer of canonical literature instead. A pilot and a group of mechanics are flying and their plane crashes in the desert and they're perched between life and death. They ask a chorus of learned Marxist-Leninists—who are the audience—should they live or should they die? And there are a series of illustrations asking does man help his fellow man? And the mechanics, who represent the working class, consent to being part of the necessity of history and live because of their consent. That is, they die and are reborn. But the pilot, who is an individual, is destroyed. He's dismantled. He refuses to die and so they have to kill him over and over again. The repetition is kind of creepy Stalinist, but what he's getting at is the absolute refusal, the marvelousness of the individual ego, and the pain and torment with which we imagine taking it apart. Is there a process other than revolution, other than bloodshed, agony and pain—which is fundamentally masochistic—by which we can transform ourselves into socialist subjects? That's a big question and it turns you toward things like Zen.

That's the question of the play: what is there beyond pain? Is Utopia even imaginable? And the loss. It's the thing that I don't understand at all, which I think is under-theorized and under-represented in the problematics of the left. If our lives are in fact shaped by trauma and loss—and as I get older it seems to me that life is very, very profoundly shaped by loss and death—how do you address that? And how does one progress in the face of that? That's the question that the AIDS epidemic has asked. Because there is nothing more optimistic than America, in the most awful way (like "Up with People"). It makes so many people queasy and it's the subject of so much sarcasm because it seems so dumb. But identity is shaped, even racial identity. If there weren't bigots, there wouldn't be a politics of race. That there has to be a politics of difference speaks to the presence of enormous oppression and violence and terror. What do we do? It's an interesting thing because the more we know about history, the more we realize—and this is an important thing about sado-masochism—that it really does return, it never ends. You can just see in our present moment a thousand future Sarajevos. You just know that when you're ninety, if you live so long, they'll still be fighting. Even after the Holocaust, the monsters are still among us. And can you forgive? That's why I ask this question of forgiveness because its possibility is also, I think, under-theorized and under-expressed.

Relating to the question of forgiveness, why do you use Mormons in the play, along with Jews? Because the angels are so clearly Old Testament angels, angels of the vengeful God. How does that tie in with the Mormon religion? There are interesting similarities between Mormonism and Judaism. They both have a very elusive notion of damnation. It's always been unclear to me, as a Jew, what happens if you don't do good things. Presumably you don't go to Paradise. There is a Hell but, even among the Orthodox, there isn't an enormous body of literature about it—it's not like Catholicism. Mormonism has a Hell but it has three layers of Heaven, four actually, that I know of. Also, Mormonism is a diasporic religion. And as far as I'm concerned, the most interesting thing about Judaism is the whole diasporic, secular culture. Mormonism is of the book. It draws its strength very much from the literal, physical volume, which isn't sacred like the Torah, but it's all about the discovery of a book. They say that Joseph Smith had a Hebrew teacher who was a rabbi. Also, Judaism, like Mormonism, is not a religion about redemption based on being sorry for what you've done and asking for forgiveness. The hallmark of Mormonism is, "By deeds ye shall be known." As you said, ethics are defined by action. And that is also true in Judaism. Your intentions make very little difference to God. What counts is what you do and whether you're righteous in your life. That appeals to me. It also feels very American. I wanted to have an orthodox religion that someone was having a lot of trouble with but I didn't want Orthodox Judaism. And I wanted something American.

I started the play with an image of an angel crashing through a bedroom ceiling and I knew that this play would have a connection to American themes. So the title, *Angels in America*, came from that. And I think the title, as much as anything else, suggested Mormons because the prototypical American angel is the angel Moroni. It's of this continent, the place that Jesus visited after he was crucified. It's like Blake and the New Jerusalem. Christ was here and this continent does have some tendrils snaking back into biblical mythology. It's a great story—not the Book of Mormon which, as Mark Twain said, is chloroform in print—but the story of Joseph Smith's life and the trek, the gathering of Zion. That's so American. The idea of inventing a complete cosmology out of a personal vision is something I can't imagine a European doing. I guess Swedenborg and Blake sort of did that but it didn't become this theocratic empire. And unlike Swedenborg, which is rather elegant and beautiful, and Blake, which is extraordinarily beautiful but mostly incomprehensible, it's so dumb. It's so naive and disingenuous. It's like Grandma Moses, the celestial and the terrestrial heavens, with all this masonry incorporated into it. It's so American Gothic. I wanted Mormons in this play. I find their immense industry, diligence and faith moving. The symbol of Utah and of the Mormon kingdom of God is a beehive, which is, in its own way, a socialist, communist image. And there were a lot of experiments in Utah of communally owned property, which is what Joseph Smith originally dictated, with wealth held in common, and experiments with controlled economies. Their social experiments were independent of, but similar to, European socialist, communal notions of the nineteenth century.

Now, they're so right-wing and horrible. Although the Mormons I've met I've actually sort of liked. I've found something dear and nice about them—they have good strong families, with all the horror that that implies. But I think, as with Judaism, there's not an enormously high incidence of grotesque abuses of patriarchal power, incest or wife-beating, for example. So they come out as nice people with centers while most conservatives are so horrendous. When I was working on Joe, I wanted to write a conservative man that I actually liked. I didn't finally succeed. [laughs] Although I feel that he gets somewhere and will ultimately be redeemable—in *Angels*, part three. Along with bits and pieces of Mormonism, I used the Kabbala for the angels. They're mostly from Holy Scripture and the Kabbala, except in their method of delivering the epistle—purely Mormon. The idea of a man who gets a set of spectacles from an angel—only in America: *The Fly* as theology.

So you envision writing more parts to *Angels in America*?
I'm a little nervous about it because I think *Angels* is my best play because with it I started writing about my world. There's a kind of safety in writing a history play—you can make up everything. And it insulates you to a certain extent from the the assault of everyday life. But I've also decided to write more *Angels in America* plays and those may be the only ones in which I deal with contemporary reality. When I was writing *Perestroika* this summer, I got very, very angry at the characters. At first, I thought it was because I was sick of them, but now I've come to realize that I hated the idea of not being able to work on them anymore. I want to know what happens to them. I already have most of the plot of part three in my head. It won't be continuous, but I could have a cycle of nine or ten plays by the time I'm done. The characters will get older as I get older. I'll be bringing in new ones and letting characters like Roy go. So, I'm excited about that. I think it's harder to write that kind of play than a history play.

Although I think of *Angels in America* as a history play.
In a sense it is. Although when I started writing it, it wasn't. But it receded into the past. As it gets older, it will become increasingly about a period of history. There is a danger for me of writing too much out of books because I'm sort of socially awkward and not much of an adventurer. I don't want to write only about the past. Brecht never wrote anything about his contemporaries. Did he?

Arturo Ui.
Except it's set in Chicago and they're speaking in a very different way.

What about the learning plays?
But again, they're drowned in pseudo-Confucian poetry and set in China and other places.

But in all of his work he was historicizing his particular moment.
Exactly. That's all you can ever do.

November 7, 1997—Tony Kushner's office, New York City

In interviewing playwrights for this book, I've discovered that it is in part about ghosts. And this has led me to think about how ghosts figure in your work, the fact that they are so crucial in *Angels in America*. And *A Dybbuk* [1995] is all about a ghost. Do you think of your theatre as an act of mourning?
I've come to understand that as part of the *Angels* phenomenon. In the places where it has settled in, it's become a site for people to make a kind of collective mourning ritual. And the play has its churchly aspects, ending with the benediction.

And including the Kaddish.
And the appearance of the angel has got a kind of comfortably secular-theological quality, inclusive of several traditions, so it doesn't exclude anyone, and it's agnostic, for the people who aren't entirely sure where they land. I think any theatre about AIDS or any great historical calamity is going to have a commemorative function.

I've been thinking about this in relation to Freud's theories of mourning and melan-cholia, and about how for Freud identity is founded on loss. One internalizes what one has lost, either consciously or unconsciously. It seems to me that in some ways your work is much more related to mourning because it's a conscious process in the play.
My understanding is that melancholia is a blocked process. It's mourn-ing that has turned in on itself, has lost its fundamentally dynamic nature and has become badly, injuriously eroticized so that it can't be let go of, and one sinks into a kind of despair. I'm interested in the rela-tionship between the political and the funereal and the ways in which grieving and commemorating are also politicizing processes—the close encounter with death, despair, melancholy and an abandonment of the world that one makes when one is grieving a terrible loss. The struggle that one makes to find one's way from Hades back to the daylight, and not get caught down there with the shades. That process in a million little ways rehearses and travels through every day of your life. Confronting the struggle against the violence and overwhelming despair of our times, and the quiescence of any active oppositional

force, any utopian alternative. You go through this every morning to get out of bed, so when somebody dies there's something terribly familiar about grieving, because you've been doing it all of your life. It begins in childhood with the processes of separation and individuation.

So mourning can be done not just for an individual but for a particular kind of politics. *Angels* looks back to the oppositional politics of the sixties and the thirties, as well as to the Rosenbergs and McCarthyism.

Mourning even a single AIDS death connects you to an entire generation of people who have died and to a certain kind of innocence that contained radical political possibility. Sexual radicalism before AIDS represented a kind of dangerous innocence but that loss of innocence must still be mourned. There is a certain problem with unfettered sexual activity, but the biological problems shouldn't keep one from recognizing, at least theoretically, what such a life suggests about the structures of political economy. When the epidemic came along, we lost a tremendous amount of daring and courage and the power to imagine what was possible. And one must grieve for that.

I find myself in a weird position now as a kind of a socialist nostalgist, a purveyor of lamentation for what still seems an incredibly important and vital idea and tradition. When one is talking about socialism, one tends to slip into the worst sort of sentiment and nostalgia. But one can't go forward without looking back. One can't be political without a sense of history. Remembering means mourning politically. I am in constant mourning for not having been able to participate in the sixties as an adult. I feel angrily defensive about having been a kid in a small town in Louisiana. But I still feel like a child of the sixties and that it's as important to defend the sixties as to defend the notion of the communal, or socialism or centrally planned economies. There's a constant assault by right-wing cultural and academic forces that has to be weighed-in against.

Often in theatre, memory and history are imagined as being at odds with one another. But in your work memory opens the door to history.

Memory is where lost history begins. There's a great quote from Yerushalmi: the antonym of justice is not injustice but forgetting. And we see today how critical memory is in the pursuit of justice and the creation of history. The re-creation of war crimes in Bosnia is based entirely on stories that people have been telling which prove to be astoundingly accurate. The history of all holocausts is based on memory. But it's not misremembering that frightens me, but an inveterate psychoanalyzing that insists that all memory has to be read and interpreted. I'm not a fundamentalist in either religion or history, and I don't believe in a literal reading of anything. But I'm nervous about this attempt to discredit memory. Badly produced history can do tremendous damage. The scary thing to me is when the act of remembering is demonized, which one sees in the assault on political correctness, on the left academy, on African-American studies, on lesbian and gay studies and feminism.

When I spoke to you three or four years ago, right after *Perestroika* opened on Broadway, you were more sanguine politically then you seem now. I certainly was much more hopeful then. It seems to me that Clinton has brilliantly repressed and marginalized the left. When you were writing *Angels in America*, ACT UP and Queer Nation were active and vital forces. There's not a great deal of queer mass-movement politics now. There's not much mass-movement politics, period. Or we have events like the Million Man March.

And the Promise Keepers. In the lesbian-gay movement this weird turn really surprises me: diversity has become a way of dismantling the movement. I just participated in a reading of *Gay Men at the Millennium*, put together by Michael Lowenthal, with Bruce Bawer, Michelangelo Signorile, Gabriel Rotello and people like that. Everybody gets up and says, "We're not one community, we're many communities." That sounds great because we all know that when gay men talked about "the community," it meant the community of white gay men, and no one else was welcome. Now they're embracing the notion of many communities, but one almost feels that it's more in the name of balkanization and tribalism. We're not many communities with one common cause, or with several common causes, we're just many communities. You feel they're saying, "You play over there and I'll play over here. You leave me alone and I'll leave you alone." That's not at all the idea behind the recognition of difference and diversity. It's a new kind of separatism that's unnervingly appearing at exactly the moment when, on the cultural front, "the movement" is racking up some astounding successes.

But it's a very disturbing time. All the political energy of ACT UP seems to have gone into the Big Cup [gay coffeehouse in the Chelsea neighborhood of New York City] and Chelsea body building. And what killed it, horribly, was racism and sexism, because ACT UP died when the demographics began to change and women and people of color became the new targeted group of the epidemic. And when women and people of color in ACT UP began to demand equal time and attention, everybody picked up their toys and went home. Also, no political group is going to have more than a few years of brilliant success, and ACT UP certainly had its share. Queer Nation had no line of analysis. Looking back historically it just seems a spin-off of ACT UP.

It's a really weird political time. Maybe because I've just turned forty-one and I can look back. I go to college campuses and talk to kids who were born the year Reagan was first elected, and I think, "God, that seems like yesterday." So I'm experiencing time-shift feelings that have to do with becoming middle-aged and feeling my mortality and so on. I feel very confused politically. Clinton did all the damage that people on the left, who were worried about having a centrist, neo-con, whatever-he-is Democrat in the office, thought he would do. He did demobilize most of what was active and vital in the opposition, because people trusted him. A lot of people on the outside, who had powerful, strong voices, just hung around the White House while he signed the Welfare Bill. But then, on the other hand, I genuinely believe things would have been worse had there been a Republican in office. There would have been a Welfare Bill anyway. The Democrats would have mounted their resistance to it, but they'd have compromised with or without Clinton. The left—and that's the terrible thing—had no legislative ability and no power in the streets to oppose something like the Welfare Bill or the dismantling of the NEA or the other hideous initiatives. We can't even get angry when it's reported that they're not going to turn around greenhouse gas emissions for a hundred and fifty years, which will clearly mean the death of millions of people. That demobilization of the population is frightening.

But I look at Israel. Netanyahu is a disaster. What he's doing is so damaging, and will continue to be in so many complicated ways to the possibilities for a peaceful resolution in the Middle East, to the soul of the Jewish people—so destructive to life. And of course, Peres and Rabin were compromised, but there is a lesser of two evils. As incredibly angry and appalled as I am at Bill Clinton, and with many doubts about Gore, I don't think it's nothing that Gore defended *Ellen*. You can turn on ABC and see a woman kissing another woman and talking about being a dyke. That is progress. I completely disagree with people who say it's just co-optation and bourgeoisification. It's not great art or great culture, and it doesn't end dyke-bashing or AIDS. But it's cause for celebration. On one level, we've been working for that kind of bland acceptance. And having the vice president get up and say that *Ellen* promotes diversity is not nothing. I mean, I danced at the White House with a boy. These are significant changes in the fabric of our society, and I don't think a Republican would approve them. *Ellen* probably would still be *Ellen*, but I think the Welfare Bill would be even more hideous than it is, if that's imaginable. Once it's clear what this bill actually means, people living on jobs that pay seven dollars an hour and trying to raise a family, they're going to have to do something to fix it. And I think we have a better chance with a Democrat than we do with a Republican.

It's certainly a very grim time. The thing that scares me, I look at this recent upswing in the stock market, and the fascinated coverage, the way that everything is so cosmetic. You really think, "Is there anything other than economics?" Maybe it really is what Marx said, just market fluctuations. The only story is Wall Street. You can make a drama of it, with Thatcher and Reagan and Gorbachev and you can say it has to do with North Sea oil, and the failure of Russian oil exploration, the collapse of OPEC. You can really do a geo-economic analysis and say these personalities don't matter, but that there's a kind of barely managed chaos created by economic fluctuations. The whole drama of political personality is just a big distraction. I don't know. It's beginning to feel to me, as Gore Vidal says, as if the next presidential election is really about who gets the next four-year lease on the studio.

But if you do see the political in terms of the economic, then aren't the real emperors of the world the CEOs of multinational corporations?
But it can be argued that they're not even the real emperors. Giant corporations that invested in Asian stock are now looked on as disasters because of the downturn there, whereas a year ago, they were the ones you had to buy. These pundits who get up on *Nightline* and say, with absolute authority, "There's the Tiger Market and the Yellow Peril and the future clearly belongs to Thailand." And then suddenly the bhat is worth as much as the gum on the bottom of your shoe. They're starving over there and this cloud of poisonous gas has settled over half of Indonesia because of slashing and burning rain forests. Michael Eisner or Ted Turner or Bill Gates has no more of a clue, they just have bigger cushions. It's not even the aggregate corporate entities anymore. As Marx said, economics is a ridiculous pseudo-science that is a mode of description, not analysis. It's become like El Niño, a weather system. I can't come up with a conspiracy theory according to which it's beneficial that the Asian markets collapsed, although I'm sure at least the stockbrokers made kajillions of dollars last week. That's where a lot of my work now is moving. I've really become obsessed about money and economics and I'm trying to figure out if there's any way to talk dramatically about that because I feel that that's the real picture. Maybe I'm just becoming senile and I'm reverting to the most clichéd kind of Marxism as a way of feeling safe. But it really feels to me like we're puppets.

Isn't that what Caryl Churchill's *Serious Money* is about?
That was an interesting attempt. But it starts out talking about money and winds up being more about psychology and people. *Other People's Money* [by Jerry Sterner] is not a good play, but it stayed with an eco-

nomic problem and worked it. Even its big denouement—although it got very Frank Capra—stayed focused on money, which is a cold, heartless thing. I'm curious to write about it for the stage. It was exciting to work on a version of *The Good Person of Setzuan* for Lisa Peterson. It's completely and relentlessly about haggling and negotiation. Even more than *Mother Courage*, it's just one deal after another. And you can't cheat it—exchange value and use value—you can't get away from the economics. I really adored working on that script because unlike *Chalk Circle* or even *Courage*, which is a greater play finally, this one never let's you off the hook. It describes human nature as essentially transactional.

In the face of these challenges to the left, how do you keep utopian thinking alive? Because your work seems so dedicated to that impossible project.
That's an important function of imaginative literature. *Galatea 2.2* by Richard Powers is an incredibly moving novel I've come to like enormously. Very interesting guy, very complicated webs of history, memory and technology in the twentieth century. And he's clearly caught on to the dialectic of grieving. This goes back to what you asked in the beginning. The suffering that comes with loss and mourning, more than anything else, obscures a view of the utopian, of the far horizon. And yet, of course the utopian is very much borne out of loss and desire, out of the unacceptablity of loss and the absolute hunger that loss produces for a place where everything is restored. I was just talking to my students about a documentary about Winnie Mandela from before we knew she was a crazy person. When Nelson was still in prison, Miriam Makeba's daughter died of cancer in exile and Winnie Mandela—apparently they were very, very close—sent her a telegram saying, "Don't despair, because when apartheid is defeated, all of the dead will come home." And Benjamin is of course so full of that dialectic, that the past and the dead and the lost are waiting on us, have endowed us with a weak messianic power, hoping for us to redeem them.

On the one hand, it's a bad time to talk about the utopian. But on the other, it's clear to me what the political usefulness of the utopian is, and that the nefarious bastards are resolute on destroying it. You see Clinton talking about school uniforms until he's blue in the face, and people trying to kill off an important Enlightenment accomplishment, the introduction of the idea into politics. There is a loss of belief in metatheories, in the explicability of the human condition, and in a specifically articulated ideology that guides human action. The battle cry of the gray middle is now: "No ideas." Since ideas are bad, you surrender yourself to the everyday, because the everyday is unchangeable, and you address specific, small problems and find their solutions. This is the way to paradise—except of course this comes from people, like Fukuyama, who don't believe in paradise, who believe we've already arrived. Andrew Sullivan once said to me, "The free enterprise system is really the best way for an individual to realize himself or herself to his or her fullest extent." People have really come to believe this, so it's unbelievably important.

There's a despair and horror and misery produced by not having a vision. When you're told that there will never be anything better than this, that's the end of mourning and the beginning of melancholia—a blockage of hope that leads to rage and a rebellion of the most satanic variety, a rebellion against life itself. There's a creepy ad in the subways right now. I don't even know what it's advertising. It's just blue—they've taken over a whole subway car—and it says, "Imagine the subway filled with fallen angels." I find it terrifying. The devil has come to New York and set up an ad agency. But there is a spooky love of evil. I look at kids sticking all these things through their ears—and these are very complicated cultural forms, so I don't know exactly what they're about. But when one is told that one's effectivity is entirely bounded by one's own skin, that revolutionary part of one's soul that desires change starts to act inappropriately. The lure isn't a sex game for these kids that are slashing themselves with razor blades. I think it's all part of a closing off of the borders that lead to the utopian.

Lesbian and gay movement people are now stunned. What happened? Now we all wanna get married—but there's more to politics than that. It's like removing God from religion, and as Unitarians and Reformed Jews found out, nobody shows up for services. The harder it is to find hope, the more important it is to look for it. The more impossible it is to find an occasion for it, the more necessary it is to talk about it. When someone in a play, like Astrov [in *Uncle Vanya*], looks to the future, he imagines, "I see something out there." In Beckett, you know there's something moving out there. Even when we see the crab louse in Clov's pants [in *Endgame*]. Or all the little leaves on the tree. It's sentimental in a way, but it's a sentiment that people can't do without.

This is yet another reason why the death-by-attrition of the NEA is so distressing, because it is precisely in culture—whether high culture or mass culture—that these utopian hopes are kept alive.

This is an abandonment of what the federal government has stood for, the possibility of making leaps forward has been replaced by a very, very slow democratic process. This is historically inaccurate, a misreading of the twentieth century, of American democracy, and a misunderstanding of a representative republic. This abandonment of leadership, just grinding on in a dull-lidded faith, is turning everyone into Dr. Pangloss: eventually it'll all work out in this best of all possible worlds. The stakes are incredibly high, and some of the causes like the NEA are all but lost. What's terrifying to me about the NEA is the absolute lack of response of the artistic community to its own destruction. I had lunch yesterday with the head—I won't say who—of one of the two biggest major regional theatres. And he's going on and on about how he's so unhappy that he doesn't have money to develop plays anymore. I handed him a script and his first question was, "How many people are in it?" It's this damnable thing about the human race, you only realize once they've knocked down your door and dragged you off screaming that you should have done something years ago. Right now there's something like twenty-six musicals on Broadway and one play, Neil Simon's *Proposals*. That's really bad news. And, it should be said, almost all the musicals are unlistenable crap. The regional theatres are dying.

I read the NEA's new report, "The American Canvas," because I got so angry when I saw that thing in the *Times* blaming the arts: "It's all the fault of proscenium arches and museum walls." I couldn't believe that's what the thing actually said, and the *Times* misreported it. What's really depressing is that the report completely uses the language of balanced budgets, it uses the smaller deficits that theatres are running as a measure that things have gotten better. But of course these same theatres are having to let everyone go from their staffs and are doing *Having Our Say* and that play about the dog, *Sylvia*. That's what's keeping them afloat right now. We're balancing our budget by throwing everybody off welfare and there's no national healthcare and no air traffic control and it's all, "Whoop-de-do, we're dying, but we have a balanced budget!" What's appalling about this "American Canvas" thing is that it's like talking about the weather on the island of Montserrat while the volcano is eating the entire place alive. All during the Clinton years there has been a bland acceptance of a holocaustal decimation of the arts scene in this country led by the destruction of the NEA.

Faced with this horrible situation, which makes it more and more difficult to envision a future, I have to ask you, what are your plans? Your current projects?
I finished an opera libretto this summer that I've now decided is a play. It's a 120-page play in verse I'm developing based on Heinrich Von Kliest's short story, "St. Cecilia, or the Power of Music." And then I'm doing another libretto to replace this one for Bobby McFerrin and the San Francisco Opera. I'm writing a couple of films, and a few smaller projects here and there, and trying to get *Henry Box Brown* finished and ready for the Royal National Theatre. I did an adaptation of Goethe's

Stella, his first play, that the National's going to do next year. But I'm frustrated because I'm overdue for a real new play. There hasn't been one since *Slavs!* and I feel like it's really time. And I have to pay the rent. *Angels* is now absolutely, unqualifiably a thing of the past. So I'm returning to being a working playwright, as opposed to a gentlemen of leisure with a very lucrative rental property. I have to create new rental properties. For one thing, *Henry Box Brown* is gigantic. It's much larger than *Angels* in terms of cast. It's half African-American and half British speaking a thick Yorkshire dialect, so it's written for a very specific situation. I have absolutely no idea what will happen to it after it's done at the National, and it's far and away the hardest thing I've ever attempted. And that's good, that's what you should be doing.

What's the full title?
Henry Box Brown, or the Mirror of Slavery, which was the title of the panorama that he toured around. I really love that title.

Do you think there's going to be a film of *Angels in America*?
No, I don't. The last I've heard—and this is as of two days ago—is that two studios would make it if I would make both parts into one film. But they've become completely terrified of making both films. They absolutely won't agree to make just *Millennium*, which is my solution. Now that they can read *Perestroika*, they say, "But this is only halfway." And because they're incredibly vulgar people, they really believe it's possible to make both parts in two or three hours. It's possible in the same way it's possible to take a big fat novel and do it, but you lose so much. The play was about an epic journey and part of that epic journey requires an audience to sit in its seats for seven hours. That's just part of the play, and I'm not going to let them do it. I'm sad about it but also relieved, because it's so hard to do. I was always a little afraid. There are some things, like not having Stephen Spinella's performance on film, that are very sad. Every time a gay movie does well at the box office, there will be a frenzy of activity about *Angels in America*. The most recent frenzy that resulted in the two unacceptable offers came about largely as a result of *In and Out*. And there was one around *To Wong Foo*, and another around *The Birdcage*.

For the first time, I have three or four ideas that actually are films and not plays. Universal's hired me to do an adaptation of a children's book that was enormously important for me when I was a kid called *The Pushcart War*, about a battle between pushcart peddlers and trucking conglomerates in New York City. I'm really excited about working on that. It's political and it's fun.

Terrence McNally

Growing up in Corpus Christi, Texas, Terrence McNally spent his youth hanging out at the drive-in and the beach, skipping Sunday Mass to play poker and listening every Saturday to the Metropolitan Opera radio broadcasts. He also became fascinated with the theatre. "My first play was made up from the background notes on a George Gershwin record album, and I had George marrying a pretty girl named Ira. Doesn't it strike you as odd that not one of my teachers knew enough to say, 'Nice play, Terry, but Ira was George's *brother*'?" Moving to New York to attend college, McNally was able to nurture his passion for opera, camping out at the old Met for three days in October 1956 to buy a standing room ticket for the Met debut of Maria Callas, a figure who would reverberate through several plays. He made his Broadway debut with *And Things That Go Bump in the Night* (1965), a dark comedy about a young man who brings home his transvestite boyfriend, which was savaged by the critics. This was followed by a string of much more successful comedies that led up to *The Ritz* (1975), a farce of mistaken identities about a garbage man who seeks refuge from gangsters in a gay bathhouse. Following the disappointment of his second flop, *Broadway, Broadway* (1978), McNally went through a fallow period during which he wrote for television but was unable to finish any plays. Finally returning to the theatre, he not only turned *Broadway, Broadway* into the hit *It's Only a Play* (1985), but also inaugurated a series of more serious and ambitious plays that have made him probably the most successful dramatist to have come of age during the 1960s.

McNally is also the great chameleon among contemporary American playwrights. Over the past thirty-five years he has written an extraordinary range of plays, from the sinister farce of *Next* (1967) to the operatic tragedy of *The Lisbon Traviata* (1989), from the edgily romantic *Frankie and Johnny in the Clair de Lune* (1987) to the mystical *A Perfect Ganesh* (1993). Despite its diversity, all of his writing is characterized by a quizzical, comic touch (in even the most serious situations), by a frankly presentational style that delights in all the possibilities that the theatre offers, and by a tendency to construct a play by piling up what seem at first to be almost innocuous events. As a builder of artfully artless dramatic structures, he brings to mind playwrights like Chekhov or Tennessee Williams, who manage to turn the minutiae of everyday life into a richly dramatic and moving spectacle. For McNally's plays have a way of creeping up on you, as patterns begin to emerge out of the interplay of conflicting voices and the incidental details of characters' lives. Eschewing the big dramatic events that punctuate the work of many writers, he focuses instead on the almost random, almost insignificant, personal choices that produce momentous consequences.

Since the mid 1980s, McNally's plays have become increasingly preoccupied with questions of meaning and mortality, his characters more reflective, and his use of theatrical conventions more subtle, elastic and bold. Thus, for example, his Tony Award-winning *Master Class* (1995) calls up the ghost of Maria Callas in order to explore and speculate on the function of theatre, the nature of an artist's calling and the impact of one's life on one's art. Coaching three students on three different arias, Maria painfully and obsessively revisits her great roles and relives her relationship with Aristotle Onassis. For Maria is a woman truly possessed by both her art and her own ghosts and she takes her students' arias as a cue to recall a past filled with fury, erotic passion and loss. The play uses opera, moreover, as a way of proving the antiquity and immortality of great art: "When I sang Medea I could feel the stones of Epidaurus beneath the wooden floorboards at La Scala." At the same time, Maria's total dedication to her art—and to her past—is the sign that the artist must be prepared to sacrifice everything. Trying to explain Verdi's Lady Macbeth to a complacent student, she asks, "Is there anything you would kill for?" The student's inability to answer proves that the great artist must be prepared both to kill and die for her art. For *Master Class*, written during the ongoing controversy over the NEA's funding of allegedly indecent art, demonstrates that real art is always excessive, brazen and dangerous, and that to shackle or censor the artist is to destroy her.

Despite the always ingratiating quality of McNally's plays, there remains something slightly dangerous and even confrontational about his work. For many of his recent plays focus on the proximity of sex and death, comedy and tragedy, the terrible and sublime. Thus *Prelude & Liebestod* (1989) exposes the dark and menacing subtext of Wagner's far-too-readily desexualized opera [*Tristan und Isolde*] by using it as a key to unlock a conductor's memories of wild sex and an inspiration for his bloody (and comically scandalous) suicide. Or *Love! Valour! Compassion!* (1994), in which the joys, desires and disappointments of eight gay men are set against a knowledge of mortality and the inexorability of loss. Or *A Perfect Ganesh*, which brings two American women, who have both lost sons, to India to confront their losses. Moving from the terrible beauty of the river of death, the Ganges in Varanasi, to the blazing radiance of the Taj Mahal, they finally recognize that Ganesha, ·the elephant-headed deity for which they had been searching, has in fact been traveling with them all the time; that he is simultaneously man, beast and god; leper and prince; the Lord of Obstacles and the deliverer. For so many of McNally's characters, like the immortal Maria, are possessed. They are haunted by their memories and by stories (and rationalizations) from the past that they use to structure their lives. And the plays in which they appear, despite their sometime improvisatory feel, are similarly haunted by opera, musical comedy and classical dramatic forms. For McNally's is a theatre in which characters grope toward transfiguration just as the darkened stage itself seems to await a blinding flash of light, like the one that illuminates the end of *A Perfect Ganesh*, in which characters and spectators alike are given an intimation of the divine. In an almost perverse way, it is a holy stage. And even in the face of the death threats that greeted the tabloid press's misreprentations of *Corpus Christi* (1998), McNally remains committed to a dangerous theatre: "Write plays that matter. Raise the stakes. Shout, yell, holler, but make yourself heard. It's time for playwrights to reclaim the theatre. We do that by speaking from the heart about the things that matter most to us. If a play isn't worth dying for, maybe it isn't worth writing."

June 23, 1998—Terrence McNally's apartment, New York City

DS: You could start by telling me how you got interested in theatre.
TM: Got interested in theatre as opposed to just enjoying it—I've always enjoyed theatre. My very early memories as a child involve theatre. Right after the war we lived for a while in Port Chester, New York, and I remember watching *Kukla, Fran and Ollie* and *Howdy Doody* on television. And I didn't care for *Howdy Doody*, because I thought he was too real, with the strings and mouth moving. But I loved *Kukla, Fran and Ollie*, which took place on a little stage within a stage—the interaction between Fran Allison and these archetypes. That stage was very real to me, and I made my own theatre down in the basement. I had copies of Kukla and Ollie. Once I read an interview in which Edward Albee talked about no one ever detecting the great influence of Kukla and Ollie in his work, especially the early plays like *American Dream*. And then when I was really young, my parents took me to see *Annie Get Your Gun*, which was the first play I guess I saw. This would have been about 1944 or '45 when I was six or seven years old, and that had an enormous impact on me. When we moved to Texas, Corpus Christi had no television station. Even all through high school, it only had kinescope television, so I didn't get to see those very popular shows that most of my generation loved—we were still watching the old kinescopes of *Kukla, Fran and Ollie*.

So even through high school I still listened to radio, *Masterpiece Theatre*, the *Shadow*, the *Phantom* and comic book versions of *Treasure Island*, *The Prince and the Pauper*, those kinds of things. That was a great appeal to my imagination, and also by that age I had fallen madly in love with opera. When I was in the sixth grade a nun played some recordings for us and I just liked it instantly. I didn't have to learn to like it. I listened to the Metropolitan broadcasts and I made a stage, and I would stage *Aida* and *Rigoletto* while they were broadcasting. Most of my stages weren't very original, I would just copy the pictures in *Opera News* magazine. These were also places my mind wandered.

I started buying a lot of show albums. My parents were native New Yorkers and came up to New York at least once a year and would always come back with programs. My father liked shows like *South Pacific* and *Kiss Me, Kate*, and Edith Piaf, whom he played a lot, which I think developed my taste for rather eccentric, rather identifiable voices like Callas rather than a generic soprano sound like Tebaldi or Sutherland. There was no theatre in my high school. The only play I remember seeing was *Picnic*, because this sad spinster teacher was playing Rosemary, and we just wanted to see her go to pieces and rip the guy's shirt off just like in the movie. And for all the wrong reasons, that's about the only play I remember seeing in Corpus Christi. Opera was as much an influence on me as theatre. For a period we moved to Dallas and they had this huge theatre for operettas, Starlight Operettas, they were called. They had a reputation for getting stars to do shows they never would have done on Broadway, or developing shows that went on to Broadway. They had to compete with june bugs, big beetles that fly around and are particularly attracted to light. And there was a famous night when one flew down the front of June Havoc's dress and she literally went berserk on stage. She was on the floor, she had little convulsions, she was so upset at the idea of some beetle crawling around in her cleavage and brassiere, whereas most of us were used to these flying bugs and batted them away. This was before we had air-conditioning, so the only bearable theatre would have been outdoors.

When we moved to Corpus Christi, opera was more accessible than theatre, the San Antonio Opera, the Metropolitan Opera toured to Dallas. A bunch of us who liked opera conned one of our mothers into driving us up to Dallas on the weekend to see three operas in two days. Opera was a form of theatre, but theatre was *Annie Get Your Gun*. When we lived in Dallas, stage shows would come through periodically. I remember Mary Martin in *Annie Get Your Gun* and Carol Channing in *Gentlemen Prefer Blondes* and other Broadway shows, but also *Red Mill*, *Naughty Marietta*, *Rose Marie*. This was long before I thought of becoming a playwright. I remember once I said something terrible to my brother, and my punishment was not going to see *Paint Your Wagon*, and I was really, really upset. I remember I couldn't believe it when my parents took off to see it without me—that was like capital punishment.

So, obviously the theatre spoke to me on some deep emotional level and I still don't know what it is. It's like Boy Scouts sitting around the campfire and the scoutmaster tells you a story and you get open-mouthed, wide-eyed. I don't think I considered writing for theatre until sometime after college. When I was at Columbia I wrote the varsity show my senior year, but that was more of a lark. I still thought I was going to be a journalist, and that seemed more appropriate for a pre-journalism major because it was a spoof. It was about a lot of the celebrities of the day. There was a film company that went to Africa where they were making this film and exploiting the natives, but what they didn't know was that the natives were cannibals. And one by one they were eating the crew until only the ingenue and juvenile were alive at the curtain call. Evil people from Western capitalism had been destroyed, and Ed Kleban, who wrote the lyrics for *A Chorus Line*, wrote the music and lyrics, and Michael Kahn directed it. I was always involved with writing. In grade school I was writing puns and stories, and in high school I was the editor of my school newspaper and founded a literary magazine.

The summer of my junior year in high school I went to Northwestern. There's a famous program where they choose twenty-five outstanding students from around the country, and you go there free and pretend you're a real journalist for six weeks, and it's the first time I'd really been away from home and it was very exciting. My roommate was Jerry Rubin. It was fun when he became Jerry Rubin. I have one friend, a poet, to whom I've stayed close all these years. I had wonderful influences and opportunities as a young man to explore the feelings I had for the arts. My parents were probably as supportive as they could be, even though their idea of becoming a writer was probably writing for *Time* magazine. They thought anyone who wrote independently was asking for poverty. It was certainly not the nineteenth century, "You will become a doctor," or something like that. And there were always playbills on the table. I remember them talking about *Death of a Salesman* and *Streetcar*, they saw shows I think all of America saw, when Broadway was still where you went for intelligent writing. Movies were kind of a step-child.

There were always people to point the way, a teacher in high school in Texas who cared about the English language and taught us the glories of Shakespeare. I'm one person who was not traumatized by her introduction of Shakespeare. Quite the opposite, she had such a humane and simple approach to him, she taught him as a playwright and not a poet. I'm just so grateful. I read Shakespeare a lot and he's such a profound force in my life, and so many bright friends of mine can't stand Shakespeare—and these are very good playwrights who read *Hamlet* or *Macbeth* in high school. I spent a lot of time at Columbia with him, the whole works and then a seminar just in *King Lear* for a year.

Coming to New York was very fortuitous. I applied to Harvard, Yale and Columbia, and I needed a scholarship and Harvard didn't give me a scholarship, and Yale and Columbia gave me the same scholarship. My best friend and I flipped a coin, because we thought it was silly to go to the same school. He got Yale and I got Columbia, and as it turned out, part of my education became being in New York. I got here in the fall of '56, the tail end of the "golden age" of Broadway, plays by Tennessee Williams and Arthur Miller, and musicals by Rodgers and Hammerstein, and Frank Loesser were still happening with some regularity. You couldn't see all the shows in a season unless you were a critic. It's like Off-Off-Broadway now, there's so much product. I saw a lot of shows. I also went to the opera and the ballet a lot. It was a great day for Balanchine at the City Ballet, and at City Opera Beverly Sills was fabulous and no one knew who she was yet. And the debut of Callas—all those things I would have been denied had I been stuck up in New Haven.

I've never studied playwriting but I've seen a lot of plays and I took some courses in theatre at Columbia. Eric Bentley had a course in modern drama which was pretty much his paperback volumes in modern Italian, French and German theatre. Other than the Shakespeare, I think that was the only theatre course I took. Besides New York, Columbia didn't have a lot. Theatre was totally extracurricular. Michael [Kahn], with all of his work, was extracurricular. The only time I've ever acted was at Columbia when Michael directed a production of *The Little Prince*, and I was taking a lot of French courses and he encouraged me to be in it, saying it would help me lose my inhibition of speaking French in public. Everyone else in the cast was a native Frenchman, and coming backstage, I only understood enough to hear them say, "It was wonderful except for that terrible American with that horrible accent playing the fox." Skipping ahead, the only other time I did act was in a little workshop at Actors Studio, and I was physically ill on the day we did it. I knew everyone in the audience. It was like I was hurled out onto a Broadway stage. My knees literally shook, and I had uncontrollable twitches in my face, and I think I threw up a few times before the play began and it was so horrible. That cliché, you could see his knees trembling through his slacks—you literally could.

How did you get involved in Off-Off-Broadway?

I wrote a one-act after college called *This Side of the Door* [1961], which I sent to Actors Studio. And because of that I got a job as stage manager at Playwright's Union despite the fact that I had no practical knowledge of theatre. I had no idea how a director worked with actors or anything like that. But Molly Kazan, Elia Kazan's wife, said, "There's a job here as stage manager and I think you'll learn a lot about how a play's put together, how actors work, how directors work." So I did that for two years and learned a lot. And then Barr-Wilder-Albee did *This Side of the Door*. That was the first time I ever heard my lines spoken by professional actors. Estelle Parsons—she was magnificent—played the lead. It was done at the Cherry Lane for two weekends. And that was not even considered

Off-Off-Broadway in those days, it was considered a workshop because Off-Broadway was very healthy. There were many more theatres and it was when Beckett, Albee, Ionesco and a whole generation of American writers, Jack Richardson, Arthur Kopit, Jack Gelber, were all being done Off-Broadway. You could be at the Cherry Lane or the Actor's Playhouse or the Provincetown because these theatres were so small.

So Off-Off-Broadway came out of Off-Broadway facing the same economic problems that Broadway was to face in the seventies and eighties. But in the sixties, Off-Broadway was very fertile—hundreds of theatres and lots of activity. This was the height of Circle in the Square reestablishing O'Neill as a writer, the Brecht-Weill evenings, *Brecht on Brecht* and *Threepenny Opera*. It was seen as an alternative to Broadway, and the difference in ticket prices was enormous. Everyone forgets. Right now, to go to the Manhattan Theatre Club costs five to ten dollars less than to see *Art* or whatever play happens to be on Broadway. It used to be, if a Broadway play was twenty dollars, Off-Broadway was five. Now, no one goes to Off-Broadway because it's cheaper. It was the only way to see all this great surrogate European drama, the Theatre of the Absurd, Genet and people like that. Those plays were not being done on Broadway. So the question is really how did I get involved with Off-Broadway, because my first play was on Broadway. In many ways, everything's changed and nothing's changed.

My first play that I put in the credits, *Things That Go Bump in the Night*, was a very long one-act, an hour and a half, three scenes, and it was too on-the-nose autobiographically and emotionally. Too much airing of family business. I didn't enjoy watching it. I thought, That's not the purpose of theatre. I should be able to watch the play with the normal discomfort of seeing my work up there as opposed to, Would this upset my mother and father and brother if they saw this? It just seems an inappropriate use of theatre. While I was at Actors Studio, I wrote *Things That Go Bump in the Night*, which we did there with minimal sets and props and a very good cast. Then in Minneapolis we had a full production and a new cast. So in a way, I did a workshop, an out-of-town tryout, and then New York. Which is what happened with *Ragtime* [1996] or *Master Class*, which we did originally in the town of Big Fork, Montana, then at a little theatre in Philadelphia, then at the Taper, then the Kennedy Center. So things are the same but they're wildly, wildly different, too.

Reading your work and hearing you talk about opera and theatre, I've noticed that your plays are so self-consciously about the theatre and dramatic literature. I'm thinking about the highly theatricalized relationship between Steven and Michael in *The Lisbon Traviata;* or *Lips Together, Teeth Apart* [1991], a comedy of infidelity

with its references to *Cosi fan tutte*, another comedy of infidelity; and of course *Master Class*, with Maria looking back at her different roles. How conscious are you of that in your writing?

Maybe not as conscious as you think. For example, I never thought of *Cosi* as a comedy about infidelity until you just said it. But *Lips Together* is a play very much about fidelity and infidelity. I chose that music because that trio to me is a prayer for safe passage. In the context of that play, life is very fragile and it's a moment of prayer. Going back to *Kukla, Fran and Ollie*, I'm not interested in naturalism, my plays are always plays, and the actors I work with most successfully are not internal, Actors Studio method actors. They enjoy being in a play and you know they are acting for you and it gives them great pleasure. That doesn't mean they are any less honest than the method actor who loses himself and it's all about truth, truth, truth. "This is exactly how I felt when my mother died." I would rather see that theatricalized, made into a little larger gesture. Almost every actor I've worked with I've learned from enormously. If you look at people like Zoë Caldwell, Nathan Lane, Christine Baranski, actors I really admire, they're aware the audience is there. I like that dialogue. I like being welcomed to the theatre. Lately I've started using narrative more, but always think, We know you, the audience, are here, let's find out what connects us. When I write a play, I don't write the truth, a documentary, a proto-real experience, I write a play by Terrence McNally. I like the devices of Shakespeare. I have asides, monologues, soliloquies in my plays. I like the devices of opera: arias, trios, cabalettas.

Usually actors say it's very easy to learn my dialogue. The only play where they had trouble was *Lips Together*, because there are a lot of trios, quartets, four people with different conversations, under the house talking to people on the deck, talking to people in the bedroom, behind the screen. I was trying consciously to work like music there. In the last act, after John goes into the pool, it becomes a verbal quartet. I don't know if it really works, but I wanted a canon, overlapped dialogue, four people doing interior monologues. In real life people do not verbalize four monologues in a situation and then freeze—so I would say my theatre is theatrical. My art is painterly realism, and my theatre is very real to me, but it's theatre and a different reality from you and me sitting here. That seems who I am. I never wanted to write a fourth-wall play. Or totally didactic theatre—I'm not terribly drawn to the works of Brecht. I feel I'm being lectured, and things are being demonstrated to me. You see three or four plays as a child, you listen to two operas, you have this high school English teacher, you go to Columbia, and that all adds up and you write this sort of play.

If I have any sort of artistic credo, I would say it's almost entirely *Master Class*. That's in many ways the most autobiographical play I've written, and I just put all these outrageous thoughts about art into Maria Callas's mouth. I honestly believe she probably wouldn't have said them but would have agreed with them. She wasn't known for her articulation about the world of art. But it's a very autobiographical play of my feelings. I went through a terrible period after I wrote it, after seeing it. I thought I would never write another play. It seemed very valedictory to me. But that passed, and I moved on to other projects. I like writing, I like being in rehearsal. Almost everything else about theatre has gotten very unpleasant. The commerce of it, the business, the fact that a show has to become an institutional hit, run for twenty years, to be considered successful. That's not a new story. People don't want to see a new play by a good writer, it has to become a media frenzy. *Corpus Christi* has become a "story," and that's totally the doing of an irresponsible journalist at the *Post*. It's not something we welcome or love.

I'm interested to hear you talk about the importance of a theatre that acknowledges its theatricality because you sometimes seem intent on bringing up things that are difficult to articulate in other ways. And I've noticed a change in your writing. Your plays of the past few years strike me as more risky, both in terms of form and subject matter, than most of your earlier work.

I'm not sure I would agree with that. I think they're less judgmental of the characters. I'm less conspicuous than I was in my early work. You could divide my work into that which promotes my opinion of the characters and that which tries to let the characters be themselves. There's a big difference. Friends even say, "Your work used to be so much riskier." They always point to *Tommy Flowers* [*Where Has Tommy Flowers Gone?*, 1971] as being so risky and experimental. Those are exactly the kinds of things, one, I don't think about and, two, it's bad to think about, because you get writer's block. "Is this play risky enough?" That's for critics, people like you. *Master Class* is really not a play. The program said, "A Master Class with Maria Callas in the Singer's Program at Juilliard." The play's taking place in real time. Certainly, *Corpus Christi* is very theatrical, and *Ragtime*. The first line is to the audience and in the first number they all sing about who they are in the third person. These are all techniques, maybe I'll discard them. The next couple plays I have in mind are plays where there is actually a fourth wall. So maybe I'm going back to something.

There are only two plays I wrote overnight, *Next*, the play that got me out of journalism and earning a living as a playwright, and *Master Class*, where I just had a vision. I knew the first line, "No applause," and the last line, "Well, that's that." I was at a benefit dinner writing on a program. I think about most of my plays, like *Corpus Christi*, for two or three years minimum, and then I wait and turn on the computer when I feel like I'm not just going to sit there and think, Now wait, how am I going to write a play called *Corpus Christi*? How do I write this play about Christ? I don't think, This should be more theatrical. This play's not going to have monologues, but address the audience instead. This play's going to have audience participation. Every so often I do. In *Master Class* she talked to the audience quite a bit, and in the original draft of *Love! Valour!* there's much more of that. I think they were self-conscious. I like the *idea* of talking to the audience, but in reality I hate it. I hate it when an actor addresses me, especially when he wants a response from me, so it's especially sadistic of me to put it in my own plays. There's four or five passages from *Love! Valour!* that didn't make it to the first preview.

So there's writing that comes easily emotionally to you, that's maybe just a technical thing. And there's making the play work. Basically you want to keep the audience in their chairs for two to three hours. That's the primary goal and everything else is just talk. There's nothing worse than seeing a play and sensing that massive indifference, that absolute void of nonenergy between stage and performance. I think that's the most horrible sound of silence in the world. There's also the very painful thing of seeing audiences leave at intermission. Lately, I've done two three-act plays where you have two chances to lose them. So much of rehearsal is about how do we keep this alive and interesting, not intellectual conversations about meaning. You never discuss meaning with a director and an actor, you discuss why a line doesn't work, why an audience is restless at a certain point. Theatre is incredibly tactical, and it's the only art form where you are so involved with other people. It is a collaboration.

I don't know exactly what percentage of the draft that goes into rehearsal becomes the final product. I sometimes think it's not much more than fifty percent. When you go to *Master Class*, you experience the set, the lighting, the contributions of Zoë Caldwell, Michael McGarty, Lenny Foglia. It's not all me. If *Master Class* had been done with a different director, designer and actress, it would have been a very different experience. I've been very good lately about getting what I want on a stage, that's why I write for specific actors. I know the directors I want to work with, and the designers. John Guare and I were teaching playwriting for a year at Juilliard and our theme was: be responsible for who does your sets and costumes. I don't design the sets and costumes, but I have a stake in it. It's difficult working with really good people that share a vision. So many playwrights get passive when it comes to production. "They're giving my play to Peter Brook. They're letting Martha Graham do the choreography." Well, maybe Peter Brook and Martha Graham are not the right people to do *Pal Joey*. You've got to say, "No, I don't think this work is in their vocabulary."

People talk about the theatre as if the text were everything. I think it's just a part. I don't think you can talk about a play without talking about the production. When you talk about *Streetcar*, you're talking about Marlon Brando and Vivien Leigh and that movie. How can you erase these memories? It's not this flat, two-dimensional thing that we read. That's what's special about theatre. *Moby-Dick* is in two dimensions, but when you experience *Hamlet* you experience him in three dimensions, and it seems to me you cannot separate notions of what Hamlet looks like or is about from Gielgud, Burton, Olivier, Kevin Kline. It makes it a very special art form. I think you can interview Ernest Hemingway and get the essence of anything by Ernest Hemingway. I don't think you can talk to me about theatre without talking to a thousand other people that contributed to what I consider to be theatre.

I'm thinking of *A Perfect Ganesh*, for example, and how crucial the lighting is in producing a sense of the sublime.

Lighting is very, very important to me. Only recently have I started to get the lighting I want. That was an example of being disappointed in the lighting, but not speaking up, thinking, That's technical. Now I feel that a lighting designer is a collaborator and I'm much more eager to hear his impressions of the text, how lighting could enhance it, but also to give him my ideas for it. Brian MacDevitt did my last play and Jules Fisher and Peggy Eisenhauer did *Ragtime*. It's extraordinary work. I used to work with a lot of different people who said, "Here are your lights. Good-bye." Now these designers are there through previews, when the critics come in. I want to work with people who care 101 percent and I know that's obvious, but a lot of people don't. I've gotten in trouble when my own aims are 101 percent. It takes enormous effort on everyone's part. Nothing is good enough in the theatre, unless it's right. You can't be almost right.

Sound is very important to me. I sometimes have to say, "There should be a dog barking here." "Was that important to you?" "Yes, or I wouldn't have put it in." I have no stage directions, I never write, "Crying through her tears sardonically." I never write those kinds of descriptions. When I write, "A dog barks," and it's the only sound effect in the entire act, I want to hear it. I think Lee Strasberg did a terrible disservice. I hope his influence is starting to fade, because I remember him saying to actors and directors, "The first thing to do is to cross out all the playwright's directions, including set descriptions and indications to the actor." And maybe that's where the barking dog gets overlooked, or the lights rise to a blinding intensity. Lee Strasberg was always contemptuous towards playwrights' punctuation. To me, it's the same as reading a Mozart score: that's a quarter note, that's an eighth note. If you make them both eighth notes, it's not the same melody. Zoë Caldwell said to me, "You're very easy to act, I just follow your punctuation." Nathan Lane, another actor with whom I've worked very well, just says every word as I wrote it. The actor needs just to show up and say it. You don't need to embellish it with "oh," "ah," "I mean," mucking about it. In the cast of *Ragtime*, no one adds a comma to the script. When actors add all this other music, suddenly it's not me anymore. I get so crazy about that. I think it's sloppy. The music of a play is there. You try to find people who say, "You've given me all I have, the script, the words, the music, let me sing it to you." As opposed to actors who say, "This is your script, let me make it mine." That's the kind of actor I don't work very happily with.

A lot of actors and directors don't look at the basic stage directions. It's really unimportant whether a character is standing or sitting. Playwrights who still write "crossing downstage right" are wasting time. Who cares? That's not what makes a scene work. The actors will find a place to be if the scene is well written. These other details are part of what I consider the score of the music and the lighting. I'm not very good at describing things, which is maybe why I'm a playwright, not a novelist. I couldn't look around and describe this apartment, but I could have a drunken divorcee in her early fifties who's thinking about having a facelift describe it, or a teenage boy describe his apartment. I write dialogue as opposed to a more objective observation, so I try to give an indication in my first stage direction of the style of the play. I remember the beginning of *Love! Valour! Compassion!* was nothing like what Joe [Mantello] and Loy [Arcenas] came up with. But they could tell I did not want a realistic set. Before Joe was going to direct it, I'd spoken to directors who said, "We're going to need two turntables." I said, "The first stage direction makes it so clear that I don't want realistic scenery. A chair becomes a car." They just didn't get what I wanted. So a stage direction is a description of the kind of set which is a way of saying, "This is the kind of designer I think is right for this show." The first thing an audience sees is the set. The psychology of scenery and colors and light—there's no getting around that. A stunning example of that would be *The Ritz*. We did it in Washington, and it got very, very few laughs. We thought it was hysterical. Someone came to see it and they said, "The set is three stories tall and battleship gray, it looks so foreboding." The producer ordered a paint call, and stayed up all night and painted the whole thing red. The next night, with no other changes at all, the laughs started right away. I thought, You can write five hundred plays and never know that the battleship gray set will not be conducive to a sex farce.

So much of this is about taking the audience on a ride, and your job is to engineer that in every way, including working with designers.
It's our job, yes. Every play has different rules. Writing *Love! Valour! Compassion!* only helps you write *Love! Valour! Compassion! II*, not *Master Class* or *Corpus Christi*. Actors can create a persona and do it for ten movies and get away with it, but playwrights can't. Everyone talks differently. If you read Shakespeare, you may not know a passage is specifically from *Othello*, but you know it's not *Hamlet*. They're all different sound worlds. You make that a goal: how do I create this world through my words? It's got to be in the text, if everyone talks the same from play to play, it won't work.

And there are other elements that also produce the unique character of a play. I was thinking about how the nudity in *Love! Valour! Compassion!* is so important in producing an almost transcendent, sublime vision of sexuality.
The design helped. Randy [Becker]'s nice ass to look at up there. The lights just go and the crickets chirp louder. Joe and Brian really worked to give me what I wanted. I didn't even write the stage direction, and I've seen other productions where the lights just stay the same through act two. There's not that moment where they're struck dumb by nature. It also comes during that speech about Alaska and the glacier and there's this incredible silence. In other productions that moment doesn't exist. It's supposed to be nonverbal for a moment or two. Silence is very important in my work. It's there, I can't make a director do it. They did a production of *Lips Together* up in Providence, and at the end of the play, the actors saw the shooting stars and then Mozart comes on and then the lights come up in the audience just as they do on stage. It was a very good production, the music plays, and they're frozen, and the lights start coming up in the auditorium and three and a half, four minutes later, we're all in the same room, in the same light, and then everything went out. It was thrilling. They didn't do that in New York. I said to the director, "Why did you do that?" He said, "It's in your script." It was in the published version, and I'd forgotten I'd left it in. It's so interesting to see someone do what I actually wanted, and I thought it worked. It's pretty scary to stand there for three and a half, four minutes, but it worked. You've just got to take risks. I think a gesture like

that says, "This play's about you, these are human beings groping through marriage, fidelity, infidelity, mortality, homophobia, all the things that trouble these people. They're not actors, they've just been tap-dancing out here all night. Let's all listen to this sublime piece of Mozart together. We're all in this thing called life together."

The theme of *Lisbon Traviata* is people trying to connect and failing. I think there's some real connection between people in *Love! Valour!* There's virtually none in *Master Class*—she's trapped in a world of art, as much as Mendy is in *Lisbon Traviata*. There's a world of beauty and wholeness when she sings, but when she's Maria Callas she's as fucked-up as anybody who ever lived. She's a terrible teacher in trying to communicate what she has that made her great. It's her secret, and she can't give it away because she doesn't know what it is. So she gets very angry, "I want some of your genius, your fire. I'm not here to give tips." It's like when I'm teaching playwriting. "How do you get an agent? How do you get your play produced?" No, let's talk about why your scene doesn't work. Frustrating. I don't think it's impossible to communicate with another person, but I think it's difficult. That's really important to me. I find theatre very visceral and very central. I want theatre that has the immediacy of a good lasagna or an exquisite wine. To me you can feel it and taste it, the theatre is not a place to exercise your mind. I want the theatre to introduce me to people I would not meet in my own life, shock me, startle me, but I don't want it to tell me what I should be thinking.

It should seduce.

Yes, theatre is very sensual. And ballet is a form of theatre I'm very drawn to. I go to ballet quite a bit. My favorite painters have a very strong dramatic sense, like Giotto, who is an incredibly dramatic painter. And the relationships between people, how do you get to that moment of the Judas kiss? Writing *Corpus Christi*, I'm very aware of that moment in the Giotto fresco of the life of Christ. The paintings are well staged, he is a masterful director. The angle he chooses, his point of view towards the material is dramatic and useful to me as a playwright. Every playwright has to go his own road, and maybe there are very good playwrights who don't go to the museum or the ballet. I have a lot of friends who are excellent playwrights who don't go to the theatre much. I happen to enjoy going to the theatre, and also that's where you find the Lenny Foglias and Joe Mantellos of tomorrow, by going to workshop productions. If you wait until they're on Broadway and being nominated and winning Tony awards, then everybody wants them and they're not going to go to Big Fork, Montana, to work on *Master Class* with you.

It seems to me that in the years you've been writing, the American theatre has really become much more explicitly gay. It's almost as if it's coming round to you rather than the other way around.

I don't know if I agree. People happen to be out and there are a lot of damned good playwrights who happen to be gay. I don't think that American theatre is becoming gayer. Even ten or fifteen years ago, Paula Vogel's play [*How I Learned to Drive*] would have been done and she would probably have been out. I just think there's a lot of really good playwrights now who happen to be gay, I don't see theatre getting gayer. There's always been a very significant number of great actors, writers, directors who have been gay.

I agree that there've always been a lot of gay men and lesbians active in theatre. But it seems to me that people are more out now than they were a decade ago, and also there's a certain sexual frankness that's more permissible.

Unquestionably.

You couldn't have written some of the characters and events in your recent plays twenty years ago.

My very first play, *And Things That Go Bump in the Night*, was considered really shocking because there were two gay men in it. In a way, I feel I've even been punished for it. That certainly wasn't a masterpiece, but people were really shocked by the relationship between the two men. I think people have stopped being shocked by gay characters. Now it has to be a good play. Additionally, they've stopped saying, "Mr. McNally's a homosexual and the women characters are inauthentic." I think a gay playwright can write gay or heterosexual characters without that kind of comment. I'd like to believe that. Anne Heche has opened in a romantic comedy without anyone going hysterical about it. I really think the climate I grew up in has changed. You remember about Tennessee Williams and Edward Albee, the horrible, horrible homophobic critics. I'm so glad they can't get away with that anymore. They either like *Tiny Alice* or they don't. I just think that's terrific. I'm all for everything that's happened in terms of frankness in writing about sex. I'm surprised heterosexuals haven't been quite as frank in writing about sexual relationships. Sex is very important in my work. And then there are other writers for whom sex never seems to be of interest. It's the difference between apples and oranges.

The only criticism of, say, *Love! Valour!* that offended me was that the nudity was gratuitous or it was an attempt to please a gay audience. That really angered me, it just wasn't true. The nudity is an incredible part of *Love! Valour!* I'm saying these people have dicks—just like you—

some of them have flabby asses and some don't—just like you. When a theatre says, "We'd love to do *Love! Valour!* but we can't have nudity," I say, "Don't do the play then." If it can't be a spontaneous, "Hey, let's go swimming!" Now if someone comes out nude or in a jockstrap and starts erotic dancing to turn the audience on, that is a very different use of the naked body than skinny-dipping, which is the most innocent pastime—that's when we all become children, we rip our clothes off and jump in the lake. I've had theatres say, "We'd love to do your play, but there's too many four-letter words, can we take them out?" I say, "Don't do my play." That's like saying, "We're gonna show the *David* here, but we're gonna put pants on him," then you're not showing the *David*. I have no problem if you don't want to do *Love! Valour! Compassion!* because of the nudity and the four-letter words, and the physical contact between men. I'm sorry you have that problem in your community. You should aspire to resolve these problems, but don't do the play with bathing suits and the men never kissing or touching each other and someone not saying, "Fuck you." Then it's not my play. Do my play or don't do it—don't do a bowdlerized version.

So, I don't think there's gay theatre anymore. I think there's less now than there was fifteen years or so ago. We begin with *Boys in the Band*. I think people say whether plays are good or bad. People say, "Is yours a good play? It's about three lesbians. It's about eight gay men." Not, "Let's go see it, there's naked men, these cute guys take their clothes off." The whole gay community has changed. In the sixties we used to go to restaurants because they were gay and the food was horrible, but we thought it was so important that two openly gay men could sit in the middle of the restaurant on X Street. Now, we're too integrated, a gay restaurant has to be as good as a straight restaurant. A gay play has to be not as good as a "straight play" but as good as a play should be. There's no more special favors. I can't say I feel there's a backlash, like, "We're so sick of gays in theatre." Someone told me about the night *Kiss of the Spiderwoman* and *Angels* both won Tony Awards—the parents of a playwright that didn't win said, "What have they got against normal people?" I think that kind of thinking is gone, too. I think we're very fortunate to have so many good writers around. And so what if some of them are gay? To say that gay works are not of interest to anybody but gay men and gay women is absurd. *Love! Valour!* would not have had the life it did if it interested just gay men. If *Master Class* were only of interest to opera queens, it would have run three weeks.

So it's very healthy and it's great that so many gay people have taken that big step out of the closet. We still have a way to go in that department. In theatre it's gotten pretty good, there's one or two people who, even if they don't speak openly about their sexualities in public, don't deny it in interviews anymore. We're so over it at the Tonys. Everyone who's gay is there with a partner of their sex, you don't have to invite girls or guys so that when the CBS cameras are on you you look okay. There are a lot of gay people kissing their partners on the Tony Awards now, too. Why gay people have found a life in the theatre is another issue. That's for psychologists. I like to write plays, I don't like to psychoanalyze myself. I have a few patterns I'm not terribly proud of. I'm in therapy. But the crucial thing is not, "Why am I drawn to the world of theatre?" Because it's fun, I always learn from it.

When theatre works, I find it deeply moving, it can be very funny, very bold, very dramatic, touching, you feel connected to people around you in a way. Whether there are ninety-nine seats or fifteen hundred, when a play works well, there's a sense of community and you feel connected to your fellow humans. That's how it should be. You don't have that experience when you're home alone reading a novel. You can be moved, but you don't say, "I'm in this with all these people around me." If a play's really good, people talk going up the aisle, "Didn't you enjoy that?" "Wasn't that moving?" "God, that was funny, wasn't it?" "I really got a lot out of this, didn't you?" When a play doesn't work, we don't talk to each other. Some connection has failed. I think we go to the theatre out of a very basic need to be instructed, enthralled, to learn something. There's a reason the scout master tells little boys these stories. There's a little learning in all of that. That's why we go to see something live at night. Even a very unsophisticated person knows it's not just like a movie, that unlike *Gone with the Wind*, they can't reopen it on Friday with a restored print. There's more theatre in New York now than when I came in the sixties. Broadway has shrunk, but Off-Off-Broadway didn't exist. Off-Broadway really meant the Theatre de Lys, twelve theatres in the West Village, one or two in the East Village, one or two on the Upper East Side, Circle in the Square, and that was the extent of it. About twenty Broadway theatres have been taken down since I came to New York, but a lot of those theatres that were considered Off-Broadway in the sixties and seventies are gone because they're considered impractical. So you have the really small, letter-of-agreement, Equity, 99-seat venues that didn't even exist ten years ago, a lot of them happening in Chelsea right now. But they can only run so long.

So it's important to you that theatre be free, uncensored. And it will be supported, one way or the other, because the kind of communication they facilitate is so essential.

I thought you meant free—no ticket price—that would be nice, too. The cost of production in New York is truly frightening and also, as you get older, it's less possible to work for no money. A twenty year old out of NYU or Juilliard is more inclined to do a workshop production for no pay than someone who's got a family. As you get older, you have more responsibilities financially, and it's very hard. But I think the cost of putting on shows now is so out of hand. It's so disproportionate. I know that prices have increased incredibly, but not like it has in the theatre. When I came to New York, the best seats for *My Fair Lady* were $7 or $8.95. That's not comparable to the $85 for musicals now. I saw a lot of plays on Broadway and $2.90 was the going price for the balcony. Now the cheapest balcony seat for a play is $45 and it's $50–75 for the orchestra. That does not reflect the inflation in the rest of our society.

With the NEA slowly fading away, theatres get very conservative. "Let's keep our subscribers happy." People didn't make enough of a protest about losing Circle Rep. It was terrible to lose that theatre. We just can't afford any loss. We should be welcoming the Vineyard at the same time we're celebrating Circle Rep's twenty-fifth anniversary, not its closing. The Manhattan Theatre Club has certainly gotten more conservative. Any subscription theatre is conservative, because young people don't say, "I want to see a play September 12th and May 11th, and here's the hundred dollars to do that." They make their plans that week. You get the old crowd there. It's sad, these are middle-aged audiences. I certainly don't want Lincoln Center, Manhattan Theatre Club, or the City Ballet to go under. But if you took away the subscriber base, all those companies would really be out of business, including the Met and the Philharmonic. The person who knows they're going to see *Tosca* on January 1st is always less excited than the one who says, "Cool, they're doing *Tosca* with Pavarotti, I've always wanted to see it," and stands in a line for ten minutes or two hours. At the Manhattan Theatre Club, the audiences just aren't as thrilled to be there. But I couldn't have been allowed to produce *A Perfect Ganesh* or *Love! Valour!* at the level to which I've grown accustomed, with that quality of actors, designers and directors, if we didn't have that subscriber base. You don't get Joe Mantello and Brian McDevitt to work at a little loft in Chelsea for fifty dollars. You just have to accept that. So that's the biggest change, subscription didn't exist then. Good plays used to open on Broadway. All of Arthur Miller, all of Tennessee Williams, most of Edward Albee after the sixties opened on Broadway.

Suzan-Lori Parks

Over the course of the twentieth century, African-American theatre has repeatedly addressed what W.E.B. Du Bois so memorably identified as double consciousness: "This sense of always looking at one's self through the eyes of others . . . One ever feels his twoness—an American, a Negro; two souls, two thoughts, two unreconciled strivings; two warring ideals in one dark body." From the tragic mulatto of melodrama to Adrienne Kennedy's Negro-Sarah, the African-American protagonist has been imagined as an irreducibly split figure, torn by pride and self-hatred, contradictions and conflicting allegiances. For how can any American avoid internalizing—and, one hopes, resisting—the values of a once slave-owning and now profoundly racist culture? And African-American writers, confronting a history of racist representation that has so often made African-Americans the objects rather than the subjects of art, have worked to fashion their own distinctive forms not from scratch (what art, after all, can ever be made from scratch?), but by drawing upon and mixing different cultural traditions, "A European or American literary tradition," in Henry Louis Gates, Jr.'s words, with "One of the several but related distinct, black traditions."

Most African-American playwrights, from Langston Hughes to August Wilson, have taken double consciousness as their subject matter and have created divided protagonists who are forced to make moral choices. Suzan-Lori Parks, on the other hand, creates a very different kind of theatre. Drawing on the work of artists as dissimilar as James Baldwin and Gertrude Stein, Ornette Coleman and Bach, she insistently stages the very doubleness of the African-American, his or her status as both subject and object. She thereby dramatizes the very act of "looking at one's self through the eyes of others," which is to say, the process by which the self is produced as an object not only for others but also for one's self. For in Parks's plays, sight is the privileged sense and it is hardly accidental that she describes *Imperceptible Mutabilities in the Third Kingdom* (1989) as "African-American history in the shadow of the photographic image." Or that the pivotal moment in part one of the play occurs when three women, watching *Wild Kingdom* on TV, suddenly realize that Marlin Perkins's camera has become a gun when they see him "SHOOTIN THUH WILD BEASTS!" Set in counterpoint against this event, Parks juxtaposes a sequence of scenes in which a (white) naturalist quite literally bugs their apartment by placing a camera inside a giant cockroach and then sprays the women with pesticide. By relating these two actions—both of which suggest that looking can be an act of violence—Parks provides the ground for a critique of an allegedly disinterested, but in fact paternalistic and racist, social science that ends up killing and poisoning the very subjects it pretends to protect.

Parks's plays are not, however, polemical tracts but rather complex and deeply resonant poems. Using a minimum of stage directions, they are in the profoundest sense texts whose very being resides in the texture and materiality of language itself. And they are structured more by poetic devices—repetitions, puns, incantations, plays on words—than by traditional linear narrative or by characters whose motivations and goals can be neatly formulated and represented. Thus language is the site of real action in her writing. Language produces character, not the other way around. This is not to say that Parks's plays are undramatic. On the contrary, they are exhilaratingly theatrical. But they will frustrate a director who approaches them expecting to find a text that can be simply and literally illustrated. Like the plays of Kennedy or Stein, they demand that directors and readers conspire with the playwright as active producers of meaning. For they do not construct stable and fixed meanings but set the self in dialogue with itself, offering contradictory possibilities for meaning. They, in short, stage (double) consciousness.

At the heart of Parks's dramaturgy is the process of "Signifyin(g)," which Gates defines as a kind of doubling of language. For all of Parks's plays are written in a distinctive orthography that draws upon both standard English and black vernacular and plays one off against the other. According to Gates, Signifyin(g) is a kind of "guerrilla action," "the slave's trope," which allows a speaker both to take up and critique "the nature of (white) meaning itself." Using innuendo, riddles and puns, it functions to undermine and unbalance a master discourse and to play on the difference between writing and speech, approved English and unapproved dialect, acquiescence and resistance. In part one of *Imperceptible Mutabilities*, the character Molly/Mona, having been kicked out of school because of her penchant for Signifyin(g), agonizes over the difference between "ask" and "ax," never quite seeing or accepting "thuh sense uh words workin like he [her teacher] said." For Parks, Signifyin(g) becomes a way of representing "the speech patterns of a people oppressed by language" who have, in retaliation, as it were, developed an idiom that is "so complex and varied and ephemeral that its daily use not only Signifies on the nonvernacular language, but on the construct of writing as well." Signifyin(g) is thus a profoundly literary and political operation, a way of taking a sometimes stigmatized language form and using it both to enact the doubleness of consciousness and to resist the forces of oppression.

Parks's plays are uniquely important for pressing a drama of Signification into service for a historical project. She explains that a play for her is always "a blueprint of an event: a way of creating and rewriting history through the medium of literature." But she rewrites history not by chronicling a prepackaged event from the past, but by dramatizing the very act of re-membering: putting things back together, finding what has been lost, imagining what could have been and what should be. In her hands, the theatre "is the perfect place to 'make' history— that is, because so much of African-American history has been unrecorded, dismembered, washed out." In so re-membering the past, her stage functions as a place where time itself is placed in the spotlight and where ghosts tread the boards. "One of my tasks as playwright," she observes, "is to locate the ancestral burial ground, dig for bones, find bones, hear the bones sing, write it down." For all of her characters are ghosts, the dismembered spirits, neither living nor dead, that haunt African-American history. And all are possessed—by their unrecorded ancestors, by the chronicles from which they have been erased and by the continuing power of racism in America.

Thus part three of *Imperceptible Mutabilities* is the tale of the Saxon family: father, Charles; children, Blanca and Anglor Saxon; and a fourth figure, Aretha who plays the roles of slave and servant, wife and mother. But the ambivalence of her position is not the result of any indecision on Parks's part. Rather, it results from the fact that the action takes place in at least three different locales and times simultaneously: on a slave ship, on a plantation when news of the Emancipation Proclamation is finally heard, and in a modern luxury condominium. By performing these scenes simultaneously, the play provides a different way of thinking about time and (lack of) progress. It demonstrates precisely how the present moment is always haunted by the past. Or in *The America Play* (1993), Parks summons up the spirit of Abraham Lincoln as impersonated by the black Foundling Father. Stranded in The Great Hole of History, digging his own grave, he is a consummate "faker" who actively represses the knowledge that "our inheritance"—the promise of freedom and equality—is only a void, an absence, a Hole. Or *Venus* (1996), which performs an autopsy on Saartje Baartman, the so-called Hottentot Venus who astonished early nineteenth-century Europe, to analyze the effects of a racist medical practice on the persons under its care and the theatre's unwitting complicity with this science.

For Parks, theatre lies at the crossroads of memory and history. It is the site at which one is able to remember, to enact the doubleness of consciousness, to resist the forces of oppression, to open the graves of the dead, to call up ghosts and to repeat. For repetition, she insists (drawing on a "jazz aesthetic"), always necessitates revision. As one repeats something, one changes it. However provisionally and incompletely, one is able to acquire a degree of mastery over the past, to make it mean differently, to rewrite history. For "in drama," as in politics, "change, revision is the thing."

DS: How did you get interested in theatre?

SLP: I'm not sure that I was interested in theatre when I started writing plays. Some people start from a love for theatre and go on from there. But I was a short-story writer in a class with James Baldwin when I was a student at Mount Holyoke College. He was teaching creative writing at Hampshire College and I took a class with him. We had to read our stories out loud for the class and I loved reading aloud. So he said, "You should try playwriting," and I said, "I'll try it." That's how I got into it. So the love of theatre and interest in theatre came after, came through the writing.

What got you interested in writing?

I used to write as a kid. I thought all kids were writers. That's kind of how my mind works, I guess. And the more I read, the more I loved to write. When I was in high school my English teacher said, "Whatever you do, don't major in English in college," because I was a poor speller, a phonetic speller. I still am but I'm getting better because I figured out that spelling is more visual than aural. It's pictures. You just take pictures with your head. So, I was a chemistry major at Mount Holyoke College for the first year. I always liked science. But then I took a class in which we read Virginia Woolf and I loved *To the Lighthouse*. And I thought, "I really want to write." So it was that book and other books that got me back into writing.

When you started writing in the eighties, what theatrical work particularly interested you? Or other kinds of writing?

When I was in college it was more that I loved literature. Virginia Woolf. I didn't read Faulkner, Joyce or Proust until long after I graduated from college. Or much of Baldwin's work. Or the Greeks. It was more writing itself, not necessarily a specific book I'd read or a play I'd seen. Theatre made me very nervous. When I was in college, it was populated by students who wore funny clothes and had a lot of attitude. Men and women alike. And that put me off. I didn't feel comfortable around them. Not that I felt more comfortable around English majors because they had another kind of thing going on. I used to say that theatre's full of people with funny hats. So I didn't really go to plays at all. The first real time I spent in the theatre at Mount Holyoke was when I went up there in March [1997] to direct *Devotees in the Garden of Love* [1991]. I studied some theatre at Hampshire College because you could take courses there. I remember I read *for colored girls* and directed it in college—but not in the theatre. We just brought some people together and put on a show. I remember I liked Edward Albee and thought, that's cool, funny, weird. I had a real thing for Faulkner.

I find it interesting that many of the writers you name, like Faulkner and Joyce, are in part writing about writing.
Right.

Writers for whom the materiality of the text itself is so important. Because that's so important for your work, too.
It is because those writers, like Toni Morrison, trace the human mind. There are things going on in the world, like in *To the Lighthouse* the war happens and people die and in *Beloved* the war happens and people die. And slavery happens. But you're tracing the fine lines of the human mind. It's that kind of writing I love. It's not less concerned with things going on outside but I use them to understand what's going on inside. And it is a lot about the text. With Faulkner, the text and the story are equal. For writers I'm not interested in, the text is just a way to tell the story. And even in some plays, the story is the most important thing and the way it's communicated, the text of it, the form, is secondary. But the thing I like about Faulkner is that they're equal.

What about Adrienne Kennedy?
I'm a fan of hers. I remember a teacher of mine in the English Department at Mount Holyoke. I was walking down the hall one day and she saw me coming and ran in her office and came back out with a book and kind of held it out like I was a train and she had the mailbag and I just took it and kept walking, and I got to the end of the hall and it was *Funnyhouse of a Negro*. So I read it and reread it and reread it and reread it. It also had a hand in shaping what I do. I thought anything is possible. I could do what I wanted to do instead of what I felt I had to do. I was having some problems because the first play I wrote was for my senior thesis and it wasn't well received. My first bad review. But I had a problem with the set. I wanted lots of dirt and digging and stuff like that. And one of the guys on the committee said, "We don't have dirt on

stage." And knowing nothing about theatre—because I didn't go to the-atre—I said, "Oh, okay, guess not." And then I found all these plays, like *Happy Days* and *Bury the Dead*, with dirt on the stage but I didn't know enough to defend myself. So I said, "I just wrote it, I don't know. You guys don't like it, that's alright." I think she gave me Adrienne Kennedy to encourage me to do what I thought I had to do instead of what people expected.

When did you come to New York?
In '86. I graduated in '85 and went to London for a year and studied acting because I thought I was going to be a writer. I had the confidence but not the ambition. That's why I look at kids—I call them kids, but college students, younger people whom I teach—it's like they have amazing amounts of ambition and less confidence. But I had a lot of confidence for someone who had just been thrown on the trash pile by the English department. James Baldwin had been very kind and I had great private moments as a writer, times when you really feel, Wow, I'm in that other world, writing, and this is great. So I had a lot of confidence. So I said if I'm going to do this playwriting thing which I enjoy, I should study acting. I didn't want to study writing because I didn't think it was going to help me—I'd already gotten burned. So I went to London. Then, because my parents live in Syracuse, New York, I moved back there and within a month or two I moved to New York. I didn't know where else to go. I knew one person, Laurie Carlos, whom I met in Texas at summer theatre. She let me stay in part of her huge apartment on Riverside Drive as one of her several roommates. That was in '86. So I've been here eleven years which is longer than I've lived anyplace because my dad was in the army and we moved around.

When I saw *Imperceptible Mutabilities*, I was really struck by its relationship to a lot of New York experimental work: Richard Foreman, the Wooster Group, Lee Breuer. When you were here in the late eighties, did you see much of that work?
I think at that time, to be honest, I was ignorant of it. I moved to New York and got a job as a paralegal because I had to make money. I'm very good at typing and office work and shuffling papers around. So I got a job and I hung out around the Poetry Project because Laurie taught there and she invited me to take part in her class. And she helped me get started. But I was really ignorant. I didn't know what an OBIE was until I'd won one. I wasn't one of those people who read the *Village Voice* or went to see Richard Foreman. I worked from nine to five every day and would show up at the Poetry Project in these little kilts and tights, because I'd come from the office, and try to mix in, and people would

make all these comments that I wasn't cool, that I was just this goofy kid. And I still had this funny feeling about theatre people. It's just a different vibe that makes me uncomfortable.

Still?
Sometimes, yeah. I don't go out very much. I haven't seen ninety-nine percent of the shows in a given season. So I hadn't seen all these fabulous people. I forget what was the first Wooster Group or Foreman show I saw. I was decidedly uncool. I just didn't know. Didn't see anything on Broadway, of course. I went to poetry readings.

So you came to theatre through language, through poetry . . .
And fiction.

Which is perhaps one reason why language is always foregrounded in your plays. I've noticed the lack of stage directions and I know that that's frustrating sometimes for my students. I don't find it so, but I've seen several of your plays performed. Why do you use so few stage directions?
There are two answers. The first is that the Greek guys and Shakespeare didn't use many stage directions. In *Medea*, Creon, I think, says something like, because she's begging him, "Get off your knees and let go of my robe." And there's no parenthetical thing, there's only Creon's line, which I always thought was really weird and interesting. Suddenly the actions were coming from the guts of the people. I was taught that anything in parentheses you could do without. So if you put the action in the guts, in the stomach, in the bodies of the characters instead of in this parenthetical thing hanging on the side, it's more integral. That seemed to make sense to me. It seemed to make sense to them. It seemed to make the language more exciting. Too many plays are full of lines like, "So it must be very hard for you. *(She picks up her glass and holds it to her lips.)*" And he says, "You know it is." That bores me, I sit there and think, "Live! Do something!" Not that what I write is more realistic but most of the action is in the lines. The Foundling Father, for example, will say, "A nod to the president's bust." And that's exactly what he does. Sometimes it's in parentheses because he doesn't always say it. For a long time people thought I didn't know what I wanted. Someone told me about an article in the *Times* last year that came out after the reviews of *Venus* that said, "Obviously she's too wishy-washy to have told Mr. Foreman what she wanted." People always assume that I don't know what I want. The reality is that I do know and I put it in the line. When I can't get it in the line, I put it in a stage direction. And when I truly don't care or want to see what the director comes up with,

I won't put in anything. Because it could be anything. I'll put in something like, "He's in the big hole which is an exact replica of the Great Hole of History." I want to see what the director says. And the director's going to say, "It's a museum, it's a black hole, it's a fishbowl." That is magical to me, when people think for themselves. It's not when I have to write down every single little thing.

So your plays demand that actors, directors, readers take a more active role, unlike contemporary naturalism where everything tends to be spelled out. There, it's just a matter of illustrating the text. But to read your work, to understand it, you have to take possession of it. Most people are not used to playing such an active role.
Right.

But that's also related to the content of your work. In the essays in your book of plays, you write about your concept of repetition and revision which makes me think of Henry Louis Gates's theorization of Signifyin(g): repeating, transforming, displacing. In your work I see people, through repetition and revision, taking possession and changing their relationship to the past, to each other.
I spend years writing a play but I never think it out like that. So when someone says something like that to me, my mind scrambles to understand the play in those terms. For example, I got *The Signifying Monkey* years ago when it came out and though I've read snatches of it, I still haven't finished it. And after I wrote *The America Play* I was flipping through it—because every once in a while I like to flip through that book—and I read something about a gap: in the identity there is a gap, a hole, or a chasm, something like that. And I thought, "Ah, interesting." Because I wasn't thinking about the chasm of identity when I wrote *The America Play*. I know what you're talking about but I can't say that.

So you don't sit down consciously to use or to write about these things.
Some people do. I've heard some people talk about their plays, or some visual artists say, "I'm going to do X, Y and Z," and you see it and it's pretty much what they said.

And the figure of the chasm is repeated and revised in many of your plays. Isn't The Third Kingdom section of *Imperceptible Mutabilities*—middle passage, being torn away from Africa—also about a chasm?
Right. That's a wet chasm. In *The America Play*, it's a very dry chasm. In *Venus* there's a chasm that is filled with a speech: the intermission. And we put something there, right between the butt crack. In *Imperceptible Mutabilities in the Third Kingdom*, there was no Third Kingdom. And Liz [Diamond], who would always tell me about people I didn't know

like Robert Wilson, told me about his *Knee Plays*. And she asked for something in the middle that would connect the parts. Or you can look at it as something that goes on while we change the scenery. Anyway, that was that chasm.

After I wrote the plays, I was trying to help people find their way into them so I wrote the essays. If someone in the play repeats something, they repeat it because they have to but I don't necessarily know why they say it so many times. Because it sounds right, they have to say it. In *The America Play*, there are lots of echoes: the bust, the cut-out, the Foundling Father, the memory, the son who comes and follows in his father's footsteps.

But as lines and actions are repeated, the meaning changes. I'm thinking, for example, of the multiple assassinations of the Foundling Father.
Right. I took that from the jazz thing of repetition/revision. Jazz musicians were the first people I knew who did that, but then later on I found Bach. *The Goldberg Variations* is one of my favorite examples. Pop music does it. Everything does it. First, I heard someone talking about it in terms of jazz and how you can repeat a phrase and then change it. A piece that has a beginning, middle and end structured by repetition makes more sense to me than one structured by a lead-up, climax and resolution. Because for me plays are more like religious experiences than secular ones. The excitement in a play doesn't come from wanting to find out who did it? Who killed him? Or will they stay together? Or will they get divorced? The excitement comes from watching happen what I already know is going to happen. Like the Greek plays. They knew all the stories. They knew Oedipus. The thrill is to see him crumble. So it's more like a religious pageant. That's much more exciting to me.

That's why there's so much in your plays that can be understood as ritual. Ritual repetition. And you also write about spells and possession—both of which are also connected to ritual.
Theatre makes more sense to me like that, and not because of any historical link to Greek plays or anything. I was thinking about that even before I'd read a Greek play. My family is Roman Catholic. And there's a lot of drama—holding things up, and bells are ringing, and holding something else up, and the bells go off again. It makes much more sense to me that that's what theatre really is, rather than a whole bunch of people pretending to be people they aren't. The audience and the players are involved in this recreation of something that could have happened, didn't happen, will happen, is happening right as they're creating it. That's why repetition makes sense to me, why I keep employing

it. I just finished the first draft of my first novel and it's the same thing. It's a circle book. Not that they start where they end, but it's like *The Goldberg Variations*. Or like Ornette Coleman. You play the beginning and then you don't know where he is and you're getting nervous and just when you think you're lost in the wilderness, there's the reprise, there's the aria, or there's Coleman playing the end of the song which is sort of like the beginning. And you go, "Wow, I was there all the time, just for a moment it looked mysterious."

Was Gertrude Stein and her use of repetition an influence? Or the way that some of her works take apart the distinction between narrative and dramatic forms?

I'm a big fan of Gertude Stein. I've read her work and I used to teach *Ida* in one of my classes. But I haven't read her or Faulkner in a long time. I never read critical analysis of her work, so I don't really understand it except that it sounds good. It feels right. Maybe I don't read her so much anymore because I'm more interested in character. It's not an idea or concept or message or place. They might start with any of those elements but what they really start with is character. With *The America Play*, there were two people looking for another person. With *Imperceptible Mutabilities*, it was the three women together in the apartment with the roach problem. Who were they? *Venus*—of course she's the center of that play. I'm really much more interested in characters than I am in language. Language is just something that comes out of the people. I say certain things in certain ways. Like if I vomited right now all of a sudden, the vomit, I think, would be a lot less interesting than me, who I am and why I threw up. So, too, it's who these people are. In *Last Black Man* [*The Death of the Last Black Man in the Whole Entire World*, 1990], who are they? They talk funny because they're in a really funny place. They're walking a line between the living and the dead, or he is anyway. Most of the people in the play are dead. They really don't make sense a lot of the time because they're dead. It's not anything more than that. And the woman, his wife, just wants him to eat, because she's alive: "Eat, just eat, that's what we do when we're alive. And we try to figure things out. We sit here wondering, where were you? Why are you dressed like that? What's your problem?"

When you came in today I was talking to a film person. The first thing I said was, "I figured out who these people are. We can't go forward until you hear who these people are." The story, who cares? The message—concerns about the race issue, the women issue, all these issues—I don't care. Once I figure out who these people are, then I can figure out what happens. Because the characters talk to you. I don't, like, decide it's going to be about something. Once you lock in on a character then the character, or that part of your psyche, or that character who is part of you, will dictate what it is about. And you just have to listen.

So then you, as a playwright, become possessed when you're writing?
When the going is good. As I wrote in the essay, it's not a voodoo priestess kind of thing—I wish it were that exciting, but it's not. It's more like a Zen thing where you just have to remove yourself from the path. I'm in the way of the play, I have to remove my Self so that the play can be what it wants to be. It's like that, which is very hard, because you have all these things that you want it to be about, or that it should be about. You have to just let it do its thing. And it's always interesting, a nice little story.

Do you write many drafts?
I did lots of drafts of *Venus* over five years or something. They were all just really bad. And then I got a fellowship to Bellagio—it's very beautiful, very inspiring, magical. But it wasn't magical when I was there, it was horrible. I was trying to finish this play there and it took me two weeks of flipping out and then finally the stone just rolled away from the tomb and I wrote a whole draft in less than a week. And the language was totally different. The same thing with *The America Play*. What was going on in the second act is exactly what I was doing. Two people were looking for this man while I was looking for him. Who is he? Where is he? We don't know. We have these pieces of things. And then suddenly, there he was. Then the first part of it was easy: he's in a sideshow. Clean up the edges and there it is. Sometimes I wish I could talk about my work more theoretically. I listen to Richard Foreman talking about his work and he uses all these impressive words and I think, "Dang, I might think about doing that." Then I think about my characters and think, "No, they don't need me to talk like that about them." That's not who they are.

What makes a good production of one of your plays?
If it's imaginative. There are good productions that I have been involved with and others when I haven't. I once saw a very good reading of my work at the University of Chicago. The Onyx Theatre did a reading of *The America Play*. Great job, totally different from what Liz [Diamond] and I had done. It was the gut bucket version. It was funny. It was like black funny. And I thought, "Dang, this is a real like, side-slappin' play." Marcus Stern did a really great job with *The America Play* at A.R.T. that I wasn't involved in which was bizarre, very imaginative. The productions I've done with Liz have been great and incredibly

imaginative because the director works with the play. She doesn't do a number on the play. That means like a bowel movement on the play. Because you're looking at the bowel movement and not the play. I guess that's fine if the play is well known like *Hamlet*. Then you do it in a bizarre way and that's fine. But newer plays should be seen in an imaginative way, in a way that makes them pop, but not in a way that obscures them. Because then you're just watching the window dressing, which I don't think is a good idea. Because then the audience is not enjoying the play. They're just watching things that obscure the play. And I think that life is difficult enough. And challenging theatre is challenging enough without having it made more challenging by some stuff that a director or a playwright wants to put in the play to make it more interesting. Playwrights do that, too, and I am getting to be a very good editor of my own work. I always cut so much it scares people. I'll go in to production and say, "Let's cut that scene, it's not necessary. It's a lovely scene but it makes five layers instead of three." The people who have trouble are the people who think it's got to be weird and avant-garde and abstract. When I directed *Devotees in the Garden of Love* up at Mount Holyoke, people up there were just beside themselves. They kept saying, "I can't believe it's just this straightforward." I said, "Look, two women on a hilltop, what do you want? We're gonna put them on a hill." "Are you sure you want to put them on a hill? Shouldn't we put something up there?" "Why put something up there? They're on a hill. In wedding dresses. Watching a war. Just like it says. And every once in a while that third woman runs her mouth." They couldn't believe it. They were just beside themselves. It was a great experience and I couldn't get over it. I thought, this is telling me something. We had a beautiful green hill, kind of flat on the top, enough room for the wheelchair. It went around and around.

And it was peaceful?
Except that we had an underlying soundtrack of war which would come up and go down at certain times. I'm sure *Last Black Man* is hard because you're thinking, "What am I doing with all of those people? Where do they go? Where do they move?" If all else fails, let them stand still. Why do you need stage business? I think whoever invented it is just goofy. Because I think that ruins lots of really great plays. You can have people standing there, just talking. If it gets a little bit like a chorus or a concert, so? They can stand and be still for a minute and just speak. They don't have to be lifting up glasses and adjusting their bifocals.

A lot of people I've never met have done wonderful productions because I don't go around the country and see my plays. People get mad at me or they think I have an attitude. If I write a play, say, in 1986, like *Imperceptible Mutabilities* and some wonderful person does it in '96, great, I'm so happy they're doing the play. But I'm in the middle of writing my novel.

I ask this not to be voyeuristic but in part because I understand that your work, like *Girl 6* [1996], is a critique of voyeurism. I know that all writers' works are autobiographical in some ways. They use elements from their own lives. I know, for example, that you grew up in a military family. . . .
My dad was in the military. A military family: we all packed guns and did drills.

So I think of that when I read "Greeks" [part four of *Imperceptible Mutabilities*]. But can you talk more generally about the autobiographical element in your work?
Looking back, there are a couple of different things I'm interested in. One is the question, Who am I? And that has a lot of answers. I was talking to a friend of Liz Diamond, this East German guy, and I'd ask, "How can you be sure of that simple thing, who the hell am I?" And he'd say, "You're you, you're Suzan-Lori Parks, you're a writer." So that's the jumping off point for all these plays. That's why I gravitate most to character and why I don't write poetry. Because I often think, "I could be anybody." I really believe that. But after "Greeks" people would say, "Gee, your dad got his legs shot off in the war?" And I'd laugh. Even *The America Play*. Someone was interviewing me and really kept pressing, "So, this is really the story of your family?" Every time I would try to answer, she would come back to it as if I were avoiding the subject. I finally said, "My dad abandoned our family when I was very young and went off to play Lincoln." And she said, "Really?!?"

But the question in these plays is, "Who am I?" I could be anybody. I'm reading all these books on yoga or Zen or Jung, and I'm carrying around the *Portable Jung* and he talks about the collective unconscious (and I'm paraphrasing), that primitive consciousness, that under consciousness, that bedrock. That's the territory I explore. The story of the Foundling Father, Abraham Lincoln, that's me. I feel like I'm as much him as I am Brazil or I am the Black Man with Watermelon. A lot of people will ask, "Why do you write all these men in your plays?" Well, I don't know. Or they'd think *Venus* is more autobiographical. You have to talk about love. People kept saying, "I see so much of you in that play." I would laugh. I mean, I'm everywhere, we all are. And that is what's so difficult to believe. We are everybody. Everybody is us. We are all one person. I don't think I'll ever write a play about the years I went to a German school. But who knows? I'm growing, I'm changing. I might.

And it may be that your experience in German schools has filtered into your writing in terms of your use of English.

Exactly. I think the problem I have with the question about autobiography is that some people assume that the line between the writer and the material is a straight line. Sometimes it is, especially these days when everybody seems to be writing a memoir. I heard it called a me-moir— me, me, me. If I were a housewife who had a drunk husband and lived in Iowa for ten years, maybe I'd write about it. But unfortunately fiction writers and people who concoct stories are getting pushed aside in favor of real stories. You see the ad for *COURT TV*: no scripts, no actors, it's all real. Or *Rescue 911* or *Cops* or any of those shows that focus on real people doing real things. The space left for imagination and fiction is getting smaller and smaller and the imagination is being de-emphasized in favor of real life, which I think is not good because what's under the surface? . . . I mean reality is very fleeting and, I don't know, I can't describe it. The spirit and the soul of people reside in the imagination, not in the stories that fill up the six o'clock news. "One Man Shot in Harlem." "Two Boys Mutilated Downtown." What is that? That's just like fuzz, it's interference.

As I was reading your plays, I was thinking about how frequently TVs appear, as a sign perhaps of realness and banality, and how important it is for you to keep them, if not in the foreground, at least in the background.

There are a lot of TVs, aren't there? Even in this novel, lots of different characters are referring to the television a lot and how, "He was just like on TV"—how we're beginning to imitate this constructed thing. In *Imperceptible Mutabilities*, a horrible thing is happening on television, as opposed to the horrible thing that's happening in the women's own living room. Or in *The America Play*, dad is suddenly on TV. And in *Devotees* too: "The modern-day bride ought to be adequately accoutrementalized for the modern age" by watching the war on TV! It's not an evil thing. I enjoy television. There's lots of great shows, lots of movies I wasn't old enough to see when they came out, and an overwhelming amount of garbage.

What do you see as the main differences between theatre and film or television? Theatre, of course, caters to a very small, selective audience.

I think theatre's best when it's like church. And I think it's the worst when it's like TV, or like a movie. I saw that *ER*, one of the hot shows, wants to film it live like they used to. Some sitcoms are live now. TV used to be live—I think it probably was much more interesting. It had that *life* in it that film doesn't have. And I like movies, and not just arty ones. There are plenty of popular movies that I just love, but movies are dead, I think. That's the difference. Theatre's alive. People are living, they're right there doing what they're doing in front of you. The people in movies could be dead, might be dead, are often dead. It's a different kind of experience. I think theatre's much more interesting when it's a religious kind of thing.

Do you think that has to do with the nature of spectatorship and the fact that the theatre audience is more of a real community, they're more participants, more active than a film audience?
I talk to the television. A friend still remembers when George Bush was giving a speech about something or other and I was over at her house watching. And she keeps reminding me that I just kept talking to George Bush: "I think you're so stupid!" I was yelling at this man as if he were in my living room. And I've been in movie theatres where people talk to the screen. Mostly black people for movies that have lots of black characters. Or anybody can be on the screen and they'll talk, "Watch it!" or "He's stupid!" They'll yell things out. So movies and TV can be active in that way. There's call and response there too.

Theatre's the only place where the people on stage know that you're watching them and that's the difference. When you're on stage and you look out there, you know that somebody's looking at you and that, to me, is weird. In *Mutabilities*, when they realize they're being watched, they-be-gin-to-talk-like-this-because-he's-watch-ing-us-it-all-be-comes-ver-y-con-trolled. It's a strange moment. Venus is being looked at. The guy in *The America Play* is there for you to look at and interact with and kill. That's what it is in theatre, it's not so much that the audience is shouting or watching but that the people on stage are parading themselves and enjoying being involved in this kind of thing—look at me, look at me, look at me—which is kind of creepy.

So then one of the most important moves in your plays, as in the first scene in *Mutabilities*, is the change from subject to object, to being looked at.
Right.

But I also get a clear sense in your plays of the violence that accompanies that process. "Marlin Perkinssgot uh gun." Looking can be a kind of violence.
It's sort of like the jungle, stalking—you know how cats do it, they watch, they look, they get you in their sights. But it's not something that's conscious. It's just what happens with these people. The women on the hill in *Devotees* are watching. Their stuff gets taken, or they're encouraged to give things away, and they're watching something that's

very violent. But that's very much a cultural thing. I love to sit and watch people watch violent things. There's a fight going on and people are standing around. I love to watch the people watching the fight. I don't know what that's about. Bad things happen in my plays because unfortunately that's what happens to the characters. But they're also independent of each other. In *Last Black Man*, there's no one really watching but there's such a difference between the living and the dead. The watching thing is independent. People are being watched because it's theatre. And that's what theatre's all about—watching. In the novel nobody's really watching anybody. People are just talking, they're telling a story.

You also use that in *Girl 6*, to show what happens when she's auditioning, the violence of the look of the director.
In plays I have more or less total control but in that screenplay, Spike [Lee] added stuff. I didn't like that part where she takes off her clothes and exposes her breasts. I didn't want it in there, I didn't write it, and I told him. He wanted that because it said some things he wanted to say. It was his baby so you just let it go and don't worry about it. That movie to me had more to do with the question of identity. She's everybody. "Who am I? Who do you want me to be? You want me to be blonde, I'm blonde. I'm a brunette, I'm Asian too." So that is really how it lines up with the rest of my work, how the self is malleable.

She's constantly changing, with all the wigs. . . .
All the costume changes. That's what I love about that. The same with *The America Play*. Who is he? *The Last Black Man*. Where is he, who is he, what is he? Is he alive or dead? He doesn't know. He's both, he's neither. All those people, they could be anybody. All those Third Kingdom people.

Are these questions specifically linked to your ideas of African-American identity?
Maybe. I don't know. I'll make it a funny answer: it could be, but because I believe in the universal consciousness, no. I think that everybody, if they're able to let go, just for a moment, of the person they assume themselves to be, will realize that they are anybody. On the surface, it's tied into the African-American experience because that's who I am. But one step back, it's part of that big, primordial soup.

I don't know whether this is related to your answer, but I've noticed that in addition to the lack of stage directions, you don't often specify the race of your characters. And Liz Diamond's production of *Imperceptible Mutabilities* used a white actor to

play a black character in part four. Alisa Solomon wrote about the confusion that that choice engendered for at least one spectator at a post-play discussion.

Because the boy was white, they thought the mother had cheated. That was the first and last time I yelled at someone in the audience. I said, "How stupid are you?" For a while, I didn't do post-play discussions. But I have learned to turn any question from the audience into a good question. It's a real feeling of power, that you can take something incredibly ridiculous and say, "That's a really good question." And then you talk about whatever you want. And the person in the audience says, "Thanks." Yeah, the race of the characters. I guess I don't specify. Maybe I should so that everyone will know they're black. But in other people's plays, they don't say they're white. Sam Shepard [she picks up *Seven Plays*] . . . let's see, he's a damn good writer. "Dodge, in his sixties. Hallie, his wife, mid-sixties. Tilden, their oldest son." The problem is that as the years go by, people will continue to assume that these people are white and assume that my people are whatever they want them to be—a lot of lightening up as time passes, or whitening out. Just one more thing I haven't thought about. Some people say, "Anybody could play the Foundling Father as Abraham Lincoln." And I say, "Anybody can play it but I don't necessarily have to watch every production of this play." Or *Devotees in the Garden of Love*. They could be three white women. There's nothing especially in that play, or in *The America Play* that requires the characters to be black. Not like *Death of the Last Black Man*. Black Man with Watermelon. Black Woman with Fried Drumstick. The rest of the people, who knows? In those plays, the characters could be anybody. And that's fine. But I guess I want to see . . . I have my preference, everybody else doesn't have to share that preference. People can do whatever they want, but I don't necessarily have to go to opening night of their production.

On the other hand, your use of black vernacular makes it pretty unmistakable for an attentive reader.

Sometimes. But again, with *Devotees* or *The America Play*, not necessarily. And I think of my use of black vernacular as a sort of borrowing, like I borrow from everybody. Black slang is changing so rapidly and I really am not up on it. I work with kids in Harlem during the school year, young kids, and we get together and play on computers. And every once in a while I pick up some words from them that I've never heard before and don't even understand. Black vernacular is like a place where you can go and borrow from. Some people read Mac Wellman's work and think he's black. I don't know what he's borrowing from. I know he doesn't speak the way his characters do, but I don't know if he's borrowing from black vernacular or Midwestern-speak. There's a kind of joy with language shared by a lot of black people I know and a lot of Southern people I know, white and black. The joy of playing with words and the sound of words. It's not black or white, it's just a love of saying things and saying something twice if it sounds really good. But I started by talking about the Self, and if that's an African-American thing. I think it's more of a human thing.

When, in "An Equation for Black People Onstage" you write, "Within the subject is its other," it leads me to think that the different identities that characters take on are in part fantasies—a racial identity, a gendered identity. Do you think of them as fantasies? Although I realize that just because they're fantasies doesn't mean they don't produce real effects.

I don't know if it's fantasy. I think it's more that that's the way it works on this planet. That's how we live. To play a part in a play and be on stage is a fantasy because you know as you are doing it that it has its limits. The phone sex thing, that's a fantasy. You know when you're engaging in it that it's a fantasy. You know that you're not really there. But I don't think race or gender is a fantasy. Gender is a reality but I don't think it's the be-all and end-all reality. There are other things beneath the surface that are also important, that are also present.

And you point out that these identities are not homogeneous. There's not only one kind of blackness or femininity.

Right. I think it's different now but there are what I call the black police, which are not black police officers but the people who are making sure that you're black enough. I guess other groups have these police, too. People who are making sure that your writing is black enough, who you're dating is black enough, and what comes out of your mouth is black enough, and what you wear is black enough. There are some people in the community and it's their job to monitor others, making sure you're up to snuff. That essay was more talking to those people who would ask, "Why don't your plays deal with the real issues?" And on the other side, there are the people who are not part of the community, white people and other folks, who think that black plays should only deal with certain issues. Like every black play should be another *Raisin in the Sun* or another *Fences*. They should deal with the struggle, uplift the race, in a kind of basic, twelve-step way. There's a light at the end of the tunnel and we are walking toward it. I don't know about that. I haven't really looked too hard but I haven't seen that kind of policing going on in other groups as much. It seems to me that others have more flexibility or allow their members to do lots of various things.

Why do you think the black police are so stringent?
I think there's more at stake in keeping black people contained. It's a question of international security. Because once the whole group realizes that they're actually free, wonderful things could happen. And I think that things would change in a way that a lot of people don't want them to. Because the accepted roles of black people are so entertaining and stimulating. The fascination with basketball players, the way that people on the golf course bow and scrape before Tiger Woods. I watch that and go, "This is a weird country." Other people in other groups have a little more room. Everybody knows about the policing of black people by white people, but the other side of it is equal and strange. 'Cause once anybody jumps out of their skin, of their identity, and swims in the underground sea of the unconscious where everybody is and it doesn't really matter who you are and everything is mythic and strange and large—I don't know, I'm not sure what would happen. That would be the end of the world.

How do you see your relationship to feminism? Because all of your plays have what I would call feminist content. *Devotees,* **for example, seems so clearly a critique of a kind of masculine aggression.**
Perhaps to a theatre scholar. But it isn't necessarily for me. I get funny when I hear that language. I don't think that way. To me it's not a critique; it's a show. In my plays most of the time everybody's bad. And everybody's good. Venus is bad and good. The women in *Devotees* are just as bad as they are good. And the men you don't see are just as stupid as they are interesting and brave and doing what society says they should do. People say I wrote *Venus* because I'm really interested in colonialism and the objectification of the female body. And it was none of those things. I wrote it because I wanted to give this great character two hours of a play with her name on it. And I wanted to give a black actress a chance to play a really cool part and be the star of the show.

So, feminism—I don't really have any language to talk about it. I like to see strong women characters because stupid women characters bore me. I like to see strong male characters—stupid men, on stage and off, bore me. I like to see characters who are complex, black or white, Asian or Native American, or whatever. Well drawn and multifaceted. Clichés are dumb. And I don't think that's feminism, that's just intelligence. I don't think it's being Afrocentric, it's being smart. I also don't like to see female or black characters more intelligent than they should be because the playwright is using the character as a mouthpiece. They have faults. It's Venus who says yes to going to England. Granted, she's in a tough place. But she wants to make a mint. She thinks she can win.

She is no more intelligent than she needs to be. I wanted to see a black woman on stage with a really cool part. Or three black women in *Devotees*. Or sure, they could be white women. White women need good parts, too, where they don't have to take off their clothes. Boy, if I see another woman take off her clothes, I'll scream—or fall asleep. My boyfriend Dave and I have a game that we play with movies. When the movie starts we ask, "So who's going to be the titty girl? Who's going to be the poor woman, most likely a newcomer, who's going to have to show her breasts?" We'll guess and invariably it's one of the ones we expect. I think people deserve better than that—audiences, writers, actresses, actors alike. More than just violent black men on TV or in the movies. Or sympathetic black women.

Your talking about stereotypical representations of African-Americans leads me to think about your use of history. All your plays are really history plays. But your idea of history is very different from what we see on TV, for example, with its fixation on celebrity, on the clash of personalities, all told with strings of depthless images. You're so attentive to historical struggle and the violence in history, whether it's the offstage war in *Devotees* or the murder of Lincoln or lynching in *The Last Black Man*. Your work is so steeped in the violence of history.

Violence is what happens in plays. If I model my plays after anything, it's Greek plays, where he's stabbing his eyes out, she's put the poisoned dress on and the horses jump off the cliff. Sure, it's linked to African-American history but it's also borrowed from the Greeks. All these *Wild Kingdom*-type activities would be the center of the play rather than psychological dramas. I can watch them but I don't understand them in a way that allows me to write them. I don't get it. *The America Play* was so much about Lincoln having been shot while watching a play so you have to put it on stage because that's just fun. And the *Devotees* thing is so Greek. The action is off stage. And *The Last Black Man* is a Stations of the Cross. There's Jesus going through his changes. That's where the interest in violence comes from.

So history functions for you the way that myth did for the Greeks.
Right.

You know that your audience knows it, so you can present it in a different way. It's repetition and revision again.
And if they don't know, I'll tell them. When I was a kid I used to love to read Greek myths. That was my favorite thing. My parents got me all these illustrated books—I love books that are illustrated. And then biblical stories—Jesus doing things and Moses doing something else.

Larger-than-life people doing very basic things, but almost childlike in their simplicity. Or fantastic—there's Persephone minding her own business and the world opens up and this guy comes out and drags her down to hell. That's a good story.

Why do I like history? It sounds sappy: to give voice to people who are voiceless. I don't know about that because all these characters are parts of me. I think we're all one person. History, I don't know. Why is *Devotees* what it is? David Hwang wanted me to write a play about inter-racial relationships to be a companion piece to a play he was writing for the Humana Festival. I said, "Okay, let me go home and think about it." And we hung out for a little while and he asked, "So what have you got?" And I said, "I've got three black women in white wedding dresses. And that's interracial, right?" And he said, "Sort of . . ." So we went ahead. But I wrote that play because I wanted to give black actresses a chance to wear pretty dresses, wedding dresses. When I did it at Mount Holyoke—and this is a women's college, with women scholars very serious about their work—I had forgotten why I wrote this play. We went costume shopping and the designer took us to a bridal salon with racks and racks of bridal dresses. You should have seen those three actresses! They were ecstatic! I remember seeing them try on these dresses and seeing their faces light up. I want dresses with trains going down the block! So the plays have all these weird reasons. It's not so much that I have an agenda as I want to see women in pretty dresses. I want to see a black guy dress up like Abraham Lincoln because I think that would be really funny. There he is walking around having a good time. I'm not thinking so much about history. He is, though, about the past and how the past is behind you. How you follow in someone's footsteps and how that doesn't make any sense because they're actually behind you. So you're walking the wrong way. But that's really the drama of being alive. It's passing through time. That's what we do. That's what people do when they're watching a play. They pass through a certain amount of time together.

I see your plays as rituals of remembrance, bearing in mind, of course, that re-membering is always a function of dis-membering. You must dis-member in order to re-member. As in *Imperceptible Mutabilities*: "A mine is a thing that dismembers/ remembers."

That's what it is. You put things back together. People say, what's *The Death of the Last Black Man* about? It's about these people who come together and remember him. They gather together and put on a play and every night they remember the last black man. That's like church: "This is my body, this is my blood. Do this in memory of me." And

Venus is very much a re-membering and a dis-membering. The dis-memberment happens right in the middle. The intermission speech is called "The Dis(-re-)memberment of the Venus Hottentot." And he does her autopsy. That's the lecture that he gives, right in the crack of the play. So he cuts it. Basically, re-membering is putting things together that don't always perfectly fit. For example, the re-membering of Lincoln and his story by The Foundling Father who embodies him and puts him back together, and also by the son and mother who look for both of them and re-member them. And at the end, when everything is together, there's a huge (w)hole inside a huge hole. There's the hole in the guy's head while he's sitting in a replica of The Great Hole of History. So it's not neat and tidy.

Because history is not a seamless narrative, it's a hole, an abyss—and a whole.
Right.

In *The America Play*, The Foundling Father talks about history "as it used to be," in which everything is "by the book" and nothing is "excessive." Yet all of your plays tell a different kind of history: history as excess, the history we don't know what to do with. There's either a vacancy, a hole—or there's too much of it.
That's funny. I forgot about that line. It's history that you don't know what to do with or history that's hiding in the shadows or is being pushed to the edges, or it's in the margins, the gaps, the crevices. It's not the big story, it's the fringe stuff. Particles of things. Writing for me is so much like archaeology. That's why I like *The America Play* so much. The whole action of the play is exactly like what writing it was. Brazil is digging because I was digging. They put things together as I was putting things together.

So the play is also about the act of writing.
Yes. History is not just the Great Wall of China, the Pyramids of Egypt, the Neuschwanstein Castle, Stonehenge. It's all the little bits and scraps. That's how narrative seems to be working for me. With my novel, there's a narrative but it's not just someone telling you a story. It's all this little garbage and little pieces of dirt and dust that just kind of fall on the page. It tells a story but it's just remnants, and the little things that people throw away if they could. Or that you did throw away. Or saved too long. As you can tell, I have all kinds of weird stuff, like pieces of my hair when I had red dreadlocks. I love characters from the big History, like Lincoln. What a costume! I'm working on something I'll probably never finish because it's one of nine million things I'm writing, but it has Napoleon in it. Why? Another great outfit. I don't know any-

thing about Napoleon except he was French—which is another obsession of mine. Venus speaks French, and the ladies do in *Devotees*. So I love building a play. You start with a character, then you hollow him out, then you fill him with all the knick-knacks that surround him, all this stuff, and make him walk and talk, make him black. They don't start as history plays but history kind of creeps in and lies there and takes over. But writing movies is different because most of the stuff I've written thus far has been on assignment, which I actually prefer because then I'm just doing a job and can write my own thing on my own time.

So they give you a story?
I'll give you an example. Someone hired me to do an adaptation of this book called *Gal* by Ruthie Bolton which came out three or four years ago. You read and reread the book and then you do something with it. People call me up when they want good characters. So I figure out what the characters are doing. At least they don't call me up for car chases.

And you're working on your novel.
I am. And I have a couple of commissions, one from the Wilma Theater of Philadelphia and one from the Public. I don't know what they're about yet. But I'm most excited about the novel now because I've always loved novels more. That's what I read most. And while I know I'm going to write several of them, I'm not going to stop writing plays.

How long does it take you to write a play?
It depends. I started *Venus* in 1990 and I finished it in '95. Then we did it in '96. It takes about five years. A screenplay takes less time because the form is not up for grabs. But plays take so much longer because I have no idea what it's going to look like. Not what it would look like on stage but what the shape of the play is, which means what it is about— the two are connected. *Venus* will have more stage directions than the other plays. I like writing stage directions like, "She's pregnant." "She's pregnant again." Things like that are really fun to put in the margin because they're not simply telling you what's going on on stage. The writing is very clean so I put things off to the side. And some things I want to happen and I don't want them talking while they happen. So I just wrote them down. Someone saw *Imperceptible Mutabilities* and then *The Last Black Man* and said, "You're writing is changing." And I think that's a good thing. I keep retracing the same steps or the same themes or the same interests but I do it in different shoes. The tracks look completely different from one play to another. It's all about, "Who am I?"

As you know the American theatre is not in very good shape right now, despite the fact that there are many different theatres in this country. How do you feel about that? Do you feel that you're writing for a dying art? You're lucky in that you're getting your work produced.

I guess if I didn't get produced I would still write. But when did it start dying? I guess it's been dying since I started writing plays so I haven't really noticed. Although they take funding away here, there and everywhere, which I think accelerates the dying.

One thing that I find so interesting about your theatre is that it's almost as though it's about the state of theatre itself. Yours is a haunted stage. You have all these characters who have come back from the dead. That's an important way of remembering.

And if theatre's dead, it won't be possible to remember in this way anymore.

All the playwrights I've interviewed thus far have written plays about haunting. What does that say about you?

I'm really fascinated with thinking about theatre as a site for remembering, for bringing back the dead, for staging the past, for coming to terms with loss.

I think it's because theatre is so close to religion. I don't know all religions but I have a feeling they are bridges between the Self and the people you're not, or the people in your past. It's natural to have plays that are haunted. It's part of the hard wiring of theatre and that's what theatre's for. *Hamlet*'s about a ghost. And the more we can do to capitalize on what theatre's for, the more theatre has a chance of surviving. The more we put on plays that look like movies or TV shows—

Why not just watch TV then?

It's a lot cheaper. People are writing plays that should be movies or TV to try to get a leap into Hollywood. That's not helping either. I'm most concerned with the death of the imagination. Because if that goes, I'll really be sunk.

José Rivera

In José Rivera's plays, the visible world is just a small part of the universe, like the tip of an iceberg floating in an unfathomable, metaphysical sea. And although it may be the only part that his characters can directly apprehend, it is at best deceptive. Using the invisible to illuminate the visible, Rivera's plays reveal the miraculous causes that we know only because of their familiar yet mysterious effects. Mixing the magical and the mundane, they demonstrate that the two always interpenetrate and transform each other. As a result, his plays—using what he calls a form of magic realism—constantly expand the horizons of theatre and are filled with stage directions that, at the very least, challenge the imaginations of directors and designers. What other playwright would dare call for the wings of an angel to dissolve in a character's hands or for a skinhead to cross the stage, pour gasoline over a homeless person and incinerate him?

Rivera's recent plays represent a significant expansion of the style of his early work. His first play, *The House of Ramon Iglesia* (1983), makes use of a straightforward, kitchen-sink realism to tell the autobiographically inspired story of a Puerto Rican family on Long Island ruled by a raging alcoholic father. His later turn to magic realism is in part the result of his studies with Gabriel García Márquez, in part his attempt to come to terms with the richness of traditional Puerto Rican culture. "I was exploring my cultural heritage by writing in a new form, employing the myths and legends of my grandparents. That was a real liberation for me." Rivera emphasizes that his turn to magic realism does not simply represent an attempt, like that of the surrealists, to use dreams to unshackle the unconscious and celebrate the arbitrary. Rather, Rivera uses magic realism partly to rethink his relation to his cultural roots. It is, as he explains, a representation of Puerto Rican folk culture that is more truthful for being more extravagant. For magic realism shakes up traditional notions of time and space. Thus *Marisol* (1992), for example, expands time, taking one second, the moment of Marisol's death, and turning it into a lifetime. And *Cloud Tectonics* (1995) does the opposite, taking a lifetime and compressing it into one night. In the same gesture, the latter play literalizes metaphor: it shows what happens when two people fall in love and time stands still. And so many of his magical scenes and events in fact represent the literalization of metaphor. In so bringing metaphors to life and shaking up time, Rivera necessarily disrupts spatial relations. In *Marisol*, the Bronx and Manhattan are "light-years" apart while in *Cloud Tectonics*, Montauk and Los Angeles are merely a drive away from each other.

Rivera's turn to magic realism represents even more, however, than a means of formal experimentation and cultural archaeology. For as he notes, his work provides a profoundly, if unfamiliarly, realistic picture of American society. "My plays," he suggests, "are not exaggerations." *Marisol*, in particular, which Rivera describes as his "most self-consciously political play," provides a devastating portrait of American urban culture. The play's dystopian vision of New York, set in what Rivera stubbornly insists is the present, is a nightmare city in a country and a world gone completely out of control. The moon has left its orbit, coffee is extinct, men become pregnant and a massive fire in Ohio blots out the sun in New York. The title character is a young Puerto Rican woman living in the Bronx who endures a series of physical and emotional assaults by characters who are brutal, psychotic and yet terrifyingly ordinary. Longing to quell the ubiquitous violence, this new Everywoman is visited by an Angel who, before going off to wage a cosmic war, explains to her the cause of universal crisis: "God is old and dying and taking the rest of us with Him." But even this "senile" world is a recognizable version of a globalized economy in which a chasm separates rich from poor and Marisol ends up the victim of class warfare, mowed down by the Woman With Furs, a lawyer from the suburbs who hawks for "the new world order" and packs an uzi.

If *Marisol* is more than just a dystopian fantasy, then its title character is more than a mere mortal. For she is—impossibly—killed in the play's opening scene (several characters discuss the TV reports of her death), and she wanders through the devastated city as a kind of ghost whose body "fits into [her] clothes all wrong." Similarly in *Cloud Tectonics*, Celestina appears as a kind of ghost, refusing to age, pregnant for two years, stopping time dead in its tracks. And certainly, these figures take their central place in Rivera's magic realism in part because of the way they disrupt the boundaries between life and death, the visible and the invisible. But these two figures also bear a crucial relation to questions of cultural identity. For Marisol has more or less given up her identity as a Latina. She has "amputated neat sections of [her] psyche, [her] cultural heritage," only to find herself choking on the "pain kept inside" and vilified by the Woman With Furs as a "brown piece of shit." This ghost, in short, is haunted both within and without by the very cultural and racial heritage she has unsuccessfully repressed. Trying to "glide through the world and not be a part of it," she is the proof that one can never completely assimilate. A sign of what has been lost, she discovers belatedly that to forget means to lose one's self. And the "unearthly" and "angelic" Celestina, like Marisol, hovers between life and death, but unlike Marisol, she provides a link to the past and a life-affirming eroticism. And this link, moreover, distinguishes her from the assimilated Aníbal whose girlfriend works at Disney and whose mind is bound by the laws of "common sense." Because Aníbal has forgotten Spanish, he is unable to translate her infinitely tender speech to him and so understand how love stops the passage of time. For it is only by resisting the forces of cultural homogenization and reimagining history that Marisol and Aníbal are able "to reach up, beyond the debris, past the future, spit in the eye of the sun, make a fist and say *no*."

The function of ghosts in Rivera's plays as both mnemonic devices and the casualties of amnesia suggests a deep ambivalence in his work in relation to the past. This ambivalence works itself out most clearly perhaps in *Each Day Dies with Sleep* (1990), in which the nuclear family is imagined as the primary means for the transmission of culture, and the figure of the father, Augie, represents both a link to the past and a willful and potentially murderous machismo. Like a ghost, Augie haunts his daughter, Nelly, following her across the continent and working to turn her husband, Johnny, into his own brutal facsimile. Although an emanation from the past, Augie is himself an instance of the failure of memory insofar as he is unable to remember his daughter's name until the end of the play. This ambivalence in regard to the past and to the family is matched by a constant geographical instability in Rivera's plays.

His characters are always on the move, always looking for a place to call home. On the one hand, their mobility suggests that Rivera's brand of magic realism is in part his way of representing a nation of transients and dealing with his own geographical displacement—born in Puerto Rico, growing up on Long Island, living in Los Angeles. On the other hand, and more intriguingly, it is also the mark of his attempt to imagine a new multiracial America whose epicenter is a post-earthquake Los Angeles that has become the "capital of the Third World" with clean air, the "largest subway system in the world," fully integrated neighborhoods, and "no more poor sections." A utopian vision indeed.

November 15, 1997—Doral Court Hotel, New York City

DS: Can you start, José, by talking about how you got interested in theatre?
JR: I think my interest started when I was about ten years old. I went to public school, and a group of traveling actors came and did *Rumpelstiltskin*.

Was that here in New York?
It was out on Long Island, where I grew up. They came in and it was a big school event. I'd never seen a play before—neither of my parents was educated in any way. My father finished the second grade, my mother finished third. We had no books in the house to speak of except the Bible. In fact, my grandparents, who lived with us for many years, signed their names with an "X," which I was called to witness several times. So we had no written tradition in the family, and absolutely no theatre tradition. The only kind of mass media was television.

So I went to this thing and there were live actors doing *Rumpelstiltskin* in front of a lot of sixth graders. I remember now even where I sat, how far I was from the stage, and I just remember the final moment when Rumpelstiltskin's body falls apart, and his arms and legs were flying through the air, and I thought, "Oh, my God." I thought that was the most incredible thing I'd ever seen, and it completely wiped out all the years of TV I'd watched. It was more exciting and more liberating than all the *Batman* episodes I was growing up with. I remember thinking that we were all joined together, that the communal aspect of the event was somehow electrifying. The person up there could make all of us laugh or think, and I thought, "Wow, this is fascinating." Then I didn't have another theatre experience for many years until I was in junior high school and saw some old chestnut, British drawing-room comedy that was being done by the junior high. And I had exactly the same experience, I remember where I sat and I remember thinking, "We're all laughing together." That's what got me started. I'd always written, and was encouraged by my teachers to write, from a young age. For some reason—and I don't remember why to this day—it was a dialogue. My short stories were dialogues. And I wrote a novel when I was twelve about baseball because I loved baseball, and it was all dialogue. I used to draw cartoons, like superheroes, and that too was all dialogue. For some reason, that's how things came out.

TV was an influence. I forget what year it was, but I was very young, and a production of *Steambath* was on television. I'm Puerto Rican and I'd watched TV all my life and never seen a Puerto Rican on television that wasn't a drug addict or a criminal, and suddenly I was watching this incredible piece of writing—absurdist and funny and God was Puerto Rican! I thought, "I've waited all these years to see a Puerto Rican on TV and he's God. That's okay." I'd never had this experience watching television before. So those two experiences really nailed it for me. And then reading *The Glass Menagerie* sophomore year, I think, in high school. That was the final push. I loved that play. I remember one of my friends doing some of Tom's speeches in a scene study class and finding them moving. I think Tennessee Williams gets knocked around a lot, and probably rightfully so for some reasons, but he did something incredible in that play and I'll always remember it. That's what made me want to be a writer, studying that play, doing scenes from that play. I wrote my first play that year in high school, a one-act play, and then I just kept writing from the time I was seventeen years old until now.

When you started reading plays more seriously, and thinking about drama, what work excited you?

The earliest work was almost all American or British. I picked up a volume of plays in the library which had *Summer and Smoke*, *The Iceman Cometh*, *Death of a Salesman*, *Darkness at Noon*, and I read all of them. They were a powerful influence on me at that time, because I thought playwriting meant social and political awareness and activism. *The Crucible*, which I actually like more than *Death of a Salesman*, was a huge influence when I was young. The language of *The Crucible* is beautiful. Those were my earliest experiences. I didn't branch out into European writing until I was in college, and then I saw Genet's *The Maids* which really knocked me out. I was an actor in college, so I performed in *The Good Woman of Setzuan*, *The Cherry Orchard* and the Peter Handke play, *The Ride Across Lake Constance*. So I got my education as an actor. I never took a playwriting class. There were no playwriting classes, actually, in college. I took one writing class, poetry writing, which I hated. So all my training as a writer really came as an actor in college. Then I did one of those junior years abroad in London, and it involved a French theatre company that was doing really bizarre experimental work. I was the dramaturg and swept the floors. And learned a great deal about new British playwriting. One of the shows they did that year—this was 1976—was a play by the writer of *The Rocky Horror Picture Show*, whose name I forget. It's about Mickey Mouse, who is a has-been actor, and Minnie Mouse is sleeping with everybody in Hollywood. The whole play's about how Walt Disney fucked Mickey Mouse. And there's Mickey Mouse in a bar with Donald Duck, and Donald Duck's a great producer, and Mickey is just a bitter Hollywood has-been.

The crowning experience of my theatregoing from that time was seeing the closing night performance of *Buried Child* down at the Theater de Lys. I think it was the night before it won the Pulitzer and I had never seen anything like it. Most of what I'd seen had been fairly realistic, nineteenth or twentieth century work, and it was the first time that a play made me wonder about the elements of a play. For instance, when they came in and said that the backyard was full of corn that no one had planted, my realist brain said, "How can that be? That doesn't happen." Then I realized, Things in the theatre don't have to be what they are in life. It was a revelation because I had not gotten that lesson from other writers I'd read. Then I started to think about fertility and the buried baby, and I thought, Who is this Sam Shepard? And I began to read him like the Bible, including *Icarus's Mother, Chicago, 4-H Club*, those early plays no one ever does and which I love. That was the same year I read Márquez's *A Hundred Years of Solitude* for the first time. In fact, it was in the same month. It was the convergence of Sam Shepard and Gabriel García Márquez in my mental library that really formed me as a writer. I was twenty-two or twenty-three at the time. To this day, I would say that my two godfathers are Márquez and Shepard.

It's interesting to hear you talk about this because I think of your plays as very much plot driven. Or you can think about this in terms of narrative structure, your use of the quest form, for example. But at the same time, you use an incredibly plastic stage on which things and people can be constantly transformed. I'm fascinated with that plasticity. And it makes me think of *Rumpelstiltskin*—or Sam Shepard.

For my generation, you can't underestimate the power of television. Story has always been very, very important—telling that story. One critic criticized *Marisol* for having a thin narrative, but I think it has a very strong one, a very clear arrow that she's moving on. I like a good story, a rip-roaring fun story. I used to work at a bookstore in the Village, a chain that no longer exists, Bookmasters. I was in the fiction section, and I picked up this strange-looking book—I'd never heard of the author before—called *Gravity's Rainbow*. I said, "I wonder what this is. It's the thickest book on the shelf. I think I'll read it." God, did that knock me out. That was another great influence. Pynchon's sense of story and plasticity, his ability to elongate character and mess with time and space. His sense of space is extraordinary.

There's a kind of double responsibility that writers have. One is the responsibility to take the audience on a journey, saying, "Come with me, we're going somewhere." And that means treading a path. It could be straight, it could be curvy. The second responsibility is to play, to really play. You dim the lights, you put on a funny mask, you throw some music at it. Those are the elements that become extended or mutated into something else. The element of time in *Cloud Tectonics* and *Each Day Dies with Sleep*—trying to play with a heightened sense of cause and effect. For instance, when the young lovers move to California, an orange tree grows out of their living room. They're passionately in love, and their love causes the oranges to grow, and the oranges are aphrodisiacs, and so their love causes the oranges to get thick. And then they open up the oranges and eat them and the aphrodisiac of the oranges causes them to have more sex and more passion. But their marriage is troubled and begins to fall apart in act two. And the trouble in the marriage, as represented by the father, causes the oranges to turn black—so it's cause and effect. And then the blackness of the oranges causes the juice to turn to gasoline, which becomes the fuel, literally, which burns the house down. I was really interested in that play in toying with our notions of cause and effect in a completely non-naturalistic way. I didn't give a fuck about the rules of physics. Especially with Nelly who has different color eyes and the difference in the color causes her to have prophetic dreams. As playwright, I like to take you somewhere and play with you.

I hadn't thought about the relationship between cause and effect and the journey. But both involve questions of form, of arousing and fulfilling certain expectations, which are so important to you. In the first scene of *Marisol*, you essentially map out the whole play. Each of the elements is there, it's just a matter of how they're going to work themselves out. Except, of course, you don't realize until the end of the play that they've been there from the start. So in playing with form, you're also playing with time, expanding time and collapsing time, most obviously in *Cloud Tectonics*, which is precisely about that. That play is almost putting time under a microscope. Right. Some of it has to do with the visual arts, and conceptual art in particular, in which artists deal with concepts like balance and tone and size. For me, there's nothing wrong with the concepts in a play being as abstract as cause and effect, time and movement, or darkness and light. These can be themes, and we can examine them by altering them so they become recognizably foreign. Therefore, we have to look at them with fresh eyes. It's funny you should mention the first scene of *Marisol*, because going back to traditional narrative and nineteenth century structure, it's a very old-fashioned way to start a play. Our hero's on a subway—she's literally on a journey and a madman comes and tells her the story of the angel, and she doesn't believe it. He says, "You're going to suffer this, listen to me." And she goes, "Go get a job. You're crazy."

It's like the beginning of *Macbeth*, for example, with the witches' prophecies.
Exactly. When we were in rehearsal Tina Landau said, "You know, many classic works begin with heroines who are literally on the road, in a wagon or a canoe or something."

I've just written a new play called *Sonnets for an Old Century*. There's a speech a man gives that reflects an experience I had when I was in high school, when I had a summer job at the Brooklyn International Laboratory. There's a place in Brooklyn called the Gamma Forest, where there is a source of gamma radiation in the middle of a forest, and everything around it for a hundred yards is dead. It's been a twenty-five-year experiment—I don't know if it's still going on. One of my jobs was to go out into the Gamma Forest—when they'd lower the radiation source into a lead box—with two researchers and take measurements. We'd measure the moths, we'd catalog the dead birds. And everything was dead. It was like a postapocalyptic environment, and was beautiful in its eeriness. But there was still radiation and they gave us no protection whatsoever. We wore a film badge that was checked at the end of every month, after the fact, to see if we'd been exposed to too much radiation. Every month they told me I was fine. Going back to cause and effect: in the monologue I wrote, the character who has this experience has a red-haired daughter many years later. There's absolutely no red hair in his family. And one night he hears his daughter crying and goes into her room and she is found floating above her crib. She's floating in the air and glowing. Looking at her, wondering what is going on, he runs over and catches her, holds her. She kind of whimpers a little bit and nothing else happens, but he begins to think about the time in the Gamma Forest, and the unpredictable effects over many, many years. What makes magic realism are the unpredictable effects produced by myriad and common causes. It's the orange tree as an effect of love. It's the two-year pregnancy as the effect of a woman who cannot tell time. These are the extraordinary effects from common, everyday, substantial, realistic causes. I've been thinking about magic realism for so long, and I've come to that definition.

I wanted to ask you a question about your fascination with chance and the arbitrary, but you've already answered it. Arbitrary happenings produce consequences that are absolutely necessary and inevitable.

You're right. My parents had moved back to Puerto Rico when I was about twenty, and my friend told me about something that happened in their hometown. I use this as an example of magic realism. Somebody in their little town had committed suicide, had hanged himself on the roof of his house. Okay, that happens. Word got out and people thought, We've got to go see Fulana, he's hanged himself. And so here's this little house and at the door there's an orderly line of people who've brought snacks, who have babies in their arms—it was like a movie theatre. And people would walk in and look at the man hanging from the ceiling and go, "There's Fulana. Looks pretty bad." And some people would go back to the end of the line and come in again. To me the magic of that is the line, that ordered response to this incredible, horrible thing. In North America the response would be completely different.

So often it seems that magic realism is understood to be a kind of nonsense, or as a willful and arbitrary setting up of discordant elements. But what you're talking about is how necessary it is, and how it's connected to particular cultural traditions.
I think people confuse magic realism with surrealism. I remember when I first read Ionesco, I recognized it, but I knew it wasn't my culture. I knew it had nothing to do with the stories I heard growing up, which were fabulous and full of magic. He was doing a collision of dream imagery. Frida Kahlo, who, as you know, was a great Mexican painter, was very beloved by the French Surrealists. They would say, "Come, be one of us." And she'd say, "Absolutely not. I am a realist, I paint what happens. You paint what you dream or imagine." That's a powerful distinction. Sometimes I've had quarrels with people who say that magic realism is just an arbitrary way of theatricalizing a play. And I say, "Absolutely not. It's as important as the clothes people wear."

And for you it comes out of your personal history and your cultural heritage.
I've heard this said by others—but it's not my belief—that magic realism springs from poverty. There's something about the Third World in Latin America where the normal rules of decorum don't apply, and where life is random and often violent and capricious. My father was a janitor, a gardener, he drove a taxi and had six kids. We weren't impoverished although we were right on the edge. The working poor, they call it now. My life was full of capricious events that seemed to have no logic at all. For instance, I had a grandmother who once burned me with a cigarette as a joke. I would go to school and tell my friends and they would say, "That shouldn't happen." But life for me was full of things like that. There's a great deal of violence in my plays, and I'm not a violent man. I despise violence, but I've seen enough of it growing up,

and I was subject to it. I know how essential it is to human existence. I went to several productions of my plays, especially *Marisol*, in the same year and I felt battered by my own play. That's why I wrote *Cloud Tectonics*, as an antidote to the violence. Even now there's still violence in the new work.

I find the connection of magic realism to your class status and personal history really intriguing, but your plays, especially *Marisol*, are also so clearly about the different cultural collisions that make U.S. society. And I thought it a remarkably realistic representation of the violence that seems to be everywhere around us. Particularly the violence that is not acknowledged, that people turn their back on. I'm thinking of the building that June sees from her window, a torture center for people who have gone over their credit card limit. And while that's an exaggeration of sorts, it points to the staggering level of economic disparity and economic violence in this country that we are trained not to see.

Marisol especially. I started that in 1989—I'm not sure if the Central Park Jogger was that year, but it was around that time. There was a rash of burnings of homeless people. I remember reading the crime statistics, and 1989 was a peak, a terrible year for violent crime. My wife, who was pregnant at the time, was punched in the stomach on the subway by a man who wanted to get in while she wanted to get out. She lay in a crumpled circle on the ground until some old lady helped her. Things like that were happening constantly. A lot of *Marisol* was actually about the years I lived in the Bronx, which were very violent years. I was attacked by a man with a golf club in the subway. I was burnt out of my apartment by an arsonist who had discovered his girlfriend was cheating on him, so he threw gasoline on her bed and set it on fire—twice.

Often, as writers, we look for patterns, and I tried to discover if there was a pattern to all this violence. I didn't discover it, but I began to feel an analogy between the little day-to-day violences between us and some big cosmic violence, something huge. I don't particularly believe that the year 2000 has an apocalyptic resonance, but it's certainly a historical moment, the end of the century's always viewed that way. It seemed like an appropriate analogy to draw. Especially in *Marisol*, because I was trying to examine my Catholic upbringing, and feeling in a lot of ways that we were just abandoned by God. Something happened—he's not around. Not in the Tony Kushner sense of God being away or on vacation, but because he's outlived his usefulness, he's now too old to be God. When I was writing the play I was also reading *The Golden Bough* and other sources of primitive mythology, and a lot of that mythology has been around for a very long time. God or gods were seen as the agents who keep the universe going, but they age and when they get too old, they must be eliminated and replaced. And it's our responsibility. We have a ritual sacrifice of the old god, and out of the blood that we sprinkle on the ground comes something new and young and powerful. So I took that myth and applied it to some of our Roman Catholic imagery, angels and things like that. I didn't want the god of my play to be the God of the Catholic Church, so I grafted the god of this mythology to that.

So it's a non-Christianized theology, but a theology nonetheless.
Very pre-Christian, very primitive. There might be some confusion—I remember talking to people who were violently offended by the play and said that angels would never do that. But they were coming from a Christian perspective, and I tried to get them to think of God in other terms.

Of course, in *Marisol* you're colliding many different mythologies, both old and new.
I like sometimes to think of these mythologies as having some kind of reality to them. Even though I know they don't. In my new play there's a monologue about a girl who sleeps next to a big hole in her bedroom. Out of the hole comes a man called Aceman, and Aceman is half Mexican and half Native American. All his friends are mixed blood, and they're all dead, but they don't know which afterlife to go to. So they're confined to this limbo and this hole in the girl's bedroom. So I wonder, What happens when gods intermarry? How do they raise the children? In *Marisol* I was playing with the idea of visitor beings, and on this particular day this one god cuts through all the borders and throws everything off. Suddenly, all these things become visible and real to this girl. A menu of mythology to choose from. I have two children, and my wife and I expose them to myriad beliefs. We go to the museum and look at Buddha, and say, "This is Buddha. This is Vishnu. This is Aphrodite," to give my daughter at least the impression that I don't know the absolutes, and nobody really does, even though many claim to. And it's her job to read them and pick. So much of *Marisol* is based on that journey. For a long time she believed in Zeus. She said, "Dad, I believe in Zeus, he throws so many thunderbolts."

So the America you're writing about is a hybridized one, populated by characters who are mixed culturally and racially and have diverse backgrounds. Like Nelly with the different colored eyes. I was also thinking about this in terms of assimilation. *Marisol* suggests that the title character is suffering in part because she's amputated her cultural heritage. If Aníbal had not forgotten Spanish, he would have understood what Celestina was saying. So, I detect a real ambivalence in your plays

about assimilation. On the one hand, there is a sense of loss, but on the other, there's the possible discovery of a new world by a new, hybridized subject.

I often think of America as a hyphenated place. There are many hyphenates of many combinations. Within the same person there are a variety of cultures. I can't escape my immigrant experience—born in Puerto Rico and moving to New York when I was four years old, and always being aware of our differences. Being on Long Island. If we'd grown up in the Bronx it would have been one thing, but for years we were the only Puerto Rican family in the neighborhood. So we were treated differently and ostracized. Somebody threw a firecracker through our living-room window once—it was horrible. We were constantly told we were different. So there's a real ambivalence on the part of my characters about knowing they are different, and seeking to be unified somehow. I remember desperately wanting to be a townie, to be like all the kids. When I was a child, I didn't want to listen to Tito Puente and things my parents loved, I wanted to listen to the Rolling Stones. That was my quest to assimilate, to be united. But like Marisol, especially in my twenties, I really felt like I had cut something off that was lost and precious and beyond my grasp. Marisol is twenty-five in the play, and I remember in my twenties thinking, What was it I lost? And having psychically to go back home to the stories, the culture. One of the strange by-products of having grown up in a family that is not literate or literary, is that I never got a sense, when I was growing up, of my Latin literary heritage. My mother wouldn't know Gabriel García Márquez if she hit him. So I grew up with no sense of our literary culture, the great works of Puerto Rico and the Caribbean, the great Cuban writers. It was a loss on my part. I had to discover those as an adult. Now I feel like I know much more than my parents or my relatives about Latin culture, and especially literary culture. I read one review that described my characters as urban wanderers. I guess that's true, they wear several kinds of clothing, but they don't really fit anywhere.

I think it's important to think about this in terms of loss. Marisol dies, but doesn't die, in the first scene of the play. So she is a kind of ghost, haunting the rest of the play. And Celestina also is a kind of ghost. But she does know Spanish. So it seems to me that your plays are haunted by a loss of cultural history, and through the ghosts they perform a kind of ritual reenactment. They remember. The ghost is a figure in whom personal memory and history collide. So Marisol is a product of your memories, a past you're haunted by, but also of the history in which she's immersed, contemporary New York.

The plays are exorcisms in reverse, they're bringing to life things that are dead or may have been considered dead, but aren't dead, and we didn't know they weren't dead. In the larger context of Puerto Rico, one of the things I'm haunted by is the fact that the island has not resolved the issue of its status. I think that is haunting many Puerto Ricans, the romantic part of us that wishes it were an independent nation. With all the pride and sovereignty and future-oriented energy that being a nation would give the island. There's a feeling of missed opportunity, in 1898, when it was briefly independent, before the U.S. came in, a lost opportunity for a truly independent identity. In some ways that's part of the Puerto Rican predicament. The haunting of a nation that never was.

I think that gets translated into the plays. Because the plays aren't too political or historical, but those issues get played out in terms of family. Nelly and Johnny are haunted by Augie, who won't go away, in his wheelchair, with his dirty words. And Aníbal becomes haunted by Celestina, and the ideal of Celestina, even when she's gone, and when Aníbal is an old man. It's the ideal of the island he doesn't have. And in Marisol, the trick is that she's haunted by herself, in a way. She's haunted by the recurring news of her death. Which is an experience I had when I was living in Brooklyn. There was a José Rivera who was murdered in Brooklyn because he wouldn't give up his bicycle. My phone rang all day: "We thought it was you." Because it was even in my neighborhood. And they said, "You would die for a bicycle." That literally transfixed me for a very long time. Like a doppelgänger, it could have been me. Marisol suffers from that mental thing, and she is haunted by the fact that it could have been her.

You were talking about the family and how the past comes to us through our family and our parents. But we never find out much about Marisol's family. It's almost as if she's an orphan.

Her only family really is June, her friend. I wanted to write a character that seemed completely disconnected from her past. In rehearsal we spoke at length about Marisol and I know we came up with a biography. But that is something an actor uses, subconsciously, and it was never incorporated into the text because I didn't want to know it. People often say—I don't know if they mean it critically or not—that she's more archetypal than actual, that she's an Everywoman. I guess that's true, but for some reason creating a biography for her seems banal, less interesting than what's going on in the play.

You mention the symbolic dimension of Marisol, but I find that true of many of your characters. They're moving in the real world, in a recognizable version of American culture, but at the same time there's often a mythological dimension to them. In

***Cloud Tectonics,* the last names of the characters, de la Luna and del Sol, have an unmistakable mythological resonance.**

I've always been fascinated with the theatre as a form of almost religious ritual. And the theatre space is always more interesting when it's about larger issues than serving coffee. I think writers like Sam Shepard who can turn the kitchen sink into a temple or a shrine or a burial ground perform wonderful tricks of alchemy. I've always had a deep love of world mythology and read it constantly, because there are so many wonderful stories out there. I think it also is what connects us. Coming from Puerto Rico, learning English when I was five years old, seeking to find what I had in common with my Italian neighbors. I think Hercules is the same as Rocky, and I think those things speak to us because they're almost part of our genetic makeup.

So you're looking for a common thread?

Yes. What is it that connects me to another writer. What is it that George Wolfe or Eric Overmyer and I might have in common—what are our common obsessions? I think we drink from a well that contains all this mythology. My favorite director to collaborate with is Tina Landau. So here's a—I think she's Jewish—woman, and ostensibly we have nothing in common. I'm a Puerto Rican man, but we have a world culture in common. We love the same kinds of music and the same kinds of artists. There are transcendent artists who speak to humanity rather than to their particular time and place. I would like to think my plays act on a world stage as opposed to a specifically American or New York stage.

And of course they do insofar as they're about a hybridization and internationalization that's undeniably taking place—we're all multicultural now. I realize you don't think about these things when you're starting to write, but can you tell me how you start a play? Do you come up with a plot, an idea, a character, a journey?

I keep a little notebook in which I write down interesting things. I'll give you a recent example, but I don't know if it will actually turn into a play. I live in Los Angeles, and we had a cat, and I'm allergic to cats, so it was a big thing getting this cat—I didn't want it, but we got it. My kids loved it, and one day the cat disappeared, gone forever. It was a stray, anyway. My wife found the cat's collar in the backyard and we live near a big park, and oftentimes during droughts coyotes come down to drink. So we think a coyote got the cat. That was my theory anyway. I kept thinking, I could not imagine a cat and coyote together. I wrote down "cat and coyote" in my notebook, that's all I wrote. Oftentimes plays start as small as that. That became a scene, cat and coyote, which led to another scene in which a woman dances with the moon and the moon is talking to her about art and says his favorite artist is Salvador Dali, and she says, "Oh my God, references to Salvador Dali make me hot." And that became the title of the new play I'm working on. So, cause and effect, one thing leads to another. It started off as a strange event in my children's life, this missing cat, and now it's become a play.

Things start that way for me, very innocently, with an overheard conversation, a piece of imagery. For *Cloud Tectonics*, it was flying through the air looking at clouds, thinking, "How could I describe that shape, what would it be?" And coming up with the phrase, "cloud tectonics" as a made-up scientific field. One of the things that started *Marisol* was a conversation I had with my mother about a friend of hers named Marisol who claimed she was visited by an angel and had a very specific description of what the angel looked like. It was so real and vivid, and that became something I obsessed about. Generally there's about a two-year gap between writing a phrase in a notebook and starting the play, in which those two years are spent dreaming about it, or thinking subconsciously about it, or thinking, How about the cat and the coyote, what are they doing now? It becomes a playful whirling of ideas and images around something central. We carry this bubbling stew of disconnected images. For *Marisol*, it was being attacked by a guy with a golf club, watching smoke trickle over New York, hearing the news about homeless people, seeing a story on TV about a cemetery for AIDS babies. And then something happens, like taking iron filings and sticking a magnet under them. A pattern appears and suddenly I have a play. All these things that seemed to be accidents are all of a sudden interconnected pieces of something. Like those drawings you see of viruses and T cells.

Once I get to that moment, when something forces a pattern to emerge, I know I've got a play to write. I start at the very first scene and I don't stop until I get to the end. Usually I write longhand, three or four hours a day, and I force myself not to read what I've written. Just to write and keep going forward. The plays have a kind of drumbeat: move forward, move forward, tell the next event. That will take three or four months of constant work, and that will be the first draft. And then what I do—which some people consider to be a complete waste of time but I think is very valuable—is copy the play over longhand, and in the copying, make changes. I do that three or four times. It's such a boring thing to do that a word has to be wonderful and fascinating to get to that fourth draft. I cut like crazy, usually the first drafts are way too long. So it's thinner and honed by the time I make the fourth handwritten draft. That's a habit I've had since I was eighteen years old—I've never deviated. Then I put it in the computer. By the time it gets to the computer stage, I feel it's ready for reading or for someone to look at, but I'm very stingy about showing early work. You can't get it out of me until I think it's producible. I have too much ego to show the skid marks and the bad, ugly writing.

I like the idea of as little development as possible. I've been lucky, I'll write a play now and it will get produced. I don't really do the developmental circuit. I may do it this summer with a new play I'm submitting to Sundance, but that's a special occasion. I haven't been to the O'Neill Conference. I actually had a big argument the first time I met August Wilson at a party. I had just been accepted to the O'Neill, but I'd also been optioned by Circle Rep for production. I turned down the O'Neill and August Wilson was so mad. He said, "You're not good enough to have your play produced. Development is part of the process." I think there's a lot of validity to that. That's his way to go, that's the way for many people. But it hasn't been good for all writers. People get stuck in that, and then theatres feel like they've done you and won't take it to the next step.

Going through the developmental stages, a playwright can sometimes lose his or her way and suddenly find the play is almost being held hostage. Or suddenly he or she is only co-author, and sometimes there's a lot to be said for holding onto your original vision.

I agree, although the risks are obviously great. I've taken some hard hits because of that, but I don't regret it. The New York opening, for instance, of *The Promise* [1998], which Frank Rich—sorry, it was Mel Gussow who hated that one. That could have used some development. I took it right to The Public—both The Public Theater and the general public—and it got soundly beaten up. You run those risks. I think development is a highly personal thing, like personal hygiene. The things you choose to tinker with, the voices you decide to develop, the impulses you decide to honor—they're internal. Those are personal choices. It's hard to understand how outside people can be a part of that. The exception for me would be when I'm in rehearsal with Tina. She has a great deal to say and I really respect her mind. And Morgan Jenness—two great thinkers. I trust actors, I trust actors' impulses. One of my favorite actresses is Cordelia González, whom I wrote *Marisol* for. I would learn so much by watching her face in rehearsal, because she couldn't help wincing if something wasn't right. I would make notes about the places she winced and I would think, I wonder if there's a flaw here. Did I miss a step? Is it too much transition? It was like canaries in a coal mine.

What do you think makes for a good production of your plays?
Take *Marisol*, of which I've seen many, many productions, running the continuum from very gritty and urban-textured to something far more abstract, poetic and theatrical. That's a very broad span. I personally like the productions that are theatrical, poetic, lyrical. It's an easy trap to read the play and think, I want to shock the audience with how graphic the violence is going to be. It's going to be a screamfest. That bores me to death. Tina's production of *Marisol* at La Jolla was poetic and beautiful. There were times when I thought Cordelia was dancing with the text in the space that Robert Kroll designed—gorgeous. I like visual beauty in a production.

But even violence can be beautiful.
Quite, ask Stanley Kubrick. There was a production of *Cloud Tectonics* in Atlanta that was directed by Julia Carillo and designed by Christine Jones that was literally very dark, and very beautiful and stunning in its own way. I like set designs that are works of art. I don't like kitchen-sink realism. Also I like music, but I sometimes feel music abuses the production. I don't want to be too aware of sound. Marcus Stern directed the world premiere of *Marisol* at Louisville. We were talking and he asked, "What influenced you?" I said that when I was writing the play I was listening to a lot of Jimi Hendrix and Lou Reed. So he did this fascinating thing where he would take five seconds of a Lou Reed guitar riff and loop it, almost hypnotically. I love things like that that are stretching the medium. Marcus is also a master at using industrial sounds, the clang of metal. The film *Eraserhead* has this incredible industrial consciousness—girders and steam—and Marcus used some of that in the play very effectively. It wasn't the obvious choice.

I'm not surprised to hear you say that. From your writing it's clear that it's not the grit that really counts but finding the beauty in and of the violence. And it seems to me that by staging it nonrealistically or more abstractly, it's easier to evoke the symbolic and ideological resonances.
It goes back to the idea of ritual as opposed to routine or naturalistic behavior. It's a heightened sense.

I realize you've already talked a bit about this issue, but do you think of your work as autobiographical?
To some degree. *Marisol* is very autobiographical in its specifics. A lot of that really happened, and I'm often hesitant to include events that didn't happen. If they haven't happened, I have at least to have heard about them, so I can claim some connection to life. Like the story I told you

about the man who hanged himself in Puerto Rico. I wasn't there, but I believe it happened so I can write about it. There's a play not included in my collection [*Marisol and Other Plays*, TCG, 1997] called *The Street of the Sun* [1997], which deals with my experiences in Los Angeles and is very autobiographical. And the new play, *Sonnets for an Old Century*, has a great deal of autobiographical material. The story about the Gamma Forest, for instance, is in that play. I constantly draw on things that have happened. I'm shy about pure invention, but sometimes that can be a lot of fun. In *Each Day Dies with Sleep*, the oranges are obviously made up. But I remember having an orange tree when we first moved to L.A., and the character of Augie is based on my uncle who had sixteen children and my aunt who was in the hospital having her sixteenth, and he was nowhere to be seen. And she got a phone call from my uncle's girlfriend saying, "You had his baby, but I fucked him last night." And coming home from his girlfriend's house later that day, drunk, he was hit by a car and ended up in a wheelchair. My aunt took him in, but then she took a boyfriend, just like in the play.

I was fortunate enough to go to Sundance in 1989 and did a two-week workshop with Gabriel García Márquez, who was in the country on a visa for two weeks. He taught a screenwriting workshop, because his early experience as a writer was as a film critic. He sees his work as a form of journalism, even to this day. As fantastic, as unbelievable as it seems, he will ground everything he writes in some kind of experience, even if it's overheard. I abide by that as well. If someone believes in it strongly enough, then I can write about it as reality. The woman whom I met who'd claimed to have met an angel—that seemed so real to her. I'm not going to tell her it's not real, and so I feel like I can write about it with some authority.

You've talked about the influence not only of theatre on your work, but also of mass culture. And I know you've written for TV. Are you suggesting that theatre for you is more or less an antidote to mass culture? As opposed to the realism and the facticity of television, it seems to allow for a certain valorization of fantasy. You also talked about the influence of theatre audiences. It seems to me that a community is formed in the theatre that is completely different from the television audience. What social function do you see theatre taking up? What can it do?

I think on a basic level it affirms the validity of the public event. Even though it costs a lot to get in—which is too bad—theatre is a public space. Mass culture has slowly, slowly eradicated public spaces, except for malls, I suppose. I remember looking at pictures from the turn of the century where there'd be a rally on Wall Street, and there would be literally thousands of people standing out there listening to a politician.

We don't have town criers, we don't have those public opportunities and theatre gives us that opportunity again. That's one of the things it gives us as an antidote to mass culture. I don't feel the community in a movie theatre. When the lights go down, I feel like I'm all by myself. But not in a theatre, even if it's as dark as a movie theatre. I feel those people. I like to think that we in the theatre can still do things that no one else can do. We still have the talent and the skill to perform, before a live audience, acts of magic, as it were, that no film will ever be able to do. And I cling to that, it's the hope I have, and one of the reasons I continue to write plays. That's a valuable and precious thing. I still count on the theatre to present moments of awe. I count on the theatre to tap into a nightmare, to delight my mind.

Sometimes an entire play will go by and no moment like that will happen. I watched a Chicago company called the Lookinglass Theatre do a production of the *Arabian Nights*. One of the stories they told was about a woman who was the smartest human on Earth and she goes around challenging all the men to feats of intellect. She has a kind of intellectual duel with a very lonely sultan who asks, "What can destroy a kingdom?" She thinks for a second, and then says, "Words." I remember watching that moment and being hit by an idea that was so beautiful and unexpected. That's what I look for. Seeing something symmetrical, seeing an idea developed, the way musical themes develop, so that by the time we get to the end of act two, the idea is rounder and fuller and more complex. I look for the theatre to give me those kinds of things. It's food for me. There are great films, but I find films to be microwaved. Whereas the theatre, even if it's a hotdog, is still not microwaved.

From hearing you talk about this, I think there is a sense of the sublime that you can get from going to the theatre that you cannot get from film. There's something about having live people in a real space that allows for the production of formerly unimaginable possibilities.

The genius of theatre is in its dialogue. It's a dialogue between the characters on stage, and between the audience and the characters. It's knowing that in some miniscule, subconscious way, my gasp or laugh at a certain line will change the performance. Tomorrow that moment won't be there, because I won't be there. Knowing that I and the person five rows behind me are part of this performance together. Like flocks of birds flying in formation and changing directions together—that's what we do. There's too much loneliness in life, too much isolation, and I'm grateful for anything that creates some kind of current between us. Some people don't go to the theatre, but they go to rock concerts or poetry readings or dance—a live event. Or even hearing some guy on the street corner telling jokes. We'll never outgrow the live event. It'll always be a form of transcendence. My mother never goes to the theatre unless it's to see a play of mine. But I think she gets the same thing from the church, that same live event. I may tell her jokingly that the priest's in a costume and he's reading from a script—it's very irreverent—but there is a sense of theatre in that church.

Unfortunately, with the NEA controversy, both public and private funding seems to be drying up, and theatre audiences seem to be dwindling. Do you think there's much hope for theatre in this country?

Whenever I read new plays by writers I don't know, I get hopeful. I don't know about audiences—obviously they're getting old. I was recently at a theatre—I won't mention its name because I don't want to insult them—and I remember the audience being very upscale and feeling depressed because there were no people of color in the audience, no one like me. Nobody from my socioeconomic background. I remember having a play in New York that was running downstairs and there was a play running upstairs, and the upstairs play was attracting everybody in their twenties. I was watching these people going upstairs, thinking, That's my audience. But the older crowd was seeing my play, and why should that be? That's very depressing. I don't know what to say about that. I have some optimism that the live event will always be attractive, and new voices seem to keep emerging. I'm teaching graduate students at UCSD, and they keep coming from God-knows-where, they keep showing up to write plays.

I was in Chicago because the Goodman was doing *Cloud Tectonics*, and after the show, the director said, "Do you want to go see this thing? It starts at midnight. It's called *Too Much Light Makes the Baby Go Blind.*" And I said, "Sure." So we went into this space and it was packed. I was the only person there, I think, over twenty. On the ceiling were numbers from one to sixty. And the idea is that they do sixty plays in sixty minutes. The audience shouts out a number, they pull a number down, and it has the title. The plays are scripted, they're not improvised, and the cast does keep duet plays in order. There's a big clock on stage, and if they can't get sixty plays in sixty minutes, the whole audience gets their money back. If there's a full house, pizza is delivered. They actually call the pizza guy and he comes during intermission and everyone gets a slice. It was exciting, it was raw, some of it was stupid, but it found a vocabulary that got these MTV-generation people to pay attention. And some of the plays were very good. Some of them were very social, very of-the-moment issues. So if people can somehow make the form do different things in unexpected ways, there is hope.

You have to fight the battles against the Right. The funding battle is really terrifying. I was in Washington for a week and was on the NEA panel. We were giving out grants for specific projects, and there are great people that work for the NEA who are under siege. They're following rules they didn't make. The system's very anti-artists. Individual artists can't apply for grants anymore. And what tends to happen is that the stars of the theatre will be funded, and those lesser-knowns will not.

Do you think of your theatre as a political theatre?
In the broadest sense. Any time you write even obliquely about assimilation, or about gender conflicts or power struggles, that's political. *Marisol* is probably the most overtly political, and part of that is because when I was finishing it I was in England at the Royal Court Theatre, which is a very political theatre. It was also the time when the Iron Curtain was falling in Eastern Europe, there was so much rhetoric of revolution in the air and it infects the play. But transactions between people are political, especially if there's a disparity in power that is a result of age or sex or class, and there are many situations like that in my plays.

I've noticed your use of women heroes, most clearly in *Marisol*, but in other plays as well. In many of them, women are the primary figures that undertake journeys. I find that a very interesting tactic because in drama men undertake them more commonly. Do you see yourself as participating in a feminist project?
To some degree. I was trapped by an actor at a party who asked, "When are you going to write a guy play?" But I think there are several reasons why I haven't. The most practical is that my early plays are written for Cordelia González, who is an extraordinary actress, and I wanted to put her front and center in the work. And I was very aware of the women I grew up with who were really powerless. Nelly is based on a cousin of mine, and in this family of sixteen children she was in the middle and had to be an adult at a young age and be responsible for feeding and clothing the kids. I'm not a sociologist, but I do think a group of people will not advance until the weakest in that group advance. In Latin culture, women are the weaker sector, and we as Latins are not going to advance until we help women advance. There's always going to be a disparity in power, and disparity is not good for us. I think in a lot of ways that's the cause I'm writing for.

On the personal front, I'm one of six—five boys and one girl. I grew up feeling such sympathy for my sister, because we got away with murder and she had to be perfect. I remember vividly a day my father found some love letters that had been written to her by a boyfriend, and he read them to the whole family. It was a humiliating experience. I wanted to give voice to that as authentically as possible. In some ways it's a reflex against being too autobiographical. I could easily have written *Marisol* as a man living in the Bronx, working in publishing, which is what I was doing for many years. Maybe it's the fear of being too exposed, or of having the easy label of autobiography planted on your work, so that everyone thinks they get it. Only it's not that simple.

All of my brothers were in the military. Two of them fought in the Persian Gulf War, and there's a character in *The House of Ramon Iglesia* who goes off to the Marine Corps. I've been fascinated by their stories, especially of the Persian Gulf War. My brother, Julio, was in the 1980 mission to try to rescue the hostages from Iran. He was on the aircraft carrier where the helicopters took off. I missed the Vietnam War by the thinnest of margins, in fact my number came up the year the war ended. My father was in the Coast Guard, so there's this whole war conscious-ness in my family. I've been thinking of that in relation to my family and the fact that in Puerto Rico you can be drafted and made to fight in a war, but you cannot vote for President. And thinking about the peace-ful Tahinu Indians that were extinguished within fifty years of Columbus's arrival. So I've been toying with a play about the nature of the Puerto Rican warrior. And about Puerto Rico not being a country. What do warriors without a country do? What battles do they fight, where do they test their method, where do they find opportunities for heroism? My brothers are pretty screwed up now because of their war experiences. So that is going to be a guy play.

It's interesting to hear you talk about warriors because I almost see each of your plays as a kind of crusade or holy war.
There are definitely life-and-death struggles. I find that being a quote, unquote "minority" writer in this culture, you have to fight to get your voice heard. Each play is a declaration of my right to speak and to be included, it's sort of like throwing down a gauntlet.

I guess that's what it takes to get to the front lines.
And when you do get there, you get beaten up a lot.

Ntozake Shange

Growing up in a professional household (her father was a physician, her mother a psychiatric social worker), Paulette Williams was always in motion. Her parents, she explains, were "so mobile" during her "early childhood" that she "never expected to have anywhere in particular to call home." Meeting figures like Dizzy Gillespie, Muhammed Ali, and W.E.B. Du Bois during those years, and performing in Sunday afternoon variety shows in which her mother read from Shakespeare, Countee Cullen, T.S. Eliot and Paul Laurence Dunbar, she "heard so many languages, so many different kinds of music." ("i live in language," she writes, "sound falls round me like rain on other folks.") Later, during the 1960s, she was radicalized by the antiwar and civil rights movements and the struggle for black liberation. Yet like so many women of her generation, she found that these movements "didn't treat women right" and she gravitated increasingly toward feminism. Feeling "a violent resentment of carrying a slave name," she changed it to a Xhosa name in 1971. Ntozake: she who comes with her own things. Shange: one who walks like a lion. "Poems and music come from the pit of myself, and the pit of myself isn't a slave."

Out of the pit of herself, she developed the choreopoem as a deeply political mode of theatrical expression. Combining poetry, prose narrative, song, dance and music, the choreopoem represents less a simple synthesis of these arts than an attempt to use them to energize and transform the human subject. For as Robbie McCauley notes, "The form demands that the performer have an organic, physical relationship to the words and images of the poems/narratives." Personalizing her relationship to the text, she does not so much act the text as become it. For the choreopoem is less an object than an act and its performance is by definition a transformative (and sometimes even therapeutic) experience for both performer and spectator. Shange developed it, moreover, as a result of her involvement with a broad range of cultural practices: from the poetry of Shakespeare, Langston Hughes and Amiri Baraka; from Latin-American magic realism; from both modern and African dance; from jazz and rhythm and blues; from ritual; and from the consciousness-raising groups of the 1970s. As its sources in ritual would suggest, the choreopoem is less a highly individualized mode of expression than a communal form. Not only did it emerge, as Shange makes clear, out of her collaboration with many different women artists and performers, but it also represents her attempt at "creating new rituals and new mythologies for people of color." Insofar as the choreopoem is a ritual act, it is at once an expression and a consolidation of community, "a movement toward realization of self, in a collective sense that had been sorely missing in [her] youth."

Shange first made her mark with *for colored girls who have considered suicide/ when the rainbow is enuf* (1975), which was the first Broadway play to spotlight African-American women, to "sing a black girl's song/ bring her out/ to know herself." A collection of poems, songs and narratives, *for colored girls* represents a communal act in which seven women, arrayed in all the colors of the rainbow, take up many roles, celebrate their joys and mourn their losses. Shange explains, however, that the individualized characters that momentarily crystallize are, in a sense, accidental. Because "the women," as she acknowledges, "are indivisible," the poems could have been divided up among any number of performers. For finally the piece is less about these artificially separated individuals than a community of "colored girls" who triumph by acknowledging, owning and finally passing through their pain and struggle. And while, initially *for colored girls* sparked a controversy in the African-American community because of its sometimes negative images of black men, Shange counters by emphasizing both the feminist particularity of her reaction to the machismo associated with black cultural nationalism and her dissatisfaction with African-American art that foregrounds "our relationship with the other (that is, white people), as opposed to our relationship with ourselves."

All of Shange's choreopoems take up a project that is perhaps best described as decolonization, in which various "colored" subjects confront and liberate themselves from different kinds of oppressive structures. The historical specificity of this project thereby reminds us that Shange developed the form coincidentally and in confederation with the rise of various decolonizing activities, from Third World liberation movements to antiracist and feminist struggles in the U.S. Unlike the latter, however, which aim for political and social revolution, the choreopoem effects psychic and spiritual revolution. Focusing on the internalization of oppressive attitudes, images and agendas, it exposes, combats and transforms "the throes of pain n sensation experienced by my characters responding to the involuntary constrictions n amputations of their humanity." Despite the utopian impulse behind the choreopoem, however, it by no means turns its back on history. For all of her pieces can be considered archaeological insofar as they commemorate the different experiences of people of African descent, ranging from slavery in the U.S. to Toussaint L'Ouverture's struggle for the liberation of Haiti. Thus *spell #7* (1979), a piece about theatre itself, dramatizes the difficulty of breaking with the negative stereotypes of African-Americans derived from minstrel shows and perpetuated by the culture industry. *a photograph: lovers in motion* (1977) uses a quasi-naturalistic, almost photographic style to stage the choreography of love, the dynamics of desire and jealousy, "the contours of life unnoticed." *From Okra to Greens: A Different Kinda Love Story* (1981) most explicitly conjoins antiracist struggle with Third World liberation movements. Imagining a pair of lovers as guerrilla warriors, it stages the link between erotics and politics, the fact that every decolonizing project must be motivated by a love for the people. At the same time, it illuminates the potentially transformative power of erotic love, its suitability both as a model for and incitement to revolution.

Despite Shange's insistence on the composite nature of the choreopoem, language remains its basis, in part because of the long association between life and breath, in part because language is more easily and precisely recorded than dance. And in her writings, Shange repeatedly emphasizes the crucial function of language as a decolonizing tool and a utopian force. Inventing a distinctive orthography clearly based in black vernacular, she aims precisely "to attack deform n maim the language that i waz taught to hate myself in/ the language that perpetuates the notions that cause pain to every black child as he/she learns to speak of the world & the 'self.'" By so deforming language, Shange repossesses it, transforming it from a "straightjacket" slipped "over the minds of all americans" into "a liberator." Drawing what (citing Frantz Fanon) she calls "combat breath," she refuses to capitalize the first person singular pronoun, imagining and writing the disappearance of the individual ego into "a collective voice." By so speaking as part of a collective, in concert with a generation of "colored girls," she endeavors "to trip" language "and trick it and use it in ways 'they're' not expecting." She thereby transforms theatre poetry into a form of activism: "a poem shd fill you up with something/ cd make you swoon, stop in yr tracks, change yr mind, or make it up. a poem shd happen to you like cold water or a kiss."

August 13, 1998—Ntozake Shange's house, Houston, Texas

DS: Can you start by talking about how you got involved in theatre? I should preface that by saying that I know you think of yourself primarily as a poet rather than a playwright, but one thing I find so fascinating about your work is the way you call those categories into question.

NS: How did I get started? I just did a piece about this for the Poetry Society of America called "First Love" about what made me want to be a poet and I said—if I have a correct recollection of myself, which is real hard for me—that I was exposed to a very strange combination of poets as I grew up because my mother had been sent to take elocution lessons. She knew all these Whitman poems and Wallace Stevens poems, as well as Sterling Brown, Langston Hughes, Arna Bontemps and Countee Cullen. So there's this huge mixture of things going on and we'd hear, "Oh Captain, My Captain" or "Speak up and express yourself" from Paul Laurence Dunbar in the same afternoon. I loved listening to her and I loved finding these poems, but I never thought that I would become a poet. I always had such reverence for them that I had imagined myself as a journalist, and I wanted to be a war correspondent because somebody had come to our fourth-grade class to talk to us about Laos. I had been raised on World War II movies and I knew that there were all these independence movements in Africa because a lot of the residents and interns with whom my father worked were from Africa and were in exile because of their political activities. So I wanted to cover the experience of people from Africa, Latin America and Asia as a war correspondent. As an adult, in college, I ran across a group of young men called the Last Poets and their presentation of their work had such movement and such cadence, and was so politically inspiring to me that I decided that's what I would do. So I wanted to be a propagandist. This was another way to be a propagandist and get the word to the people. So I worked as a warm-up act for a bunch of other people, to warm up crowds before the Young Lords political-party speakers would actually talk. I honed my skills in parks and project playgrounds, and project community rooms, outside demonstrations at Lincoln Hospital, for example. This is where I began to learn how to work a crowd.

This was in New York?

In New York. This was during the anti-Vietnam War movement, so I also belonged to the National Black Anti-Draft Anti-War Association or Committee or something, I forget what it was. But we needed poems for that, too. We needed poems about Rhodesia, we needed poems about Guinea-Bissau. We needed poets to rouse the people so they would give money and prepare for when the political people came. So that's how I moved around so-called artistic circles before I went to Los Angeles. At that point I was perfectly happy to be what Americans derogatorily term a poet of the people or a poet of the masses. There were specific things I was fighting for, specific things I wanted to do. I knew I had precedents in Neruda and Mayakovsky, and in the Dadaists. I said, "This is the route I've decided to follow." It wasn't until I moved to Los Angeles, where I knew no one, and found the political movements relatively naive, even though some of the more really stunning revolutionary acts took place there. The thing with the Soledad brothers, putting Angela [Davis] in jail, the murder of Fred Hampton, all these things were much more viscerally propelling than what was going on back East. But back East there was a more sophisticated thought process, or so I thought.

When did you move to L.A.?

To go to graduate school in 1970. So there was a play called *Free Angela* on South Main Street in South Central L.A., near USC. They wanted a poet to open up before the political act. Having moved myself from a culture I understood, where there were no Puerto Ricans around, no black people who spoke more than one language, I had to make some sense to this audience. It was the first time I was challenged to find what I now consider to be my own voice and my own way of interpreting language and music. In New York I was part of a whole school of people, and I didn't have to work terribly hard unless I was actually on the stage, because there were certain assumptions about the aesthetic that I knew everyone shared and I didn't have to make one up. In Los Angeles I had to begin to do that.

I found a Chicano who lived down the street from me who played guitar. This guy was a tortilla maker, I think that's what he did in the daytime, but in the night I could hear him playing the guitar from down the street. So I asked him, "Davíd, will you come and do this with me?" And out of total isolation we went and did three poems with the guitar. I didn't want drums because that would invoke another aesthetic that I didn't want the Los Angelinos to think that I was part of, because it was too male, too harsh, too rigid. And I worked with the Young Lords

Party because they had an antisexist platform and a platform for bilingualism. As opposed to the Black Panther party which had nothing like that. So me and Davíd did these three poems and it turned out that I meant the "I" in these poems to be a collective "I." But because I was an Easterner and a graduate student, it was harder for the Californians to accept me as a voice of the masses. So I had then to decide if I cared about this or not. I decided that the only thing I was responsible for was what I wrote. And what the reader took from that was their responsibility. And I've lived by that ever since.

I continued to do readings around Los Angeles and found some people who worked with Horace Tapscott's Arkestra, which was similar to Sun Ra's Arkestra, so I got to play with what I call new music. Ishmael [Reed] published my first short story. I started to feel I was going to become a poet, even though I was still grinding away in graduate school as a cultural historian. I didn't want to be a poor starving artist because I didn't believe in it. I knew French poets weren't starving, so if the French poets weren't starving, I had no reason to be starving. If Sartre and Simone de Beauvoir could teach forever and ever and not be looked down upon, then I could do the same thing. None of my models were American in terms of how I wanted to live or what I wanted to do except for the poets of the Harlem Renaissance. They, I almost felt, were my contemporaries because I continued to read their work and teach them, and they were so much a part of my life. It's almost like I was never introduced to them because I came to them with my mother.

What about the Black Arts movement?
I was genuinely inspired by the Black Arts movement, but I had to be protective of it, because it was so male and, I thought, so condescending to the public in some instances. I never found it necessary—and I still don't find it necessary—to condescend to my audience, be they from the projects or from Fifth Avenue or from River Oaks in Houston. There's no need to do such a thing. I felt a lot of that in stuff guys were writing. It was too simple, too surface, everything was telescoped for the audience as opposed to allowing them to discover with us what we were going to experience. I didn't want to be a part of that, which is why I didn't work with conga drummers, because that's what the guys did. I wanted to make sure that when I came on stage people knew something different was going to happen, so that they wouldn't get mad at me. If I came on with conga drummers, I was disturbing their aesthetic. If I came on with a Chicano guitarist, we had an open field. So I was eventually assimilated into the Los Angeles poetry scene, and was accepted on my own terms.

Then I moved to Boston, where I worked with the Collective Black Artists' Café. That's where I heard Marion Brown do his "Karintha" the first time and it had a tremendous impact on me. I also heard Archie Shepp's "Blase" with Gene Lee for the first time up there. I started to think, Wow, the words can hang in the air the same way a note hangs in the air. The rhythms can alter the same way the rhythms in the poem alter. So music doesn't have to be a backdrop, it can be a collaborative effort between me and the musician. The poem seems to be coming out of a chord or a note, as opposed to coming only out of me. Next to me there's this separate entity. And that was essential in helping me find the way that I still use to work with musicians or dancers. I really began to write there on a consistent basis. We would work in these small cafés in Cambridge and I would literally walk around with a tambourine with ribbons on it, and that was how we got paid. Sometimes we got paid so little we had to hitchhike back to Boston. Then I started developing little bands. I started forming these large musical groups and writing a lot so that I had a large repertoire of things that I could experiment with. I would work with the musicians and in rehearsal I'd find out if something was too wordy or sluggish or unnecessary or redundant. But front of the audience was when I could really edit. Because I would start to do the poem and I'd hear something from them, and I'd say to the musicians, "I can skip to the next stanza or come back to this one later." I started to be able to play with things in a way I hadn't been able to before.

From Boston I went to New York again and then to Northern California. And there I really started coming into my own. I applied to graduate school at UCLA to work with ritual music and dance. I had applied to the dance department, but they gave me a fellowship in playwriting. I said, "I don't want to be a playwright. I don't like plays. This is why I want to do rituals and write poetry. This defeats the whole purpose of what I want to do." So I didn't go. I stayed in San Francisco and taught part-time at two colleges so I would have some money. Previously, in New York I had started seriously studying African dance and drama technique. So I moved to California and I immediately picked back up on that and I worked with several dance companies: Raymond Sawyer, Ed Mock and Stanze Peterson. Between those three, and Halifu Osumare and Ruth Beckford, I got phenomenal training and experience, and was able to discover a new way to relate to the drum. I didn't have to use it the way I heard poets working with it before. I could use a drum with my body, I could use it with my words, which was very spontaneous and free. And there were signals from the drum that could spur something linguistically or in terms of movement. That was my first experience in theatre per se, in the sense that the dance companies I worked with were innovative to the point that poems would be going on top of drums while there were twenty dancers on stage. And this was in 1972–73, so people weren't doing it then. There would be poems in two or three different languages. The company was multiracial, it was Filipino, Native American, black, Hispanic, Chicano and white. What kept it from being a statement was that we were only involved in doing the movements, and if we did them correctly, that was all the audience could be involved in. They couldn't be involved in thinking about who was what color or anything like that. And so that's why my first company, I guess, of *for colored girls* was Native American, Asian, Filipino and black. That's why it was *for colored girls*, because it was for women of color, and I didn't think anything of it.

I started wrestling with myself because I would be going to dance classes or going to dance concerts and then I would be rushing home to write. I said, "Why am I making this big distinguishing dichotomy here?" I change my mode of thought to become this writer person. "Why don't I just use the energy that I have from dance and go write? Or use the energy from writing and go to rehearsal—stop trying to make these two separate things." Once I did that, it was very easy for me to envision working with dancers as my collaborators, because I would find myself moving at the typewriter or imagining specific types of movements going on in my own body while I was writing—and that's the beginning of the choreopoem, at my desk as I was writing. I was lucky that I had so many friends who were not only competent dancers but had been trained really well in improvisation and being able to listen, whether to a musical instrument or a voice. Paula Moss, Elvia Marta and Rosalie Alphonso were the three I worked with primarily, and Halifu, of course.

Then Paula Moss and I started calling all the readings *for colored girls*. I would just change the poems every night. I worked in all the cafés in San Francisco you can work in. I got paid three drinks a night or I could invite somebody else in, or we got a meal. The only place that actually paid us was the Poetry Center at what was then San Francisco State. They actually paid money, which I thought was amazing, but that was for working a huge crowd in a cafeteria of college students who were eating and chatting each other up, which was really, really good training for me. As well as working bars where people came to drink, or cruise, or whatever they were going to do, and trying to keep at least three-quarters of the population paying attention to me. The only way I could do that was by finding passages in the language where repetition was called for, or playing with the syllables in the lines. So Paula Moss and I would do these things called *for colored girls*, and we would change it all the time. And finally, one time I had one bunch of stuff, and a Haitian band and a white avant-garde sort of band that's now called Rova. So I had these two different bands and I had these dancers and we did the same show four times in a row. Except that Paula and I had these meetings where we would say, "This is too long, we have to cut this." So we were honing it, but we weren't changing it—I had become accustomed to just doing whatever I felt like doing.

Then we decided we were ready to go to New York. My sister, Ifa Iyaun, knew actors. I didn't know any actors, or anybody in theatre per se. I only knew musicians and poets, that was my world. My sister and Oz Scott knew actors and producers. And so they found me some actors whom they claimed could move, which turned out to be true. So we started doing the same thing I used to do, changing the show every night, every Monday night at the Old Reliable Café over on East 3rd Street, across from where La MaMa used to be, in the back room. And that was so pitiful that we had a bucket back there where we had to weewee. I was freezing and there was no heat. And people started coming, primarily artists, but it was packed. We'd make enough money on the door so I'd have fourteen dollars or something at night after we'd divvy it all up. This to me was success. And down the street we moved to DeMonte's Café, which was even more success because it had real chairs and tables and real lights, and it didn't have sawdust on the floor which made it very difficult to dance. When we got to DeMonte's, Oz Scott started shaping the piece to more what we know as *for colored girls* and it became a more theatrical entity.

Because we were working with real actresses, I didn't do all the pieces myself as I had always done. There was this new bunch of people with multiple skills and that was scary to me, I didn't want my voice taken from me, and these people didn't look or move like dancers. They looked like women who weren't necessarily clumsy—they had a spirit about them—but they weren't dancers. And I didn't like that. But then Woodie King came to see us and said he could give us so many nights at the New Federal. I said, "Hell, let's go for it. I can always write something else." When somebody asked Duke Ellington if he was angry at Paul Whiteman for stealing all his songs, Ellington said, "I don't have time to be angry at Paul Whiteman, I just write another song." So that was my idea, I said, "They can take this and do whatever they want with it. I'll just write something else." That's essentially what happened. Then I got to the point where I didn't consider it my piece anymore, it was just something that I had written that got stuff done to it, and I needed to go do something else so I'd feel like myself again. Once we got to Broadway, we formed this group called Negress, because we felt we were being commercialized entirely too much. We would do new pieces because the actors I was working with were also writers and/or different kinds of dancers trained in postmodern dance, so they had a different aesthetic than I had. So we did that for a few weeks after the show at the Booth Theatre. That started to wear us out, we couldn't keep that up too long, then I left the show and left the country. Went to Paris and didn't do anything. Went to see art and get out of that environment. I came back and Joseph Papp asked me when I was going to write a play, which ticked me off, so I said, "I'm gonna write one right away!" I didn't have the slightest idea how to go about it, so I wrote *photograph*, which was a critical failure but which I still think contains some of the most beautiful passages I ever wrote.

***photograph* is also the most realistic of your plays.**

It is, and I actually came here to work at the Equinox Theater, because they loved *photograph*, and I said I just wanted to fix it a little bit. And that began my relationship to the Equinox, where I was free to write, and they wanted me to write theatre pieces, but I could also write poems if I wanted, so they gave me these residencies that were totally open. As long as I ended up with something by the end, it didn't matter. So I was an artist-in-residence more often in Texas than in the state of New Jersey, where my birthplace was, which I find very funny. I was paid better in Texas, and in Texas I found the good mix of Hispanic and black and Asian people that I was accustomed to in California, and not overwhelmed by Anglo culture, which I sometimes feel in other places.

Then I went back to New York, *photograph* was up, *for colored girls* was up, and I still wasn't doing any poetry and I was mad. And so Jessica Hagedorn, Thulani Davis and I had this idea to do *Where the Mississippi Meets the Amazon* [1977] as the Satin Sisters. We worked with incredible musicians during that time: David Murray, Anthony Davis, Jay Hogarth, Fred Hopkins, Henry Threadgill. There were places in there for improvisation and that was a wonderful experience. So I said, "See Zaki, you can do a piece that they accept as theatre where you feel free to be yourself." Which I had been looking for since I became involved in theatre. I just couldn't find any solace in making up these other people. It did not move me terribly. That was not my forte, I didn't feel comfortable doing that.

So all of the characters in your plays are parts of yourself, fragments?

They begin like that, and then I have to adjust them and give them names. I take a poem and then I say, "Okay, this is a magician or this is Lou or this is Dahlia," but they all started as poems or prose poems.

Now when I started writing *Sassafras, Cypress & Indigo* [1982], I wrote it as a horn solo. Luckily, Ishmael read it before anyone else did. I had written *Sassafras* without any punctuation whatsoever except the slashes because I wanted people to read it without stopping like the way you hear a horn solo. He said that was so fascist and dogmatic that I had to put punctuation in, and I fought him. But people just couldn't read forty-five pages without stopping. They just couldn't, and they would get lost because there was nowhere to go back to. You couldn't say, "Well, I was at this paragraph," because there weren't any. So I knew what I was doing, and it was dictator-like, so I compromised and gave *Sassafras* some standard punctuation. The little group of women I worked with would do excerpts from it at poetry readings.

I didn't make distinctions, because what I wrote could always be danced to, could always have music to it. I even believe that of my so-called critical essays—you can play music with them. I call it carnal intellectuality. That's my philosophy of the kind of passion I write with. For some reason, I think it's a very French idea, but it just might be in my head. I gave a paper on that at a black writers' conference in Pittsburgh about ten or twelve years ago. It's either "visceral intellectuality" or "carnal intellectuality," depending on whom I'm talking to. I'm working on the *Lulu* plays right now, so anything might come out of my mouth. I might say sex about anything. I just finished act two of an adaptation. Sex is on the brain because of *Lulu*. I think people in this house are beginning to get tired of it. I think I'm a can-can dancer all day long.

When you talk about your antipathy to theatre, you describe it as the weakest American art form. Why?

I love Tennessee Williams but everything's so sad, and there's no hope, there's no joy in life, and I didn't want to be an unhappy white person. All the theatre I saw was being written about that. I did find some inspiration in that group of young English writers that they called the angry young men. I found a lot in common with Irish and Welsh playwrights, Brendan Behan, Dylan Thomas and those guys. So we had these working class people, Irish people, who were infuriated about their situation. But when we dealt with American white people who, except for Lorraine Hansberry, were the only people on Broadway, I didn't have any feeling for them, I didn't feel sorry for them, their lives were not universal to me. So it wasn't necessarily boring, but it was emotionally dead. I believe theatre should be living. I was inspired to believe that, because I saw *Marat/Sade* and I knew you could do intellectual pieces that were historically based and full of passion and full of amazing, surprising music and movement. I had seen it with my own eyes. I knew that white people were capable of more.

I've been thinking that although the choreopoem draws on different arts—poetry, music, dance—it's wrong to call it a synthesis. Because it's really about the physicalization of something that comes from deep within the body.
I believe movement can finish a phrase of language. I have seen that happen on stage. I have felt it. The interaction is symbiotic, if it's really being done correctly.

How would you define the choreopoem?
Didn't I do that once already?

I have it right here.
I shouldn't stray from that then. I get myself in trouble when I change my definition. They say, "She contradicted herself when she da da da," and I probably did.

So it's about using the body, the whole body, as a kind of switch point.
Language and movement are both based on breath. The breath that leads us to talk is the same breath that leads us to move, to have flight, to have balance or to defy gravity. So they're related in a very primal way, in a spiritual way, too.

So, the choreopoem, to some extent, undoes the opposition between mind and body, spirit and flesh.
I can't emphasize how lucky I was to have some of the finest African-American dance teachers who ever lived. And the loss of two of them for me was devastating. I have to mention Fred Benjamin and Dianne McIntyre in New York. I studied dance until I lost my teachers because of AIDS. I hadn't even needed to take ballet with white people until the AIDS epidemic. And so the habit of going to class became a kind of terrifying and stultifying ritual in the early eighties. I was kind of lost because my grounding in my body was disrupted, but now I feel better because I go to class to keep what I had learned. It didn't matter so much anymore who taught me. It was my responsibility to create things.

So your work really comes out of a collective, working with multiple collaborators and teachers, and it is about expressing the will of that collective.
Wonderful, that's good to hear.

It's as if you're using the Self as an almost accidental point of intersection, because the work is really about community. I know with *colored girls* you said there was a certain arbitrariness in dividing up the lines among seven women. You could have done it with more or less, because what's really important is the collective "I." I think this is true of all your work.

I would hope so.

For me, that's where ghosts come in. The "I" that's produced is so permeable, so porous, so much a part of larger structures, more an effect than a cause.

Anna Deavere Smith wanted to know something about the "I." I said, "It's very slippery, I can't tell you exactly what I think of that because it's constantly changing for me." It's metamorphic.

So in expressing a collectivity, the characters you produce are both one and many.

I think that has a lot to do with the fact that I've been in analysis for decades. My relationship with the unconscious is very intimate. When I design characters, when I see characters, when I see people, I'm not as concerned with what I'm looking at as what's going on in their unconscious. I went through a phase where I couldn't write on subways, I couldn't write on trains with all those unconsciouses, I didn't know what was going on with them. Not that somebody was going to kill me, but that they might be thinking about it. That was as real to me as if they had done it.

This makes me think of the way your characters occupy different realms—conscious and unconscious, literal and symbolic. So actions are always happening in different registers simultaneously. I'm thinking about how in *spell #7*, when Natalie is talking about killing her child, she is talking literally about infanticide, but she's also enunciating a fantasy about producing the Self. It seems to me that your characters are almost ghostlike in the way they inhabit several different realms.

They are because I don't find the real world terribly interesting. There's so much that resonates from movement and music that I don't find in the written or spoken word. A lot of times I try to reach out for other possibilities of interpretation, so that we don't have to follow only one path that a character takes. We can go somewhere else with him or her, which I think is more fun. And also allows for deeper understanding of who the character is, because we are not only what we do and what we think and what we feel and what we smell and what we notice and don't notice. What we remember is very important for who we are. So I'm very obviously concerned with memories which don't so much haunt as exist in some simultaneity with our current actions.

So the past surrounds us.

Yes, I have a very intense sense of déjà vu that I used to think of as a distraction from being in the moment, and I now understand it as an added element to my life. So my characters often carry the spirits or the pain or the desires of their forebears, either without their knowledge or with their knowledge. They either fight with them or embrace them, but it's very much a part of who that person is.

And so memory is the key.

Yes, you have to remember that I was raised in a place where in my high school history book there were literally two sentences on slavery. Two sentences. That obliterated my grandmother and my great aunts and my great-great grandfather—they didn't exist. There was no more mention of black people after slavery, we just disappeared. So I became very involved in trying to learn what happened to all those people, where are they now, and how can I keep them alive? How to keep them alive in us and offer our ancestors some wholesome resting place? If, in the souls of black folks, we have no land, can they have a resting place? I'm one of these people who believes in buying back black farmland, because we lost so much of it. And a landless people is a desperate people, as the Palestinians show us. Is that what we want it to be? Going around asking Americans, "Can we please control our water source? Can we please be allowed to go in and out from the city to the suburbs without passes of some kind?" Which is not that farfetched. You can't get into certain office buildings in America, even as an artist or sculptor, without a pass. So all that's very important to me, and all that can be used to inform the reader of the character's wildest dreams and most peculiar actions.

Which are connected to memory and the struggle to get some of these things back. As I was reading through your work, I kept thinking time and again that it really is about decolonization. In the introduction to your *Three Pieces* [St. Martin's Press, Inc., 1992], you quote Frantz Fanon writing about the process of decolonization. I see all of your work now through this lens, with its concern for taking possession of one's memories, one's history, one's desires, one's fantasies.

If you look at my beginnings, at my work for the Young Lords Party, and remember that I was raised at a time when my father knew people from Nigeria, Mali, Cameroon, Algeria, all of which were becoming independent states. It's a logical progression for me. My dad and I listened on the shortwave radio to Fidel coming into Havana. Because that's the only way we could find out what people of color were doing in the world. No one here was going to tell us. It was not news. So on the shortwave radio we were able to experience these monumental events for people of color in the Third World.

In much of your work there is a sense of community among the peoples of the African diaspora. Which is why I see it connected to certain liberation movements of the sixties, in particular black cultural nationalism with its grounding in a theory of internal colonialism which sees African-Americans as suffering under the yoke of domestic colonial forces.

My senior thesis at Barnard was about the essentially urban reservations that were called inner cities. And one of the myths of the American frontier on these reservations—that were the black centers of cities— was that there wasn't much to burn down on these reservations because they were nothing but barren land. But they burned themselves up with firewater, and what's firewater but burning oneself up?

It seems to me that your understanding of decolonization includes not only race but also gender.

I went to a high school where they had a meeting of all the girls in the auditorium to tell us that premenstrual and menstrual cramps did not exist, and that the nurse was no longer going to allow people to stay in the nurse's office. You were no longer allowed to get medication or stay home from school because of menstrual pains. I lived in a house with a father who, benevolent though he was, and amazing though he was, would tell me things like, "That's too hard for a girl." I wanted to be a doctor. "That's too hard for a girl." I wanted to be a musician. "That's too hard for a girl." What could I do? Even up to *Love Space Demands* [1992], my father was like, "Couldn't you get someone else to take that part? It looks really hard." I've been working all my life to have a piece like *Love Space Demands*, and he still wants me not to work so hard.

Which is why there is always a feminist dimension to your work. I'm curious how this relates to your experiences with seventies feminism. When I teach *colored girls*, I think of it as being in some ways a critique of seventies feminism which has sometimes been criticized as having been very white and middle-class.

That's where I differ. I might be misreading history, or maybe I'm just arrogant, but I never thought that white women on their own defined what feminism was. I've never given them that power. I was part of the first consciousness-raising groups at Barnard. So I don't have that problem. The problem I do have has to do with lesbian separatists and ideal communities, and women who ran off to be among themselves, which would decimate our community. It would tear our community apart.

We don't need more kinds of gender separation than we've already got. At that time, according to the rules of welfare, you couldn't have a man in your house. We didn't need lesbian separatism, because heterosexual separatism was already being enforced by the state. I was highly theoretical at that time. I was reading Susan Griffin, Mary Daly and Adrienne Rich, who were friends of mine, so I knew major white feminists. What we were working towards, as far as I was concerned, was liberating women. I was there to represent the people I had to take care of. The title *for colored girls* was a phrase my grandmother used to use. It was the same thing as when we used to take back words. We took back the word "bitch" and "hag" and "witch." I wanted to take back the words "colored girl" because it was important to me to do that. Someone would say, "She's pretty for a colored girl." And my grandmother would say to me sometimes, "You're such a pretty little colored girl," and it would make me so proud. And I wanted to give that to the youngsters I was working with. They did not have that. No one was telling them they were pretty. They were black and they were proud, but they couldn't say anything about being female. We didn't have these voices speaking for us, or if we did, my community didn't know they were speaking for us. The one thing I can do is make sure another generation doesn't come along and have no sense of self. The first poem in *for colored girls*, "dark phrases of womenhood," was written for a class of Chicanos I had at Long Beach, there wasn't one so-called black girl in it.

I'm interested in how this process of taking back is related to what you're doing in your plays with black vernacular. In the introduction to *Three Pieces* you write about wanting to deform language.

Judy Grahn inspired that, she's been an amazing influence on me. She was performing her piece *The Woman Who* while I was developing *for colored girls*. I'm very much connected to that, the local women's collective and the Shameless Hussy Press. I was involved in those things, and I knew all those people. We influenced each other without being territorial about it. I've always thought that Judy had a bit of genius when she wrote that our point was to destroy the King's English, because in the King's English we were tortured and maimed and deformed, so therefore I simply carried that to a level where black people could understand that part of black English is doing that. We didn't have to start from scratch. We already had a language.

"Signifyin(g)"?

Yes.

And I think you write that your deformation of the King's English and the vernacular gives you a way of thinking something new. It calls forth the unthinkable, the unimaginable. Which means that language is decisive for your project.

Absolutely, to use the same building blocks to go somewhere else where nobody thought you could go with these building blocks, these things.

Hearing you talk about the political dimension of your work, makes me think how in *From Okra to Greens* **[1981] the political and the erotic come together in such a compelling way. I know that** *colored girls* **was criticized by some as an attack on African-American men.**

That's because they made the whole cast black. It had never been black before we went to New York. That was an afterthought, it wasn't my thought.

At the same time, Beau Willie is a rather prominent figure in it.

I knew guys like that. I had been to the VA with guys like that. I had watched a Chicano man in San Francisco hold his babies out the window. Then I was sitting there one day and thinking that we're taught as little girls that the most important thing a man can ask you is, "Will you marry me?" It got twisted here so that by asking this child to marry him he was killing her spirit. Which is not a new idea, just a new way to put it. That story came out of the tension between what we'd been told and what I knew.

That's such an important element in all of your work, the violence done by men to women, but I'm also struck by the joy of eros, its transfiguring power.

Euripides is my favorite Greek playwright. I like Greek tragedies because of the passion and the inclusion of the element of Dionysus in *The Bacchae*. That had always been very attractive because it seemed similar to the idea of the black person as the other, the unconscious. Therefore I was left to exploit everything having to do with sexuality. We owned it in this country. That's why young black girls are taught to be so proper, to defuse the notion that we are sexual creatures. Part of what I was getting rid of was that oppression. I don't quite know what to say except that it's ever-powerful and ever-present. One of the things we still haven't done as women is take control of our own sexuality and our own sexual images and desires. The evidence of that is the spread of AIDS. We still will not say to somebody, "You have to wear a condom." We give in constantly, and we know this from the statistics. The only way this could have happened is if, in a room by herself, a woman has no control over her sexuality. It's very important that I keep banging away at that door. To make sure we're not afraid of it, we're still so afraid of our own bodies. I have students who write in their journals that they have never touched themselves, never caressed their own faces.

So the erotic for you is a site of transformation, allowing for women and men to become themselves.
Right, because without freeing the sexual within ourselves, we're only using a quarter of our being. And that quarter is not trustworthy.

In *From Okra to Greens* you also link the sexual to a political project, the taking up of arms. And reading that made me think how eros is connected in all your pieces to warfare and violence.
It really is, in *Liliane* [1996] it's there. She makes labia boxes out of dirt. What do black people need? Earth, soil, our own land, self-determination, what does she make out of this stuff we need? She makes labia boxes. One of her first statements to her psychoanalyst is, "I made these labia boxes and he laughed at me." What would she want to make out of her own land? Our vaginas are in some ways our land, after all they call us mother earth. They are absolutely connected for me. Sexual liberation, in the sense of being liberated from shame or guilt or fear about sexuality is very important for women. I don't understand the real chiaroscuro men have about women and sex. I don't get it, so I can't speak with any definitive authority about that. I do know how it affects women. I've worked with them, I know myself, and I've seen enough emotional torture, and enough repression of real brilliance to know that this is something I need to do.

We grew up pretty much at the same time—I'm a couple years younger than you are—but we're both products of the sixties. Isn't the linkage you draw a product of that period?
Yes it is.

At times, in the past, you've described yourself as an Afrocentrist. Do you think of yourself as one now?
I must have been in a bad mood when I said that, because I've always said that I define myself as an African of the New World. My relationship to Africa is just now becoming clearer to me. I was this person who wanted to know about every slave community in the Western Hemisphere before I went to Africa. I didn't want to go there until I knew about the rest of us. I might have cousins, I might have relatives, I wanted to put myself back together from all these slave communities and slave societies before I went over there. That's not what happened. I ended

up going to Senegal before I'd done everything else I'd wanted to do. I've got a book back there on Afro-Argentines—they hide us everywhere. I've got a book on Afro-Uruguayans. I'm on a mission to find us and put us back together. I'm not looking for the dick of Osiris, I'm looking for the hole in our being because it's not North American slavery. We're so chauvinistic to imagine that our experience of slavery is universal. Slavery was universal in the Western Hemisphere, but not this particular kind. It's very important to have knowledge of and respect for the suffering and disappearance of the rest of us. I have Afro-Peruvian folk songs. Black people in North America don't know there's such a thing because nobody lets us know. That's part of my job, to let people know we're not alone in this, that there are more people than just us and James Brown, "I'm black and I'm proud."

So for you it's more of a historical project.
Absolutely. You know, I wanted the first foreign country my daughter went to to be Cuba, that was very important to me. If it hadn't been for the Duvaliers, I would have taken her to Haiti, but I couldn't take her there then, it was too dangerous for her. I took her to Nicaragua, to Cuba. These are liberated places of people of color. This is where she must go, this is what she must know. It must be in her soul that she has been there. White people can't tell her that we can't do, that we're not ready to run a country. We've been running a country for thirty-five years. I also had her blessed by a Santeria priest in Cuba, because I wanted to make sure that the spiritual and the cultural and the political were all done at the same time. This is not something that Fidel loves for people to go doing, but I was allowed to find a priest to bless my daughter in Havana. I want to take her, later, not quite yet, to Haiti, I want to go with her even though she's a grown-up now, because it's still very difficult to negotiate Haitian culture—a small faux pas can be very dangerous, especially for black Americans who have little or no historical understanding of what the significance of Haiti is. The first embargo was against Haiti, not Cuba. It started in 1804, all the European countries stopped sending necessary goods to Haiti. That's why it's so poor, it wasn't an accident, it's been a two hundred-year embargo. Nobody talks about this. They say, "It's the most impoverished country in the Western Hemisphere." Of course it is. They were determined to show us from early on. There are documents in the Library of Congress saying they're going to stop these Negroes now, end this: if you can't get rid of them, starve them. That's essentially what's happened. Except that the same vitality that you find in the work of Africans of the New World, wherever we are, is manifested in Haitian music and Haitian

painting. That's what I meant by the joie de vivre that I couldn't find in Anglo-American culture. The viability of the sensual, of their joy, is so tenuous.

American foreign policy has been terrifyingly consistent.
Americans don't even know that Haiti was occupied for thirty years by American troops, that's why there are all these Haitians with American names. They segregated Haiti. The most bizarre things. They put Duvalier in power and then accused him of witchcraft. It's just a pack of ironies and contradictions, but with one constant, "You cannot rise above us. You cannot rise up against it." That's what happened to my piece in the Shakespearean sonnet play *Love's Fire* [1998] when we went to Britain. They just dismissed it because it was in the vernacular. One gay paper in New York actually understood that it was a street-savvy love piece, and they enjoyed that. But when they want it to be white, they've got to get rid of me, because I make the English language do things they don't want it to do. It was real clear with *Love's Fire*. It was dismissed constantly, even though I know it works because I watched it and I watched the audience. And I know it works because Latinos told me it works. So as long as my work does that, I'm a happy girl.

Hearing you talk about this, I think back to the beginning of the interview when you spoke about wanting to become a journalist and a war correspondent, because in a way you have.
I am, I'm a cultural war correspondent. I'm involved in cultural war, and I know it, I understand it very well.

That also marks a change in the role of journalist, because we usually imagine them as being detached from what they're reporting, while you've always been on the front lines.
Oh yeah, and I also believe in propaganda. You just keep banging on the door. You just keep telling them. That's one of the reasons why I'm so happy to be at Prairie View [Prairie View A&M University, Texas], because I have students that are just hungry for this kind of information. We are walking around a former plantation. And we can go to slave burial sites on our campus. How dare we not remember! Literally, we're standing on their bones. This thing's built on their bones. This is a phenomenal responsibility, and honor. I got mad at my students when they didn't go on the slave walk to see the grave sites. Told me it was raining. I said, "You gonna tell massa it's rainin', I ain't cuttin' cane today?" "It's rainin'." That's how lax we've gotten and that's why I have this whole sense of urgency. Which goes back to that thing about com-

bat breathing. That's why I have to practice relaxation and meditation every day, because I get too revved up. So I had to learn not how to take it out of my work, but how to take it out of my body so that it didn't become dangerous to me. It can become dangerous to other people, but not to me.

Yesterday, when I was interviewing George Wolfe, I asked him how he felt about the future of theatre, because it seems theatre has been shrinking so much since the 1960s, and he said that for him, the lifeblood of theatre is community, being connected to community. Does that apply to you as well?
Absolutely, that's why I haven't ever turned down a request from a black community group in my life. I haven't withheld rights from a black, public high school ever in my life. Because that's what I wrote it for, it's for them. I haven't held back anything from Puerto Ricans, they haven't held back anything from me. They wanted to do *for colored girls* in Appalachia, those poor women needed it, so I said, "Sure." They were so surprised. I said, "I'm not crazy. I was raised in Missouri, I know how they treat hillbillies. I know how they treated them when they got to St. Louis. I know how they laughed at them when they found out they came from Arkansas and North Carolina." So absolutely I believe that. I feel very much a part of a community, even if it's far-flung. My aloneness is the aloneness that Ngugi Wa Thiongo talks about or that Fanon talks about, which is the aloneness of sensing this oppression in isolation. Fanon made it clear that oppression is a felt, personal activity, and that is the root of my loneliness. That's why it's so important to me, out of my own despair, to re-create the joy and the fervor of the lives of the people I know who still survive. . . .
    In my *Lulu*, all her lovers are henchmen of Batista.

That's fascinating to set your adaptation of that play in a revolutionary moment.
It was a very decadent place, in a lot of ways, the same as Germany.

That also brings together the erotic and the political.
Absolutely, there are generals walking around after this girl, and the animal tamer at the beginning is the head of the secret police. The circus is the jail where they keep the political prisoners.

What is it that makes for a good production of your work?
The spirit of the actors, the vision of the director, the support of the theatre and absolute respect and reverence to the text itself. Which doesn't make it any different from any other play. If you don't deal with my text seriously, you'll miss it. The historical references and the name

references are essential. People have done *for colored girls* and they have no idea who Arsenio Rodriguez is, and they miss the whole thing. They miss the whole element. If you don't know that Charlie Mingus wrote a book in which he said he wanted to be a pimp, *My Life as an Underdog*, that line doesn't make any sense to you. You don't hear Archie Shepp play music, then you can't do the transition from Willie Colon to jazz. So a real respect for the text, every word in it is important.

And understanding all those historical differences.
Yeah.

Do you think of your writing as forming a kind of psychic or spiritual or emotional or intellectual autobiography?
Well I would hope it would form a something, because I know they all progress, one from another. I use them as parapets to get from one place to the next. I hope it would do that. I used to read one author obsessively. I could go through everything so I could see what would happen in his—usually they were his—thinking and way of looking at the world. That's what I would hope people are able to do with my work as well, not only to enjoy the pieces individually, but also to watch a life in progression. If I stop progressing, then I die. Or they put me in the hospital, one or the other.

Is there anything you want to add?
I want to add—for women writers and male producers—that women who are mothers have different support needs from women who are not. I needed baby-sitters in the greenroom, I needed space in the lighting booth for the crib, I needed extra time to finish a project, I needed rehearsal times when I would be able to find a nanny, I needed a place in the theatre to write because I could not write with a crying baby at home, I needed them to understand that for six or seven years, I couldn't write theatre per se, because I couldn't do anything with other people as freely as I could when I got a child in school. And not to dismiss us because we have these segments in our lives when we simply cannot be involved in the theatre community as much as when we were single or as when our children are grown. It's physically impossible. I think I suffered for that. People thought I had stopped working or I had given up. I was raising a child, which simply demanded picking up and dropping off and feeding and washing and going to the school, and made it impossible for me to be available to do what we call normal theatrical work. I think it's very important that women know that this is a true

Nicky Silver

One of Nicky Silver's earliest memories is of being dragged by his parents to a psychiatrist at the tender age of four because his teachers found him a distressingly campy toddler. His therapist not only failed to cure him of his effeminacy, but also may have inadvertently encouraged his interest in theatre, that most disreputably homosexual of the performing arts. "I remember playing with puppets, an alligator, and I remember [the doctor] had one leg longer than the other so she walked with a limp. But they were apparently mistaken about curing [me]. Where there's a will, there's a way." Graduating from alligators to people, and from the psychiatrist's office to Off-Broadway, Silver has become a dexterous manipulator, a black farceur in the tradition of Oscar Wilde, Joe Orton and Christopher Durang. Like these playwrights, he delights in pushing the bounds of propriety, in celebrating the inanities that crowd his characters' lives and in dredging up the desires and enmities we are taught to repress. Thus, for example, *Fat Men in Skirts* (1988) is not content with blithely consummating the Freudian family romance. Silver does Sophocles one better by having the son, Bishop, not only sleep with his mother and murder his father and his father's mistress, but eat them, too. For Silver's world is one in which no one is safe from devouring mouths; in which desire leads to ecstasy, despair or death, or more usually, all of them; in which taboos are made to be violated; and in which a tyrannosaurus skeleton towers over a living room to remind its inhabitants that human beings are an all-too-perishable species of carnivore.

Silver's plays mix genres and styles promiscuously, combining *Suddenly Last Summer* with *Gilligan's Island* to make *Fat Men in Skirts* ; or *The Philadelphia Story* and *The Birthday Party* to make *Pterodactyls* (1993). Not content with these perverse amalgams, Silver throws all sorts of other ingredients into the mix: *Medea, Helter Skelter*, the Bible, thirties musical comedies. For he is the first to admit to a fascination with "cross-pollinating genres." A play "may start out as a comedy of manners and become a farce and then a black comedy, then a tragedy." *Free Will & Wanton Lust* (1991), for example, "should be approached as a conflict of theatrical styles." Because Claire is written in the style of Noël Coward and Philip in the style of Brecht, the final struggle between them becomes "a battle between these two aesthetics." And although his appropriation of conflicting styles is less marked in his more recent plays, he still delights in flirting with different aesthetics.

Not only are Silver's plays composed of shards of high and low culture, but his characters also are eccentric, fragmentary beings. "I happen to be a writer," Silver confesses, "who creates people from some very fragmented part of my own personality. Luckily, I have a *very* fragmented personality." These splintered people, not surprisingly, are profoundly mutable. Their names often change, or like Todd in *Pterodactyls*, they are identified by two different names. At the same time, they are almost pathologically unfaithful and liable to fall in love at the slightest provocation. Yet these skittish figures are not pasteboard characters, but obsessive personalities who, in pursuing their unrealizable goals, will sometimes and unpredictably change their object of desire. These characters, like the playthings of some cruel god, never know quite what to expect. Not only are they constantly surprised by what goes on around them, but they are always liable, like Amanda in *The Food Chain* (1994), to "fall into a hole in the time-space continuum." They may suddenly find themselves in a strange location with people they thought they knew who are now doing peculiar, and often inexplicable, things. Or else a ghost will suddenly materialize, as Emma appears to Todd in the last scene of *Pterodactyls*, to remind him of what he would rather forget. For Silver's ghosts function pointedly as mementos of past desires and entanglements, and it is telling that while Emma was alive, she forgets things pathologically, dividing her time between repression and panic. But when dead, "The pain is gone and I remember everything." For death is profoundly utopian, the only state in which love can be fulfilled and the past can be both magically restored and laid to rest: "I remember everything and find that nothing matters." Only by remembering is she able to put all of the pieces together. "I forget . . . that we were ever alive. And everything makes perfect sense."

The disturbances in Silver's plays around questions of memory, the mutability of names and the many potholes in the time-space continuum have a curious way of suspending the laws of cause and effect. Because his characters are so obsessive, the choices they make seem more like reflexes than choices. Most, moreover, remain oblivious to the consequences of their actions. Thus, for example, Ford in *The Food Chain* falls in love with Serge and walks out temporarily on his wife without providing any motivation or explanation for his behavior. Indeed, Ford is distinguished from the other undyingly loquacious characters by his studied silence. He shrugs his shoulders, nods, paces and thinks, but "uh-huh" is the closest thing to language he can muster. Unable or unwilling to explain or justify his actions, this central character—the one who makes a pivotal choice and is also the primary object of others' desire—would, in a more conventional play, be the soul-searching protagonist. Here, however, he remains a cipher. His blankness allows Silver to focus on others' reactions and to imply an equivalence between his silence and their obsessive chatter. For in both cases, characters remain oblivious and inviolate. They talk to each other but don't really listen. As a result, the extremely precise language of Silver's plays tends to careen between stychomythia and monologue—both, in his hands, exercises in disavowal and avoiding confrontation.

Silver's reinvention of surrealistic comedy has the effect of turning conventional ideas of family life upside down. Rather than being a source of stability, the family is imagined (and how Freud would be proud!) as a socializing machine that never quite works the way it is supposed to and so produces all different varieties of perverse desires. It is hardly surprising then, that Silver was so intrigued by a report on *Nightline* of a species of ape that is uniquely nonviolent and omnisexual. His account of simian family life could inspire a dozen, as-yet-unwritten plays: "You throw a banana among ten of them, and there's no fighting. They do, however, have continual, nonstop sex, of every sort—heterosexual, homosexual, mother-son, father-daughter, aunt-uncle—every possible mutation. I thought, hmmm, what a fascinating premise for a play."

June 5, 1997—The apartment of Scott Teagarden (David Savran's partner), New York City

DS: In the introduction to your collection of plays, *Etiquette and Vitriol* [TCG, 1996], you explain that there was no one experience that got you interested in theatre. Why were you attracted to it?
NS: I have no memory of a moment when I was not interested in theatre as form of playacting. I was not like Katharine Hepburn who put on plays in her backyard and had the Hepburn family playing out different parts. But I think I saw it instinctively as a form of escape. Playacting in the schoolyard allowed you to be someone else. But I don't have any memory at all of an event and, as I say in that introduction, the first couple of plays I went to see I don't think I cared for very much. No offense to their creators and artistic staff. But I was too young. We went to see *You're a Good Man, Charlie Brown* when I was in junior high or something. But I was, like, six, and it was too long to sit still. And I didn't care that much for *The Fantasticks* either. My mother had to take me for a walk around the block in the middle. So I think my parents tried to introduce me to formal theatre a little too young. But I remember being in school plays, like, in third grade, and I found it very addictive. I think I always knew I wanted to have some career in the theatre. When someone would ask me, "What do you want to be when you grow up?" I probably went, "I would like to find a career in the theatre." [laughs] I knew I wanted to find some place in that community.

So then rather than plays, it's playacting and performance that drew you to theatre?
Yes. Like most people in the theatre and most people in the arts, I thought it was a safe place in which you could become someone else. Later you find out it's a safe place to vent your spleen, under the guise of literature, and take revenge on those who harmed you. And it was fun—I don't think I was intellectual about it. My initial interest was not sparked by the traditional literature of the theatre. In the new play I've just finished, a character talks about how, when they were little kids, their version of playing house was playing *Dark Shadows*. Do you

remember that TV show, *Dark Shadows*? I used to play *Dark Shadows*, taking all the parts. That's where it begins.

When you were older and started going to see more plays, what work did you find particularly interesting?

When I was in junior high school, I spent my summers at a theatre camp. I'm forever running into people who went to this theatre camp. It went through various names because they would go out of business at the end of every season and so then they'd have to drum up a new name. It still exists, I think, under the name Stage Door Manor. And in those days it ostensibly was a hotbed of sex and drugs—so sue me, I'm only reporting what I heard. I was completely unaware of it. I was very involved in what I was doing and everyone around me was having some kind of maturing experience that I wasn't partaking in. So this place was run by a man named Jack Romano, who has since died and, were this another kind of book, I could fill page after page with sordid details about his life. But I will stick to the facts. And Jack took ten- to fifteen-year-old kids, and you were in five plays in eight weeks. One summer I was in ten. And we had classes during the day and were in plays at night. And he had you doing plays like *Follies* or *The House of Bernarda Alba* when you were ten years old. And this was of course far too sophisticated for us and probably scarred us emotionally but it did alter our aesthetic completely. Because I was aware of Garcia Lorca and Stephen Sondheim at age eleven, which is a little odd. And that's where I think my aesthetic as a theatregoer actually came from.

When I was about ten or eleven my father took me to see *Equus*. I picked the play. It was very thrilling because growing up in the suburbs of Philadelphia, I'd never seen a play in which people talked to the audience. I certainly had never seen naked men on stage, let alone one masturbating on the back of someone else dressed like a horse. I enjoyed this to no end. [laughs] Who could ask for more than Peter Firth stripped to his birthday suit reaching climax at the end of act one on Nugget? It was just a thrilling experience. They talked right to the audience. And I thought this was great. And we went to see *Pacific Overtures* and *A Chorus Line*. This was all still when I was in high school, I guess, or junior high. And then I moved to New York when I was sixteen. I skipped twelfth grade and went early admission to NYU. I didn't think I'd be a writer then and I still didn't know what I would be. I certainly didn't think I was remotely viable as a commercial entity in terms of earning a living as an actor. I knew there were lots of brilliant actors who were a lot better looking, thinner and more gentile than myself. But I came to New York when the New York Shakespeare Festival was at Lincoln Center—there was

Streamers and *Threepenny Opera* with Raul Julia and *The Cherry Orchard* with Irene Worth and *for colored girls* was on Broadway. I think it was just about that time that Christopher Durang and Wendy Wasserstein were emerging at Playwrights Horizons. This was an incredibly exciting time to be going to the theatre in New York City. And I assume a lot of it had to do with economics. I find the theatre now much more conservative and afraid to develop new writers or take risks. And that has engendered a more conservative aesthetic on all fronts.

And studying at NYU—I went to the Experimental Theater Wing—the idea was that you did a play with Liz Swados for four weeks, then with Charles Ludlam, then with Mabou Mines, and we were supposed to be picking an aesthetic that appealed to us. Rather than doing that, I picked from each aesthetic something that I could then manipulate in my own writing to create my own kind of theatre.

As I was reading through your work, I was really struck by the numerous references to so many plays and playwrights. And it seems to me that there are particular texts that really haunt your work, like *Suddenly Last Summer*.
As in *Fat Men* .

The mental institution, incarceration . . .
But a lot of it's unconscious.

Yes. And *Long Day's Journey into Night*.
And what do those have in common? Katharine Hepburn! It's not so much plays, just the career of Katharine Hepburn.

But not only plays, also *Gilligan's Island*, thirties musical comedies, Noël Coward, Brecht. You talk about not choosing an aesthetic but manipulating several. It seems to me that your method is to take elements from these works and put them together in unexpected ways.
I would agree with that. But I am probably moving away from it a little bit. I was much more interested in that technique when I started. I've always been very specifically aware of genre and juxtaposition of genres in theatre and what that does to an audience—how it helps an audience into the world of the play, how it upsets them once they're there. But to go back to your first point, I have absolutely no classical education whatsoever. It never ceases to amuse me when *Fat Men in Skirts* is produced and I go on the Internet and read these reviews—you keep razor blades and sleeping pills nearby and read them only to satisfy some masochistic streak. And critics are constantly pointing out Greek references. And I know that Oedipus was in love with his mother and he killed his father—is that accurate?

Yes.

And Electra is the opposite because in Freud it's the opposite, so I'm assuming she was in love with her father and killed her mother. And a lot of Greek people put their eyes out. But I never read much Shakespeare. I was in *A Midsummer Night's Dream* once. I have no classical education whatsoever which means that all of my literary heritage begins with movies and television. I mean, Philip Barry is, to me, the classics. And *Philadelphia Story* is very heavily evoked in *Pterodactyls*. That to me is a classical reference. I know that Aristotle wrote *The Birds*.

Aristophanes.

See, there you are. Aristotle was the one who slept with little boys.

They all did.

Oh, to have been a Greek! But seriously, I have no education in this area. So the aesthetic that informs my writing and the history that's evoked in it goes back only as far as about 1930. But I think I am moving away from it. There are clearly identifiable genres in *Fat Men in Skirts* but if you look at *Fit to Be Tied* [1996] or *Raised in Captivity* [1995], they're juxtaposed—hopefully—in a much more fluid and seamless manner. I don't know what else there is to mix. I'll have to learn some more aesthetics before I can mix any more of them.

I've also been thinking about your work in terms of a tradition of gay male playwrights, from Oscar Wilde to Noël Coward, from Joe Orton to Christopher Durang.

Which just goes to show you again how powerful the collective unconscious is. Christopher Durang was being produced when I first came to New York so I saw a lot of his plays. And I really like Bea Lillie's voice so I have Noël Coward CDs. And I saw *The Vortex* upon which *Free Will* is based. I think that was the only Noël Coward play I'd ever seen. I've never read or seen an entire Oscar Wilde play. Joe Orton, on the other hand, luckily . . . I was just going to say, luckily he died [laughs], so I've read everything. Had he lived a long time and continued to write, my attention span would not have made it. But it was certainly not lucky that he died young. And he's the most important figure of the twentieth century to me. He's somebody who really learned to use accessible comedic form in a subversive manner. That had never, as far as I know, really been done before. So he's like the grandfather of all of them. Oscar Wilde—somebody, I think at the Huntington, gave me this giant, fat book about Oscar Wilde, but it would make my stomach hurt because I would read in bed and it was very heavy [laughs], so I never read much of it. The artistic director of the Huntington said that he assumed that I was referring to Wilde in the opening scene of *Pterodactyls*. There's a scene in *The Importance of Being Earnest* in which, I assume, someone brings his fiancée and is interviewed by the matriarch of the family. I had no idea of this, but what it shows is the influence of Oscar Wilde in our culture because it has become an archetypal scene. You don't have to know where it started because it's just filtered down. This interview should be encouraging to all those little children who don't pay attention in school.

But one thing that distinguishes your work from these playwrights, even Durang to some extent, is the way you play around with different styles and devices, using direct address, flashbacks, fantasies, dreams. And I find that plasticity of your work fascinating.

It is plastic, isn't it? [laughs] Because I would say I'm just trying to tell stories in interesting ways. It has never been that interesting to me, for example, just to amuse, although I think it is most important to amuse. Unless you amuse you don't engage. And I think that part of it has to do with the era in which I'm writing. We have a shrinking and jaded theatrical audience and I think that plays have to do more than they used to. They're plunking down their forty-five dollars for an Off-Broadway play that they have to laugh at and cry at and be intellectually stimulated by at the same time. When you went to see *Tonight at 8:30*, it was quite enough to chuckle.

As I was reading your plays, I kept thinking about your characters' names.

A more goyish group of names you'll never find. This is a completely conscious thing. There are some Jewish names, like the Woodnicks. After I graduated college, I wrote a play called *The Bridal Hunt* [1982] and I gave it to a friend of mine who worked at the Phoenix Theatre company and she gave it to the head of script development and they did a reading and it went great and they went out of business the next day. And then David Copeland, who was the head of script development there, optioned it personally and tried to get a commercial production. So here I am fresh out of college and this is really great. But he couldn't raise the money largely because it was about an overtly Jewish family and it was extremely negative and hostile. I remember we did this reading of it at The Dramatists Guild and Estelle Getty was very unpleasant about the whole thing. She said she'd do the play but she found it offensive. And I remember people sort of accusing me of being anti-Semitic in writing the play and I explained that I wasn't being anti-Semitic, I was just writing about my own parents. That was my flip answer but people were offended by it. And I looked around and I realized that what gets produced—whatever its real origins are—seldom looks Jewish. There's such a big Jewish audience and they want to see themselves reflected and yet they want it to be distanced. And I very consciously decided not to write a play about Jews. I did *Food Chain* much later, in a much lighter mode when I could get something produced. Tina Howe said in the introduction to one of her books that she looked around to see what was getting produced and she saw that plays in unusual settings were getting produced. So then she wrote *Museum*, I think that's the first one, and then the thing on the beach. I'm sure it's not called "The Thing on the Beach," because that sounds like a horror film. *Coastal Disturbances*. Writing is so largely unconscious that I think you should be grateful for any conscious decisions you can come up with.

But you so frequently and deliberately foreground names. When, for example, Claire forgets Amy's name and reels off lists of names beginning with A.
And Todd means "death" in German. There's the naming the children in *Fat Men in Skirts* and *Raised in Captivity*. And there's ten years between these plays. Well, you know Nicky isn't my real name. That's probably where it comes from. Very few people—the bank and my father—know my real name. My real name is Edward Albee. No. [laughs] I was given the name Nicky as an infant. I didn't pick it.

And I was thinking about the mutability of names: Todd/Buzz, Amy—having all these different names. It's as though your characters—names, identities and all—can be easily transformed. I almost see them as these dream figures that are constantly mutating.
I don't think of them as mutating at all, or changeable. I think they are exposable, which is different. Because I think of characters as having layers that they reveal as the play continues. A really clear example is *Free Will* in which you first think Philip is comic and a minor character and you like him. And then he has that twenty-minute monologue in the second act and it starts off with very revelatory jokes. And if you're intellectually processing it, you feel, because of his relationship to his mother, that he's a victim. And at the end of that twenty-minute monologue the rug is pulled out from under you because he reveals something about himself that alters your perception of him completely— that he has actually killed someone. And I think the same thing is true of Claire in reverse. She's really amusing and she's very archetypal. If you look at that character in the first five pages you say this is a really jaded socialite. And as the play progresses, you just accept that her children are sad, pathetic figures that she's bullied or ignored and it is through her monologue that you get to perceive her as something else,

as quite human and sort of sad. So I don't think of them as changing. I think of them as revealing different aspects of themselves.

So you see that as an unmasking?
Yes.

Getting to the truth about them?
Absolutely. I've directed a couple productions of *Free Will* and I've directed other productions of my plays—but I will probably never do it in New York because you might just as well paint a target on your ass and stand in Times Square—but there are often moments in plays, and I mention *Free Will* again, when I will say to an actor, "Use this passage, if you can, just to relax and to get to a point where you're not acting and you're just you, and say it as simply as possible." Because that is when communication really happens. And that is when we'll see the real person, just existing. And it's usually when the character is most revelatory as well and comes to some kind of truth. It's an odd thing. Actors are always very reluctant to do it until they try it and say, "I see it, I know what that is." Just recently we were working on a workshop of an old play of mine called *My Marriage to Ernest Borgnine* [1996] and I said to one of the actresses, "Use this last speech to end as yourself. Go from the character to yourself in the most relaxed way that you can be." And it wasn't jarring. It was just this subtle, gradual thing. I don't think anyone watching went, "She dropped the character." That isn't what it felt like. We simply had peeled back a layer of facade. So I do think of it as unmasking and getting to some kind of truth.

What's your process of writing? What do you start with? An outline, characters, a line of dialogue, a scene?
It is different for every play. In general, I'll start to think either about a situation or a question. And I start to think about them pretty much in tandem, actually. I don't work from an outline and I start to think about characters. I'll think about a play for four or five months before I write anything. But I know a lot before I sit down to write. I don't know everything, but I know who the basic characters are and what question I'm trying to figure out the answer to. The play does not end up being an answer to the question nor does it end up only addressing the question. It is where I start. Regarding *Raised in Captivity*: I really have no religious life at this point and I don't travel with a bunch of people who do. I feel that the country is very polarized between the devoutly religious and the nonreligious. And what do we nonreligious types do with this guilt that we have for whatever reason? Having no system of purg-

ing it, how do we function? That is really what I wanted to explore. Now I had to question why I wanted to explore it a little bit, too. And other questions immediately come up as soon as you start thinking about characters. Because I do think that that is what that play is about. It is also about how do you love someone who behaves outside of your own personal moral code, which is what a lot of my plays are about. So, I start with a question and that stimulates character and that in turn stimulates other questions, and I think and think and think and think and I have a basic structural idea before I sit down to write. I have to know enough about the play so that my unconscious can function. Because the first draft is usually about half as long as the play will end up being. And the second draft is twice as long. And the third draft is what I call the first draft. And that's very quick, that's five weeks. But I wait. People think I write a lot. And they say you have to write every day, but I think the only thing you have to do every day is go to the bathroom, eat and sleep. If it works, that's great, but that's never interested me. I don't write until I have to. And there's a big difference between the play you have to write and the play you want to write and you can feel it on the page.

So it's important to you to let your unconscious do a lot of the work.
Yes.

Do you have particular exercises?
LSD. No. [laughs] When I've had to speak to students I don't know how to tell them to free their unconscious. You either have access to it or you don't, as far as I can tell. I don't ever remember my dreams, which I think might actually help. But I don't know how to make you not remember your dreams. I would say that therapy probably helps. Now I haven't been in therapy for a number of years, but I was in therapy when I was younger and it does help just to shake things up and maybe get in touch with yourself a little bit.

Are the endings of your plays usually surprises or do you know them in advance?
I know well in advance. I may not know the exact ending when I start, although I often do. I have to know it very early on or I'll get frustrated. And I've been known to work on a play for eight weeks, walk to the garbage shoot and throw it and memories of it down the shoot. Because I try not to edit myself or censor myself when I'm writing, which means that sometimes you're going to get just pure garbage. The exception is *Food Chain* which was written in three sittings to amuse myself. I mean

I had a thesis statement of the play, but it was a completely different process. It was pure unconscious and fun and there was nothing I was really struggling with. I knew what the idea of the play was—that some people are unhappy and others are happy—so it was very different.

What makes for a good production of your work?

That's really hard to answer because it's so intangible. I am more prone to answer what makes for a bad one—of which I've seen many—so I'll answer it in my head and reverse it. I've opened four plays and done five—*Fat Men* at Naked Angels—in the last three and a half years in New York. And I've been really happy with the productions. They weren't always pleasant experiences but for the most part they were, and I thought they were beautiful productions. And I have also traveled quite a bit and seen a lot of productions of plays of mine. What makes a good one is first of all intelligence. As stupid as I've said I am—and I've said it in terms of my classical training and background—you have to be at least as smart as that to know how to do the plays. Because they have a lot of style, so you have to know how to play various styles and remain emotionally connected and appreciate how the styles are going to rub up against each other. A lot of really, really fine actors have auditioned for plays of mine who are naturalistically based in their training, particularly film actors, and they're great actors, but they don't know how to connect to the material and have it look and feel like a Noël Coward play and then suddenly pull the rug out from under it and have it feel like naturalism at the same time. So that's really hard. The most important thing is being smart. Simplicity helps quite a bit because I think my plays are really, really hard. I'm forever asked, "What do you learn from readings?" I learn nothing except that they're too hard to do readings of. [laughs] None of them requires much money. They're small shows for small casts. Sometimes they're big shows but they're physically small, a small number of people. They've sometimes been done grandly in New York. *Food Chain* certainly had a lovely turntable but it was also done in Washington probably for a quarter of that money to thrilling effect. In other words, you don't need money. You need to be smart. You need to be clean.

It seems to me that they may be difficult for a lot of American actors because they're not really American naturalism.

No. Naturalism is a style that is relatively new in the theatre. But I thought it was dead. It seemed dead a few years ago and it's having quite the upswing at the moment. I guess it's important to know how to do it but I don't know why. It costs almost nothing now to get a video camera and make an independent film. Just do that if that's what you're interested in. Ooh, don't I sound bitter. [laughs]

Whom do you write for?
Me. I try to make myself laugh. I try to move myself. And I think I'm an average theatregoer. All you can do is make a piece of theatre that you would like to see.

In your plays your characters often confess, and although your work does not seem especially autobiographical to me, I know that playwrights happen to write their lives as they're writing their plays. Could you talk about that?
There are a lot of autobiographical details scattered throughout the plays. And I think that probably happens with every writer no matter what you're writing about. That's your frame of reference. I was raised in the suburbs of Philadelphia and I set *Pterodactyls* there. I was not raised in the country so you'll never see a play set, say, in the hills of Wyoming. My father was a businessman. He's retired. My mother did run a needlepoint store. I worked in Barney's as a salesperson where I learned what rich people are like and the names of designers. So there's always a lot of specific autobiographical detail in plays. There are also, in most of my plays, one or two moments when it goes beyond detail, when I am painting an image or showing something that I lived through. Fran Liebowitz once said that growing up is realizing that your life would not make a good novel, and I think that is accurate. However, I think that there are images in one's life that, when manipulated for the sake of storytelling, are best simply related. In *Raised in Captivity*, the description of Simon as he looked upon dying was simply a report, as accurately as I could relate, of being with someone whom I loved very much upon dying. Now, not having murdered someone, that I know of, Dylan's description of what it's like to murder someone came largely from my imagination and from talking to someone who has murdered someone. So there is a mix of conscious detail and conscious memory. Also, I think all plays are reflections of how you view your position in the world at that moment and so in that sense they are auto-biographical. *Fat Men in Skirts* is a very angry and unforgiving play, filled with self-loathing. The anger of *Pterodactyls*, five or six years later, is no longer turned inward. I'm not aware of this at all while I'm writing, it's only with some distance. By then the anger is turned out, culturally. But I was in therapy between *Fat Men in Skirts* and *Pterodactyls*, and I think I did learn to say, there's nothing wrong with me, it's the world or the government, such that it is. I think *Pterodactyls* is a very political play. And I felt that *Fit to Be Tied* was, among other things, the

end of that cycle. Because it's a play that is completely forgiving. And it does say we've done these things to each other in the past, but at the end of that play relationships are restored and characters have surprised each other by being more decent than they ever suspected they would be. So in that sense they're autobiographical. They're never about what happens to you, or my life would have been much more interesting and colorful. But they're autobiographical in that they reveal your view of the world.

One reason why I don't see them as being especially autobiographical is that there are so many empathic characters in your plays. There are many characters whom we both identify with and recoil from.

That's craft and taste and, hopefully, dignity, because it offends me to see plays—and I don't want to name names—in which you can spot who the playwright thinks he is and it's usually a noble person who is the victim of the rest of the world. If *Pterodactyls* were going to be seen as autobiography, I would clearly be Todd. He's the Tom character of the play. He opens the play with a monologue and thus is your way in structurally, but I make it clear in the notes, and I think it's clear in the writing that, if anything, Todd is the most morally reprehensible because he seems to know a little better and does horribly destructive things anyway. It's very important to me not to paint yourself as a victim of a culture and without flaw because we're all flawed. Anyone of us could be the central character in the play. And I always say to actors, "All the characters always think it's a play about them." And that's partly the reason they talk to the audience so much because they're a little bitter when anyone else gets the audience's attention for even a moment.

As I was reading through your work, I couldn't help but notice the incest, the cannibalism. . . .

There's not cannibalism in a lot of the plays.

Principally *Fat Men in Skirts*.

There is incest in several plays.

Incest or almost incest.

The whiff of incest. Cannibalism and incest are often coupled together but they're so different. They're coupled together because of *Fat Men in Skirts*. Incest is, I think, rampant in our culture. I don't really think cannibalism is rampant in our culture. [laughs] I mean maybe something's going on that I don't know about.

But isn't there the Brechtian cannibalism of men eating men?
As in that song, "What Keeps a Man Alive?" Yes, granted. But I'm talk-ing about real, let's put-it-on-a-spit-over-a-rotisserie kind of cannibal-ism. I try not to get uptown past 75th Street and I'm sure maybe it goes on up there, but I'm not aware of it if it does.

But one thing the two have in common is a violation of boundaries.
"Boundaries are for countries on a map, not human beings." *Raised in Captivity*.

So much of your work is about that, troubling boundaries, characters violating boundaries.
I have no boundaries. I *do* have boundaries. I have a lot of boundaries personally. Tremendous boundaries. Someone once, in a newspaper, asked me of my inability to edit myself as a human being. And I said, "I am in complete control. I can edit myself, I simply see no merit in doing so." Even that answer was edited. It was carefully calculated for what-ever effect I wanted it to have. I would say, though, that I was raised with insufficient boundaries and I have developed stronger boundaries, probably, because of it. And I think that there is a lack of boundaries in the culture in general.

So you see cultural boundaries as being very important.
I think we're better off. More boundaries. More manners, less realism, less honesty. Wouldn't you rather be in London where everybody's pleasant and doesn't mean it? [laughs] What a much better way to live!

I also noticed how much your work is about loss, characters thinking about death or coming back from the dead. Virtually all of your characters have lost people and things that are dear to them.
It's sad, isn't it?

But they all find ways of dealing with that. I read your plays as being about memory as an antidote to loss. Emma forgetting her past and having to reconstruct it. And then she herself returns to haunt the living. And this strikes me as a very Jewish preoccupation.
Really?

Since there's no official belief in an afterlife, the way you keep people alive is by remembering them.
I certainly think loss is one of the most vast of common denominators, and that theatre is a way of staging those feelings of loss. That's what

theatre's for, to make things better than they were to begin with. *Fat Men in Skirts* was written before anyone I was close to had died. And then between *Fat Men in Skirts* and *Pterodactyls*, several years passed and AIDS comes into America and I immediately lost many people, including the person to whom, at the time, I was closest. The reason I bring it up is that I don't know necessarily . . . mom comes back from the dead in *Fat Men in Skirts*. So there is already the sense of trying to recapture something and yet I don't think I had experienced any obvious and tangible loss. So I think it has to do with the fact that you can lose things (a) without knowing it, and (b) without them being tangible.

It seems to me that theatre is a very important site for that, for remembering. I'm not sure why.

My guess would be that theatre allows for abstraction so much more than other media. It's a freer journey for the viewer. A movie is a flat, two-dimensional thing, a photograph. In our culture the theatre has learned to represent things in abstract terms. And that allows a community of people to look at something and to see it differently, even though they're all looking at the same thing. And I think that makes for a more profound experience. My God, I don't know what I just said or what I meant!

Didn't you used to ask people about critics? I want to talk about critics.

I did for *In Their Own Words* [TCG, 1988], but the best answers the playwrights then decided they wanted cut from the book.

Here's what I would say. I want to talk about it because I just had this experience and I can't imagine that people can understand what it's like. *Raised in Captivity* is my favorite of my plays that you've read. It did very well in New York. There are people who hated it and it has its champions. In the past year I've been to see it in Germany where I thought it was dreadful. I think it did well, however. I know that it did well in some Scandinavian country. And I've just returned from Washington. I've done three plays at the Woolly Mammoth Theatre, two of which I've directed myself. And this time I saw two or three rehearsals and I really felt that I was battling and struggling to get the show into shape. Lloyd Rose, who's the lead critic of the *Washington Post* has always been very supportive of me. The daily review came out and I called the theatre and asked, "Is it good or bad?" And they read me the first couple sentences and apparently they didn't like the play. And I said, "I don't want to hear any more," and hung up. You are constantly, constantly, constantly emotionally vulnerable. It's not that the play opens in New York and you're done. Every two weeks in this country someone is attacking you. And granted, it's not like being on television and being attacked, but it feels the same. People ask you all the time, "Do you learn anything from reviews?" Yes, you learn how much money you're going to make from that engagement and if it's New York, you learn how much money you're going to make that year around the world. How could I learn anything from Lloyd Rose? I don't begrudge critics their job. People used to decry Frank Rich for having so much power. Well we gave him the power. We said, "We're too stupid to make up our own minds. Please tell us what's good and what's bad." And I think it's great to be a consumer advocate, even a shaper of aesthetic on a big spectrum. But young writers who buy this book, like I did your first one, should understand that rehearsals are the most fun you're ever going to have in your life. Writing is occasionally pleasant. And the rest of it is a continual emotional horror. The joy of opening to a great review lasts about three hours. And tomorrow the audience can hate it anyway.

You mentioned before that you consider Joe Orton a subversive writer. Do you think of your own work as subversive?

Not remotely. I do think that Joe Orton was trying to be subversive. He defaced library books. I've never defaced a library book nor have I ever returned one. [laughs] No, I don't think I'm subversive. *Pterodactyls*, more than any other play, was a little angry. But I don't think it's possible to be subversive anymore, certainly not in the theatre. *Fat Men in Skirts* is done constantly by small theatres—people do it and they think it's shocking. But I don't think it's so shocking. There are certain things you could do on stage that would shock people. The problem is, you wouldn't get it produced, and if you did, it would be preaching to the converted. I guess performance art can be shocking, but I don't go to performance art and it doesn't interest me. And I think only the unshockable go. So I don't think that theatre can be subversive. *Pterodactyls* and *Raised in Captivity* are very political. *Raised in Captivity* is very antideath penalty. As we do this interview, the world is waiting to see if Timothy McVeigh gets the death penalty and I can't help but feel sad for the world. They should kill him if they want to kill him. But we are in a giant Roman colosseum waiting for the emperor to go thumbs up or thumbs down, as if this were some joyous, fun carnival. It's very grim. I don't think there's much I could do to shock a world in which this is our entertainment. How could you shock anybody?

Perhaps more shocking would be to tell people what they know, but have repressed or forgotten. *Pterodactyls* begins with Todd's history of the world. . . .

But he's gotten it wrong.

Yes, but it's one of the few places in your work in which history is invoked. And I don't generally think of your work as historical—it's all set in contemporary urban culture. But do you think of it as engaging with any historical issues? Or you might want to think of it more broadly in terms of social issues.

Yes, political issues, social issues. I feel that *Pterodactyls* is dated, for instance.

Why?

It isn't dated in its bigger issues but it is dated in its attitude toward AIDS. People, thank God, are living much, much longer than they used to. It's now a period play. But it's also very much about the politics of denial and its costs. *Raised in Captivity* is absolutely against the death penalty. It says, punishment helps the punisher. It has nothing to do with the punished. *Fat Men in Skirts*, *The Food Chain*—so many F titles—explores the might of the beauty myth. Although it doesn't really explore it, it's a given—it's like writing a play that's against death and pro-birth. As a play, it's very pro-gravity. [laughs] A lot of the plays consider how we love someone who falls outside of our moral world. And it's dealt with in lots of ways. The father in *Pterodactyls* who calls his son Buzz thinks he loves his son very much. He of course doesn't. He loves someone called Buzz. And then there's the idea of abstracting people to suit our own emotional needs. You can only kill people when you manage to abstract them. Just as Arthur in *Pterodactyls* can totally love his son when he can abstract him. You can't kill someone when you know them, only when they are "the murderer" or "the Nazi" or whatever.

A fantasy.

Right. I think that all of it comes down to our uninterest in seeing each other.

And your work is very much engaged with that problem.

What isn't?

Which I guess makes you a moralist.

I don't think of myself as one but I don't have a problem being perceived as one. I think of myself as nonjudgmental. But everybody's judgmental. I'm just not judgmental of what most people are. Like, I think sleeping with your father—good for you! [laughs] Leave a twenty-dollar bill on the bureau and don't slam the door. If it doesn't affect me, I couldn't care. Most people have loud opinions about things that have no bearing on them.

As you know, theatre's not doing very well these days. Broadway is dominated by a few megamusicals. So-called straight plays have a hard time of making a go of it. You're lucky, but you're one of a handful.

I know I'm lucky. Although I will tell you about an interview I gave with someone named Leonard Jacobs for *Encore* magazine who showed up about an hour late and didn't apologize. His first question to me was, "Why do you think you have such a big, fabulous career when there are so many talented writers out there?" Mr. Jacobs is apparently a writer of some aspiration. [laughs] "Well," I said, "you're wrong on both counts. I don't have such a big and fabulous career and there aren't so many talented writers out there." The whole interview then went to hell in a handcart. But I think that it's a vicious cycle: the theatre doesn't nurture writers and therefore writers don't write for it. So everyone will say it's all economics. Oh God, I don't buy it and I'll tell you why. And I know how lucky I am. But I wanted a life in the theatre. I worked at a place called the Vortex Theatre Company for six or seven years, it was a showcase theatre that Sophie from *Sophie's Choice* would have taken one look at and said, "I'm not working here." It was so grim. It's beefed up a little now, but they do mainly soft-core male pornography plays called, like, *Cute Boys in Their Underpants Go Bananas*. I haven't seen them, so I'm not bad-mouthing them. But it was grim. Nobody got paid. I worked two jobs sometimes and did plays with my friends when I paid for the rehearsal space and we rehearsed three nights a week for four weeks and then the man who ran it gave us the space and a handful of lighting instruments. And he did this because he saw something in my work. But had he not given it to us, I probably would have rented it with my earnings. I still live in the same apartment, but I had a roommate then. And it's tiny, tiny, tiny. I didn't have a vacation that I paid for myself until I was thirty-four. That was what I wanted to do. And all my friends were in the plays and none of us got paid. We built the sets ourselves the night before. And I eventually bulldozed my way in to the American theatre community.

So yes, there are fewer opportunities. But I don't know that I buy that it's just economics. I think it has to do with the fact that a lot of people, after a year of that, would have said, "Either I can get a job where I make more money or I'll go try to write sitcoms." And that has to do with love of the theatre. And we don't engender it. It's really not important to the country. And we're fooling ourselves if we think it is. It's a wonderful thing. It's important to me. It's important to some. It's not important to most people. I'm not suggesting that it should be. It doesn't affect their lives. It doesn't speak to them. They don't understand it. They don't want to understand it. More power to them. And people are always saying that theatre is dying. I don't think theatre is dying. Theatre is changing. It has evolved into either amusement parks or an intimate kind of theatre that speaks to a small group of people. What we will no longer have, it seems to me, are big plays that speak to a few people. I've never really written big plays, so it's not going to affect me much. Every now and then, maybe, somebody can pull it together financially. *Angels in America* may very well be the last big play that spoke to a handful of people. It was a big success, but next to a Spielberg picture, it played to a handful of people. At the end of *Pterodactyls* when Todd is saying that the dinosaurs died and some people think it was this and some people think it was that and some people think it was just evolution and no tragedy. It feels sad to me, but is it sad? I don't know. I don't know what will replace it or what our culture will be like. I tried to be big about it and say, if nobody wants it, is it my right like a spoiled baby to say, "You gotta give me money to make it happen." From my position, I'm supposed to say, "The NEA has to support more theatre and we have to make sure the theatre doesn't change or die." And I have benefited from funding, not personally, but I've worked at Playwrights Horizons and the Vineyard Theatre and have had plays produced that I'm sure would not have been produced were it not for grants. And so I'm grateful for it. But I don't know what gives me the right to say, "You have to give me money," if you don't want to. So I see both sides of it. It's been in a period of very slow transition for a lot of years and I think it will continue. As for my plays: five characters, can be done on a bare stage. Enough people want to see that so it will still be around. It's the big spectacle play that will be gone. So if it goes, it goes. It's been going since Kaufman and Hart.

Have you written for Hollywood?
I've written for the city of Hollywood, yes. [laughs] I have written some pictures. They have not been made.

Are any of them adaptations of your plays?
Just for fun I wrote a screenplay of *Raised in Captivity* in which there has been interest at various times and that may yet come to pass. I do not count on that happening. I don't need it for money because I have the opportunity every now and then to get hired to write a big goofy Hollywood movie. But they don't get made. Eventually I hope one will, or they'll stop hiring me.

Why haven't any been made yet?
For various and sundry reasons. I don't think that quality has much to do with the making of Hollywood product in general. I have worked

extensively with Goldie Hawn, who has taken a liking to my writing, which is probably an odd thing to think about, and found her to be remarkably generous and supportive. I haven't worked with any other big actors. The fact of the matter is that when you get notes from studios, sometimes they're hideously stupid and you read them and can't believe it. I'd say that about a third of them—in my opinion—would make it a worse movie. A third of them are neither here nor there, they're just taste, like should she be brunette or blonde? And a third of them will actually make it a better movie. They're the boss and you try your best to accommodate them. And even if you think it's going to make it a worse movie, what do you know? If everybody knew what made a good movie we'd only have good movies. So you do your best to accommodate them and the fact is when you get those notes, it's a bad hour. After that, the act of writing is pleasant. I don't buy writers who go, "It's so horrible, they're so mean." Then don't do it. Who's making you do it? You'll never, for instance, see a play from me about the vipers of Hollywood. They pay you too well. It's hush money and you should just hush [laughs] because it always hurts to get notes. It's not bad. You get to fly first class to Los Angeles for meetings and sit next to, like, Anne Bancroft and Marky Mark. That's really groovy. I have a very good time with that part.

What are your theatre plans now?
I have a new play called *The Maiden's Prayer* [1998] that I will be doing at the Vineyard in the January-February slot. I had originally decided not to do another new play until the following season, feeling that I had done too many plays in too short a time. That's a career concern. And I don't think you really can plan your career. You can only plan your work. And before I had a career, when I was just making plays, I would have done two more plays in the past year. And it's completely different from my previous work. It's about two sisters and the various men in their lives and it's about need and unrequited love. Are there any ghosts? I don't think there are any ghosts. There's no mother. No mother is even mentioned. One of the things the play is about is the difference between need and love. And some of them actually learn it and some of them don't. And it's very ugly for the ones who don't. [laughs] And I look forward to doing it because I think of it as the flip side of *Food Chain* in many ways because there's a beautiful man and a beautiful woman. They're not comically beautiful as in *Food Chain*, they're just beautiful, but it's about how they use their beauty to get what they need in life and how it hasn't ultimately served them well. But it's always fun to sit through those auditions.

Anything you want to add?

I'm just afraid because of that tirade that I sound bitter. I just think I am so lucky to earn a living doing what I wanted to do since I was a little kid. There is no greater experience than the first read as far as I'm concerned, or going to rehearsal every day. I do love what I do and I will do it until nobody wants me to do it anymore. Then I'll just eat a lot.

Anna Deavere Smith

Anna Deavere Smith's work is all about crossing boundaries—bound-aries between black and white, female and male, Jew and gentile, privileged and underclass, fact and fiction, playwright and actor, theatre and performance art, participant and observer, self and other. In cross-ing and recrossing these boundaries, she offers a searching and unset-tling examination of how identities are consolidated and performed in a nation grown increasingly fragmented. Imagining society as a kind of theatre, she fills the stage with the many people she has interviewed as part of her ongoing project entitled *On the Road: A Search for American Character*. Impersonating a panoply of personalities, letting them tell their own stories, she endeavors "to find American character in the ways that people speak." Her impersonations are often startlingly accu-rate and probing, and thus quite different from the caricatures of a Tracy Ullman or an Eddie Murphy, being far more nuanced, exact and exacting. For unlike most impersonators, she is intent less on produc-ing a smooth, convincing—and highly judgmental—representation of an ostensibly coherent personality than on revealing the fact that peo-ple never do exactly what they think they're doing, that intentions and actions never quite line up, and that effect does not issue from cause as straightforwardly as one would think. Implicitly foregrounding those moments when words fail, she focuses on the hesitations, the stammering, the "syntactical breaks" inside of which "American character is alive." For her, language is the key because it provides a "photograph" of what is "unseen" in an America in which identity is always "in motion." In an era in which questions of identity—racial, gendered, sexual and otherwise—almost completely dominate the discourse of leftist political culture, she interrogates the boundaries that have been drawn to produce the illusion that our identities are stable, coherent, essential and unchangeable.

Smith explains that although *On the Road* emerged from many different experiences and endeavors, TV talk shows were a pivotal influence. Tuning in *The Tonight Show* one night in 1979, she saw a "very uncomfortable" Johnny Carson interview Sophia Loren. The latter was "so quiet and in control" and "sexy" that she "managed to disrupt the whole show by just refusing to participate" in its rhythm. She was followed by a "hysterical" Joan Rivers who, disparaging herself in relation to Loren, rattled off a string of self-hating jokes that made Carson laugh so hard that he cried. Finally, the Hines Brothers came on and tap-danced. "I turned off the TV set," Smith remembers, "and said, 'This is America.' A European beauty comes on and suddenly we have no voice, no culture. A comedienne comes on and talks about the European beauty. And some black men come out and tap-dance." For Smith, the power of this performance comes in part from its processional nature, from the stark contradictions between and among the different guests and from the very format of the talk show itself. For her work clearly issues from and illuminates an America defined not only by conflicting identities but also by a compulsion to speak, to confess. For talk shows have in recent years become the dominant feature of daytime TV and the mark of a culture that has become obsessively confessional, in which one exists only insofar as one is able to tell one's story, in which everyone has a secret and secretly relishes playing both exhibitionist and voyeur, and in which the public sphere has been overwhelmed by the personal, the private and the sexual.

Talking back to this culture of confession, Smith's work pointedly explores the collisions among the different narratives that people use to construct their selves and justify their actions. *Fires in the Mirror: Crown Heights, Brooklyn, and Other Identities* (1992) is an exploration of the tensions between African-Americans and Hasidic Jews after a Caribbean-American boy was killed in Crown Heights by a rabbi's motorcade and a Jewish student slain in retaliation. Having interviewed most of the principals (and many others) whose opinions and points of view both dispute the chain of events and illuminate what is at stake in Crown Heights, she lets these contestants, in effect, sit down and talk with each other for the first time. By focusing on the deployment of language by each of her subjects—the avowals, evasions and circumlocutions—she holds a mirror up to the persons and the events, foregrounding the powerful, and indeed tragic, emotions produced in all those affected by the double homicide and the relationship between these emotions and the uneasy coexistence of two radically dissimilar cultures on the same streets. Yet, the purpose of this interrogation is not to discover the guilt or innocence of the parties involved. Quite the contrary. Instead, the collision of points of view in *Fires in the Mirror* constantly broadens the scope of the inquiry, demonstrating that one cannot hope to understand the tragedy of Crown Heights without knowing the complex and intractable histories of racism, anti-Semitism and economic deprivation.

Twilight: Los Angeles, 1992 (1993) focuses on an even more complex series of events, the uprising that followed the first trial and acquittal of the police officers whose savage beating of Rodney King was video-taped and broadcast around the world. By presenting an extraordinary array of persons from many different communities, the piece dissects what Smith calls a "new racial frontier" that "isn't about black or white" but "multiple conflicts. Latinos. Blacks. Asians. Police." Unlike *Fires in the Mirror*, whose linear structure moves inexorably toward the almost unbearably moving testimony of the father of Gavin Cato, the slain boy, *Twilight*, like the city it reflects, is more diffuse, circular, sly. It also focuses more explicitly on the very construction and deconstruction of boundaries, on the moment when the light is fading, that "surreal time of day," the "moment of ambivalence/and ambiguity." In the time of twilight—which is the time of America at the end of the millennium—the "hard outlines of what we see in the daylight," the belief in the power of light to clarify and enlighten, is called into question. For the piece also suggests that twilight is the time when ghosts walk, when we remember and we forget, when history presses in upon us, when we are haunted by the loss of our own private dreams and another more pub-lic dream (so memorably envisioned by another King) of a multiracial, equitable America.

Smith emphasizes that her work is far more about "looking at the *processes*" of "social problems" than "looking for *solutions*." For both *Fires in the Mirror* and *Twilight* allow the spectator, like Smith herself, to participate in social and political process, to empathize, analyze and understand that all conclusions are provisional in an America that is also very much in process. Literally standing in for a host of social actors, she puts her body on the line, using it to invoke the shadows of

DS: How did you get interested in theatre?
ADS: I don't think I can remember my first play, but whenever I would go and see a play—as opposed to presentations at church or skits or school things—it was a very big treat for me. I wish I could remember the first one. Of course in some ways it began with puppet shows. Even when I was little, at parties there were puppet shows, and to me that was great and special. I think I understood the difference between that and the movies or television, which were also a very special thing. We didn't watch a lot of TV, hardly any, and going to the movies was a really big deal. I think the first movie I saw in a movie theatre was with Hayley Mills and Agnes Morehead, *Pollyanna*—was that it? Or *Bambi*. We were a fairly religious family, so I couldn't go to the movies on Sunday or anything like that. And probably other than being in school plays or scenes or skits, my first feeling of the pressure of performing in front of an audience was at church, of having to recite and not forget. Because those things felt special, my interest in theatre developed, in a way, over years, although I didn't do anything that was taken seriously until after college.

I'm interested to hear you talk about how both the secular and the sacred were responsible for your understanding of theatre. In a number of interviews, you talk about your own performance as having an almost mystical feeling to it at times.
People brought that to it. I know by now I feel—without really having words for it or knowing why—very nervous about people who don't believe. I mean, I'm not talking about atheism because that is not about believing in nothing, it's about not believing in God because of a belief in something else, whether it's Communism or whatever. I find that I do dismiss people—not in terms of whom I interview, but whom I choose to work with or not—who talk about not believing, about a prevailing doubt or skepticism. But my church was all I had, all I was exposed to, because I wasn't in a vibrant situation in terms of theatre. Given that I grew up in segregation, my mother was interested in

exposing us to stuff whenever she could. I was in children's groups that also attended to that. Segregation becomes significant in terms of the church being the first place of presentation and the limited access to theatres one could go to or participate in. So I think it would be important to think about why the church became a place to begin to investigate my voice. But it was nothing compared to those people from evangelical backgrounds. I'm always really interested in talking to those people.

What about when you were older, in high school and college, and starting to read plays?
Well the first play I remember having a big effect on me was *The Glass Menagerie*. I can still remember sitting at a sewing machine my mother had that flattened out and served as a desk. I don't remember what grade I was in, but I remember that there was such a special feeling— again this word, "special"—of reading that play and feeling as though I'd been there. And I knew that it was something very different from a novel. I remember in high school reading *Who's Afraid of Virginia Woolf?*, and being in a car with my mother and her saying, "You like plays, I like novels better," and having this conversation about what it was for me that seemed so alive and so special about a play.

In the beginning, because my high school was an all-girls high school, it didn't have a fabulous drama club or anything like that, and we didn't do big productions. It was a good school, but it was a public school where the population was too big, so we came to school in shifts. It really decreased the amount of stuff that we did in an organized way, except for student government. We didn't have a drama club or a dance group or any of those kinds of things because teachers weren't available to run them. There wasn't much theatre. The extent of it was reading a play for class and getting to act out some of the characters, which was something I did well—people told me I did it well—so of course I looked forward to it. I didn't do a lot of other things well—or at least people didn't tell me I did them well—so it felt good. I wasn't even in a situation where I could be a leading lady of my school. One of my best friends, who was also African-American, went to a very good private school. In fact, my niece goes there now, the Roland Park Country School. It had plays all the time, and it was an all-girls school. I loved going to those plays. When I think about how much was adequate for me then, compared to what's adequate now, it's just astonishing that I would go to those plays and think they were fantastic and be completely engrossed. That tells me something about audiences and their expectations and how little can please some audiences, and how so much more is required for audiences like you and me. I remember seeing *The Stage Door* and the first time I saw *Twelfth Night*, it was in a high school girls' version. It almost makes me want to go back and do something like that with high school girls, but for real, at a professional level. Maybe that's where my interest in cross-dressing and all that comes from. But again, you would have to take into account that that's all I had to see. There was a children's theatre affiliated with Center Stage that I went to a couple of times, and once the people from Center Stage came to our high school and did readings from Oscar Wilde, and again, I couldn't believe how natural and how real everything sounded even though it had been written many, many years before.

So you became habituated to seeing . . .
. . . amateur theatre . . .

. . . and seeing people perform roles that were very distant . . .
. . . from them, that's right. So the question would be how to make a production like that be not about the incapacity of a group of actors, but their capacity to comment on what they were playing. And that may be something I'm working through with my new play, *House Arrest*, because I'm taking what I used to do alone and using other actors to do it. And I'm absolutely not interested—and I think the producers would have loved it if I were—in having a multiracial cast do what I do. But I am interested in using that multiracial cast to create a reality that appears to be playing the play. Right now it's incarcerated people playing the play. But I'm realizing this interest may have to do with primary experiences in the theatre, with people playing things they were not. Or the one black theatre in Baltimore, which I didn't get to go to often—I don't think they played too often—was called the Arena Stage. They were playing white plays. I remember seeing *Sorry, Wrong Number* played by black people pretending to be white. And then going to see that same company do a Langston Hughes play—that was a different feeling. Ultimately, when I came into professional theatre in New York in the late seventies, early eighties, I was profoundly bored by these little plays—I should be careful because these are important playwrights—that were extensions of people's personal lives, where everyone plays what's appropriate to them in terms of race, gender and even social class. I was profoundly bored by all that, which was the status quo. I felt it was very oppressive and more interesting to me were the theatres that were about the restrictions on who could play at all. Right from the start, it's, "Whoever could possibly do this?"

Isn't your interest in this kind of theatre related to your project of problematizing the one-to-one correspondence between actor and character in psychological realism?
Right. It seems to me that our theatre has to become in part about that. There is something inherently theatrical about our problem of many people inhabiting the few chairs at the table. There aren't enough chairs, so it's going to be that the wrong people are in the chairs that were supposed to be occupied by white, straight, well-educated men. To me, that's the theatre in life, and theatre has to absorb that, has to be that, instead of continuing to try to put people in their "appropriate" roles.

I'm interested in how these issues of identity tie into questions of confession, because *The Glass Menagerie* is a confessional play. Tom narrates in the first person. You've spoken elsewhere about the importance to your work of Johnny Carson and of talk shows more generally. Although your theatre uses confession, I wouldn't call it confessional theatre.
The people are confessing. The big difference is that when you read Tennessee Williams, August Wilson, Lorraine Hansberry, many others in that tradition, you are reading one intelligence moving into a variety of forms, like the intelligence of a dream. When we dream, we dream about all these varieties of characters, but they are still coming from us, we are the single author. In my work, it's not just points of view, it's multiple kinds of intelligence. So it's not one confession. Williams, in a way, is using Tom to make a confession. Everyone else's confession is under the guise of Tom's and he must have chosen Tom as an organizing factor, a vehicle to make that house. I've used the tape of Tennessee Williams saying Tom's lines as a part of the auditions for *House Arrest* because I was trying to create an accent for Thomas Jefferson, whom we don't have on record. And I thought that Tennessee Williams's is one of the more pleasing Southern accents. Frequently when we use a Southern accent, we caricature it as a redneck and I thought we should give Jefferson something elegant, and Tennessee Williams is so gorgeous, and those lines are so magnificent, when he comes forward to talk. So that confession is Tennessee Williams's, if that makes sense.

I think the reason that I loved *The Glass Menagerie* was that I was probably identifying to some extent with Laura, although she would never be the first character to come to mind when I think about that play. Also, as with all of psychological realism, as when I read *Hedda Gabler* for the first time, the sense of place is so astonishing that I felt that I was really there, in her apartment.

I'm interested to hear you talk about multiple intelligences, multiple perspectives, multiple subjects, multiple identities, because it seems to me that your work is so

much about that—on the one hand, trying on different identities, intelligences and perspectives. But on the other, it's also about the coercive power of identity, the way identities are forced upon people. I see your work as negotiating between these two conditions, identity as malleable and identity as coercive.

What do you mean by coercive?

Because we are perceived by people in certain ways, they give us an identity. Because, for example, you are seen as an African-American woman, people have certain expectations of you when they see you walking down Mass. Ave. To the extent that you become this identity, that you are forced to become it, it is coercive.

Who's coercing?

The society in which we participate. Do you think of your work in relation to this opposition?

Probably, yes. But it's not just about my own personal work, it's part of what's happening here at this Institute. My latest idea is that we're trying to castrate the president in public because it's inevitable we're going to have a female president one day. And the potential lack of the white male as the great explainer is huge. That is not an empty chair, it's not a chair for hire, but it's a contested chair. It's like the chair in the middle of those circle games that you had when you were a kid. It's not up for grabs, and there are still more white men in the circle who are faster to get to the chair and more vicious in keeping other people away. But there's something that's gone forever about who is occupying that space of the great explainer. It means we'll have contentious times, and times when he's still in there, but it will never be forgotten that from time to time he was pushed out. Even though no one else can occupy the chair right now. So, I don't think it's just my work, it's a bigger problem, and my work is coming from the place of my conscious and subconscious concern about the fact that there is no great explainer anymore.

If every single thing you and I and our friends have done to try to shift the canon around gets pushed by the wayside and we go back to how everything was when you and I were in elementary school, this is still on the record. We're sitting in a very well-endowed place called the W.E.B. Du Bois Institute, which has among its professors two University Scholars, which, in my understanding, is the biggest honor you can have at Harvard and probably in the world. They are African-American men and everything that Skip [Henry Louis Gates, Jr.] is doing here is about the seriousness of this group of people in our culture and in the world. If there's a downside to this, it's that when it became clear that there were going to be multiple intelligences available, and that one man would speak, which was at the end of the sixties, whoever was in power, the great "they," managed to create identity politics out of the debris of the sixties. I don't think that was completely of our own desire. We had our own desire, but somewhere someone must have seen that as an opportunity to organize the debris. We were not able to form our own coalitions, our own alternative ways of being. It's extremely convenient to structure things so that you've got the person on the faculty who's the gay expert, the person who's . . . even at Brown, let's face it. When I was teaching with you and Paula [Vogel], you asked me to work with Aunjanue Ellis, who wasn't even a student of mine, and was offended by George Wolfe's play. At the time she didn't know who he was. Interestingly enough, after she graduated, he gave her one of her first professional jobs [in *The Tempest*]. I can remember fighting with her about *The Colored Museum*, about how derogatory she felt the images were, and the need on the part of young students to hold onto their identity. I'm questioning even that, because it is a very efficient way of managing something which could have led to more chaos.

So when the white male is not in that chair in the middle, it's not like everybody really runs at the same time, because we're organized into certain places where we're expected to be. Except those of us who refuse to be in one place, and I'm one of those people. I'm not even aware of the degree to which I pay for not sitting in one place. I know I pay for it. It's just not acceptable. That's what my work is, my resistance to staying put. It has to be very naive, because I'm a grown-up. But I also naively believed from my training in Shakespeare, that if I said something with diligence and accuracy, I could appear to be that character. That's what they taught me in Shakespeare class. They didn't have a class that said, "But you can never be that character." They don't talk about what you can never be. I could get in a lot of trouble as a teacher if I taught that, and so could you. Want some bad student recommendations? And at the same time the students know it's true.

They may know it's true, but they hope that they will be the exceptions.
But they're not doing, or being trained to do, anything about it. I don't mean just that Aunjanue couldn't be in *The Tempest*. Of course, she can—there's other people like George. And I want to have that kind of theatre, and I think half the people in your book probably want to have that kind of theatre. But I'm talking about a bigger thing, which is the degree to which they are ultimately coerced because they believe they have something to gain.

This whole problem is so clearly connected to questions of multiculturalism, a word, I've noticed, you tend not to use.
No, not frequently. If I do, I put it in quotation marks.

Certainly in the past five or ten years there have been critiques from both the right and the left leveled against various ideas of multiculturalism.

I've certainly benefited from "multiculturalism"—a perfect word to use to get funding. I've surely benefited from those kinds of funding, I wouldn't be sitting here talking to you if I had not. Because I'm almost fifty, I'm not as interested in it as a drama as I am in appreciating the fact that I lived in segregation. I'm sort of really glad that I had that happen to me. The move from segregation to integration. In my life, so far, that was much more dramatic than multiculturalism. I really think multiculturalism is more what I described, the organization of a nation whose authority was falling apart. Nixon was brought down, the Vietnam War and the murder of Dr. King. As Gloria Steinem points out, it actually took three murders to put Nixon in office: John, Bobby and King. It was a bloody, bloody time, and I think that blood was being shed about who gets to be in that chair, and who gets to be around that chair. So I don't know about multiculturalism, I don't really use it. It's an overused word, so it's a dead word. Are we really talking about multiculturalism or are we talking about the ways that alternative voices have been organized and managed?

And perhaps the key word is managed. Hazel Carby has a wonderful essay in which she writes about how far too frequently the fascination with African-American women writers comes to substitute for any kind of engagement with an antiracist politic. She understands that so-called multiculturalism can actually work to defuse antiracist struggle and activism. That's why I feel uncomfortable using the word. For me this is significant in terms of your work because you emphasize the importance of inaugurating a particular kind of process rather than suggesting a solution.

Cornel West talks about so many images, the bloodstained banner in the struggle of resistance, and your awareness that these things don't happen without struggle or bloodshed. In *Twilight*, the difference between hope and optimism, optimism being when you look outside and you go, "Looks pretty good out there, I'll go ahead and do this." And hope, on the other hand, saying, "It doesn't look good at all, I'm going to try to do this anyway, to try to create visions that become contagious, that inspire people to do heroic actions." So none of these are easy—humanly, intellectually, financially, spiritually. They take a great deal of courage. I'm interested in those things probably because I did feel that drama of the end of segregation and the sense that something had to die in order for something else to be born. I think we're probably in a different moment now, but that battle was never really completed. The danger of words like "multiculturalism" is that it leads us to believe that we should be working for an environment in which we can all get along, or that when we see a problem, we should leap to say, "Where's the hope here?" That's just like Hollywood, that's not the work, and how can you make art unless you look at things upside down for a moment? Changes take lifetimes, but in the moment when the artist has turned things upside down, maybe something has shaken out that helps you and the audience think differently. And maybe it moves you to some kind of action. But we need all kinds of networks of activity, and art is only a part of that network.

Now, that's one way of looking at art. I'm sure that many of the other people in your book can talk about art for art's sake and other kinds of things. I envy that. We're talking here about art and its relationship to civic dialogue, to the public place, to social issues, to activism. A very interesting visual artist named Shu Lee Chang stood up one day and said, "Why is it that the colored people always have to be worried about this kind of stuff?" We could say, in a way, that my interest in moving identity around is no different from my tradition and heritage, that as a black individual, I have to work double-time, to try both to do the work and to create a new kind of world for the work. And that's always the predicament of artists in other than mainstream situations.

Carrying the burden of race.
It's not just the burden of race, but the burden of perception, how we think about identity—not just race—differently in our world now. And theatre and movies, because they use the human, spoken form, are dealing with identities and creating identities. If one really is interested in looking at how differently the world is going to be occupied, even within my lifetime, one has a responsibility to try to concoct different kinds of memorable characters. So the best thing I knew how to do was to go to the streets to find those people.

Thinking about this in terms of your *On the Road* project, which you describe as a search for American character, it seems that you're trying to keep alive a certain utopian idea of America—also understanding, of course, the horror of American history of the past three hundred, four hundred years—an America of almost unlimited possibilities. That is why, I believe, your work is dedicated to questions of process, to getting people to think, to wake up, to see. I think of Tony Kushner's work in similar terms, and both of you have enunciated your projects in national terms. *Angels in America* is also a search for American character.
I'm very concerned about America, even as we're in a world in which nationhood will become less and less important. Maybe it's alright to be concerned, because one wants to document a dying thing. But I'm partly concerned because of race and wanting to retrieve or think differently

about a catastrophe and to give America the benefit of the doubt. To give America the possibility of saying, "We made a mess, we made a tornado and we can rebuild this in a fascinating way. In fact, now that it's blown apart, how about not putting up that back wall at all and having an open window?" We first have to say it was terrible, instead of trying to say it didn't happen, or, "I wasn't there." I wasn't there either, but I'm sure traumatized by it, and I feel that the culture around me is.

We're constantly living the consequences of our history.
There's this stunning part of *House Arrest*. One of the interviewees is talking about Jefferson and the Louisiana Purchase. They could have forbidden slavery there, and this scholar says about Jefferson, very angrily, "We could have had our mess not this bad." I'm more and more interested in historical moments not only in terms of what happened, but also in terms of what *didn't* happen. Even the way I'm talking about the "birth of multiculturalism" is to think about what would have been the alternatives? Why is *this* the one that was so popular all across the country? Why do you and I know that if we're going to some arts association or university, we can be sure they will have some version of the office where the Latino people and the black people sit?

I think one reason for that is that when multiculturalism is enunciated it seems to focus specifically around race, gender, sexuality—the identities, particularly race and gender, that are understood as being the most visible. While the more invisible identities, particularly class, get left out. We've always had such a hard time seeing class in this country. And as I was reading through your plays, I was thinking about the importance of visual metaphors. *Fires in the Mirror* is a visual metaphor and a number of your interviewees talk about mirrors as distorting images. *Twilight*, as well, is a visual metaphor which you use as a deconstructive tool to question those things that appear to be stable. And you write about language as a photograph of the unseen, again using a visual metaphor. Why do you think these metaphors are so important for you?
Because they have something to do with beauty, and struggling always to find beauty. Wherever I am, I'm aware that the beautiful image stimulates our imaginations. So, fires in the mirror—that image is not a terrifying image but a beautiful one, as is twilight, something that Homi Bhabha would call that in-between state, or the state of limbo, the liminal state. I feel that's where we have to negotiate these ideas and if you can grab an audience in there for even a brief amount of time, you can do some work with them. And for me, the creative process is so beautiful. It's stormy, the more human beings you add to it, the harder it gets, the uglier it can get in terms of relationships—it can be painful, it can be terrifying. But there is something about it which, I would have to

admit, is mystical. How is it that we create something out of nothing? By now we've cut probably forty-five hundred tapes to create *House Arrest*. That's a lot of things, but the things in and of themselves won't create a work of art. The work of art will be the gaps between those things and the degree to which those gaps are short and long, all that invisible stuff, all those breaths, all those spaces are what make the evening. Because they have to go in with the audience's ability to receive—to go in, to come out, like breathing. I don't theorize, I just know that that's the real stuff. And so when I come up with an image like that, I just don't let it go and hope that everybody in the theatre thinks it's okay as a title. There's always a terrifying moment when you propose it.

And this relates back to questions of process, of doubt rather than certainty, of trying things on, of looking for liminality and ambivalence again. I'm intrigued by your equation of those processes with art.
I don't understand a whole lot about metaphor. In my mind, it's just these two things or any number of things which we never would have thought about together, and we put them in proximity to each other. And then the mind makes those associations and you have a new meaning.

I'm curious about how you conceptualize your performance. The first time I saw you perform, I understood your performance in Brechtian terms: you were holding up a character rather than becoming him or her. And you then told me that it's quite different for you. Can you explain how the process of impersonation works for you?
I would have to say that in the long run, I *am* trying to become the person. One helpful thought about that came from your colleague John Emigh, who, when I came to Brown to talk after I'd written *Fires in the Mirror*, said, "It's not that I see you becoming the character, but I see the effort that you make to become the character." And so I am making the effort to become that other. I'm not bringing the other to me and assuming it can be found within me, rather I'm reaching for it outside of me. Now, all of me goes along, and the more of me the better. But I don't presume to own that thing. I have a problem about ownership. I don't think any of us own anything that has to do with human beings. I even have a bad feeling that, as actors, we come to a project and want to know what our parts are in the play. Maybe one day I would like to create a way of working with actors that is about coming to know not the part but the whole, with the Self contributing to that whole in a variety of ways. So I don't think I could ever own a character. Ever. Ever. What I try to do is relive a real moment that that person had and that they have on my tape. I could try to illuminate the more compelling images in the stories they tell, but they don't belong to me.

Recently, I had to call several people I interviewed for *Twilight* and I realized how much I loved them—including Daryl Gates. It's like a love affair where you write all the letters and don't get anything back. There's always an incredible feeling of warmth. They know me, because they find out, either they saw the play or somebody tells them they're in it, and there's something profound about that to them, that they have turned themselves over to me for a while. They let me borrow them. For the most part that's a pleasant relationship. I don't know enough about *House Arrest* yet to say, but in *Fires in the Mirror* and *Twilight*, something has been okay. I have been listening to and saying the words over and over again. So, those are all my love letters I've been writing, it's about trying to get as close to them as I can. When they sign on to it, I'm sure they don't understand that's what I'm doing. It's a really wonderful feeling to call them later and to realize that that little two minutes that I've been dealing with is perfectly well alive, and that it's bigger than me, but that I have understood some basic truth about it. It's like when I call them, I'm quite pleased that they're still playing the same opera that includes the aria I borrowed. That aria that I learned was a truthful thing. "I know you." How often in life do we get to feel that way about anybody, even friends. We know them in a way and maybe we were trying too hard to be them or have them be us, and we come back and we don't feel that closeness.

So your performance is also a way of dealing with death, with loss, with the fact that these people are no longer present for you. And, in good Freudian terms, you deal with this loss by consciously internalizing those people whom you have lost. That's Freud's description of mourning. I've always thought of your work in those terms and that's why I see it as haunted.
Very interesting.

I think you really are calling up spirits.
Except that they're not dead. They're alive. And the spirit that we're calling up is usually the moment in their life that they were trying to tell me about. In *Fires in the Mirror* and *Twilight*, those were important moments in their lives, and so it is important to have the character so close to me, because I don't care about people coming to see Anna Deavere Smith, a black woman, on stage. If I'm holding it up, as you say, I really want them to see the thing—not visit my charisma—see whatever it is that could attract their attention. It's not to watch me, but to take their attention to that thing, and through that thing to a moment that I hope they won't forget. I feel we forget these moments too often, so I would like them to have an image to remember.

I have a story in *House Arrest* that's very disturbing, about a woman who sat in a locked room while her daughter was being beaten by her boyfriend. And the baby died. A woman came up to me yesterday after having seen the play last week—we had a meeting yesterday for our so-called core audience that come to all our events—she said, "I just want you to know that I had to leave the theatre after that story and you might want to consider taking it out. I didn't see people leaving in droves, but you lost me there. I had to go home to my daughter who's epileptic and has a swollen eye. I just couldn't take that. You should take it out." Well, I don't know about that.

Because your work is so much about remembering, and especially remembering the pain, the violence, the horror, all those things we would rather forget. And you're urging us to remember, as well.

I think it's more to help us stop before we miss it. Because we have so much verbiage, so much talk on television about current events. And we talk ourselves into these frenzies. Shoshana Felman's book *The Literary Speech Act* interested me in the idea that people talk and talk and talk until they have the experience of themselves, and I feel some of the talk that's happening in the public space right now kills the possibility of us having the experience of ourselves. It leads us straight into the trap of denial, talking yourself into an identity which is not you at all. So when is there a turning point when you stop that talk of constructing an identity and have a talk which is *of* your identity, a truthful kind of talk? Since we're in this public space with a lot of talk shows, it's not true that we don't talk to each other. There's a whole lot of crap, we just don't listen to each other. When we do talk, we don't talk from a truthful place, we talk from a performative place, which makes our work as actors very hard because we're living in a society where everyone's acting. So our job must be to take all that talk and chew it like a cow and vomit it up and reorganize it and bring it out again. I just had a meeting with the interns here, who are all just out of college. They're very smart people, some of them are from New York City, from Brown, from Harvard, and several times in the conversation I said, "Let's go back to what you just said, let's tease that through a little bit." Because they're often not aware of the degree to which they're speaking without full consciousness of what they're saying. So, I've tried to find times when people are talking about something that is extremely important to them, when they find their experience rips right through their linguistic organization so that the story is not about telling truth, good or bad, but is real. And to say to the audience, "Let's listen here for a minute. Please." And to use the auditoriness of the theatre for that.

Do you think part of that is the result of what happens in the interview situation? I know you've written that when you interview people you want to get out of the way. And in your pieces, you are absent. You are not represented. A character will occasionally make some reference to you, but that's very rare, so you're signified by your absence. Which is another way of saying that you, Anna Deavere Smith, are the ghost that is haunting your own pieces. But when you're interviewing, aren't there moments when something extraordinary or unforeseen or profoundly intimate happens between you and the person you're talking to?

Let me quickly say a little bit about haunting. I think that in the cases of *Fires in the Mirror* and *Twilight*, and also with *House Arrest*, there is somebody who unlocks the door of the haunted house. In *Fires in the Mirror*, it was Ntozake [Shange], whose groundbreaking work was first done at . . . no, it wasn't first done at The Public, but The Public Theater put her on the map, made her famous, and made it possible for many of us "colored girls" to come forward. Because she declared the space as not just one colored woman who looks the way you're used to, but many others, so she opened the door of a kind of haunted house. It meant a lot to me to be at The Public Theater and I felt the only possible way to open the door was with Ntozake who had already opened it for me. And she is haunted, in every bit of her. My respect for her has to do with the degree to which she has the ability and the stamina to be haunted. And *for colored girls* was a haunted house, a horrible haunted house where I could never live. I mean, even working on those monologues would scare the fucking daylights out of me, but she opened the door, just as Jessye Norman opens the door in the most recent version of *Twilight*. And in *Fires in the Mirror*, Mr. Cato is waiting in the wings, watching. Because he ends the play by acknowledging that it's all been recorded, by saying, "You can repeat every word I say." So I always felt that he was waiting there in his raincoat watching the whole thing. The other ones might have gone off and Roslyn Malamud would have had other things to do, call people, tell them that I'm anti-Semitic. George [Wolfe] is, whatever, running down to get the *New York Times* to find out what the review is. But that man was standing, waiting, watching. And the same with Twilight Bey, the watchdog of his community, as he called himself in my interview. I felt that he was a kind of twilight. Just peaceful and sitting there, and it could get scary or rocky, but he was there because there was nothing that wasn't going to happen there that Twilight hadn't seen or couldn't see. He was waiting to come. You were asking me a bigger question about this.

But that's fascinating in terms of questions of spectatorship. Twilight as audience. I was wondering about the interview process. I realize every interview is different,

your interaction with each subject is different, but it seems to me that part of your work is in fact bringing to us that relation that you establish with your subject. It's clear that there are moments when a very deep connection is made even though, again, you are not represented.

That's really complicated because some of it has to do with what I'm doing when I'm sitting in front of them, and some of it has to do with what I'm doing later on when I'm working with the material. That has to do not just with them, but with how what they've said to me on a given day ends up having a resonance with what somebody else has said. So that the feeling that I've come close to them has a lot to do with how what I end up using sounds in relation to something else. When I'm actually sitting in front of them, I don't watch myself interview them. I'm not aware of what I do or don't do to bring an interview forward. Also, don't forget that you see maybe one-tenth of what I've collected, so I have an extraordinary amount of material and from that I try to choose the things where people are speaking from an other-than-performative place. They are performing essentially, but it's the difference between performing out here and speaking from the place inside of them where they are complicated human beings and their psyche is able to catch up with their moving mouth. So I try to find that moment when it has caught up, but even then, it's not going to work if it's not relevant to the narrative that I'm trying to create. So I have to try to find both things together. Sometimes people have said things that I need for the narrative that actually are not coming from that place and I have to try to work with it anyway. It's very hard to work with.

I'm curious how you put a piece together. As you said, you amass huge amounts of interview material. How do you go about assembling that?

Hard work. *House Arrest* is extremely difficult. We had a workshop. We had a production. We had another workshop. I just did a nine-day going-down-a-steep-ski-slope with it. Now what I'm trying to do— which is very hard because there's no model for it in the theatre—is to find a way of working with it in three dimensions. Which is to say, I have this material and in these nine days I had the actors—no director. And I ask, "What is it that other actors bring to this that I couldn't bring to it myself?" If it were just other actors getting on stage and doing the tapes, that's not enough of a departure. If I have other people, I have to examine what they bring, and it seems to me what they bring is their bodies. Not my body, but their bodies. And all the other things they bring are part of that, their voices and their bodies. So, it seems to me, the author, that to make theatre out of that, I have to be engaged with their bodies. It can't just be any old body in my mind that I'm assigning tapes to, but that black man with those muscles and with the words of a woman, or of President Clinton or a slave. That man with those words juxtaposed against a ninety-five-pound, sexy, white woman means something. And so now my problem is how to compose using dynamics. In the past I was doing it, too, but it was just on one person, so that the building of a narrative was never me sitting down and writing out the words that people had said. That came as an afterthought, because the stage manager needed a script, but it came from me with the tape and my body, moving around the room and feeling how those words with that voice went up against the weight of these words with this timbre and this inflection and this rhythm. It's always something I've been working with.

Fires in the Mirror I wrote here at Harvard, in this big work space, and people were like, why did I need an empty room? I needed a great big empty room because I was going to be throwing my weight and my body around the room, screaming those words until I learned the dynamics. Now it's much harder, because in the latest version I've got fourteen bodies on that. We came through *House Arrest* with tons of materials and historic materials and tapes and three years of me being on the road following Clinton and getting in places I didn't belong and all this stuff. All that notwithstanding, what it comes down to is: how do these dynamics work? To me that's relevant because I don't think we can even look at our race relations without recognizing that as white and black and women and men, we really are different from each other in space—that's where the anxiety about race really comes from. It's not just equal rights, or who has what another doesn't have, but how are we, as physical bodies, in the presence of one another. And what does it do to shift and alter what we're comfortable with and not comfortable with?

So in other words, your process in making the piece is in part what the piece is about. Right, it's precisely that: what does it mean to have actors haunted—to use your word—by these shards of America? It's very hard to find the time in rehearsal, given the way we do things, to address those questions, which I think are the essential questions. I think a course could be created about this: what happens when you are inhabited by America? Is there something that your body has access to that could help us understand this in a different way than what the pundits have access to? I say, absolutely yes. I would like to have your hundred and ninety pounds or your ninety-five pounds, because I'm going to trust that a heck of a lot more than Cokie Roberts, who is making a ton of money exactly to skim over the surface. I'm very concerned that for some reason in our society right now, very little is expected of performance people. You go up, put your clothes on, play your part and go home. If you say more than that, at the Academy Awards or anywhere else, you get in trouble for it. And the best you can do is come out of it and make art out of that. But we are not expected to do any more than that, and I don't know enough about the history of world theatre to know, but I do know from my friend Sandra Richards, who's written about me and others, that the clown in Africa was kicked out. Even in my earlier pieces it wasn't a big thing, because I wasn't known, but there were a variety of places where I was essentially kicked out for doing the very thing I was commissioned to do. But we're all so civilized and polite that I wasn't really kicked out. "There was a problem." They didn't really want "that" story. You're supposed to know, particularly with race, how far to go, what you don't say. So I've assembled people who come to the work with extraordinary resources. They're not frequently asked to use them. The striking exception is Kate Valk whom I was lucky enough to get for these nine days, with Liz [LeCompte]'s blessing. Someone who's a performer but who isn't just a performer and will tell you that she would lay down her body in front of the Wooster Group if anyone were going to come in and endanger that, because what it represents is so precious to her. But most of us leave that all up to the producers and everybody else, and if it doesn't work out, move on to the next play or the next theatre.

So part of this is about understanding what the actor brings, and using that, and crediting the actor, the actor's presence and power.
I don't know if I'd use the word "crediting," but I would say, trying not to deny aspects of his presence. I mean, this is not a photograph. I just had my photograph taken for an Anne Klein ad, it's in *Elle* magazine right now, big spread with all these women. And so people look at the picture and go, "My God, what you look like in that ad!" Well sure, to make the ad takes a whole day. Getting your hair exactly right. Annie Leibowitz putting all of you in the exact right pose that shows what it should show and not what it shouldn't. Of course. That's a fashion photograph. I should hope that in the theatre, where we do not have too much to gain, not money at least, we shouldn't be concerned about performing the perfect picture, we should be worried about exposing the mess of the body in our society. The body that matters and the body that does not.

I think that was also essential in *Twilight* and *Fires in the Mirror*. I don't care what anybody wants to say about me and identity politics—the degree to which I do or don't meet the expectation of what a black woman is supposed to do—the fact is that both of those plays and all of that effort came out of my concern for the lives of two black men and two white men, Mr. Rosenbaum, Mr. Denny. Very concerned about those two sets of male bodies and what happened to them. And the degree to which the media, like the war tanks, just go over the rubble, and whatever gets pushed in front of the wheels is what we see. I feel that my love for America and the time in which we live has to do with going back over that rubble for what we have left behind while we've gone on to the next thing. I've had the opportunity in my life to do a lot of self-examination, and I know what it means, what price you can pay for moving over the rubble without going back and looking at the riches of it and the problems of it.

And so, of course, the key moment in Reginald Denny's speech is when he wakes up in the hospital and doesn't remember the rubble, doesn't remember how he got there. I had a very terrifying dream about that, and usually when I have terrifying dreams in the creative process I am relieved because they help locate my anxiety. The creative process is always fraught with anxiety because of the way I work, usually trying to do a lot of work in a very short time, and the producers are breathing right down my neck: I think all of us in this country are in that predicament. My dream was exactly that. I was in a hospital room because I was going to go have dinner with a friend of mine named Blair, who is a very patrician-looking guy, Blair Fuller. Interestingly enough, his grandfather was a very famous American painter, and whenever I was with his friends they were, you know, those kind of people. So I went into this hospital room and was told, "Just wait here for Blair." And also my friend Val Smith, who's a black author who's written about Harriet Jacobson and such, Val was going to meet us, too. I had to sit in this room and into the room came an Asian man who'd just had an operation. He was unconscious and his head had been shaved in a perfect rectangle, they'd done that in order to do the operation. I was sitting on the floor with my legs crossed and I started to panic because I thought, "He's going to wake up and he's going to panic because he doesn't realize he's had surgery." It happened that the shape of his head was the exact shape of a corn bread that I used to get at this health-food restaurant where I ate regularly while I was working on *Twilight*.

That dream was a real relief for me, because I realized how anxious I was about Reginald Denny, and about how in the speech he was not in time with what he was saying, and what it would take for me to be on stage and do that out-of-time speech knowing the price he will pay when he comes back into time. Because I have the consciousness to know what he doesn't know and it's just a matter of somebody reorganizing that a little bit for him to get it: "What happened? What happened?" And George [Wolfe] used to say, "He's going to wake up one day and he's going to kill everybody." I feel that America's like Reginald Denny, and that we're so smart, I get to be around a lot of smart people, and I see all the ways we can talk ourselves out of what we are doing. Arianna Huffington—of all people—said to me recently in an interview that, "We're so smart we're not wise." Or the way that we think now about myths and other things that helped us learn the truth as lies. Or we say that the president is an actor, that people in Washington are performers, which means that the word performance—which means lying—is the word that's used for what we're doing. Somehow the telling of truth has to do with being in a position to speak Reginald Denny's gap, or to speak all gaps. And to feel the pain of what it is not to be conscious, and the danger of a lack of consciousness.

Do you think that the theatre is a privileged space to be able to speak that?
With writers, I don't know if it's privilege, or if art puts us together with ideas of safety—artists need safety, students need safety. It's disturbing because these things that I'm talking about are not safe things. I'm not sure that I believe that the theatre is a privileged space. I'm very sad that I've been told that we live in a time when we can't have acting companies anymore because actors don't want it, in this society where you can get paid a lot of money to do a little thing. And it matters that you make that money, because you want to have a certain quality of life and you want it for your children and for the people you love and you want to be prepared should you or someone else become ill.

I really think it's about the actor's body as the site of a resistance to the systems of denial. The actor's body is the place that says, "Slow down, stop! Let me say that for you again. Let me say that. I don't think I understand that. Let me say that a few times to get it right." Which is what rehearsal is—you take this obscure, complicated text and you say it again and again and again until it comes into life and meaning. And then we know what somebody meant and what they didn't mean. And we understand something about truth. And I feel that that's really what the project needs to be, more than the written word. And I know that the domain of plays is usually the written word, but you can see I've dedicated my life to the spoken word in a society where I'm not sure we tell the truth.

So what's crucial then is the presence of the live actor as a focal point, as the site of action.
The presence of the body, the voice and the building of people—spiritually, intellectually and physically—who are strong enough to carry

the truth and carry the lie, to bridge the gap. Because if we have any-thing to be concerned about in our society, which is so wealthy, it's the gap between the rich and the poor. Or when black men tell me . . . you know, it gives them chills to think that fifty percent of "them" are in jail. Then it's worrisome. My latest thought about it—I'm sure others have said it before—is that black men and black women were brought to this country to do something, which was labor, and we don't need to do that anymore, so look where you get sent. More prisons than universities are being built, so we're not thinking about education anymore as a way to equalize and bring people out of it. I don't want to be the sayer of doom, but it seems to me one exciting prospect is to prepare people to negoti-ate that gap. I'm not sure that anything in our schools prepares us to deal with that because, as we've established, we pretend everybody is everything and we know that's not true, and we don't spend enough time understanding what we're not. And reenacting what we're not.

Do you think this situation has something to do with systems of belief? At the begin-ning of the interview you talked about your distrust of people who don't believe in anything, and as you were talking about that I was thinking about how for me, belief represents a kind of negation of the self. It's about committing oneself to some-thing larger than the self, whether it's God or community or revolution. Perhaps theatre has functioned historically as a site for interrogating belief, or even for enacting belief, for making belief. Or making believe.
Ah, it's making believe, yes, very interesting.

And that connects, as well, to traditions of testifying in religion.
It's so interesting to think about the theatre being, in a childlike way, about making belief. Making believe. You could have a marvelous task in a cynical society. You have to make believe in front of people who don't believe, who've seen it all.

Ours is a pretty cynical society.
And that's probably why theatre is in trouble now. In addition to all the other diversions people have, they are willing to go and make believe in a movie theatre, cynics though they are.

It seems to me that's a different kind of event.
You don't have to believe in the event because the event's already believed in—that's what the whole Hollywood enterprise is about. A long, long time ago somebody had to believe in an event, but it was an event that was evident. It's more fragile in theatre, anything could hap-pen to disrupt the whole thing. I was at the opening of *The Makropoulos*

Affair at the Met, and in the first three minutes the tenor, who was on stage singing alone, fell from a ten-foot ladder and had a heart attack. The end, that's it, that's all she wrote that night. Anything could happen.

There's that sense of danger which makes theatre so powerful.
Potentially.

Although theatre is distinguished from mass culture by that sense of danger, most is hardly concerned with exploiting it, either as content or form.
I think it would be fascinating to learn what state the church is in right now. My sense is that people are going to church, at least the religious right would want us to believe so. The question is, do they worship God?

Americans have become so secularized and there are so many substitutes for religion, like the spirituality movement. I hesitate to think of theatre exactly as a substitute for religion, but it seems to satisfy so many of the needs that religion satisfies.
It could. We have a problem in our theatre, though, the theatre of identity politics, because I don't think it feels big enough for that, for God's world. I'm not accusing identity politics of anything, but how do you create a house of worship which is big enough to call the many? I realize people don't feel a need for that, but the people who run theatres in this country are not really trying to solve the problem of who they are calling to. I really worry and I feel very sad that they're not trying harder to ask that question. I'm not just disappointed in a political way, I'm disappointed in a spiritual way because I wonder, how could this really be a holy temple? I'm not sure I've been in a holy temple of American theatre, because it just reenacts the same thing of who gets to be there. I don't know the teachings of Christ, really, though I'm a Christian, but so many religions seem to acknowledge that the pauper belongs at the table as much as the king does.

What are your plans for *House Arrest*?
I did the nine-day thing here, and then I'll turn a draft in sometime in early or mid-September, and it's supposed to go to the Taper in the spring.

Do you want to say anything about the subject matter?
It started being about the relationship between the president and the media in Washington, but I would say that it's become more about captivity in America. And I understand the importance of not making metaphors truth—the president is not really incarcerated. But I put it together from texts that I got from some pretty privileged sources—journalists and the president and the people around him—with narra-

tives that I got from incarcerated people, and also with Jefferson and, in particular, his relationship to Sally Hemmings, because of this fascination that I began to develop with the American presidency. Why have I gone to Washington? Why do I care about this so-called center of power? I'm not on the road in *search* of American culture, I really am *looking* at it. So whereas all my other works have dealt with power upside down or people with no power, this is about looking at power. And to look at power, I have to look at the most powerless. If the most powerful man in the world at the end of the twentieth century—not that President Clinton necessarily is—but if that figure is a white male, then the other would probably be an African woman, not necessarily in our country, but an African-blooded woman. So the relationship between Sally Hemmings and Thomas Jefferson was a good way to look at those two figures and their relationship to power, and to try to take that through until now and look at the president up against some incarcerated black women.

When I was reading *Twilight*, I noticed that at three points speakers talk about wanting to have a private room, a room cut off: Reginald Denny, Peter Sellars and Paul Parker. I was thinking about that, the fantasies of these isolated rooms, almost like prisons. The question of a safe space that's also cut off. And now we are so intent on interrogating Clinton's private behavior and so undoing the separation between public and private.

At the end of *Twilight*, Twilight himself says that one of the things he understands is that he can no longer care about and identify only with those like him. So he's in this limbo state because although he doesn't know what's next, he knows he can't stay. When you put it that way, I can understand why people have to have their own rooms, because we have so little private space anymore. People don't have to be in this coercive state in terms of identity to want to have a precious place where they can be "themselves" and don't need to feel threatened that something will be taken away.

I want to tell you one more thing before you leave, and it's a story I've told a lot which is also for me the predicament of American theatre right now. And what I am trying to do in the way that I work is to bring more characters from American life onto the stage, to encourage the stage to begin to become a place where we stop reenacting who we were twenty years ago, or wish for who we were in 1955, but really grapple with who we are now. I was naive to think that if I brought people from a variety of social classes and races and places and points of view, they would be powerful enough to bring their cousins and the people like them to the audience. But it didn't work that way. The irony about

Twilight is that I named it after this young man Twilight Bey who was a gang member, and he never came to see it in Los Angeles. He lived about twenty minutes away from the theatre. A couple of years later, I was at the Million Man March, and who should I run into among the million men but Twilight. I went over to him and we kissed and we hugged and I said, "Twilight, you know, you never came to see the play."

"Yeah, I know, I couldn't make it."

"Twilight, I named the show after you."

"I heard. You kicked it, girl."

"You had the last, most important lines in the play."

"I'm sorry, I just couldn't get around to it."

So my question becomes: here's Twilight, the play's named after him—and I understand that Farrakhan's got his charisma—but why is it that coming twenty minutes feels like more than coming three thousand miles? And how can we make those twenty minutes seem like less? We have a lot to do in American theatre not just to maintain but to encourage a kind of aesthetic excellence which is more likely to be about helping us as artists both be absorbed by our world and absorb our world. That's going to be very hard, and I'm not sure that in the past art has ever had that intention. I think it will be harder and harder to keep acting for a smaller and smaller audience.

We have to get them to come those twenty minutes.
That feel like more than three thousand miles.

Paula Vogel

In her playwriting classes, Paula Vogel always asks her students to write the impossible: a play with a dog as protagonist, a play that cannot be staged, a play that dramatizes the end of the world in five pages. And while these provocative exercises stretch students' imaginations in remarkable ways, they also inadvertently reveal much about Vogel's own playwriting. For all her plays endeavor to stage the impossible. They defy traditional theatre logic, subtly calling conventions into question or, in some cases, pushing them well past their limits. What other playwright would dare memorialize her brother in a play filled with fart jokes and riotous sex, whose medical authority, a cross between Dr. Strangelove and Groucho Marx, ends up drinking his own piss? What other feminist would dare write so many jokes about tits?

For a Vogel play is never simply a politely dramatized fiction, it is always a meditation on the theatre itself—on role-playing, on the socially sanctioned scripts from which characters diverge at their peril, and on a theatrical tradition that has punished women who don't remain quiet, passive and demure. Take, for example, *The Mineola Twins* (1996), which plays deliriously and chillingly with the age-old farcical convention of using one virtuosic actor (and a battery of wigs) to play two startlingly dissimilar identical twins. Or *Hot 'N' Throbbing* (1994), which transforms a theatre into a living room and a living room into a theatre in order to dramatize the fatal consequences of stage directions gone out of control. Or her Pulitzer Prize-winning *How I Learned to Drive* (1997), which does far more than explain the effects of sexual predation on a young girl; it literally splits her into two—a body and a voice—in order to represent the radical alienation from Self that results from having been molested.

In *How I Learned to Drive*, Vogel turns the theatre itself into a vehicle for memory, using first gear to move forward in time and reverse to move backwards. By reenacting the driving lessons given her by her Uncle Peck, L'il Bit remembers her strangely—and literally—intoxicating sexual initiation. For there is no question but that her uncle's seduction has caused her to retreat "above the neck." At the same time, Peck, that most charming of pedophiles and himself a victim of abuse, is the only member of her family who makes a real effort to understand, nurture and help her grow up. For *How I Learned to Drive* is the story not only of L'il Bit's molestation. It is also a slyly subversive dramatization of how a girl—perhaps any girl—becomes an adult.

At the beginning of the play, L'il Bit remembers the suburban Maryland of her youth, completely absorbed in the touch, smell and taste of a "warm summer evening." These sensory perceptions connect her to the past, to the land and to her own body as she renders herself miraculously whole again through the power of memory. But as L'il Bit knows all too well—and any adult will tell you—this primordial wholeness cannot last and the remainder of the play shows her being taken for a drive that will lead her into another realm, one dominated by the senses of sight and hearing. For if touch, smell and taste are the tokens of intimacy and wholeness, then sight and hearing are undeniably the most objectifying of the senses; they introduce a radical separation between subject and object. This is perhaps why the very center of the play is a photo shoot, for it is in this scene that L'il Bit most graphically becomes an object for Uncle Peck and, more ominously, for herself as well. Yet this sequence is so effective theatrically because it tacitly recognizes that sight and hearing are also the senses, by no mere coincidence, upon which theatre depends. It demonstrates that the theatre, like the photo shoot, will always produce figures who are subjected to the scrutiny of voyeuristic spectators (or lascivious uncles). L'il Bit, in other words, suddenly discovers that she has become an actor in a drama that has been scripted for her by an exploitative, if well-meaning spectator who is, in turn, the product of a society that values women for their allure. Yet *How I Learned to Drive* is no more an indictment of theatre than it is of eroticism. For it is precisely the theatre that gives L'il Bit the time and the place to re-member, that is, to reconstruct herself, to put herself back to together. In learning to drive, the play shows us, L'il Bit learns how to desire, how to be in control and how to teach others. She learns, in other words, how to use the theatre, and the act of self-presentation, to put herself quite literally in the driver's seat.

In *How I Learned to Drive*, L'il Bit is literally haunted by the unquiet spirit of her Uncle Peck in the same way that Anna in *The Baltimore Waltz* (1992)—and Vogel herself—is haunted by the spirit of her dead brother, Carl. For in attempting to remember, Vogel's theatre calls up ghosts, figures lighter than air yet heavy with the past. It is obsessed with commemorating what has been lost, while understanding that loss always pays a kind of dividend that is experienced both on a personal and cultural level. For Vogel's ghosts always materialize at the place where memory turns into history, the particular into the universal. Thus, *Baltimore Waltz* becomes an exhilarating tribute and love letter not only to Carl, but to everyone who has died of AIDS, in the same way that *Drive*, by staging L'il Bit's singular journey, dramatizes the relentless process by which we are each being produced as the subjects and objects of our own dramas.

For all their precision in documenting the act of remembering, Vogel's plays are perhaps unique in the way that they locate memory in the body. For it is far more than her punning sensibility that inspires her to title her most recent collection *The Mammary Plays* (TCG, 1998). Summoning up the "full-figured gal" of TV-commercial fame, both *Drive* and *The Mineola Twins* simultaneously exploit and critique the cliché of this "stacked" femme fatale. Both tacitly acknowledge that female bodies are steeped in history, that "sometimes the body," as Uncle Peck puts it, "knows things that the mind isn't listening to." And like her other plays, they are intent on listening to and reclaiming that lost, forgotten history. For as a feminist writer, Vogel not only attends to the deeply contradictory representations of women in our culture, but also delineates female characters who are prepared to use their physical charms (if need be) to wrest control of their lives. From the sprightly geriatric prostitutes of *The Oldest Profession* (1988) who have seized the means of production; to Myra, Mineola's answer to Patricia Hearst and Patricia Ireland; to the lesbian parents of three imaginary little boys in *And Baby Makes Seven* (1984); Vogel's women are themselves playwrights who attempt to write their way out of difficult situations and script more creative, bountiful lives. Like Vogel herself, they are committed to redressing a history of oppression by rewriting the scenes they have been handed. By so turning her female characters (and

June 4, 1997—The apartment of Scott Teagarden (David Savran's partner),
New York City

DS: What drew you to theatre?
PV: I got interested in theatre in Washington, D.C., as a way of staying
out of the house. My first experience was some god-awful opera at the
National Theatre. It was a school trip, and they put us in the very upper
gallery of the National Theatre, which is way up there, and what I
remember with fascination is that the boys were leaning over the balcony
because from that point of view they could see the soprano's cleavage. We
didn't hear a note of the opera, I just remember the entranced gaze, and
I think I knew even then that theatre had to be seductive in order to work.

And that theatre was an art of the body?
From the upper gallery with those sopranos and their large bosoms,
yes, it was very much of the flesh. Then I stumbled into a drama class
and high school productions, when I was a sophomore. I walked into
the room and I felt, "This is home." I pretty much knew I couldn't be
an actress. I was petrified of exposing my own body. I also pretty much
knew my own sexuality, and in this high school drama class there were
very few boys because to take drama in those days meant you were
admitting you were homosexual. So I was chosen to play all the male
leads, and I did them very well. I thought I made a superb John Proctor,
and I was actually asked to coach the young boy cast for the high school
production of *The Crucible*. When it came time to audition I got my
courage up and I auditioned for Abigail. And the drama teacher took
me aside and said, "Please, don't do this. Don't make me go there." He
was a gay man and I think he knew absolutely my sexuality. I knew my
sexuality. So I spent three wonderful years being a stage manager. One
of the things I loved about stage managing was that you got to see backstage as well as on stage. That you were immersed in the culture of
making theatre seemed as important and vital as the actual theatre
itself. I can't say that I fell in love with *Our Town*, *The Skin of Our Teeth*
and *The Sound of Music*, but I fell in love with the process of making theatre. By the end of my senior year, when I had already had my first

affair, it was pretty clear to me that I would have to make a choice in my life, and that included my sexuality. At that point I was a good public speaker. I was class president but I suddenly became aware that if I went in the track of law school and politics, my sexuality could not be hidden, which was unthinkable during the sixties. I realized immediately in my first moment in bed with another young girl, "I can never stop doing this. I can never not have this be a part of my life." And I immediately said, "Good-bye politics, good-bye being a public servant." And what else is there to fill the gap? I really started—this was my junior year—looking seriously at theatre as a more immediate outlet. So by the end of my senior year I was starting to write. I thought I'd actually write for the Broadway stage. I loved musicals. I was writing lyrics, writing little books and revues and that sort of thing. I think I chose the theatre because it was a home that could include my sexuality.

During that period what works were particularly important to you, whether musical theatre or not?
In the sixties, I was going to things like the Shady Grove Music Fair and I fell in love with *A Funny Thing Happened on the Way to the Forum* possibly because of the flesh. The truth was being told, like the boys hanging over the balcony. *A Funny Thing Happened* told the truth about women's sexuality from a man's point of view. It wasn't polite. It was vaudeville. I absolutely fell in love with *Gypsy*, which was remarkable and splendid. As a matter of fact, I think the possibilities of being a female subject were greater, to some extent, in musical theatre than in straight drama. In *West Side Story* you could have at least some character development. I found character for women extremely flat in straight plays so I gravitated towards the music—maybe it was the singing voice that added the notion of dimension to a character recipe. So for me in the sixties, it was going to be Broadway. And I had to figure out how to do this. I already knew I couldn't be an actress, although I tried it for a couple more years. I thought I'd be a director until I went to college and the writing started to take over. I was writing musicals in college.

I know that *Peter Pan* was a big love of yours.
Peter Pan was a huge thing. Mary Martin was a huge love of mine, and not only *Peter Pan*. In the fifties, Broadway musicals were being written as vehicles for Ethel Merman and Mary Martin—and then Julie Andrews came along. It felt like a very female-centered form, and I think it was. When I fell in love with *Peter Pan* at five years old I didn't fall in love with the book but with Mary Martin's performance. I recog-

nized a possibility of disguise in the theatre. As I worked through my sexuality in my early twenties, I started thinking through the gender roles we are assigned. I thought then that actresses, heterosexual women, were at home in acting because being heterosexual for a woman means being conscious of your acting; being a good woman is acting a role.

So even then you saw both femininity and heterosexuality as roles.
And that point of view is a perfect fit with acting as a profession. I had enormous problems with it in that I didn't want to act the role. It seemed to me that acting was great for young gay men because they had to act heterosexuality in order to pass in a straight, pre-Stonewall world. For gay women, technical theatre was perfect—you were out of sight, you could watch everything. Directing seemed to be the province of straight men—prescribing the roles that everybody else played. And because figuring out where I fit was a real problem, theatre became a home that included a spectrum of possibilities in terms of gender.

More and more I thought maybe I could write but I didn't know of any women writers. By the time I got out of Catholic University, the only place I knew to apply to was the Yale School of Drama. It was the only program in the country I was aware of where one could study to be a playwright, and I was turned down. I didn't know what else to do with my life. I put my head on the table and wept. I was turned down in the class of Christopher Durang and Wendy Wasserstein. I've charted the impact that being admitted to Yale has had in people's lives and it seemed in one more way I was outside the club when Yale turned me down.

Because of public speaking and my personality skills, I figured I'd probably enjoy teaching—it was just a hunch. I then decided to apply for a Ph.D. program, got into Cornell, and pretty much used Cornell as a backdrop to continue the playwriting and try to figure out how to do it my own way and teach myself a method. The method I've taught myself was very much based on the readings Bert States gave me, finding a formalist perspective on writing plays.

Kenneth Burke . . .
Kenneth Burke, Susanne Langer, a lot of Bert States sprinkled in, a little Vladimir Propp. Roland Barthes's *Mythologies* was a huge book for me. My Ph.D. reading was very useful in that it gave me a vocabulary so that I could write in isolation.

And it gave you some of the tools you've used in teaching at Brown for over ten years.
Twelve years.

For you did go through most of the Cornell Ph.D. program. And I know that criticism and theory have had a big impact on your writing.

The love I had for theatre when I entered Cornell was not the love that I had when I left. At the time I left, I was passionately in love with Büchner, with Wedekind. I felt theatre as a concrete thing in a way I hadn't before. Before I'd been in love with the world, the way that kids are—you're in love with the flash and excitement and process. But I started thinking of playwriting and of plays as something living. That's what that program did, which is actually a great deal. A lot of programs kill the thing you love. Maybe my excitement was fostered because I wasn't in a playwriting program.

You can also think about this in terms of the balance between conscious and unconscious. Because you are so attuned to playwriting as a craft and to its formal dimensions, your unconscious is freed.

My interest in formalism, and leaving the unconscious alone, was also fostered by my reaction to the abuses that I witnessed in an MFA program at Cornell in which a bastardization of the Method was used to exploit and abuse young actors. I was so appalled by the psychic rape I saw these young actors and actresses going through that I determined that an artist's unconscious should be left sacred and untouched. It's not that they are unaware, but the unconscious shouldn't be the emphasis and focus in the art-making. I felt that by following Russian Formalism, say, Shklovsky, and defamiliarizing the known, by making yourself concentrate on your left hand, you leave your right hand free to plunge into your own psyche. Time and again I've said this: if I had sat down and said, "I'm going to write a play about my brother's death from AIDS," I never would have written a play, I would have simply curled up in a little ball and wept. But if I say I'm going to write a play on language lessons, knowing full well it's about my brother's death, you allow yourself to forget. The only way you can do that is by playing games with yourself. It's a very conscious craft.

I will admit that with *Meg* [1977] I didn't know what the unconscious was doing. It took me by surprise. I think this is a first-play phenomenon. I didn't realize what I was doing or saying in terms of my father until he showed up and saw it. And I went, "Oh my God, Vogel, you are a darned idiot!" But once I realized that that was the mechanism, I was never caught off guard again. I am still sometimes caught off guard by a hidden message to myself that I only discover on stage. And Molly Smith, as a director, has been terrific about this because she's known me since the days of Catholic youth. She says, "By the way, did you know you're doing X, Y or Z there?" and I'll go, "Oh my God, yes."

Those discoveries for me are a personal, private epiphany. There's a little shiver up the spine.

Normally before I start a project, I know what journey I'm taking for myself, I know what my personal relationship to the material is. And then I forget it. I forget as much as I can and instead get ingrained in the mechanics of plot, character, language and plasticity. Those are the blinders I put on to keep me focused.

But in some cases, as in *Baltimore Waltz*, forgetting becomes a way of remembering.
I remember at the end. More and more, I've been focusing on how, for me, playwriting is about structuring memory for an audience.

Structuring whose memory?
A communal memory. Our memory together: we start the play at eight, it's over at nine-thirty or ten. Where and what do we remember? And the only way to forget, paradoxically, is to expose your devices and keep them in front of everybody because through repetition you can make us all forget. We take it for granted and stop looking at it. So then you can make us re-remember. An example of this is the gloves in *Baltimore Waltz*. I told Anne Bogart I wanted the Third Man constantly in latex gloves. And she said, "Isn't that awkward?" And I said, "If he's constantly in latex gloves we will forget that he's wearing them, and people will gasp at the end of the play when he pulls them off." As cultural animals, we do not forget because something is hidden, we forget because something is in our face and we don't want to see it anymore. That's what forgetting is. Forgetting is a way of not looking.

In other words, a form of disavowal.
Because theatre is a wonderful mechanism for denial and escape, it's a wonderful mechanism for confrontation. This is all in Russian Formalism. When you get to Brecht, you get the Alienation Effect. So I have always been very, very careful as a teacher. Sometimes I will say to someone, "Do you know why you're writing this play? Don't tell me. Figure out why you're writing this play for yourself, but don't tell me. It's none of my business." Frankly, it's none of the audience's business either. If you know why you're writing the play, the audience will know why they are watching the play. They will construct a personal journey for themselves—if a playwright constructs a personal journey through the material.

Do you think that one of the advantages of using a narrative voice, as you do in *Baltimore Waltz* and *How I Learned to Drive*, is that it allows for a more explicit personal identification on the part of the spectator?

The narrative voice came about from concerns I was feeling in the seventies when I began. The empathic mechanism works differently for women characters and women playwrights. This goes back to the Aphra Behn thesis that playwriting and theatre are seen as public acts, and hence not very hospitable to women, who have been seen historically as belonging in the private sphere. There's nothing private about the theatre, even with the fourth-wall convention. It is really political speech. Women therefore have invented, or at least gone toward the lyrical expressions of the novel, the short story, essays and poems. You get women like Aphra Behn being able to say "I"—you're not speaking publicly for all people, you're saying "I," a private voice written in privacy—and that leads you right to the rise of the novel and the woman novelist. You write it at your parlor desk, and you can hide your writing when your father or your husband comes in. This goes straight to Virginia Woolf and *A Room of One's Own*. It's a room of one's own, not a stage of one's own, so for me the narrative voice is a way for women playwrights to imbue the whole notion of dramatic persona with the lyrical immediacy of saying "I" on stage.

The second thing about empathy, of course, is that I think that women have been trained to empathize with male subjects, so we are always translating our personal response from one gender to the other. Men have not learned how to empathize directly with a female character. They're constantly looking for a male subject. They don't know how to translate their empathy. So if you have a female subject, they will say, "You know the secondary male character, why don't you make him the protagonist?" They see the whole journey through him, whereas women see the journey through women's eyes. That translation means also that women playwrights have a great deal of difficulty creating a three-dimensional character because we don't have a stage vocabulary for it. "I don't know how women talk together when they're alone on stage." It's because we don't have a legacy of women alone on stage talking to each other, with the rare exception of works like *The Bacchae* or *The House of Bernarda Alba* or *Three Sisters*. When Jane Austen was told that she didn't have any scenes between two men in her novels, she said, "I don't know how two men talk to each other." It's exactly the reverse on stage: the sphere of authority in the novel and the poem is the female "I," which is also the e-y-e, versus the stage, where the sphere of authority is the masculine public space. How do I learn to empathize directly with female subjects? Another way of putting this is to adapt Anne Righter's thesis on Shakespeare and the idea of the play, in which she said Shakespeare basically took the morality plays, the vices and virtues, and started down the road of individuation until you end up with *Hamlet*. But you can still see the seeds of vices and virtues. You might say that women characters to this day are closer to the vices and virtues. You still see the seeds of our abstraction. You see our functions within the play world rather than our individuation. Another way I put this is that every time a male character walks on the stage, whether it's in a bit role or it's David Mamet, he is trailing the mantle of Hamlet. But when a women character walks on stage, she's trailing Gertrude or Ophelia or Lady Macbeth. They are abstractions, they're not fully dimensional. It's functional in relationship to family and the private sphere. The notion of a female protagonist is a very, very recent event that starts, in my mind, with Ibsen and with Chekhov, to some extent. But *Hedda Gabler* was astonishing. There's a very small legacy for women dramatists to use.

So the most decisively feminist aspect of your writing involves trying not only to produce women as subjects, but also to go back historically and reimagine the female character.

That's exactly right, and trying to think, How can I seduce both the men in the audience to identify directly, to empathize directly with the female subject, and to retrain women in the audience to identify directly with the female subject? It's a problem of retraining.

Or to get men to identify with Uncle Peck, a very sweet man who happens to be a pedophile?

Excellent, although I don't like the "P" word. The influences on *How I Learned to Drive* are not only *Lolita* but also Michel Tremblay's *Bonjour, La, Bonjour* and Louis Malle's *Murmur of the Heart*. I think this is an American phenomenon, thinking in the interests of empathy, keeping the good good and the bad bad, and letting the audience know exactly where they are—to moralize. It's what Mac Wellman has written about beautifully in "The Theatre of Good Intentions." Basically, in America, because of the Hollywood system, we still remain fairly entrenched in the well-made play. That's the way you produce mass cultural work. For me, that makes a very flattened-out drama. One of the great things that James Clancy gave me was the aesthetics course in which he talked about the early twentieth-century aesthetics of Vernon Lee and Theodor Lipps, and the whole notion of negative empathy, in which we resist the empathy we feel towards the protagonist. What you're really talking about is tragedy, because all tragedy is, by necessity, negative empathy. If you don't have fear and pity, you don't have catharsis. To me any serious drama is negative empathy. At the end of the twentieth century in America, we have purged that from Broadway plays, certainly

from studio movies in which the only kind of empathy you feel is positive empathy without any resistance. To me, empathy is a muscle: it gets
tired, it gets worn out. What I think has resulted from just feeling good
and knowing who to root for is that we've ceased to feel at all. You need
obstacles and obstructions to your empathy in order to make empathy
stronger, to make the muscle stronger.

**Do you think this is one of the basic differences between theatre as a form of cul-
tural production as opposed to television and film? Is negative empathy specific to
theatre?**

It's not just specific to theatre. The movies I most adore, whether it's
Chinatown or *The Grifters*, absolutely are based on negative empathy.
I'm often coming out of movies going, "Oh my God, I didn't know you
could get that made in a studio." *Thelma and Louise. The Producers*,
which I adore, could never be made today, it's filled with negative empathy. A man who's going around seducing old ladies, saying, "I love you,"
into their hearing aids and producing really rotten theatre? I love it!
What happened to me in that period of three years of classroom study
with Bert States, Marvin Carlson and James Clancy is that I fell in love
with *Spring Awakening* and *Woyzeck*, pieces that were all about negative
empathy. Classic theatre is all about negative empathy; it's saying that
the function of theatre is to go into the problems, the pains, the darkness of society and hold it up for reflection. I don't want to be a moralist about it, but I think it creates an aesthetic response. When I've had
discussions with people like Mac Wellman, he often thinks I am a
moralist, and I'm actually not. Shklovsky says you can use any contemporary subject, the subject is unimportant. The importance is that it's
out there in the public view, and therefore, it's ripe for forgetting. So
the interesting thing is to remember to expose that which is in the public view. What is in the public view? AIDS, pedophilia, child molestation, domestic violence, homosexuality. All of these subjects people may
say are sensationalized—"sensationalism" is another way of avoidance
and denial. It's ripe material for a Russian Formalist. It's right in plain
view, it's topical, it's what's hurting us right now and therefore we're not
looking at it. What are we not looking at? All you have to do is walk out
the door. Look in the street and you'll find twenty or thirty subjects to
write a play on.

**So then negative empathy, as a form of disidentification, is a way of shifting the
focus from the individual subject to the society of which he or she is a part?**

In essence, yes, although I see that more when the curtain is down and
the lights come up and the audience walks out of the theatre. I think the

personal journey inside is to resist the identification and then give in to it. The identification is more overpowering for having been resisted. The power for me sitting in [the Wooster Group's] *Route 1 & 9* is not realizing, "This society is racist," but, "Oh my God, I am a racist. I have participated in this. I have sat here and watched an evening of blackface." To have that ugliness exposed is overpowering because I resisted it.

Do you see this process in relationship to Brecht? That's one figure you haven't discussed yet. So much of what you're describing could be seen as a kind of Brechtian defamiliarization.

I have a love/hate relationship with Brecht. At some point in the next couple of years I'm hoping to sit down and reread Brecht. I really, really had a negative empathy response to him, to his theory. I don't see history as a distancing mechanism at all. I agree with Brecht only because he was basically robbing Shklovsky. I think history allows us to historicize the immediate concerns that we don't want to look at and therefore actually creates empathy, brings us closer. I was thinking, for example, in terms of historicization: what is it that's in my face right now that I want to look at? Okay, let's talk about capital punishment. How would I write a play to really look at and talk about capital punishment? Well I wouldn't do it the way that *Dead Man Walking* did. Wonderful movie, actually, but it's using a different mechanism. I'd probably write a play about Mary Surratt, the mother of John Surratt, one of the conspirators in Lincoln's assassination. She ran a boarding house in Washington, D.C., a good Roman Catholic mother, and her son brought all of his friends there. She was a confederate sympathizer, as were many in Washington. After the assassination, John Surratt was one of the very few conspirators to successfully flee the country. So they arrested Mary Surratt. Nobody believed at her trial that they were actually going to kill her, but they did. In 1865 she became the first woman executed by the federal government. The man who invented stenography took all the notes and he knew she was innocent from the transcripts. But the transcripts were edited, suppressed. Julia—who wrote *The Battle Hymn of the Republic*—she did an all-night vigil on the White House doorstep trying to get Andrew Johnson to commute the sentence. No one believed she'd be executed and yet she was. The most powerful argument that I can think of against capital punishment is the Matthew Brady photo of the four bodies hanging in the Navy yard, in which Mary Surratt's body is hooded. There she is in a Victorian dress and they had to rope her dress to her ankles so soldiers couldn't look up her dress when the body was hanging from the gibbet. They could go ahead and kill the woman but they couldn't allow Victorian morals to be violated by letting someone look up her skirt. That is such a phenomenal example of a kind of naturalization of mores that happens in history. By using history, I think you can get through to an incredible, empathic identification on the subject of capital punishment in a visceral way.

So that's why *How I Learned to Drive* is also a history play?
It's a history play because I'm observing that the notion of gender has changed for eleven-year-old girls, or for sixteen-year-old girls. I don't really quite know what that is now, so I had to go backwards in time to a point when I could speak with some authority. It's a way of asking, "Have we really changed?" It's a way of using history to see what we are naturalizing now, in 1997, by looking at what, through the perspective of history, we now notice as strange.

What's your process of writing, Paula? How do you usually start a play?
I usually start by trying to escape, closing myself away from people, going and finding a place that's remote, where I can't be reached. I start writing by spending a week doing nothing but staring at the ceiling and getting bored out of my mind. It's almost a retreat. Depending on the play, I spend a little time looking at the ceiling, finding out what my relationship to the material is, where I am. "This is what this play will do for me. Okay, I have to address this, I haven't addressed this yet." I do a lot of reading and research. For example, I read a lot about the fifties, sixties and eighties when writing *The Mineola Twins*. I did a lot of reading about automobiles for *How I Learned to Drive*, which I really enjoyed. There are thousands of books on automobiles—such a fetish— and I plunge into that. I construct a lot of tape loops. I spend a huge amount of money on music. Interestingly enough, looking around, I see all of your CDs and collections—I don't have any good music. I have only schlock for a particular play that creates a distinctive sound world. I create a sound loop that I play over and over again. It may be Strauss waltzes for *Baltimore Waltz*. It was The Mamas and The Papas' "Dedicated to the One I Love" and Roy Orbison for *How I Learned to Drive* with a little bit of Melissa Etheridge thrown in so that I could craft the end of that particular voyage. Teresa Brewer, all that kind of stuff.

Then I do a general plot outline. I try to figure out where I'm going. But I'm not figuring out the absolute ends of my plays anymore. I'm figuring out the peripeties and the beginning points. Then I usually surprise myself in the last moment. Not always, but often. Or the sequence surprises me. You let the plot take over. Take notes, and then let it rip. I usually try to get a draft out in two to four weeks. It depends on the material. Sometimes I'm lucky. *Baltimore Waltz* came out in three. And then I changed maybe ten percent. *How I Learned to Drive* came out in two weeks. I changed even less. But *Mineola Twins* is a year-and-a-half long baby. *And Baby Makes Seven*—we're talking about plays for which I wrote fifteen to twenty drafts. I also believe—and this has to do with the unconscious versus the conscious—that, on plays like *Hot 'N' Throbbing* or *The Mineola Twins*, the best thing to do before I return to rewrites is to start a new play. So I keep an ongoing cycle in which the new play tells me how to change, how to rewrite the older play.

What makes a good production of your work? Over the years I've seen so many productions, some very good, some very bad. I know from those, also from directing *The Oldest Profession*, that there is something very delicate and difficult about your work. And I know you've had some wonderful experiences, working with Molly Smith, for example. What do you think makes for a really good production of your work?
What makes a really good production is letting a play be mysterious and fragile, and having a director come in and not try to figure out what my intentions are or what will please me. Rather, a director has to figure out her or his relationship to the material in the way that I did when I started to write the play. So the director says, "This is the tale I want to tell with this script. Not the relationship of Paula Vogel to her dead brother, but here's the person I'm grieving, or the person I want to celebrate, or here's my homage to my first love affair, or my homage to my brother or sister." That's a director that's going to come in with a resistance to my play. I'm now thinking that what makes a good production is avoiding the kind of marriage model that we use in directing and playwriting collaborations. I think marriage is a terrible idea in the theatre—you get a compromise and a collaborative vision. It just creates mush. Much better is a kind of resistance, and a vibrancy, in which at times the playwright is speaking and at times the director responds. At times the designer is speaking and the actors respond. So it's more a response to the text than trying to let the text be the guiding principle. Now that may sound kind of fluid, but I'm really thinking synthesis is wrong. More interesting to see that's Bogart, that's Vogel, that's Mark Brokaw, that's Vogel, that's Molly Smith. Or to say, "Oh my God, that's Cherry Jones, that's Joe Mantello." So I'm now using the "call and response" mode of Gospel singing. The leader stands up and then the chorus responds. At times the text is the chorus, and the director is the leader, at times the actor, at times the playwright, the designer, the audience. That creates more of a collective response.

When you're writing do you have an imaginary audience in mind? Do you write for a friend, for a family member, for your lover?

It depends on the play. I don't think of an anonymous mass audience. I don't think of the theatre company, Oh, I'm gonna pitch this to so-and-so. I don't think of the market, in other words, the way that one might if one were sitting down to write a screenplay for hire. I don't think playwrights usually think that way. I do think occasionally, for example, I want to write a play for Anne Bogart to direct, or I want to write a play for Cherry Jones, or I'm writing this for my brother or I'm writing this for Anne. But usually, I'm the only audience in the room and I try to write just for me.

As a result of some nineteen years of teaching, of seeing a lot of plays in development, of being ill myself and of witnessing death, I have far less patience. What I say has to be said—I call it the "now we're two hours closer to death" principle. The last thing I want to do when I go out of the theatre is think, I'm two hours closer to death and I could have been spending that time . . . There's got to be something so compelling that I'm glad I spent those two hours in that theatre. So I'm a little more aware of sort of cutting to the chase at the top of the play. Each time I sit down to write now, I feel a greater urgency.

I know there's a strong autobiographical element to some of your plays, both overtly and covertly, and I wonder if you could just talk about how you think about that. Do your plays function as a kind of autobiography for you?

There's autobiography in it. Sometimes in unexpected ways. Since Carl's death, with every play I'm writing, I think of the Hirschfeld drawings in which he embroiders a "Nina" somewhere in the picture. There's a Carl embroidered in every play. There are places where there are small—I don't want to call them private jokes—but private communications sent to a variety of people that I love, both living and dead. But I think the plays are autobiographical in the way that actors need to have empathy and use their own bodies as vehicles in order to portray a character. I'm using sides of my history, of my own life, in order to enter a subject. For example, it's no coincidence that I'm writing *How I Learned to Drive* with a character named Uncle Peck at the time I turned forty-five. So I use that distance, between myself at age forty-five and my undergraduate students or younger people that I know, as a way of entering into the portrayal of Peck. I'm using my age, I'm using my personal memory of Maryland to make authentic the lyrical "I" so that I know exactly what song was playing when I was in summer camp in ninth grade. In the same way that actors give their bodies over, I'm giving over my memory and my history to the different characters I'm writing. That's different than saying each play has a function for me, which it does have—something released or something worked out—but it may be very indirect. This may seem a little strange, but I think the closest I will get to an absolutely autobiographical play will be the play that will seem to be the most distant, which is *Farinelli*, the play about the eighteenth-century castrato. It is, in my mind and thinking, the closest autobiography on the stage that I will ever write.

Because you feel like a castrato?
Absolutely. In the process of making artists, we make castratos. I think the castrato metaphor is a very true one. It's a way of examining myself as an artist, as a castrated human being teaching. I realized that I couldn't write the play until I quit teaching, so I've been holding off. I've had it in my head since probably 1981.

It's very interesting what people perceive as autobiography. On stage, I feel an incredible closeness to Peck. I feel an incredible closeness to Anna [in *Baltimore Waltz*], not because we were in the same position, but because, in essence, Anna is speaking the words of my brother. I use the actual relationships between myself and the material. But it's translated, it's not direct.

So all of the plays are autobiographical, but there's always an element of displacement.
Always. And I think that's the nature of theatre, too. When I want to become really autobiographical, as in the novel I planned to write this year, *Travels without Charlie*, that's the time to become, quote unquote, a "woman writer" and to write the lyrical I/eye as the fusion of the private persona with the reader. But there's a displacement in the theatrical process. It's not you, there's no such thing as a "you" or "he" or a "she." They're character recipes, not real people.

So there's always a sense of indirect discourse even when it's structured as a confessional narrative.
Absolutely. I'm very much reversing the experience I had as an actor, trying to understand Stanislavsky and the Method, knowing that it's not me, I'm not here. And the more you accept it's not you, the more you can, paradoxically, be visible and almost transparent. So you disappear and the character is what's there.

It's so interesting to me that your two plays that make the most use of the first person singular, confessional voice—*Baltimore Waltz* and *How I Learned to Drive*—are also the two that formally are the most deconstructive. So yes, there is a self that's being produced here, but it's a self that's in pieces.
And that hopefully is being unraveled.

Being unraveled through memories, fantasies, projections—different techniques. I think that's so important about your work. It's about producing women as subjects, but, particularly in your more recent plays, that subject no longer stakes a claim for the kind of prerogatives that male subjects like Willy Loman or James Tyrone have historically enjoyed. There's never a sense of that imperial ego in your work.

I always feel that all subjects—and I think this is also true of male subjects, depending on the writer—are impeachable. That's the great thing about drama. There is no "there" there. There's no authenticity. There's no absolute truth, it's who's in the room. In terms of structure, my plays are starting to use something very close to French scenes. Li'l Bit is whoever's in the room with her. Is she talking to us? Is she talking to her mother? Who is that woman who's no longer her mother? Transformational acting actually makes French scenes. One thing I always loved was when, I think it was Bert States who said, the first time you say Brutus was an honorable man, you go, "Yeah, well, maybe," and the second time you hear it you start to suspect, "What's wrong with Brutus?" And by the third time you hear it, you wouldn't buy a used car from Brutus. In a similar way, whatever anyone says on stage is impeachable. All subjects are impeachable. So there's no such thing as a protagonist structure. Whose play is it anyway? I really like watching characters fight to construct their own plays within the overarching structure of mine. This is the wonderful thing that Pinter did in *Old Times*. One of the things I love, and it just feels right to me now, is having Peck suddenly come down and say, "Uncle Peck teaches Cousin Bobby how to fish," suddenly talking about the real reason he comes back to South Carolina. Or when Aunt Mary speaks on behalf of her husband—who's the narrator? Everyone's the subject in their own play, in their own mind.

I do discern a change in your writing since about 1985 when you came to Brown. Do you think that that has something to do with your teaching, with the theory that you've been reading?

I think teaching has had a huge impact on me. Coming face-to-face with the younger generation and seeing how they don't ask permission to break the fourth wall has been very liberating. Reading a lot more contemporary dramatists has been really helpful. I'm sure theory also has. I also think it's probably a process of aging, which may sound strange. Aging does not necessarily mean solidifying or becoming more rigid. Aging could also mean, "Well, what the fuck. I don't give a damn anymore." Letting go, not being embarrassed, and in a strange way for me, aging is a process of just giving over. So a number of things are happening. One is that I think my plays are reflecting at a deep level more of a sense of loss. There's a sense of yearning and mourning.

So your plays are haunted by the ghosts of the past.

Mourning for a protagonist. Yearning for a well-made play structure or plot. There's a sense of what is lost, a nineteenth-century theatrical tradition as much as my youth or even people who are alive. You can see aging as a kind of coming apart in a good and liberating way. So I think my plays are coming apart. At some point I decided, I'm never going to get done. I'm never going to break through, let's just give it up. The second I stopped trying to please the dramaturgs and the Jon Jorys of this country, the second I accepted that I wasn't going to get through the door—and I still haven't gotten through the door of a lot of places—the more I started writing for myself. So I also think that's in there: a kind of giving up on American theatre, on commercial theatre, on pleasing people or on what people are going to think. I really don't care what people think anymore. There's greater pain than the rejection of strangers. It's an interesting thing, there's a liberation from loss.

But only as a result of acknowledging and living with loss?

Right, and trying to find a way for the dramatic form to encapsulate loss.

Which is precisely what *How I Learned to Drive* is about.

Right. To me, structure is everything. How do you make a structure that is actually the meaning of *How I Learned to Drive*? If people look at it, they can see the impact of abuses on the body. It's the way the play is told.

So that the body of the play almost becomes a substitute or a displacement for the body of Li'l Bit.

Exactly. And it is an out-of-body experience. The subject and the protagonist will never be unified. There is no unified interior for Li'l Bit, which I was struggling to find, I think, in *Baltimore Waltz*. So this is the next evolutionary stage. I suspect the castrato play will be the next. In between there are other plays. *The Mineola Twins* is very much my rethinking *And Baby Makes Seven*.

The difficulty is that it's easier to find proponents of *How I Learned to Drive* and *Baltimore Waltz*, and much harder to find supporters of *Desdemona* [1993], *And Baby Makes Seven* and *The Mineola Twins*. I'm not really sure why that is. I'm feeling that my actual physical shape on the world, being a "lesbian, female playwright," interferes with the reception of the play. I think we do this game. We look at a play and receive the play according to what we think a woman playwright or a lesbian playwright should write. There's a decorum here, and when you go against that decorum of what we should be writing, there's a real resistance.

Although that policing is, of course, primarily directed at persons of color, at sexual minorities and at women, because it's assumed that white men can write anything.
Tom Stoppard can do *Rosencrantz and Guildenstern*, but Paula Vogel can't do *Desdemona*. Recently on the Internet—there are some wonderful women playwrights in this chat group that I lurk on—a very good woman playwright brought up the topic of why it was so hard to get women's plays on. She talked about the frustration of seeing David Mamet's plays when his women characters were so abstract and caricatured. The men on the chat group changed the name of the thread to "Mamet and women." And when the woman playwright pointed out that women playwrights get bashed for negative portrayals of men, everybody then leapt in and said, "If Mamet's portrayals of men are positive . . ." completely ignoring the point that there's a decorum for women playwrights and men playwrights, for playwrights of color and white playwrights. There's a latitude given those in the majority that just does not exist for the others. There should be a word—it's beyond homophobia and misogyny—for a bias against lesbians that's very particular. It's not okay to be homophobic to gay men or misogynist to women, but it's okay to be misogynist and homophobic to lesbians. That's a peculiar combination. Certainly things aren't great right now for women playwrights, but for lesbian playwrights, it's terrible. One reason I stayed at Brown so long was that I was basically told by the theatre department to go away and it made me stay longer. I get told, "Go away," for *Desdemona*, which still amazes me—I am very proud of my failures, I don't think they're failures. But the reception just stunned me, so I decided to come right back and use those strategies again in *The Mineola Twins*. I probably would have left off writing for straight theatre long ago and moved on to movies and musicals. It's been the antagonism of the press that's kept me going.

Is this at all related to your point about the artist being castrated?
There are two things going on. In *The Female Eunuch* , Germaine Greer argues that women are seen as castrated males in society. I read that twenty years ago—I'm going to have to reread it—and it had a profound effect on me. One thing I've been thinking is that language that is particular to the male gender is now starting to attach itself to the female gender. For example, I have long felt and thought that women are virile, that there's a sense of female virility. Thanks in large part to women songwriters/singers, we're starting to see desire expressed by women in a profound way. The second has to do with our arts—we've castrated our arts. To isolate, to put on a pedestal, to make special is to take away power, to make impotent, very much the way that the female

gender is constructed: "Oh, you're special." You're isolated from the community of your peers, isolated from other people who work. And in essence, you're not going to be allowed to have children, i.e., you're not going to be able to replicate or to cross-fertilize each other because you've been ghettoized. I think of this phenomenon, for example, when *Angels in America* is isolated from all the other plays that Tony wrote. We constrain, we constrict our artists. We are so petrified of genius. Instead of saying that genius is just what happens when you work in a community for a long, long time, it's quarantined. We see art as something God-given and one-of-a-kind, and not as a way of working, as labor, something that is attached to so many other disciplines that give it meaning.

You were talking before, Paula, about the importance of history in your writing, and the function of history. A number of your plays could be described as history plays, *The Mineola Twins*, in particular. I'm curious, what does history mean to you, what counts as history? Because there's so much to draw on—social, political, economic history.
I'm a lay person, not a philosopher or a historian, but I've always been fascinated by it, and actually I started to major in history at Bryn Mawr. The connection I have with time is something that causes enormous emotional repercussions for me. Let me go way back. I remember a teacher in fourth grade—when I was the teacher's pet—bringing an early Edison gramophone into the classroom. And she said, "Paula, why don't you turn the crank of the phonograph," so that we could see how it worked. I think I burst out crying, and she said, "What's wrong," and I said, "I can't." And she said, "Why?" And I said, "Because there's a dead man's hand on that crank." I didn't want to put my hand out and occupy the space that belonged to somebody else. It was actually quite tangible to me. I don't think there's a neat demarcation, politically, ethically, between history and the present moment. It's a continuum. History is simply a way of us being enough out of the picture to analyze the shifting interconnections among politics, social history, economics, culture, gender. History is simply the name we give a discrete moment when we analyze those connections. So if you ask me about history, I guess it's about having enough distance to be able to see, for example, the notion of gender at a particular moment, the role that religion or the economic structure plays. For me, of course, it's all the present moment, just being analyzed through an Alienation Effect.

There are a number of periods I'd like to delve into more. I think that the Civil War in this country is still going on, but I don't know how or where to get into that in my work. Obviously, I've been molded by the seventeenth and eighteenth centuries. Huge changes going on, the transformation of science. I don't really see the present moment as distinct from history.

I find very powerful your understanding of history as loss, that it's about the man who used to crank the phonograph player who is no longer there.
But in some ways he is still there, and I think art makes him be there.

So art is always about ghosts.
The real power of art is to help us remember that which has been lost. That's exactly what an Edison gramophone is. Just in its physical being, impeding on our time, it draws us back into a time in which the clothing was different, in which the notion of science was different. I think writers do this a lot. Always, whenever I travel, I look into the houses and the apartments and try to imagine who lives there. How would you live in this tiny little town, with the car up on cement blocks and the laundry flapping in the wind? What does it feel like? How many children? Do they have indoor plumbing? What does it feel like to live inside that house? Environment has a profound effect on me. I think it does for a lot of playwrights. There are times when I just can't bear the sadness of being in a place—it's like a load on my spirit and I have to get away from it, because there's too much empathy. What was it like in 1725 for Farinelli? What was it like for Lorenz Hart in 1941, to have men hitting him in the back of the head, telling him to stand up when the National Anthem was being played, when he was already standing.

Since the 1960s, the American theatre has, in a large part, been defined in opposition to mass culture, especially to television, but also, to some extent, to film. I think that's been changing in the past ten years or so with the explosion of independent film.
Independent film has helped a lot.

But is there something that makes theatre distinctive?
Being with so many wonderful younger writers, I see there's no problem with theatre as an art form speaking to a younger generation. But you have to get the structure and the production out of the hands of older generations that don't want to give it over. Independent films have shown there's a way for a twenty-five year old to make something on two hundred thousand dollars and go to Sundance. So you suddenly have an art form that's addressing the current moment, and that's different from someone who's got access to studio financing. And similarly, in New York right now we're seeing a proliferation of places like The Drama Department or The New Group or Tiny Mythic Theatre. If

you turn over the theatrical apparatus to artists that have been dispossessed by the not-for-profit LORT structure, and by the Broadway and Off-Broadway structure, you're going to get theatre that's vibrant and speaking to audiences that haven't gone into the theatre.

It's almost like you're talking about the development of a new Off-Off-Broadway.
We have to have a new Off-Off-Broadway, and actually there is a new Off-Off-Broadway, and there's a new TCG forming. What do they call it? The RAT—Radical Alternative Theatre. There's a network that's connecting the Annex Theatre in Seattle to Salvage Vanguard in Austin, Texas, to Sledgehammer. It's the same thing that happened at the end of the fifties, "Okay, let's do Genet." No one's going to pay you to do Genet, you're going to have to do it on top of your day job. Is there something that's unique about theatre? Yes, there is, and I think it is making a comeback in the same way that, for example, poetry slams are suddenly being discovered by a younger generation. There is a live connection between the audience and the stage. That's the most terrific asset. Unfortunately, there's also been a connection between theatre and film at a studio level—people trying to figure out, What market are we talking about? How do we do this commercially, when they're not directly connected. But if you get any poet up on stage live, with an audience, there is going to be a vibrant connection. It's just that it's not worth anything in a capitalist country. It's art, it's not a moneymaker, and we've developed a notion of entertainment which has confused the two. That's not to say you can't have theatre that makes money and isn't also art. But the means of production in this country have been in the hands of people who feel that theatre should be a moneymaking proposition or now must be a moneymaking proposition since foundations and the NEA have turned their back, since we've forsaken the great experiment of the sixties. I do think theatre is going to specialize. Small theatres, doing what only theatre can—forget the helicopters—that's what's going to flourish. I'm not worried about theatre dying. I think to some extent, we have to die off. By that I mean our generation and those older have to give up the reins to let younger people in.

I'm feeling very, very good about recognizing that generational gap. Aging allows you to come apart and deconstruct your own generational art. You're unknitting and unraveling the commercial theatre of your time and actually speaking to audience members a generation younger than you. Your own generation wants to see everything comfortably put together in the status quo, they don't want to see it taken apart. You've got to reach the age and have the experience with the theatrical apparatus to be able to take it apart.

So you think it's essential that theatre artists start addressing these younger audiences?
We talk to ourselves, and the people, as a result, who pick up on us are younger. Suzan-Lori Parks and Mac Wellman are understood with perfect ease by twenty year olds in our classes at Brown. We have to explain Mac and Suzan-Lori to our own peers in their mid-forties because they're saying, "I want a tune that goes bum-bum-bum-di-dum." It's like Sondheim dismantling the Broadway musical, speaking to people twenty or thirty years younger than he is. It's not intentional, but as we dismantle the apparatus of our time we are speaking to a younger generation. That then becomes their legacy and they will dismantle it further. But they have to take over the means of production even to have a forum. I'm not thinking, I'm gonna go and get done at the Guthrie. I'm thinking, Gee, The Drama Department's in town and I'm in town, I oughta find out what they're about. The truth of the matter is, I don't know how to explain myself to someone who's been running an Off-Broadway or regional company for twenty years, but I don't even need to to a twenty year old.

So for you, then, the real divide is not so much between theatre and film as between the New Off-Off-Broadway and Broadway.
Or even Off-Broadway. What's interesting about independent film—and of course it's going to become the new studio film—is that now there's a way in which you can shoot *I Shot Andy Warhol* quickly, get it out there and speak to your peers without having to pay God-knows-what kinds of dues for ten years to get it through a studio. By that time it's turned into, I don't know, *The Way We Were*.

Despite all the complaints about the decline in audiences, you believe that theatre will thrive, especially a kind of poor theatre?
A poor theatre will remain. Absolutely. And looking at the last twelve years and the writers who've come through, it's extremely vibrant. What has made my hair turn white is thinking, Do I have to wait another ten years before the brilliance of a Madeleine Olnek gets through? I'll go crazy if other institutions don't arise Off-Off-Broadway to meet the Madeleine Olneks and the Donna DiNovellis who are already speaking to twenty year olds, but twenty year olds are not running Manhattan Theatre Club or Lincoln Center.

What playwrights do you think are doing the most important work now?
That's two questions. First, are my gods, who've already had a major impact on me. Second, are my peer group and younger that are doing what I think is really interesting, major work. I have three gods. One is

John Guare, the second is María Irene Fornés and the third is Caryl Churchill. They've transformed the possibilities, the vocabulary. I wouldn't be able to exist without them. In terms of who's doing fascinating, fabulous contemporary work out there, I would say Suzan-Lori Parks, Mac Wellman, Chuck Mee, Elizabeth Egloff, Connie Congdon, Naomi Wallace. I'm very excited to see what Tony Kushner writes in the next few years. It's actually a vibrant time for contemporary writers. And Philip Kan Gotanda's *The Ballad of Yachiyo* is a remarkable work. There's a rising generation that I've encountered, that excites me a great deal, like Stephanie Page Miskowski from Seattle. She wrote a play called *Feasting* that I read ten years ago, and boy, it still haunts me. It's a *Peer Gynt* of the nineties. I think Nilo Cruz is somebody I just adore on the page. Madeleine Olnek is already producing incredible contemporary masterpieces. Donna DiNovelli's work remains with me. I often think of starting a theatre just to see her work done. I've actually encountered a lot of major writers reading for panels. I will probably continue to do panel readings for the rest of my life—they're a way of restoring my faith in the vitality of theatre. It's not that theatre is unvital or on the decline. But the only theatre being produced is in such an ensconced, safe system that people aren't seeing what's out there.

What are your writing plans for the future?

I'm hoping I can finally do this full-time. That's my goal. And I've been thinking a lot more about film. I'm taking myself back to school in a way, reading as many screenplays as I can to try and figure out what my voice is cinematically. I'm starting an adaptation of *How I Learned to Drive*, which I originally saw as a movie and not a play, and I'm getting very excited by the movie in my head. So I want to continue screenwriting. I want to start to write for musical theatre. I don't think I'll be writing for straight theatre as much. I'm feeling the restrictions of the space, of the apparatus.

What is it about the musical stage now that excites you?

I think it's an emotionally overpowering form. And because it's so overpowering, it's political dynamite. When you can play with emotions like that, you can get all kinds of nifty things in politically. My father said something when I was a child that he repeated when I met him again twenty-five years later. He asked me if I liked musical theatre, and I said, "Yes," and he said, "Well that's good, because only through the American musical theatre can this country ever approach what Bertolt Brecht did in Germany." And I remember staring at him and saying, "Dad, did you tell me that when I was a child?" And he said, "Yes." I said, "I teach that now." For precisely that reason. I'm not opposed to mass culture at all. I think amazing things can be and are done on TV and in film. You just have to realize that you're not going to get certain things done on a big budget. If your budget's big, you can forget your voice. Know where your voice is. My voice happens to be in independent film or cable TV. It's not going to be in a big-budget film—although ask me again in two years. If I can't pay the rent, it may be very appealing. I've enjoyed the collaboration of the stage. I think I know how to collaborate now. Which means I think I'm ready for musical theatre and for film, where, as David Mamet once said, when they say collaborate they mean bend over. I think I'm less attached to my writing than I was as a younger woman. So I would like to write more novels. I've got about three in my head. I'm starting *Travels without Charlie* this year.

How do you see it?
It's a book I'm writing based on road trips I took to women's bars in the Deep South immediately following my brother's death. That's the first of a series of maybe three novels that I want to write. I'm hoping I'll eventually end up on the Cape, somewhere between Wellfleet and Provincetown, writing my detective novel series that we all want to do when we retire. So I think more and more I'll go into those forms, with just a few exceptions: the play about Farinelli, a play about the Duchess of Marlboro in the eighteenth century called *Wax*, and maybe a couple others. There are no longer any straight plays that I'm burning up to write. I'm mostly burning up to write musicals and movies. It's an interesting thing. A lot of people stay away from those forms because they see them as selling out. There's a defensiveness about the forms in which we write and I'm not feeling defensive anymore. I feel like I'm ready to work with more people in the room, and I'm ready to learn new forms that my Russian Formalist mind can attack.

Wendy Wasserstein

Wendy Wasserstein's Pulitzer Prize-winning play, *The Heidi Chronicles* (1988), was the first play to bring a history of the women's movement to Broadway. Since then, Wasserstein has repeatedly been hailed as "the voice of her generation" for her ability to tap into the zeitgeist with a convivial accuracy. Yet this epithet has proven as much a curse as a blessing. It is partly the result, she is the first to admit, of the scarcity of so-called straight plays on Broadway—especially plays by women. Her success thereby ironically puts her in the uncomfortable position of having to speak for a generation not only of women, but also of men, who came of age during the late fifties and sixties and now find themselves running the country. Wasserstein, after all, is only a few years younger than Bill Clinton, the obvious model for the unnamed president of *An American Daughter* (1997) who refuses to stand up for what he believes because, it is suggested, he doesn't believe in anything except his own popularity. At the same time, Wasserstein, has in her recent plays, taken up, at least as background, the kind of social and political issues that are usually understood to define a generation: in *The Heidi Chronicles*, the history of second-wave feminism; in *The Sisters Rosensweig* (1992), the collapse of the Soviet empire; and in *An American*

Daughter, the relentless personalization and trivialization of American politics. Making a "drama of ideas" out of fragments of culture, she deliberately mixes high and low, comedy and pathos, Farrah Fawcett and Bishop Tutu, proverbs and pastry. Wasserstein's main characters, moreover—in what is undeniably character-driven drama—have a certain emblematic quality. They all come from and inhabit the same social world and are all, like Heidi Holland, as much spectator as actor. They are Ivy League educated, affluent, well connected, slightly detached from the world in which they move and obstinately clever.

As Wasserstein has acknowledged many times, her plays comprise a thinly disguised autobiography: "What drives me to write, the urgency, comes from experiences I've actually had as a woman." Most of her heroines strongly resemble her in terms of background and education. Growing up in New York, the youngest of four siblings, she went to a private high school, attended Mount Holyoke College and earned an MFA in playwriting from the Yale School of Drama in the mid-seventies, when it produced a number of rather celebrated figures, including Christopher Durang, Meryl Streep and Sigourney Weaver. Like many of her heroines, she has taken advantage of the increased career opportunities for women that feminism has opened up. Like them, she travels among the rich and famous, has turned down at least one marriage proposal and has many close, gay, male friends whom she refers to as her "husbands." Her early plays, especially *Uncommon Women and Others* (1977), focus on a group of women looking forward to the rest of their lives and are centrally concerned, as Wasserstein admits, "with choice." Throughout *Uncommon Women*, Rita repeats the line, "When we're thirty, we're going to be pretty fucking amazing," only, at the end, to change the critical age to forty-five. Wasserstein's more recent plays, focusing on middle-aged characters, are, in contrast, more about choices that have already been made than a future waiting to happen.

In taking up a number of feminist issues, Wasserstein has become a somewhat controversial figure. Although lavishly praised by the mainstream press, *The Heidi Chronicles* was attacked by some feminist critics for recycling negative, comic stereotypes about women, and for fueling the backlash against feminism by blaming the women's movement for the personal unhappiness of its eponymous hero. Although a successful art historian who champions the work of women artists, Heidi prefers "humanist" to "feminist," bemoans her unmarried status and confesses to feeling "stranded" when "the point [of the women's movement] was that we were all in this together." There is no question but that her disappointment represents not only Wasserstein's own ambivalence toward feminism ("I don't think of myself as being a very good [feminist]"), but also and, more importantly, that of the many educated, privileged women who come to see her plays and apparently feel that they, too, were promised more than they got. At the same time, the equivocal reproach of feminism is clearly linked to the play's examination of the loss of idealism and political will on the part of so many children of the sixties who were determined to change the world, and now find themselves politically complacent and personally dissatisfied, yet remain unable to recognize that there might be a connection between these two conditions.

An American Daughter, Wasserstein's most pointedly political play, attempts to address that connection by interrogating the media's role in the debasement of political discourse. In an unmistakable echo of Clinton's abandonment of his nominees, Lani Guinier and Zoë Baird, the moment they became controversial, Wasserstein invents Lyssa Dent Hughes, a descendent of Julia Dent and Ulysses Grant—and liberal daughter of a conservative senator—whose nomination for Surgeon General is derailed when a slick, cynical newscaster discovers that she once misplaced a jury duty summons. Despite the focus on Lyssa's predicament, the play also foregrounds and satirizes the narcissistic, unprincipled commentators and pundits (all of them thinly disguised versions of real media stars) who monopolize the airwaves and take a positive delight in sabotaging Lyssa's nomination not for ideological reasons but because it proves their own clout. For the play clearly bears witness to the disappearance of ideology in today's celebrity journalism, the shift in emphasis from questions of belief to matters of entertainment and style. In the second act, Lyssa is distinguished from them by choosing to withdraw her nomination rather than cave in on what she believes. And in what is perhaps its most provocative moment, the play asks whether a pseudo-liberal president, uncannily like Clinton, "a good, well-educated man who reminds us so much of ourselves," may perhaps be "far more insidious than someone who hates every goddamn thing we believe in."

Although *An American Daughter* is far less ambivalent about politics and feminism than *The Heidi Chronicles*, it testifies to the increasingly retrospective nature of Wasserstein's recent plays, the tendency of her protagonists to look back on the choices they've made and to confront their losses and disappointments. And although she has no ghosts in her plays, her characters are finding themselves increasingly preoccupied by the past. Thus, for example, the assimilated, upwardly mobile Sisters Rosensweig are gradually revealed to be haunted by the spirit of their mother, by their New York Jewish upbringing, and by the men they've lost. And Lyssa Dent Hughes is haunted by her role as an American daughter, not only of the senator from Indiana but, more suggestively, of Julia Dent Grant, the Civil War, Reconstruction and a vanished, more conscientious nineteenth-century America. Yet perhaps the most haunted character in Wasserstein's work is Lyssa's friend, Judith Kaufman, a successful oncologist and African-American Jew who is mourning her inability to have a child. On the day after the Jewish New Year, she celebrates Tashlich, the festival of regrets "when good Jews send 365 days worth of their sins and sadness out to sea." Casting herself, rather than the crumbs of her low-fat muffin, out on the waters of the Potomac, she suddenly remembers the slogan of her mother's favorite donut shop, discovers a purpose and crawls up out of the river. It is perhaps the pivotal moment in Wasserstein's work (What other playwright would plumb a donut shop slogan for words to live by?), as a character remakes the past and what she has been handed, and takes an unamibivalent stand. Unlike Heidi and her nostalgic sisters, Judith discovers that only by drowning her regrets can she commit herself to the future: "As you ramble on through life, brother, whatever be your goal, keep your eye upon the donut and not upon the hole."

September 8, 1997—Theatre Communications Group office, New York City

DS: What got you interested in theatre?

WW: A number of things. Growing up in New York, in Brooklyn, and my folks taking me to theatre. I went to dancing school classes at the June Taylor School of Dance at 56th Street and Broadway. I would go there on Saturdays and then my parents took me to Broadway shows. And my grandfather wrote and acted in plays in the Yiddish theatre. He was a Polish immigrant and his stories are all sort of apocryphal. But he did, in fact, get ill while he was acting on stage in Pittsburgh, and then moved to New Jersey where he was the principal of a Hebrew school and remained in touch with a lot of people from the Yiddish theatre. My mother remembers going down to Ratner's, which used to be on Second Avenue. She remembers having dinner with Molly Picon and all of those people. I didn't know this man really, but I think there's something there. My mother is a very theatrical person. She is a dancer and her name is Lola, so there's that as well. But for me, it was very much about going to Broadway musicals. And as a girl I played with dolls a lot, and spent a lot of time making things up.

Making up situations, characters?

Yes, absolutely. It's odd, when all these things come up about, Girls shouldn't play with dolls, they should play with trucks, I think, You know what? I'd rather write a play with dolls. I had lots of fun making up things with dolls. So I think that as a child I was always funny, and that was one way to get by in life. I think that's still true.

So in other words, theatricalization is connected to comedy for you.

That's always been true.

When you were a kid, what musicals did you see?

I remember the movie of *Porgy and Bess*, also *Oliver* and *My Fair Lady*. We saw everything. We saw Ray Bolger in *All American*, I liked that. *The Unsinkable Molly Brown*, I remember seeing *Jennie*, with Mary Martin and the waterfall. I also remember seeing *Tiny Alice* with my parents, who were not, you know, the intelligentsia but they loved the theatre. They still do call me and say, "Can you get us tickets to take in a show?"

What plays besides *Tiny Alice*?
Tchin-Tchin—and I got very upset by that. Chris Durang and I talk about that a lot, and after *Tchin-Tchin*, I made myself a note not to come back home again. *Luther*, I remember very clearly, the Osborne play with Albert Finney, because I liked the idea of revolution and putting up a moral thesis. I also remember *No Time for Sergeants* very clearly and wondering, Where are the girls? And I remember thinking that the girl who got the boy was generally sort of boring whereas the best friend, the funny one, the Rosalind Russell type, was usually much more interesting.

What about classics? Shakespeare, Ibsen, Chekhov?
These are the plays I remember from elementary school. So even *Tiny Alice* when I was six years old was peculiar. I do remember my brother and I took my parents to see The Fugs in the Village. That was really funny. They just sat there. But as I got older, yes, I was very taken with Ibsen. Ibsen, Chekhov, a little bit of Shakespeare, too, but very much Chekhov. With *Three Sisters*, also at a very young age, the temperament of it must have resonated, maybe because my parents are immigrants. It has an Eastern European temperament to it, and the texture, if not Jewish, was something sad and funny. And I was quite taken by that mixture. I read Ibsen's *A Doll's House* in high school and thought about women's rights and what do you do with an intelligent woman.

In reading over your plays, I was thinking about how they're put together and the fact that most are built on almost Chekhovian principles. The plots are made up of little pieces of action and bits of choices that characters make. You don't have big events.
It's the smaller events in life, although in *An American Daughter* there is a larger event. But I feed on Chekhov. These people are smart and sort of well-to-do and they don't have big problems in life and who cares? The sadnesses of their lives, their lost moments and their cowardices as well, are things that really strike me. When I went to college I studied history. History really interests me, because it asks how do we look back at time. How did decisions get made?

It seems to me that your attraction to Chekhov is particularly important for female characters. For Chekhov's dramaturgy, with its subtleties and its almost microscopic action, allows for the production of a different kind of female character.

Yes, an unexpected female character. I'm writing a screenplay of *The Sisters Rosensweig* now, and it's very odd going back to an old play because you sit there and think, Oh my God, it's Dr. Gorgeous. Get her out of my house! You can turn on your own work very easily. You could dismiss Dr. Gorgeous as a suburban woman who just wants to wear Chanel. Then at the end what's interesting is that she is revealed to be a person of some dignity, sadness and intelligence.

I did not see that production, which I regret, but as I was reading it, I was struck by how she functions as a continual source of disruption.
That's exactly right.

The way she comes in and completely changes the mood of things. After Pfeni has been let down by Geoffrey, she comes in completely oblivious of it. It reminded me how in *Three Sisters* Chekhov always brings in characters like Solyony specifically to disrupt a scene.
Yes, and Merv the furrier is also a Chekhovian character. He's like the rest of the middle class, and Sara can't see it.

I'm intrigued to hear of your interest in history because some of your plays, most obviously *The Heidi Chronicles*, are history plays. And even *Uncommon Women and Others*, insofar as it's a record of the time. One thing I'm learning as I work on this book is that one of the main themes is ghosts. So many of the playwrights I'm interviewing have ghosts in their plays. You don't have actual ghosts in your plays, but there is a sense in which your characters are haunted by their own pasts.
Yes, I think that's true—prisoners of their childhoods! It's interesting, I wouldn't put a ghost in a play. That would scare me a little bit. I think they're haunted by their pasts and by their milieu, by the worlds from which they came and by the expectations of those worlds.

So by their families, their parents, their social class.
Social class very much so. The expectations for their lives. Those expectations stay in them—that's where the regrets come from. You don't even know if those are your personal regrets or your regrets for not fulfilling your parents' expectations.

Were you writing plays at Mount Holyoke?
I wrote plays even when I was in high school, but they were little plays to get out of gym. At Mount Holyoke I took playwriting from a wonderful teacher named Len Burkman who teaches at Smith. He's so great. He's got a long white ponytail and red sneakers—and this was

Smith College in 1969. I later found out that I was in Len's first class of students. I had no idea. To me he was like a grown-up. This means he's been at Smith for almost thirty years. He was a guy from Brooklyn so there's a connection but, because you're young, you don't know it. He was a wonderful teacher and playwright. He's in touch with this sort of nationwide band of playwrights that he's met at Sundance or wherever. That was extremely useful to me, because he was the first person who made me feel confidant with my own voice. Because I'm comedic, I'm somebody who could have ended up writing series television. Except that I think I'm too useful, or as André [Bishop] would say, "There's too much of an artiste in there." It wouldn't have worked out.

And you started Yale in '72?
'73.

What was most important to you about the playwriting program at Yale?
The people I met. Especially Chris Durang. Chris is one of my favorite people in the world, and even when I don't talk to him there's some-thing—we don't talk every day anymore as we used to. We talk maybe once a week, once every two weeks. But there's something about the fact that he's there. I used to feel when I first got to Yale that it was like the *Three Sisters*, except I was the idiot who went to Moscow. There were all these people in the late sixties at Amherst or Mount Holyoke, saying "Oh, I love the arts! I'm going to have an unconventional life, and you're just going to marry your boyfriend." They all went to law school or something. I thought, What kind of cuckoo am I? I didn't know where I was, but the thing about Christopher was he made me feel like I belonged somewhere and there was something about talking to him and how deeply bright and funny he was. We would sit for hours talking about our families. I respected him deeply.

When I showed up there it certainly wasn't, "Oh darling, you're so brilliant!" That did not happen. Howard Stein is a wonderful teacher and was very influential in my life, too. Meryl [Streep] was there at the same time and Sigourney [Weaver]. And Anne Cattaneo and I are still close, and Alma Cuervo has been in all of my plays except for *An American Daughter*. I'm very close to Tom Lynch, the designer. *Heidi Chronicles* was named for Heidi Ettinger. There's a lot of old friendships there. Paul Rudnick. There are people with whom you share an aes-thetic, and they're also friends. In many ways the character Peter Patrone comes from those years at the Yale School of Drama.

And the play's dedicated to Christopher.
The person who said to me at Yale, "You look so bored you must be very bright." Chris Durang, and André later—it's very much about the closeness of that.

Was there any theatre you saw in those years that was particularly influential? So much was happening in the seventies.
Yes, very much. Terrence [McNally] was teaching at Yale at the time. And they had what they called CBS fellowships. And Chris's work, Albert's [Innaurato] work. For our third-year project they did *The Three Sisters* with Christine Esterbrook, Marcell Rosenblatt and Alma, the three women in my class.

What about New York theatre during the seventies?
I remember coming in earlier, when I was in college, to see the Peter Brook *Midsummer's Night Dream*. But from '73–'76 I spent most of my time in New Haven. I was trying to find an identity for myself. I saw alternative theatre and Off-Broadway earlier. I remember *Adaptation*, *Next* and *Collision Course* very clearly. Israel Horowitz was a playwriting teacher of mine when I got out of college and was at City College. So I remember the playwrights of that generation: Terrence, Lanford [Wilson], Israel, John Guare, Leonard Melfi.

John Guare was writing such incredibly beautiful plays in the 1970s.
Yes, great plays. I just love *Bosoms and Neglect* and *Lydie Breeze*. I also like *Morning, Noon and Night*.

So you're fairly catholic in your tastes.
I like Lanford Wilson's writing a great deal. In some ways I can see a similarity between his work of a certain period and mine. I love *Tally's Folly* and the *Fifth of July*. I think he's a really wonderful writer. And I really like *Loose Ends* and Michael Weller's other plays from that time. And English plays are a very big influence for me because I've lived in London. I recently saw *Amy's View*, and I could see parallels between that play and *An American Daughter*. And I could see parallels, in many ways, between *Plenty* and *The Heidi Chronicles* as well.

What about women playwrights? Caryl Churchill, for example, though I realize she didn't come along until a bit later.
I love *Serious Money* and *Top Girls*—that's a vivid theatrical imagination. She's someone I deeply admire. We write very differently, but I think

she's great. I think Marsha Norman is a wonderful writer. I love *Getting Out*. And Tina Howe. I think of them very much as my colleagues. This summer I had a movie made [*The Object of My Affection*], and there's a convention scene. We thought, just as a sort of "in" thing we were going to have playwrights there. I called Tina and Marsha, I called the ladies, you know. Marsha was going to do it but she had child things, but Tina showed up. And Wendy Kesselman, too.

So you see yourself really as a part of a community of women writers who came of age in the seventies?

Eighties, too. In the mid-eighties three women won the Pulitzer Prize. I thought, that would be an interesting book if somebody wrote about me and Marsha and Beth. As personalities, too. I admire Paula Vogel's work. I was once on a panel with Paula and María Irene Fornés. It was kind of great, because I thought the three of us were wildly different people. But there's an intelligence and a caring there. Sometimes I look at the people around the table at The Dramatist's Guild and I think, "These are truly interesting people. Even interesting looking."

How do you write? What's your process? Do you start with a character, a situation, a line of dialogue?

I write pretty slowly. I'm good friends with Terrence McNally and he'll call me up and say, "I haven't done any work, I'm so worried." I'll say, "Terrence, you've written a play, a musical and God knows what else this week. Get off the phone." I'm slower than that. Once I'm writing I'm okay, but I rewrite a great deal. And sometimes my plays seem too well crafted. They're too well written, so they seem easier than they are. They're actually quite difficult to write. To get that kind of smoothness takes a lot of writing.

Generally, a play will come from an idea or something emotional. *The Heidi Chronicles* came about because I was actually unhappy, and I couldn't figure out what had happened from here to there. I couldn't understand how everyone was going one way when before they'd been going the other way. I have a very good memory. So I'll forget people's names, but I remember I had a conversation with them where they said they were doing X, and three years later I'll run into them and they'll be doing Y. I'll think, How come they immediately forgot and I remembered. I hate this. So often, it comes from something that I've been thinking about that I haven't seen someplace else. So I think, Why is nobody saying this? It should be said. I had the idea for *The Sisters Rosensweig* when I was living in London and writing *The Heidi Chronicles*. I thought it would be interesting to write about identity. I started *An American Daughter* during *The Sisters Rosensweig* and the Zoë Baird thing happened. Also, everyone was saying, "Where's your angry play? Aren't you angry?" And I thought, "Okay, okay."

And then I went through a period of a different kind of unhappiness. I'm going to write a play, but not for a few months. I also know when I'm going to start a play because I do other things. Sometimes plays are too important to me, so I avoid them. I do little journals and pieces, I also write movies or television to make money, then go back to the theatre. I'm going to write a play about money, actually. Because I felt that's a world I actually have access to that I don't see written about. I thought it's an interesting thing to write about, in a Philip Barry sort of way.

When you say a play about money, do you mean Wall Street?
No, it's never a plot like that. Again, it's about the people, I think, and the influence of money on their lives, and the romance, or what their values are. I was trying to do something about the turn of the century. I even thought about going back and forth in time to the previous turn of the century and this one, because I think it's really interesting. Hard to do.

So plays for you really come out of a sense that there's some problem for you or something you try to work through or some issue you want to examine?
Yes, I think so.

I was really intrigued by how ambitious *An American Daughter* is.
I think it's actually my best play, if there's such a thing, although it probably doesn't succeed as well as *The Sisters Rosensweig* in what it set out to do. I do remember the day I finished *The Sisters Rosensweig* I called up Chris Durang and said, "This was a hell of a lot of effort just to prove to myself what a good playwright Chekhov is. Next time do me a favor and tell me just to read the play." There is something about that play, now that I'm going back and working on it. The characters speak very honestly. And there is Gorgeous and Merv. So it fulfills its ambition. I'm still too close to *An American Daughter* to really know if it fulfills its ambition. Or maybe I am not the person who should be writing that kind of play.

What surprised me about it is that it really is a polemical work. And, I must say, I was really moved by the changes in both Judith and Lyssa in the second act. The play is so clearly about the importance of standing up for what you believe. It's very different from your other plays which tend to be more speculative, with characters having things both ways—or neither way.

Yes, they're all much more ambiguous. I know everyone changes in time, and in some ways that character Judith is very close to me. I hope she goes away! But yeah, in a certain way, it is closer to a polemical play. It'll be interesting to look at it again in about four or five years.

And watching it, I couldn't help thinking that perhaps one reason the press was not terribly kind to it is because it is so polemical and so political.
It's an indictment of the press.

A real critique of the press's role in personalizing politics and I don't think they particularly want to see that critique.
Right, and I was sort of cuckoo to think that you can do that. I mean, what was I thinking? Except you should be able to do that. What's the point of writing plays if you can't do that, if you have to say, "Well this won't work," or "I can't do that," or "I have to make a hit." That's crazy. You might as well write television if you're just going to craft a comedy. The point of the theatre is to use it for things that don't take thirty-seven meetings—to promote a voice or a view. Andrew Sullivan came to see it and said, "This is more of an English play than an American one." That was interesting as well. Closer to a David Hare play.

Because of the focus on how personal life affects politics.
Right, let's say I did take on Wall Street the same way I took on the press. That would be wonderful!

When you write, whom do you write for? Do you know when and where a new play is going to be produced? How conscious are you of an audience or production team?
I've been very lucky with André and Dan Sullivan. There has been a home for my work. And maybe when I went through *American Daughter* I didn't think, Will the press like it? Because it's hard for me to write, I think, Can I finish this? Is it doable? Then I think about whether it works for the characters in it. More than anything else, is this working for Gorgeous, or for Judith? My plays went on tour around the country and seeing who went to see them was very interesting. Do I think of women over men? Who knows, it depends on the play. I think there is a voice that is unexpressed, that's not taken seriously. Professional women roughly my age—people went to see Lyssa Hughes and Judith. They're not sexy people, but they're smart. They're people who have come of age, have some power, are hard-working, earnest. And yes, I do think of them, because those people often keep culture alive. Those people go to museums, they go to theatre, and they're not on the "Style" page, they're not the hip young things.

Maybe because of my experience at Mount Holyoke or my personal friends—it's not that I write for them, but I think about them. I do. Because it's not a question of those women being politically correct or incorrect, but they often go to plays. Even when I was young, when I did *Uncommon Women* I thought, I want to put the people who come to my plays up on stage. Same thing for *The Sisters Rosensweig*. I thought, If the Gorgeouses of life are the matinee ladies, let them see themselves on stage. Why do they have to sit there and see themselves as the wife who's a jerk and getting divorced?

When I went to a matinee of *An American Daughter*, the audience was about four-fifths women who were really absorbed in the play. Do you see your success in reaching an audience of women as a feminist political project? My own sense is that your relationship to feminism has changed over the past ten years as, of course, has feminism itself. I know that some feminists were sharply critical of *The Heidi Chronicles*.
Very much so.

What does feminism mean to you?
Maybe when a play closes and gets bad notices you get these things. But women started writing to me after *American Daughter*—Nora Ephron and Diane Sawyer and all these people—and I thought, This is really interesting. I would have expected that play to be criticized less by feminists. Much less. If there is an ideology, or if an idea can change your life, Betty Friedan's was probably the one that changed mine.

What about it?
The generality of feminism, or the idea that a woman's voice had legitimacy. I think, probably, it was something I would have come to on my own, because I went to girls' schools all my life and my mother is a deeply eccentric and independent-minded person. My eldest sister Sandy was head of the card division of American Express at a time before women did those things. She truly was a pioneer of corporate life, and I do have all these pictures of her with men in suits. In *Uncommon Women*, Katie says, "We knew we were natural resources before anyone decided to tap us." There's that sense of, "Why would you hide what you know? Why would you go and become somebody else to please someone?" That doesn't make any sense. "Why isn't my voice as legitimate as another person's voice?" That seems right to me. "Why is there no one like me on the stage?" I took the first women's history class at Mount Holyoke in 1970, which was taught by Chuck Trout, and I remember reading *The Feminine Mystique*. There's a line in there by this

girl who said she never thought she'd be older than twenty-one. If you go back, I love reading stories or the obituaries of women who were doctors in the 1920s. I think, Who was this? How did she do it? Because that's really hard. What I did was kind of hard, but not as hard as that. I find that deeply interesting. I don't know what would have happened to me. I maybe would have made an early marriage, gone to law school to make my parents happy, had kids and then started writing at age forty. I think maybe that would have been fine, too. I can't say one's better and one's worse. It's a different life experience. But that idea of equality, or of going and finding out what you can do really changed things for me.

So for you feminism is most important in providing women with opportunities that they never had before.
Opportunities—and in that it's been successful. If you look at law school classes, or drama school classes, or medical school classes, there are far more opportunities. My nieces went to law school. They've all married, but that's another story, you know, and that's the next generation. They will not wake up at forty, these upper-middle-class, educated women, and think, I gave my life to this person, what can I do now? I think more important is a personal sense of liberation. A personal sense. You have to open up opportunities. There has to be equal pay—these things are deeply important. I also think that pro-choice politics are deeply important. But the point is to be able to do what you want to do. My nieces, twenty-one year olds, say, "I don't know what I want to be." And I say, "I don't know who I am. So fine! But at least you have the right to find that out." And it's not defined by your gender, or by your sexuality, whatever that is.

One thing that struck me about *An American Daughter* is that in the first act, Judith's despair at not being married and not being able to have a child reminded me of your earlier work—the sense of loss and disillusionment that a number of your female characters feel. What surprised me was when she bounces back in the second act, transformed in a way. I thought that was a particularly important moment, because in a lot of your work, women—and I'm thinking of *The Heidi Chronicles* particularly—are striving for self-determination, for some kind of liberation from stereotypical feminine roles, but at the same time seem to be so desperate to be married, to fit in.
Judith throws that regret into the water. That's what's interesting about her. And the other thing I always found very powerful was when she showed up for the interview with Timber. And she always got applause when she left saying, "Keep your eye on the doorknob." I always felt, Here's this person who's in a state of despair, but she showed up for her friend. She's a really dignified person. And her sense of self has to be

deeper than her despair. That was the point. And at the end she goes back to work, the Chekhovian thing of going back to work. I agree with you that the change in her is a powerful change, and it's like Lyssa saying, "Your lives will continue."

But this also struck me as a real change in the trajectory of your work, creating characters who are able to take that kind of stand, because that's not something Heidi could have done.

No, it's not.

I've been wondering how you feel about those critics who have said that *The Heidi Chronicles* blames feminism for Heidi's unhappiness.

There was one woman critic who wrote about *The Heidi Chronicles* five times, and finally I thought, Go see another play. Go see *Crazy for You*. At that point I used to think that there aren't enough plays written by women. One woman—and I talked about this once with Callie Khouri who wrote *Thelma and Louise*—can't write that one play, that one movie. You can't put that kind of weight on something. During that period a great number of my friends started adopting children. Single women, single mothers. Then Murphy Brown had a baby alone. In some ways that show was prescient. So what's the single lady doing next door? She's adopting a baby. Are you going to tell her she's making the wrong choice? That's her choice, as a feminist, that's not up to you. One, there should be more plays by and about women, and two, groups inevitably look to a work to . . . I've talked to William Finn about this, that there would be gay groups that liked *Falsettos* and groups that didn't. I'm sure Tony Kushner must know all about this, because suddenly you become a spokesperson, and finally you want to say, "Honey, thank God there's a play about a gay fantasia on Broadway. And maybe next season there'll be three more, and you'll like the next one." I felt that very much about *Heidi*.

I think the point you're making about the burden of representation is extremely important. It seems that the New York theatre will allow one woman playwright on Broadway at a time, and you were in the spotlight at that moment.

I was the only woman to win the Tony Award for a play. (I'm sure Betty Comden's won one for the book of a musical.) Even some of the reaction to *An American Daughter*, when the press started saying I'd slipped on a banana peel this season. I thought, Would you say Edward Albee or Tony Kushner ever slipped on a banana peel? Would you say August Wilson ever slipped on a banana peel? What is it about me that gives you the ability to say this? Is it because I'm a girl? Is it because I'm a nice girl? Is it because I'm a funny girl? That was a bizarre thing, because I began to feel like Lyssa Dent Hughes. So, like André says, that play was prescient. I truly do believe that. And it's fine, not all plays will be successful. Maybe they're right, I don't know. It's like when Lyssa says, "There's nothing like hanging a female icon out to dry."

I was also thinking about the crucial position of gay men in your recent plays. Perhaps as a gay man myself, I'm really intrigued by their representation in your work. Particularly in *Heidi* and *The Sisters Rosensweig*—
And Morrow [in *An American Daughter*]?

I find him pretty repulsive.
I love Morrow. I'd want my friend to be endlessly interesting.

I've been noticing how important gay men are in your plays. In *The Heidi Chronicles*, Peter has everything that Heidi wants, and also Geoffrey, to some extent, in *The Sisters Rosensweig*. It's so interesting because I find that women in your plays tend to identify with gay men, and also to desire them. That's really complicated, because these gay men, like Peter, have what women want but at the same time they serve as an obstacle to straight women's desires, in part because they tend to fall in love with them.
I just did a movie about that. I adapted *The Object of My Affection* by Stephen McCaully It's about a gay man and a straight woman who falls in love with him. In my own life, there are a lot of gay men, you know. Those friendships have been my closest relationships with men, or with anyone. Especially, Christopher, Peter Parnell, André. They're in the plays as well, because they're in my imagination, and always have been. You know, I had a cousin who grew up with us who was gay as well named Katherine. So that's always been in my life. I'm forty-six, I'll be forty-seven in October—so I came of age sexually in college shortly before people were really coming out of the closet. As I recall, at the Yale School of Drama they were coming out in 1973. I was having a lot of those dinners—it's the scene at the Chicago art museum. In 1969–70, there was one guy at Amherst who was sort of a cross-dresser, but my dear friends were not telling me they were gay. That happened later. So a lot of the crushes you got on people, you got on men who weren't attracted to you, who were "sensitive" or "attractive" or you shared something with them. Jonathan Alpert used to work at the Manhattan Theatre Club and was, in fact, involved with my roommate. We used to sit in the basement at Amherst and sing show tunes. We came to New York to see *Coco*. I really liked him, I didn't have a crush on him or anything, but he was a great friend of mine, because we had that in common. So it was partially that. What's sexual love and what's romantic love, you know, that's all quite . . . maybe that's clearer to people now, I don't know. I hope so.

So your ambivalent representations of gay men come in part from your own complicated relationships with them.
I think so, and coming of age with gay men who were coming out of the closet when I was at Yale in '73–'76.

It's funny, because it sounds like your relationship to Christopher is very much like my relationship to Paula [Vogel], because we went to Cornell together, and we'd confess everything to each other—very similar.
Yeah, that's family and there's family love or whatever, and with André, too. You're lucky to have that. It's a mess if somebody's in love with you and it's not being returned.

You mentioned earlier you were a history major at Mount Holyoke, and I'd read in another interview that before you wrote *Heidi*, you were thinking about the play as a history of the women's movement. So I'm curious about how you understand history. One thing I've noticed is the importance of music in your plays, all of the songs from the fifties and sixties for *The Heidi Chronicles*, *Uncommon Women* and *An American Daughter* which you use to evoke a particular moment in or feeling about the past. But what is most important for you about history?
I was actually an intellectual history major. I was very interested in ideas, much more than dates, facts and things like that—how an idea can influence a time, or how it becomes so exciting that it changes things. Perhaps even the idea that there could be a dialectic or change. I've never been too interested in spiritual life—as an intellectual or personal pursuit, it doesn't interest me much. History: maybe it's not the structure of the play, maybe it's when you figure out where something's going. That you are very much a product of the times you live in. There's my family and stuff like that, but there's also coming of age in the late sixties, being a part of this group. I feel totally representational of a population glitch. We probably both are.

How do you feel about the sixties? I know for me, many of the hopes and ideas of the sixties were so important to me at the time and remain so. And it seems that for you, a lot of those ideas come through in your interest in feminism.
And an interest in the not-for-profit theatre. Who do you know who goes into something called "not-for-profit" these days? I have a sort of earnestness, too, that goes back to the Brooklyn Ethical Culture School. Sometimes I look at women of a certain age in the park who have hair the length of mine and refuse to cut it. Then I look at young actresses like Elizabeth Marvel and their spiky hair and I think, I know exactly who's got this length hair, I know where she comes from, I know who she's trying to look like, I know that she's trying to look like this person

thirty years ago. In terms of the sixties, there still is that idea that you could live an unconventional life. I don't feel, What am I going to do when I grow up? anymore. I think I am grown-up. If I'm going to change things, I'll change my grown-up life. Sometimes I am insanely hopeful and I just think, Why don't you look at the cold, hard facts? And then I think, Don't!

It's funny, it almost seems as if music functions in your plays to keep alive that hopefulness, because it seems so utopian. Whether it's Rodgers and Hart or songs from the fifties and sixties, these songs evoke a sense of hope and a sense of community.
There is a hope in community. But don't you get depressed when you look at our president and you think, Is this what we did? I think that really shows the hypocrisy. He's only style. I find him deeply depressing as a representative of us, if that's what he is—I wouldn't say give me George Bush, but I think George Bush, in a sense, is clearer.

That's another thing that surprised me about *An American Daughter*, the strong critique of Clinton.
That's another reason why I slipped on a banana peel.

Still, I can't help thinking about music, and how it works to keep something alive for you.
I actually think it works to keep me alive. I'm like Lyssa Hughes, I don't listen to much music past Aretha Franklin and the Beatles. Frankly, when I'm working I listen to music a lot because it wakes me up again. I also think that through the music you very much get a sense of time. Although, now I notice more and more that movies get stuffed with this kind of music, so I like it less because I think, This is a feel-good thing—now we're going to listen to Dionne Warwick.

I find in a lot of popular culture that music becomes a substitute for history. Instead of looking at what was really happening during the sixties, we'll put on some Supremes—
And then we'll put on a skirt and a mirror ball. That's exactly right.

It seems to me that this substitute for history is very dangerous.
I agree with you.

I mean, the state of amnesia people live in these days.
Yes, I think we're living in a very strange time.

I know you've already been talking about this quite a bit, but I'm thinking again about the autobiographical elements in your work. Not that I want to do a *National Enquirer* number, but—
That would be good. I was rescued by aliens.

It seems that your plays really do tell the history of your ideas.
I think that's closer to what they do. *An American Daughter* is my least autobiographical play, except that Judith in many ways comes close to how I was feeling at the time. That made me happy. I loved Lynne Thigpen in that play. Yes, they've become less autobiographical as time has gone by. *Uncommon Women*, surely, that's like a first novel, an autobiographical college play—that's my friends and me. And *Isn't It Romantic* [1981], too, in a way. *The Heidi Chronicles* somewhat less, you know—Chris Durang and me, or André and me, but it's also different circumstances. I do remember the first feminist group I went to and it was in Northhampton. *The Sisters Rosensweig*—I am the youngest of three sisters. It was very odd, I was with my sister in London this year. My sister lived in London between ages twenty-one and twenty-four, and it was odd thinking I'd invented this woman who lived there at fifty-four—and I know London much better than my sister does. I think you're right, it is more a history of my own ideas or my reactions to things.

And your questions and commitments.
Yes. And then also my trying to become a better playwright. Because you're in charge of that. I've never thought, I have to write a play, give me an idea. It's always come internally. Hmm, this would be interesting, I'd like to try to do this, let me see if I can create this thing. An interest in playwriting. That's why I liked *How I Learned to Drive* so much. I thought, This is really good playwriting, this is really interesting, this woman knows how to do this. I also thought that I would never know how to structure something like that. And I thought, We're very different kinds of writers.

It seems that there are certain things you can do in the theatre that you can't do on television or in the movies.
You bet. You can also express ideas. What's interesting about *The Sisters Rosensweig* is a man coming on stage and falling in love with a fifty-four-year-old woman. I haven't seen that in the movies or on television a lot. You might see that after something works and is commercial—*The First Wives Club*. I used to talk about the theatre using a Melitta drip theory of culture. Things come first from the theatre because it's an art form,

and then it drips into the culture. So you'll find gay plays first, then it'll be *Philadelphia*, then *In and Out*.

So despite your work for Hollywood, theatre remains your first love?
What I always love is going through customs and writing down your occupation: playwright. That's just the coolest thing. It's stupid, but yeah. I just did *The Object of My Affection* with Nick [Hytner] and I would write again for him in a minute. What I love the most and respect the most is playwriting and, therefore, it becomes the most difficult. Sometimes you just don't want to go near that. It just means too much to you.

It's the most personal.
Yes, it is the most personal. It was fun doing the movie this summer because it wasn't about me. But I guess it's theatre that interests me most, frustrates me most, angers me the most, sometimes, when I see other plays. I go a lot to the ballet, and as I get older I like it even more because I don't know much about it, because I can't sit there and say, "She's terrible, she can't lift her legs."

At this point, as we all know, the American theatre is in pretty bad shape. Do you think theatre will survive?
It really worries me. There will always be panels asking: "Is Broadway Dying?" And as long as there's a panel, there'll always be these "Women in Theatre" panels. Paula and I will grow old together. I will see this woman once every two or three years on these "women" panels. As long as it happens, you know there's theatre, and you know there are women in theatre, and that's all fine. And things will mutate and change. Talk to Edward and Lanford about the early Off-Broadway, and what that movement was like. And now we have the Manhattan Theatre Club and Playwrights Horizons—are they the establishment? Are they not? Blah, blah, blah. I think Disney and Garth Drabinsky coming into Broadway is different, because it's not just an aesthetic difference, it's also a contractual difference. Once playwriting becomes contractually like movie writing, that's bad, because then you're no longer an individual voice, you're a mouth for hire. Then there is less of a reason to write plays. If that happens to plays—and I don't think it will—that's very serious. I also think it's dangerous if it becomes like the Oscars, if Broadway becomes the province of blockbusters and real work is solely the product of independents and Off-Broadway. With *The Heidi Chronicles* I figured at the time, "Let's just keep this Off-Broadway. Let's keep it affordable," but the move made it a popular work. Frank Rich is a friend

of mine, and he was saying a play like Paula's could actually play at the Booth Theatre. I think it's wonderful at the Vineyard and it should run forever. But there's a difference between it and those blockbusters—good theatre becomes marginalized. And that worries me. We are not playwrights gearing up and doing our plays Off-Broadway so someone will notice us to give us a movie job or hire us to write *Les Miz*. We are practicing artists.

I remember the year *The Sisters Rosensweig* was on Broadway, so was Tony Kushner's play, and so was Anna Deavere Smith. I thought, "Three years ago, nobody would have said any of these people are Broadway writers." They would have said to Tony, "What, a gay fantasia?" Or this black woman doing something that's like performance art. Or this play about a fifty-four-year-old woman who falls in love? And God knows, with the NEA and slashes in funding for the arts—that's really scary. On top of that, you have the critical establishment, but that will always be. Wherever I talk people raise their hands and ask what I think of the critics. And I say it's part of the thing, and your feelings will get hurt, and your play will close—that just happened to me—but that's it. If it's one guy or another guy, one guy will like it, the other won't. It would be very nice if there were women doing that particular job in the theatre—that would be delightful. I was at the Royal National Theatre recently with Nick [Hytner] and the audience there was rather staid and he asked, "Where is the younger audience?" I think that's very important, too. Making it vital for a younger audience. Because once you get in there, theatre is moving in a way that other things can't be. You know there are all those kids sleeping outside of *Rent* to get tickets. What those people, the Disney/Garth Drabinsky people have figured out is that theatre is big business, you can make a lot of money. Playwrights should make a lot of money, too. They should make heaps.

So there are two real problems for you: one, theatre audiences are aging. Even plays like *How I Learned to Drive* or *As Bees in Honey Drown* attract older audiences. It's disturbing that young people are not, for the most part, being brought into the theatre. Two, theatre has become very hierarchical, with Broadway dominated by the big corporate producers. And I guess you are suggesting that these categories—Broadway, Off-Broadway, etcetera—are becoming increasingly hardened.
They weren't a few years ago.

And the movement between the categories keeps theatre alive.
Yes, so that every now and then there'll be a *Rent* and they'll move it and go, "Oh, wonderful." But there really isn't enough of that.

Because theatre needs new blood.

Theatre really needs new blood. And you know what's interesting at this point about a guy like Jerry Zaks? He has a life directing plays. It's very hard to have a life directing plays, acting in plays, writing plays. It's nearly impossible at this point. You have to do something else, or you can't afford it. So it really becomes an art form. What's interesting about plays is that ideas can come from them and go into the culture, and then they go into television or into film. I remember going to a Christmas party for *The Heidi Chronicles* or *The Sisters Rosensweig*, and I would think, All these people are here because somebody sat in a room and wrote a play. So I consider myself really lucky to have done it. Probably by a fluke. I think definitely by a fluke.

Mac Wellman

Mac Wellman has a wicked way with words. In 1990, while enjoying a grant from an embattled and queasy NEA, he wrote *Sincerity Forever*—a raucous meditation on art, politics, family values and Jesus H. Christ—dedicating the play to Senator Jesse Helms and the Reverend Donald Wildmon, head of the American Family Association: "With my compliments, for the fine job you are doing of destroying civil liberties in these States." A fierce defender of the First Amendment, Wellman wrote to Wildmon when the latter reprinted a speech from the play in his newsletter, charging him with violation of copyright, bigotry, willfully misunderstanding the Bible and dressing up "hatred in the language of love."

Perhaps the most provocative accusation in Wellman's letter, however—for what it suggests about the playwright—is his insistence upon Wildmon's "intense hatred of the rich and colorful language of the common people." For all of Wellman's plays represent veritable orgies of language. Stretching grammar to the breaking point, reveling in the sound and texture of words, they turn language, character and dramatic form inside out. Doing for drama what William Burroughs did for the novel, Wellman creates a unique, language-driven mise-en-scène that pulverizes the syntax of traditional theatre. This is not to suggest that his use of language is obscure or pretentious. Quite the contrary. For it is always an outgrowth—cancerous mutation might be a more accurate metaphor—of "the rich and colorful language of the common people." And so many of his characters' speeches represent ingenious appropriations and elaborations of clichés, puns, curses and prayers; lists of often wildly dissimilar names and places; and violent harangues that morph into a kind of pure poetry. What other playwright could imagine a universe teeming with planets named Plinth, Goethe, Jubilatrix, Bistro, Reddish, Galahad, Wild, Mildred and Dudu? What other playwright would dare people his plays with space aliens, dancing plates and spoons, vampires, girl huns, mystic furballs and bodacious flapdoodles?

Wellman's theatre, however, is by no means an arbitrarily designed linguistic curio shop (how difficult it is to write about his work without proliferating metaphors and lists). His 1984 essay, "The Theatre of Good Intentions," represents a kind of antinaturalist manifesto in which he attacks the traditional theatre for its manipulation of warm emotions, its impoverished dramatic vocabulary, its fake profundity, its doggedly consistent and well-rounded characters, its fixation on questions of motivation and intention, its habit of explaining evil away and its obsession with victims. It argues that the well-intentioned play "succeed[s] all too well" in producing "a perfect and seamless summation of itself and its own intentions, and nothing else." Reduced, in other words, to an easily consumable message, it becomes "a mere disposable article." In response to this moralizing, debilitated theatre, Wellman offers a theatre of excess, of deeds rather than motives, of agents rather than victims. Most important, he writes plays that cannot be summarized or translated into another medium, that exploit the theatre for its ability to amaze and stymie. Despite its gleeful rejection of the well-made play, his drama is always a reflection upon theatre itself and is haunted by popular forms—knockabout farce, melodrama, musical theatre and vaudeville—fragmenting, mocking, exploiting, holding them up for examination. Thus *Crowbar* (1990), which takes place in an old Broadway theatre, is a kind of vaudeville show for ghosts, casualties of history, who compulsively turn their lives and deaths into grand guignol, retelling the injustices, inequities, greed, poverty and the big and little murders that killed them off. Because, "All theaters are haunted" and "America/is an empty theater," the play reimagines the history of the nation as a pantomime of nervous ghosts, some of whom die rich, but most of whom die poor.

Wellman's agitation for civil liberties and his invention of a new theatre poetry are by no means separate enterprises. For his antinaturalist project represents a deliberate political intervention. Confronting what he calls the "self-destruction of the left" and the apparent dead end of liberalism—as exemplified by the theatre of good intentions—he attempts to "pursue an edgy, intuitive path to explore the full damage done by the onslaught of political lies, right-wing hucksterism and general consumer-society madness, on the inner person." Using theatre to jostle and unsettle our ideas of reality and truth, he writes plays that are mysteries. But in his version of the whodunit, the mystery is not finally resolved but deepened. His theatre, in short, becomes a spur to reimagine American culture, to rethink the connections between corporate rapine and the politics of deception, between environmental devastation and the loss of community, between art and social critique. Focused on doing rather than being, on acts rather than identities (and implicitly criticizing the ubiquitous identity politics of our time), it never tells an audience what to think or do. Sometimes, as in *Sincerity Forever* and *7 Blowjobs* (1991), politics is at its very center. More commonly, however, as in *Terminal Hip* (1990) or *FNU LNU* (1997), the political is embedded in a vertiginous reflection on performance, role-playing and the power of language. But in all these plays, and quite literally in *Whirligig* (1989), Wellman reacts against the asceticism so often associated with leftist art by taking the spectator on an exhilarating ride to the far reaches of outer—and inner—space, past Whipple and Hamburga, past Helms and Wildmon.

Wellman's most activist play, *Sincerity Forever*, represents both an unmasking of the intolerance and hatred that lie concealed beneath the language of love and a dialogue about the function of art in a time of social crisis. Set in the town of Hillsbottom on a "beautiful summer's night," it focuses on seven rather banal young men and women who pass their time wondering about God and the meaning of the universe, falling in love and being deeply sincere. They also happen to be dressed in Ku Klux Klan regalia. Their bucolic paradise is raided, however, by two Furballs who seem to have been beamed down from the East Village. Like enraged, naughty artists, they loathe the "flabby-minded, suburban, knee-jerk, bogus, flatulent, slimeball" ways of the good citizens of Hillsbottom, despite the fact that they, in their own uncouth ways, are just as earnest, well intentioned and sincere. The good citizens find themselves becoming inexplicably possessed by the furry invaders, turning homosexual and regurgitating the Furballs' speeches. In the midst of this chaos (clearly an allegorization of the right's fears about the corrupting influence of allegedly indecent art), Jesus H. Christ appears, an African-American woman carrying a heavy suitcase. In her long final speech (part of which was purloined by the good

DS: How did you get interested in theatre?

MW: It was an accident. I took my junior year abroad, this was 1965, and I was hitchhiking in Europe. Outside of the Hague. I got picked up by a woman who yelled at me and said, "You're hitchhiking in the wrong spot, if you stay there you'll get arrested." She spoke perfect English and said, "Get in." Her name was Annemarie Prins and she ran an experimental theatre company in Amsterdam. She was doing a production of Garcia Lorca, not a play, but a production based on his life, and we started talking about theatre. She was the kind of person I'd always wanted to meet in Europe, a bohemian artiste. She did the premieres of eight or ten Brecht plays, a little later she did a TV version of *The Seven Deadly Sins of the Petty Bourgeoisie* for Dutch television and the Germans objected to this version and they had Helene Weigel take a look at it, who loved it. Annemarie has pictures of Weigel staying with her, about four months before Weigel died. So through Annemarie I began to think about theatre in a different way. I studied in Washington, D.C., and occasionally I'd go to Arena Stage, but I found it fairly tedious.

Where did you go to college?

I studied at the School of International Service at American University, which is a diplomatic school. Like Georgetown, it's very specialized. D.C. in those days was a very interesting place. It had not yet become the imperial capital. This was before the riots, so there were still jazz clubs and it was fairly integrated. The color field painters were there, poets, it was a very bohemian kind of place, this sleepy southern town. And it was a good time to be in school, although by the end of the sixties it had gone completely crazy.

It took me a while to get involved with theatre. At one point Annemarie noticed I had dialogue in the poems I was writing. She said, "Did you ever think of writing plays?" I said, "No, I don't know how to do that." She said, "There's somebody coming from Dutch radio tomorrow. If you have an idea, we'll try to convince him." I thought this was an opportunity, so I made a list of things I thought should go in a play. I knew nothing about what I was doing. The guy commissioned me, and that's how my first play got written. So for a few years, my work was all radio drama, translated into Dutch, a language I don't speak. I was rather shocked the first time I heard my own plays in a language I don't understand. It was terrifying.

A couple years later I moved to New York because I was getting sick of the third-string New York School poets throwing their weight around in D.C. I thought I might as well go to New York and become one of them. So that's what I did. But even then—I moved here in '75— it took me four or five years before I really found my place. I was writing plays that I would characterize as poetical plays, ghastly historical dramas, almost no connection to contemporary theatre. But I went to see a lot—rather than go to a drama school—which I think was the right thing to do.

What work was particularly important for you then?

I went to see everything. I rather quickly made friends with Bonnie Marranca and Gautam Dasgupta. I met them at a book fair when they did the first issue of *Performing Arts Journal*. We started hanging out. I asked them, "What plays should I read?" And they said, "What plays do you have?" I read an awful lot. I saw the last production of the Open Theater. I saw the Performance Group's *The Tooth of Crime*. And Mabou Mines was really getting going then. And Richard Foreman, *Rhoda in Potatoland*. So it was an exciting time in New York theatre, and those works made a huge impact on me. Something like Lee Breuer's *The B. Beaver Animation* is still, for me, almost a perfect theatre piece. That and *The Lost Ones*, which was a Beckett adaptation.

That, too, was Lee Breuer's?

Yes. Pieces impossible to paraphrase and describe. Travis Pressmen said, and I think it's true, that there were a couple years when he was the best director in the world. I was lucky to see those works.

So you really didn't get interested in theatre until you started seeing experimental work.

That's true. I was more interested in poetry, although I think there are always instances or occurrences in life which predispose people to like theatre. I can tell immediately when I talk to a playwright if they have that sort of experience in their past. For me it was my father dying when I was a young boy. So we had one of these classic midwestern attics full of stuff, including an old gun case, a model of a clipper ship he made himself and a Punch and Judy set, with the little puppet theatre. I remember those figures being quite horrifying, which they are. The Dog-faced Boy and the Punch and the Judy and the other characters. I didn't really know what a theatre was, but it doesn't take a lot of deep knowledge to figure out a Punch and Judy show. I played with them until they fell apart. I think that was really a constitutive event, meaningless in terms of its actual content, but it predisposed me to theatre dementia later on.

This comes out particularly in terms of *Crowbar*, but I think it's everywhere in your work: the idea of haunting, the way that characters appear from somewhere else and bring a sense of a mysterious past with them, a sense of history. Which means your theatre is also very much about loss.

I think that probably goes back to the fact that those moments were associated with the death of a parent. So, theatre's connected with replacing that person, in a sense. I always ask young playwrights when I teach if they have that kind of event—not that it has to be the same. If they don't, I'm skeptical about whether they really are playwrights.

Did you see the Wooster Group or Robert Wilson when you were in New York in the seventies?

The Wooster Group formed a little later, out of the ruins of the Performance Group. I know Jim Clayburgh pretty well through Jeff Jones and I respect their work an awful lot. I think it's nearly perfect. For me it's cold, I don't warm up to it a lot. It's deliberately not about anything. And I'm a little old-fashioned. Some of their pieces I like more than others. I do think they're wonderful artists and everybody should see their work, but there's always something very studied about the way they situate themselves in the New York cultural scene and they can get away with it because it's so mediocre. If this were a great theatre culture, and it's not, they would be forced competitively to be doing work of real substance. The same is true of all those people. I think Foreman is repeating himself an awful lot. He's turning into a kind of export pills of American avant-garde, and there's nobody to push him. Wilson—I spent many years sort of hating the idea of him, but actually I think he's a great artist and enormously savvy about language, which he's not supposed to be. But he's far smarter about language than half the Pulitzer Prize winners in this country. Just because it's visually intelligent doesn't mean it's not intelligent verbally. Those are major figures. They came along at a time when it was not easy, but easier than now to establish a domain on the landscape. A lot of the lesser ones have disappeared. These people certainly had an enormous impact on my generation of writers, at least in my immediate circle of friends, for people like Jeffrey Jones and Len Jenkin. But the sort of people that interest me have had a more aggressive attitude towards writing itself. Partly, that's dictated by an aesthetic agenda, partly by economic necessity, since none of us were working in places where we could mount productions they were capable of. It took me a long time to see how radically different that kind of work is from what I was trying to do. The Woosters, for instance, want a very straight text that they can then do something crazy to. A text written in a deeply complex way that almost deconstructs itself on the page is of no interest to any of those people, because it takes away the joy of what they like to do.

Except for Richard Foreman, I think. Foreman's own texts do that.
Basically they're rather simple. The language is fairly simple. The jumps have to do with associational leaps—it's a psychology thing, it seems to me. Also, the directors I needed were not those who were going to deconstruct a text and throw it all over the place, but somebody who was going to direct it as simply and as naturally as possible. It's still a challenge to get people to do that. So, there's a sense in which I write naturalistic plays that don't appear naturalistic. I just didn't know it.

There's a kind of luscious materiality of language in your work which is very different from the other people you've mentioned.
Those people—and a lot of people who are exploring language now—showed me that theatre can be excessive. Because the mainstream theatre that I knew was naturalistic or realistic in a way I found claustrophobic and dull. It was not a theatre of excess, except for the musicals which, of course, were wonderful. It was a theatre of penury and littleness and paucity and deprivation—spiritually, emotionally and ethically. And theatrically. A lot of us responded against that. Why do theatre if it is so tame? Annemarie Prins always said, "Why do theatre unless you take risks?" I'm stunned, even to this day, by how many people I respect think that theatre is about cutting your losses, trying to present things believably and sequentially in a rational way. As far as I'm concerned that's the last thing to put on stage.

I find your notion of excess so interesting because I connect it, both in and out of the theatre, with pleasure. It's one of the primary sources of pleasure.
Exactly. It's a very, very important aspect of the theatre that often gets short shrift. For instance, I was on a theatre panel a few years ago in Los Angeles organized by the Audrey Skirball-Kenis Theatre Projects with all these major playwrights. At the end, we all had to explain what we

thought theatre was for. And all these people were saying the right things—that theatre was important politically because one had to be morally involved in the issues of the day. One after another, they were talking about social problems. Then at the end they got to me. I said I was in theatre because it was a low, sleazy and discredited art form that had to do with sex and things of the devil, and that I got into theatre for the same reasons that most people do, to meet partners and sexy people and low-life types that were having a good time when no one else in town was. The moralism of contemporary theatre worries me a lot, and that's where the Wooster Group comes in—they are dangerous, they play that card. Theatre respects no gods. It always has terrified authorities and the better class of religion. Theatrical knowledge is of its own kind. It can't really be paraphrased. I can't possibly explain what the best theatre experiences are about and when I try, I just end up saying clichés or silly things. A great production is unlike anything else.

So for you then, this quality of excess, this danger is something that really distinguishes theatre from other art forms, film, for example.
Yes. I think screenwriting—and a lot of people have said this—is more like novel writing, because you can tell a story, set up a location, have special effects that actually work. You can deal with psychology in novelistic ways. But what you never can have is the immediacy, the physical realness of theatre, the danger. There's a kind of spiritual intensity to theatre that's hard to get in film. I love film and I think in some ways it's more germane to the main narrative of the twentieth century than theatre. But I think theatre is truer and even more necessary now than film. Also film is not going through a happy period right now. I see fewer and fewer films that are any good. Even the noncommercial small films bore me. Whereas during the thirties and forties Americans couldn't make a bad movie. During the sixties the French couldn't. But I'm impatient with film now. It's all committee work, it's laborious and about money. I think that explains why it's not as interesting as it once was. But theatre, particularly noncommercial theatre, can be small, you can do it with almost no money. So I think theatre's actually in a rather good position to survive as a significant cultural mode of expression.

As I was reading some of your plays, they suddenly starting reminding me of Jacobean tragedy, in terms of their verbal and spectacular excess.
I think that's one of the great periods because the language as we know it was being invented by all these people. Shakespeare was only the smartest of a very smart bunch. The language literally could have gone

in several directions. There were so many major dramatists who are never done, like George Chapman. The spelling, grammar and punctuation were a part of one's personal writing style, which is inconceivable to us now. The love for theatricality and the intellectual daring, they had. A lot of it has to do with the fact that the first English grammar wasn't composed until twenty years after Shakespeare was dead. And then the gatekeepers of high culture take over.

I find it interesting your talking specifically about writers inventing their own language because I often sense that's precisely what you are doing in your own work. You are using the poetic line precisely as a way of breaking with certain traditional ideas of meaning, inventing a vocabulary.

I think this is what we do in life. There's a very American notion that one's life is a performance. So self-invention goes along with it. The hardest thing for me as a playwright in the early days was to figure out how to be a poet and a writer for theatre at the same time. I wrote these poetical plays of the sort that everybody in New York City has under their bed, including my dental hygienist. But it's only in the realm of the poetical, and it's false and dead and motivated by nostalgia for Shakespeare and a grand age that we don't live in. It was hard for me to figure out how to write in a way that was, in my view, poetic and involved an interrogation of language, and also was germane to what was going on in the world, and therefore contemporary, which I think art has to be. If it's not contemporary, then it's geezer theatre, it's embalmed from the start. The writer who provided me some sense of how that might be accomplished was [Franz Xaver] Kroetz. When I first read his plays I thought, This is interesting, a five-act play that's twenty pages long. The language, it's not pretty, but it's poetic. It's very gritty and very real. So I read all of those Germans and in those days there were six dozen of them writing like that. No American did. The English I've always had an aversion towards though I don't know why. Of course, Pinter and Orton are wonderful. The rest leave me cold. Their tradition makes them so confident of their cultural tradition that I distrust them. The Germans had some extraordinary work but I guess it kind of petered out after Botho Strauss. It's odd how these movements don't last very long.

What about Brecht?

I feel very ambivalent about him. A few plays mean an enormous amount to me, like the *The Caucasian Chalk Circle* and *The Good Person of Setzuan*, and a couple others. I like a lot of his theoretical writings. But

I think the work translates badly which makes me wonder how good it really is. No one ever admits this, but there isn't a good translation of a Brecht play anywhere. They're all stilted and they come across with a permeating, leering smugness. It must be there to some extent in the German, but there's something nasty about it. All American intellectuals who are in theatre love Brecht. You get it at the Yale School of Drama—you have to love Brecht. I was so interested in the scandal of Fuegi's *Brecht and Company*, how he stole from all these women. I thought, How are my feminist friends at Yale going to respond to this? Well, they just linked shoulders and denied that it ever happened, which absolutely baffled me. I still think he's great. But it's impossible to do those plays in a culture like ours that shares almost nothing with Weimar Germany. People would like it to, but that means we'd all like to have Hitler around. Germany's always been, as far as I can tell, a true pressure-cooker in a way that America is far too diffuse and contradictory and complicated a culture to be.

On the other hand, a playwright like [Ödön von] Horváth, I think is a great, great playwright, and there's no excuse for the fact that his plays are almost never done. He does everything that Brecht does, and he's a human being, too. There's somebody at home. One of the best productions I've seen in New York in recent years was the CSC/Cucaracha production of *Don Juan Comes Home from the War*. It has all of that really smart, tough theatrical intelligence, political intelligence, and it was human. Right now the whole Vienna bunch is really obsessing me, people like Wittgenstein and Musil, who are real thinkers, and Karl Kraus. I think Alban Berg is one of the great playwrights of this century, just the way Wagner is one of the great playwrights of the nineteenth century. But I'd like to take Brecht, Shakespeare and Beckett, and say, "Put them away for fifteen years. They have nothing more to teach us except mannerism. And in the case of Shakespeare, cultural smugness and complacency. In the case of Beckett, psuedo-existential something or other—depression."

As you were talking about Brecht I was thinking about his commitment to the Enlightenment project. Is this what you see as smugness? I mean, as a committed Marxist, he really believed in class struggle and in the Marxist theory of history as progress.

It is a very Victorian notion. Not only is history a process, but we are the culmination, almost the culmination, of this process. It's also something about the language of Marxist-Leninism itself, which is so dead. There are great sections of Brecht that are just as dead because they're written that way. It's not academic, it's apparatchik talk.

You're thinking about *The Measures Taken,* for example.

And essays, too. This is an extremely intelligent, witty man and yet, he's writing like this. More and more it becomes possible to consider the failure of that kind of socialism as a failure of language. If you don't make the terrestrial paradise a beautiful vision, nobody's going to buy it. And no one wants to be part of that dreary, East German, Stalinist world. I think that Brecht was hiding in that kind of talk, certainly in the last years. We're all prisoners of our culture in some way, but what a narrow, nasty little verbal machine that was. I also think of the devastation of the Second World War. I remember finishing a biography of Brecht thinking, All these poor people who lived through that nightmare. The incredible amount of alcoholism, disease and destructiveness in the Soviet Union had a lot to do, I think, with what that country suffered in the war. Something like thirty million Russians died, with the country torn up in ways that are inconceivable. And Germany, too, for that matter. I don't think you get over it so fast. Not in one or two generations.

I sense from your work and what you've just said that you are very skeptical of the Enlightenment project. I suspect this is connected to your antipathy to a particular kind of moralizing theatre.

Fairly recently I worked on a project called *FNU LNU*, which was written for the cigar factory quarter in Tampa, Florida. It started off as my version of the *Eumenides* of Aeschylus, which is a play I've always liked because it's about the foundations of the civil bases of power. If you try to exclude the furies altogether, they will destroy you. So you have to find a rational way of making them part of society. It's almost impossible to do. I saw the Mnouchkine version which I found impressive and elegant, but actually kind of unmoving and I wanted to play around with the idea myself. So anyway, I set a play about that in this suburb of Tampa where immigrants from Sardinia, from Galicia in Spain, and blacks from Cuba worked in a cigar factory making cigars because they were all anarchists. They hired people to read to them while they were making cigars. Marx, Bakunin and Shakespeare. They were illiterate. It's the crazy story of how these people built hospitals and their own mutual aid societies. I did a lot of reading of Bakunin who actually had read Marx correctly from the start. In 1868, he said what Marx cares about isn't socialism, it's setting up what he referred to as a partial Germanization of Europe. He believed in the state. I believe in a socialism, but one that is more anarcho-syndicalist.

The other line of thinking that interests me a great deal now is that of Wittgenstein, who's coming to be very relevant for a whole bunch of my friends in the experimental poetry world because of his critique of language. He also critiqued really severely the high-flung moralizing that you find in every society. It's a big area of fog between contemporary liberals' ideals about what makes sense to do, and action. He just said that's all bullshit. When you hear somebody crying out in pain, you don't interrogate them. You don't need a theory to know somebody's in pain, you either do something about it or you don't. So this is a human being who is, of course, miserable in the world we live in, because ninety-nine percent of people are involved in temporizing or acting denial of one sort or another. So he would periodically leave philosophizing altogether to work in hospitals, or as a gardener or in rural Austria teaching farmers' kids how to read. And his work is utterly free of all this ideological nonsense. I mean, the critical theory crowd would say, "No, no. There's still an essence there." But what makes Wittgenstein so interesting is that he denied that completely. For him the meaning of the world lies outside the world—in its own terms the world has no meaning. The word "I" is just one word among many, he said. There are no necessary claims on the ego, to be anything other than itself—it has to do things in order to be significant. Someone like that is really radical to me. To get out of the academy, out of philosophy, go do something real.

One of my friends in graduate school was a young man named John Malpede who was studying philosophy. He started a theatre that's fairly well known in L.A. called the LAPD that works with homeless people reading theatre texts. And that's a totally Wittgensteinian thing—you don't talk about it, because talk is meaningless. It's an extreme position that is hopelessly aristocratic and impossible, but I find it very attractive because I'm repelled by so much of the rhetoric I see in the newspapers, on TV and in the theatre. Let me relate it to something I remember Foreman saying at a panel about political theatre years and years ago. He said he didn't want to do political theatre because it ended up making him feel like he'd done something when he hadn't done anything. That's a statement I think Wittgenstein would approve of. It's why I have committed acts of political theatre, but I don't take them terribly seriously. I wanted to try them out since I spent so much time attacking political theatre.

Do you mean something like *7 Blowjobs*?
Yes, but I don't mean them as high-minded. I mean them as mudslinging, low satire. Written in a language my opponents can understand and with the intent to cause them suffering, rather than to improve them. One of the healthiest things about this country is our sarcastic, cynical side.

One of my other cultural obsessions is Ambrose Bierce, who's charged with being cynical when his view of things is merely tragic.

Beckett says that the worst thing that happens to a person is being born. Bierce says the same thing. Instead of being hailed as a genius, he's called cynical. Bierce is somebody who attacked the four leading San Francisco railroad moguls over a period of fifteen years, and one of them, Collis P. Huntington, offered him twenty-five million dollars to stop. Huntington had bilked the U.S. government out of thirty-five million dollars in railroad shenanigans to get free public lands, and Bierce went after him. Finally Huntington said, "Name your price." And Bierce said, "I want thirty-five million dollars—make the check out to my friend the United States government." Also, Bierce is, I think, the only major American writer who actually served in combat in the Civil War. Most of them bought their way out. He did it because he believed in abolition. He caught a bullet in the head at Kennesaw Mountain. He's very interesting politically. People like that I have respect for.

Conducting interviews, I've been thinking a lot about the relationship between language and politics. It seems to me that your plays are never about illustrating or advocating a fixed political position or agenda. Rather, it's as though you're using language to disrupt any kind of programmatic politics.

Yes, I think I am. Partly it's a deconstructive thing, but not like the cultural theory people believe. Let me explain. The language of plays like 7 *Blowjobs* or *Sincerity Forever* is derived from earlier pieces like *Cellophane* [1988] and *Terminal Hip*, which came out of a totally different strategy. I was then frustrated as a writer. So I set myself a little task—to write badly. A lot of people have talked about this in my work, but it's a little more complicated than that. I wanted to see what would happen, how far you could go in breaking rules. So I wrote a page of legal pad every day for two-and-a-half years. To my great surprise—and I wasn't trying to make any sense or tell a story—I found certain patterns emerging. I found a sort of lofty poetic line developing that reminded me more of Whitman than anyone else. I found that a lot of clichés, or dreadful expressions that I would make up that were like clichés, were more speakable than the supposedly literate stuff I was writing. They came trippingly off your tongue, because clichés are used a lot. There's a lot more bad language in the world than good language. Then I also found there was a spiritual dimension, a yearning that came through for a better America, for transcendence, a reaching for the stars even though you have your feet in clay. There was a political dimension that came up, too, a sense of betrayal. I didn't want to forget the betrayals, the lake poisoned by the people who didn't take care of the cooler unit at the local reactor. And class envy, too, which began to really permeate the writing. Just in the language, the voices began to become acutely aware that they were lower class and not as good as somebody else.

I then began to use that to make political statements. *7 Blowjobs* and *Sincerity Forever* are the two most obvious instances. Because it seemed to me a rather delicate way of talking about class in a way that only academics and Marxists do—people on the street have no conception of it and no interest in it. Messing around with language taught me more about my subject, or certain things about my subject. Of course, to write about these things indirectly is more interesting than expressing my opinions, because in this society one's head becomes full of junk. Particularly on the left, in the arts, we all think the same things anyway, at least on the level of opinion. I have a quote here from Wittgenstein on this: "You cannot write anything about yourself that is more truthful than you yourself are. That is the difference between writing about yourself and writing about external objects. You write about yourself from your own height; you don't stand on stilts, or on a ladder, but on your bare feet." Which is why I don't write about my opinions. I was trying to get at class issues with *Sincerity Forever* because I think they're deep in all Americans, and language is a very effective way of getting at them.

Another big influence on *Sincerity Forever* is Philip Guston, the painter. I was at MOMA yesterday and there was a painting of three guys in Klan outfits with big cigars in a car with caveman wheels. I felt that his turn to that sort of work in his later years, which everybody hated at the time, was one of the great moments in contemporary art. Actually, he'd done Klan paintings of a social-realist type back in the WPA days in the thirties. So I take my politics seriously—it's just that I don't trust my opinions. I think I'm stuck in the same problems as everyone else. The problem I have with a lot of left-wing friends of mine, and even cultural critique people, is that they think they have one foot out of the dialectic themselves. I don't think anybody does unless you're enormously wealthy, and then you have other problems.

You talked about your approach to politics as deconstructive. So often I'm reading something of yours, and I think, Who is speaking? That's such a crucial and difficult question. Even when we know literally who is speaking, we don't know who *really* is speaking. It's as though so many of your characters—all of your characters really—are ventriloquizing, as if they are haunted by a culture they don't understand and can't control.

As I said earlier, nobody knows anything. People just say things. Go out onto the street and listen to people talk. It's amazing what they say. I think the relationship of people to speech in a country like this is different than in a dense, monochromatic European culture. I don't agree with everything the deconstructionists say, because I don't think language is meaningless and there is a total slippage between the signifier and the thing signified. But you cannot tell somebody's social position or how smart they are anymore by looking at them. Context and social construction are much more complicated in our society. It's why I'm interested in journalism because that shows our obsession with representations of ourselves. I watch TV and I get angry. It's almost gotten to the point that I don't want to watch it, but I do. Same thing with the newspaper. Do I have a doctrine or a set of beliefs that I want to replace all that with? No. I used to think I should have one, but I don't think you need that anymore.

Is your own obsession with different media related to the many characters in your plays who are obsessed and driven? So many of them seem completely mesmerized or possessed—by the past, by other characters, not to mention their own fears, desires and hatreds.

I am interested in people in a possessed state. Kierkegaard said that you can tell you're becoming a demon when you start to dwell upon unlimited possibilities, because that's what a demon is, someone totally possessed by possibility. I think Americans are extraordinarily demonic. We don't understand restrictions of any kind. That operates in every cultural activity I can think of. Also, I have to confess, another reason for this use of language is that I find it sensuous, beautiful and powerful in ways I cannot analyze. So it's not satire or sarcasm or an indictment, it's something quite splendid in its own way. Which means I acknowledge a demonic attribute in myself. I am part of this morass of ill-thought-out social constructs and general lunacy.

I realize that you have several different kinds of plays, but can you talk a little bit about your process of writing. How does a play usually begin?

I have a notebook and I keep ideas in it. But I think a work of art should be unparaphraseable. So I don't generally write, "I want to write a play about the problem of . . ." Because it would then make the most sense to write an article about it, to cut to the quick and get the matter over with. So then it's more a question of ideas or images that puzzle me. I wrote an early play called *Harm's Way* [1985] because I always wanted to write a play in which everybody was angry, just to see what that would be like. Starting with that supposition, I found that the play wrote itself. I'm always more interested in negativity, because there's a lot more individual energy and associations buried in places you don't want to look. We're always trying to be good, to be smart.

Sometimes I'm interested in a word. I was interested in the word "harm," which seems to me a more appropriate way to describe social conditions, like violence, that I wanted to deal with. There's violence in love, in building; in nature it's called the sublime. But the concept of harm seemed more interesting. Sometimes I start with an image. One play began with an image of two people playing cards at a card table, only all three objects were floating above a river and that was enough for me to write the play. Lately, I've been starting more with stories. *Second Hand Smoke* [1997] and the play that follows have been obsessed with how awful the workplace is, so I construct the worst workplace and the worst boss in the world. Just thinking, It's not like it is on TV. Bosses are awful, awful tyrants, and they humiliate you in endless ways, and the work is incomprehensible and meaningless and stupid. I wanted to investigate that. Just two girls talking about nothing on the roof. I like scenes where nothing happens, because then what happens is that everything begins to take on a kind of radiance. A lot of Robert Wilson is based on that. Why that doesn't interest more American writers I don't know.

For me right now the two main weaknesses with American drama are first, that it's phony, overly dramatic in unconvincing ways. Two people yammering at somebody in the foreground and nothing is in the background. Second, American theatre writing is so sentimental. The trouble with sentimentality is not that it's silly or emotional, it's that it's a lie. And yet there's still a lot of pressure. If you write a play, it almost has to be sentimental. Everybody from the producer to the actors will want you to have a happy ending. They joke about it, but it's true. Thinking back about Bierce, one reason I think he's so great is he's never sentimental. Sentimentality is the presumption of feeling an emotion that one has not earned. So, I really start with almost anything. I usually try to make some initial outline of all I know about the play. After I make a few notes, generally I just let the thing sit for a long time. It takes a while for the associations to cluster around the ideas. When I finally do write the play, I usually write as fast as I can. I try to get out ahead of the schema so I'm not filling in the blanks. I write best when I don't know what I'm writing about, again, when I write badly. I always think I write better when I don't know where I am. Because then it's not the first, most obvious thing that comes to mind, but the second and third and fourth, the things that you don't know you knew.

Is it a kind of free association?

It's more than that, it's about being disciplined about association so that you get past the things you always think about, because most of my free associations are dull and all the same. You get stuck in patterns, from

TV, movies and magazines. All of this junk that we're saturated with. It also determines how our reflexes work in terms of what we consider dramatic. I think as I grow older, I'm less easy on myself, so I can tell now when I'm treading water, when I recycle things from other plays. If I'm doing it, I cut it out. I rewrite in a harder way. Partly, that's come from collaborating with people like Len Jenkin. We had a great time writing the last one, entitled *Tallahassee* [1991], and at one point we were doing what writers in the twenties and thirties must have done, standing around in a room dictating. You get pretty hard and mean when you do that. We're always harder on our own work than on each other's, but you come away disabused of thinking of yourself as a high-falutin writer. TV writing must be like that. I think it's healthy at some point to view yourself as a desperate hack. I don't think that's a good way to start out, but after you've been doing it for a while, you should be harder on yourself. The hardest thing when you start to be a writer is not writing something good, it's creating the ego that actually allows you to be a writer in the first place. Because writing plays is not a natural thing. Making theatre is natural, but writing is a complicated kind of imagining since it involves kinesthetic things with words and different senses. Synesthesia. I remember thinking, I don't know what I'm doing. I don't even know how to write stage directions. How would I behave if I were a genius, if I were Goethe, say? How would I write? And as silly as that activity is, I think you have to do it when you're starting out. If you do not create the ego for that, it's overwhelming. The danger comes if you get a little too comfortable with that ego, if you turn into a pompous fraud or something worse. So you have to be able to inhabit that space, and then leave it so you can deal with family and lovers and other people.

So for you then, freeing the unconscious is only a small part of it.
I consider myself more of a constructor. I'm always trying to escape my nature, always wanting to write in a slightly different way. I think my work has changed more than most of my friend's over the years, so I'm impatient with it, I try one thing and then try another. I'm not very romantic about it, I think it's just work.

I sense in some of your works that you're attempting to engage with feminism more carefully and consciously than a lot of your colleagues, the other straight, white men who populate New York alternative theatre and, I believe, in their different ways are trying to keep alive what I see as a certain cowboy mentality, as if they each want to be the next Sam Shepard or David Mamet. Do you think that's true?
I wouldn't want to say I'm more woman-friendly than the next play-

wright. I get along with women. And I'm more interested in the way women relate to women than the way men relate to men. I've written some plays about the latter—it's called "drama" in the sense that it always goes nowhere and remains humorless and grim. For a great many people that's what drama is, a father and a son, getting on and dealing with that stuff. I don't think that's as interesting as being with a woman or the way that women deal with each other. It's a different kind of drama, and it seems less limited.

I see some of your works as trying to carve out a space for a particular kind of feminine agency that we just don't often see in the work of your associates.
That's true, because the quality of the interchange seems more complex. In *Cat's-Paw* [1996]—I always wanted to do this—I wrote a Don Juan play with no men in it. The other rule was that the women couldn't talk about men. I wanted to explore that. I don't believe in dramatic essences the way a lot of playwrights do. They're duped into thinking you throw the woman off the wall in a Shepard kind of thing, and that's supposed to be visceral. It just makes me feel uncomfortable. I don't think women are superior, or have deep and mystical powers. I don't want to essentialize or romanticize women, I don't think they have demonic essences or goddess essences, or that they're inherently nobler and more connected to divine forces than men are. I like what I see as their social conventions, their manners. The way they are with each other is more complex, at least in this culture at this time.

So these behavioral differences translate into theatrical differences.
I think it's a time when women are feeling the need to extend or exert themselves in a wider realm of activities, and that's always more theatrical than the situation facing men, which is essentially learning when one's exertions are not appropriate. Which is not so theatrical to me.

What makes for a good production of your work?
I see less and less difference between my work and other people's. So it's the same things: a director to whom I can talk, who reads the script, who will ask the right questions, which aren't necessarily the ones I would like them to ask—somebody willing to collaborate. Same thing with actors. Obviously, I like to work with the most talented people I can, then you have less to worry about. I think it's best when you're all on the same page. I like to work with people who have their own agenda for the piece, too. For instance, the designer I work with most frequently is Kyle Chepulis, who never went to college. Sometimes when he builds his sets his parents come and help him. He does installations

for the New York Public Library and things like that. Something he wants to do may or may not have a direct bearing on what I want to do. That's very healthy, because then you get a richer texture. For example, *The Hyacinth Macaw* [1994] had a lot of references to a sun and moon which were always rising and setting at the wrong times. So he got this idea, and he's a kind of technical nut, he came into possession of a ten thousand-watt lightbulb, which comes in a little oak box. They last seventy years, they're filled with graphite so you shake it to clean it. And he told the director, "I want to light this play with a single source." And the director said, "That's impossible." Kyle said, "Let me try it." Well, ten thousand watts was too bright, you couldn't be in the room with it, but five thousand watts you could. So he built this machine, it wasn't a pretty romantic sun, it was a big clanking machine. It could rise and track across the set. Now that's not a literal translation of the play. On the other hand, it's an extremely interesting interrogation of the text and one that for all sorts of reasons I found useful, because it stressed the artificiality and also something about nature in this play, which was brute, anonymous, mechanical and somewhat scary. So I'd rather have somebody who's not a mainstream designer. Then I look in *American Theatre* magazine, and every picture in it looks like it's from the same production of *Cyrano* in 1959 at Indiana Rep. So it's always tricky in the theatre because you never know how it's going to work out. It's a collaborative art. With my work, just dealing with the text in the simplest way is usually the best. And that sounds easy, but it isn't, because what comes to be the simplest is often hard as hell to figure out.

I was so interested in your mentioning Kroetz because in a lot of your work I get a sense of a Kroetzian gulf or chasm between text and subtext. Characters are talking or doing things, and there's clearly stuff going on underneath but it is so deliberately unarticulated. It's crucial in your work to realize that it can't be played the way American Method actors play subtext, because that would just destroy it.
A better way to think of it is that these plays are somehow the subtext for some absent realistic play. I just dispense with writing the text altogether and write the subtext because it's more interesting.

The surface of things is so mysterious.
Actually you do get a subtext, but it's not understood in terms of motivation. Motivation is always boring to me. You need some of it to create narratives, but you need far less than many American dramatists think. The problem with motivation and foreshadowing is that if you do it in a straight-ahead way, the drama is always happening elsewhere. And it reduces all characters to something that may be plausible intel-

lectually, but it's not very satisfying. All people and actions become understandable. That's why I find the work of someone like Arthur Miller ridiculous and shallow. Success and failure turn into these interchangeable icons and nothing is illuminated. A noble man, and certainly somebody I respect, but there are literally dozens of writers of that type whom intelligent people seem to find very moving. If you consider the age we live in one of a disordered will, then you view human beings as possessed, demonic beings alternately illuminated or desecrated by their willfulness. But the willfulness is always a part of them and their activities. And us. And because we're perverse, we always want the thing we shouldn't go after. Roger Shattuck actually has a wonderful new book about this called *Forbidden Knowledge*. He has a long chapter on de Sade, and he says, "This guy isn't just a pornographer. This is true evil. And it's fine that it's not banned, but he has gone beyond the line of the human, and there is no rationale for this." He puts that into the same category as those who did not flinch at making the hydrogen bomb. That contemporary Americans think there are no limitations on knowledge, Shattuck would say, "That's demented. There are limits and if you ignore them, you do so at your peril." And then he talks about the sort of people that honor those limitations, like Emily Dickinson. That's a line of questioning that I think is inherently theatrical. How far can we go and where can't we go? That's much more interesting than this debate over motives and not-motives, success or failure. Who the fuck cares? Or people confessing—the endless confessions in American plays, all of which are meaningless.

Which leads me to: do you think of your work as being autobiographical at all?
In the Wittgensteinian sense. Since it comes from me, it is. When a writer is young there is a tendency to write about things that are close. But you have to be careful about that because you can actually use up your experience. When you write a play you do use up things in a way that is different from other kinds of writing. There are so few interesting writers of advanced age because they burn out, sometimes out of despair and alcoholism, but sometimes they simply run out of things to write about. People who know me will be able to read my experience easily. I never talk about it. Usually it's in the detail so it doesn't draw attention to itself. Sometimes it's a word or phrase that's been going through my head for twenty-five years that means something to me, and it gets stuck, and it illuminates the piece for me. I think I'm far less autobiographical than most American playwrights, certainly someone like Shepard. Even Paula [Vogel], I think, her pursuit of a kind of excavation of the Self. Or Albee. Someone like Williams is less clear to me.

I'm also more interested in indirection and how you can't help but reveal yourself in anything you do. The older I get, the less I think that self-expression is among my goals.

I'm curious about your understanding of history, because it seems to me that all of your plays recycle historical detritus in one way or another. But some of your work is more explicitly—and interestingly—engaged historically, like *Crowbar* or *Dracula* [1987]. In *Dracula* you're exposing things that are not really there in Stoker's text, the emergence of the New Woman at the end of the nineteenth century, connections with imperialism.

Those things are hinted at and there is a reference to the New Woman. The imperialist stuff is there as filigree. There's a casual anti-Semitism in the book, too. You have to look for it, but it's there. Those things seemed important to me because Stoker used them only as details, unimportant stuff. I thought it said something about the world that was important to the characters. The better class of adapter would have removed those things and concentrated on the monster, but to me, that's part of the monstrousness, this insane world that these people live in. That's just as much a part of the story as the high drama, how we're going to get the monster before it kills us all.

I'm fascinated by history, but I'm afraid of it when it becomes reductive and simplistic. So I'm more interested in out-of-the-way histories. I'm fascinated by Byzantine history which is fifteen hundred years of really complicated stuff that's as interesting as Roman or Western European history, but nobody knows it. Or the history of Islam. I'm always looking around for different takes on contemporary experience.

What is important to you about these particular histories? For example, Byzantine history.

Byzantine history is full of people that seem very contemporary and just as complex as Reagan and Nixon. And it's a history that hasn't been prettified. It hasn't been turned into a literary, established, high knowledge. So it's still available to the imagination, I think. There was a Byzantine emperor who had to deal with the Seljuk Turks, and made a deal with them to protect them against the Huns. At the same time he was dealing with the ambassadors of the Huns, saying, "I'm dealing with these crazy Turks, so they won't be any problem to you." Using both sides of an argument for political advantage. These stories are just heartbreaking. One of the last Byzantine emperors went to Venice to appeal for aid and was thrown in debtors' jail, sold all the royal jewels and made a new saddle out of eggshells. Things like that. And when the emperor was deposed, they cut off his nose, as was the custom. He went to a monastery. You're supposed to stay in the monastery, but he didn't. He came out, led some troops up a sewer pipe into the city and ruled for twelve more years. They called him Nesepharis the Noseless. These are creatures of enormous, demented, willful abuse. Also, in that world you're dealing with a very contemporary kind of cultural diversity. And these are figures that are very different from those who people the "better" class of history. But it's the complexity that interests me.

Simon Callow was talking about theatre at the TCG conference last year and why he was involved with it. He said, "For me it's not the great stories, or even the great language or the great drama, it's great characters who can will exactly contradictory things at the same moment. That to me is what theatre is about." And I think he's right. That is what interests me, because that's the way we experience our lives in a historical context. The only way to experience your life in any kind of meaningful sense is with some notion of historical experience. But we live in a country that has very silly notions of what history is. History's supposed to be somehow edifying or make sense, or lead to something, but it doesn't. What's important about it is that it's particular and strange. A lot of my friends who are playwrights are interested in the strangeness and beauty of the world, which Ovid talks about: you can be a beautiful young girl one minute and then be turned into a tree stump.

And for you that's what history is about?
That's the positive way of viewing it. When you're not in such a nice mood it's what Joyce meant when he said, "It's just a scream in the street."

But that is something that all of your plays also deal with.
Byzantine art has that look to it, which is dead-on, spiritual, absolute and emotionally very clear. The art I like most—and I always send my directors to see art—is the pre-Renaissance. My favorite are the Siennese painters, the narrative painters. A number of their narratives showed up in the Metropolitan Museum a few years back. There was a painting of a heretic being burned. It was a ghastly scene, and it was a sunset, so the setting sun looked much like the fire, and there was a look on everybody's face like, We're getting this son of a bitch, we're gonna burn him up. But the look on his face said, If I could get down off this pile of burning logs, I'd tie you up and do the same thing to you. So emotionally it was very pure, very powerful. We're not so comfortable with expressions of those kinds of emotion now. We prefer things shaded, muted, not too strong because we have to take motivation into consideration. Over and over, it boils down to the fact that in America, a bad boy's a good boy with a sad

story. The real miracle, the real mystery is what was this man thinking? It's a mystery because he has no light to shed on it.

As you write in "The Theatre of Good Intentions."
I'm not saying I know any more about it, but I do think this is very, very mysterious. And the fact that we can't understand this mystery in our lives is the reason why tragedy is essentially impossible for us as a culture. I'm not sure I'd want to understand that. It would be a clearer world, though.

It seems to me that theatre since the 1960s has been defined as an oppositional cultural formation, opposed both to TV and film and to the social and political status quo. It seems to me that your work participates very clearly in that project, refusing so much of what TV and film demand. Does this make your work subversive? Is that a useful way of thinking about it?
It's very easy for those of us on the left to flatter ourselves that somehow we're on the barricades, fighting these important battles, which I think is romanticizing the situation. I'm not sure theatre is all that oppositional. Most of it. I am always tired of the "playwright goes to Hollywood" play which all American playwrights write. "Hollywood is evil, and I was corrupted there, and I've come back a sadder but wiser man with my newfound sense of values." It just seems silly because New York theatre seems just as corrupt, just as blockheaded as Hollywood, and just as much part of the system. So I'm not sure I'm particularly subversive. What interests me more is interrogating the facts of my condition, interrogating contemporary reality as I see it, interrogating theatre itself. That might be subversive. I don't flatter myself that I'm achieving anything profound. I wish more people were interested in interrogating their experience, or questioning it or playing with it. I find the theatre as a whole to be dominated by a culture of theatre, which tries to say things that are provocative, but mostly ends up being shrill, knee-jerk and self-congratulatory.

Maybe not unlike the Furballs in *Sincerity Forever* who ironically become almost a mirror image of the well-intentioned, Ku Klux Klan-clad citizenry of Hillsbottom.
I've had people say the Furballs speak for Mac Wellman and, no, they don't. Maybe in a sense.

Because you do, of course, like public radio.
Actually, I don't. That was from the heart. Yeah, that loathsome kind of do-gooder persona that you get with a Bill Moyers. Even when he says something smart, you want to hate him.

What about Jesus H. Christ in the play? I realize, crucially, that Jesus H. Christ is not Jesus Christ, but whenever I read the play I get the sense that that's the closest you come in your work to articulating a kind of truth, an unequivocal point of reference.
It may feel like that but I'm not sure it's meant to work that way. It's a tricky play to do because of that—it's like the play tends to stop there. I think what I wanted in a Christ was someone who was like what I think the historical Christ must have been like, who came into the world not to redeem people, but to knock them on their fannies and make them think. Not a particularly nice human being, but a whirlwind of a certain kind of destruction. I think of the message of Christ, if you read the Scriptures, as being a fairly simple one: give away everything you own and take to the open road preaching the Gospel. It's not the message of Paul, to found a Church upon this rock. It's far closer to the kind of thing the hippies got us thinking about. And for that play to work, you have to believe that that person has that sort of moral authority, which is not particularly comforting or illuminating—it's not Buddha, it's something else. To do that theatrically is extraordinarily difficult. I wouldn't want to try to write that kind of a play again. It could so easily turn into a parody of itself.

For me, *Sincerity Forever* so clearly comes out of that horrible moment in the early nineties—the continuing triumph of Reagan-Bushism, the crisis over the NEA, the Gulf War—when the lines seemed rather sharply drawn. For a brief moment, there was a resurgence of real opposition.
It was a very short period. Things sort of opened up in this culture from about '89–'92, then they closed right back down again. It ended with the Bosnian war and the L.A. riots.

In the introduction to your plays you describe yourself as a cheerful pessimist. Does that characterize your feelings about the theatre?
Yeah, I think so. I like the theatre. I think it's dominated by a culture that's mediocre, that's careerist in petty ways, not even in intelligent ways. I used to think I could change it. Now I realize I'm not going to change it at all. On the other hand, there are a lot of really wonderful people in it and you can do certain things. I can pretty much go my own way and people will leave me alone. That is a good place to be. I'm actually more interested now in what young people are doing than in my own generation.

Which is, of course, connected to your teaching.
Yes. I got one of these Lila Wallace grants, for which you have to do a social component, and what I'm doing for mine is organizing a series of

presentations at the Brooklyn Academy of Music of teams of young writers and young critics in which they talk about the story of new writing, how it developed, who influences whom, what excites them. We're going to do three of these a year for three years. They have to write essays after the presentation, which will be published in various theatre magazines. Then I'll put all nine together in a book. I don't think there are enough opportunities for younger writers to talk about their work, because the press certainly isn't covering it. I don't have a lot of hope in the young, but on the other hand, I have more hope in them than in anyone else, because at least they haven't made up their minds. I also belong to a group of people who started their own theatre, the Bat Theatre: Kyle Chepulis, Eduardo Machado, Jim Simpson, Jan Leslie Harding, Mike Nolan. We want to design another kind of theatre from the ground up. It's not a little black box with shitty seats and ugly facilities. We want to make a really elegant, lovely little gem of a space. Sixty seats—that's all I need. We won't do a season or fundraising. We've got a chunk of money so it'll last us a while. We'll run it for five years and then it's done. We're just trying to figure out other ways of doing theatre than the ways we know.

So in Brechtian terms, it's a matter of seizing control of the means of production. Doing it ourselves, which means a lot of work, but the alternatives are fairly grim right now because things are so conservative. I don't think there's really a theatre community in any meaningful sense. There are a lot of large theatres trying to gobble everything up and doing a pretty good job. If I thought their work was outstanding I would applaud this, but I don't. As usual in this country, smaller works seem to be the better ones. Large-scale theatre is hard to do anywhere, and most cultures have evolved past the point at which normal cultural practice is inherently and wonderfully theatrical. That still happens at Mardi Gras and other carnivals, but those are getting rarer and rarer. But I think this country does produce very smart young people. It's what happens to them when they grow up that's very sad, and to me, in a way, inexplicable.

There is a kind of spiritual crisis that's going on in this country. A desperate lack of real faith in almost everything you can think of. Religion doesn't work the way it should. Ninety-two percent of the people claim to be religious or believe in some kind of salvation of their soul. It just astounds me—in the eighteenth century something like twenty-five percent of the people identified themselves as Christians. I simply don't believe it, because these people do not act like they believe in anything. So the writers that interest me the most are dealing with spiritual issues, or with political/spiritual issues.

Do you see a clear distinction between the two?

No. Even Tony Kushner is avowedly political in a Marxist kind of way, but I think he'll go more in a spiritual direction than a Marxist one, which would be more difficult. Certainly Richard Foreman is investing in this weird sort of Cabalistic crap, stuff that's almost Hasidic. There's a lot of room for that, because these practices are inherently theatrical. All you have to do is have someone dressed as a cardinal walk on stage and it's drama. Or any religious figure. The language of these practices is all loony and crazy, but it's still wonderful. You look at Marxist stuff and you just glaze over—I mean it's hard to read it. I hope people start thinking about the whole anarchist tendency, because those people were very smart.

And there's a whole tradition of that in American letters.

The smarter cultural analysts, people like Edward Said are very interesting, or C.L.R. James.

But James was a Marxist.

But not a Stalinist. Bonnie Marranca just gave me a new collection of plays: *Plays for the End of the Century*, it's got something by Erik Ehn, Foreman, The Wooster Group's *The Temptation of Saint Anthony*, Reza Abdoh and two or three other people. Rachel Rosenthal. But they're all kind of quasi-spiritual texts, and Bonnie's introduction is really about that.

I think a lot of that is connected to a sense of an end-of-the-millennium crisis. The end of the Cold War.

I never thought it would happen and I think the fallout from that has been extreme. Russia must be a totally lunatic place right now.

What are your new writing projects?

I'm very interested in writing more music theatre, small pieces. The *FNU LNU* piece I talked about has ten or eleven songs in it, some of which I just found the material there, which are always the best. One of my goals with this theatre is to create a more intimate music theatre that's not cabaret. The fourth piece in the *Crowtet* series is called *The Lesser Magoo* [1997], and I just did a production of it out West, and a friend of mine who was a composer did five or six songs. It opened the piece up for me, I never thought it could be that beautiful. I've always liked music theatre, but that tends to get stuck with musical comedy, or opera or something else.

I can see how that would be an extension of your poetry.
I'm also interested in puppets. I'm working on this puppet piece with Anne Hamburger and Janie Geiser. That goes way back for me, as I told you. They have a puppet festival every September and there's a lot going on in that field right now. Those are the two main directions that interest me. I think my work is in flux right now—it's going to change. I finished one line of development, I just don't know where I'm going to go now.

So, *Secondhand Smoke* marks an end?
That and *The Lesser Magoo*. I feel like there's a kind of end there. I'm not quite sure what I want to do next. I'm actually writing a novel about the theatre, I do that when I get tired of the theatre. It's very wicked.

This makes me think of your characterization in *Bad Infinity* [1985] of what I assume to be a bad play like *K2*.
Right, I'm trying to fill it up with bad play titles. Lists and lists. But theatre is such a crazy world. The creatures you encounter are absolutely hilarious. The best gossip of any art form. Priceless gossip. But after this, I don't know, we'll see.

All the gossip and obsession. Don't you think that all people involved in theatre are obsessive?
Going to the OBIE Awards is always such a scream, all the black bile and conniption going up. People get burnt out at an astonishing rate. But it's also a very friendly world, too. And very supportive, which is odd. And a rather small world, too, which surprises me. It's fairly easy to know almost everyone in it. But I feel comfortable where I am, on the periphery of things. I've been quite lucky being able to do mostly what I've wanted to do. More fortunate than a lot of people.

George C. Wolfe

Few American playwrights are as enamored of history as George C. Wolfe. During a period when so many artists—especially those working in popular forms—are turning their back on the past, Wolfe is intent on using the history of African-American culture to retell the story of America. All his plays could be described as archaeological in their concern for sifting through the sands of culture to retrieve buried artifacts and use them both to reconstruct the past and to examine its relationship to contemporary struggles. Wolfe's archaeology, however, is far from being a dry and dusty affair. On the contrary, history is for him a living, breathing presence. It seduces and amazes. For history comes not only in the form of written documents, but also in the shape of human subjects who are heirs to and incarnations of great cultural traditions. Thus, he describes Savion Glover, with whom he collaborated on *Bring in 'da Noise, Bring in 'da Funk* (1996), as "a living repository of rhythm" who, for the two-hour duration of the musical, becomes its hero and point of origin: "In the beginning was 'da Beat." And in *Noise/Funk*, Wolfe uses 'da Beat—as dramatic character, historical figure and living repository—to retell the history of persons of African descent in the U.S., from Middle Passage to the present. Reexamining both the horrors and joys of the past, from slavery to the Harlem Renaissance, from lynch mobs to gospel choirs, Wolfe stages the extraordinary richness and diversity of African-American music. For the history of 'da Beat is also the history of African-American culture.

Having grown up in Frankfort, Kentucky, during the heyday of the civil rights movement, Wolfe recalls having been "part of a generation of black children who were raised like integration soldiers . . . groomed to invade white America." As a student director at Pomona College, he became frustrated by realistic plays that fixated on the sufferings of African-Americans and he set out to write his own highly theatricalized comedies. Coming to New York in 1979, he continued his training in the graduate musical theatre program at New York University. An integration warrior, he first invaded The Joseph Papp Public Theater in 1986 when his play, *The Colored Museum,* transferred there from New Jersey's Crossroads Theatre. That play, together with *Spunk* (1990), his adaptation of three short stories by Zora Neale Hurston, so impressed Joseph Papp that he named Wolfe a resident director at The Public. During this period Wolfe continued to pursue a career as director by staging the widely acclaimed Broadway productions of Tony Kushner's *Angels in America* and Anna Deavere Smith's *Twilight*. In 1993, shortly after Papp's death, he was named Producer of the The Public Theater/ New York Shakespeare Festival and is now devoting himself to making The Public Theater "vibrate with this city's energy, and be inclusive, in a healthy, nontoken way." "I pride myself," Wolfe notes, "on being available to as many people's stories as I possibly can."

Yet it is not only as producer that he excels in being available to other people's stories. For in retelling the history of African-Americans, his plays represent a collage of different styles and stereotypes. Thus, *The Colored Museum* offers the spectator a guided tour of history as revealed through a number of exhibits—from a slave ship to eighties' black musicals, from Ethel Waters to the new black diva—each designed to reveal that which usually remains unacknowledged in African-American culture. The glamorous, perfect couple living inside *Ebony* magazine, for example, nonchalantly smile and strut while voicing their own superficiality, "No contradictions . . . and no pain." Or the fierce snap queen, Miss Roj, who, reading his audience, very calmly and flamboyantly asserts his power and shows that he knows how to get "Respect"—with or without Aretha Franklin's help. Or "The Last Mama-on-the-Couch Play," which, providing a brief résumé of African-American theatre from the "coon show" to *Raisin in the Sun* and *for colored girls*, finally reassures its audience, "Nobody ever dies in an all-black musical." Or the eighties' Buppie, Mr. Colored-Man-on-

Top, who can maintain his privilege only by literally trashing his past, by jettisoning his Afro comb, his Sly and the Family Stone records and his history as an activist. In what is perhaps the play's most chilling moment, he declares, "I have no history. I have no past. . . . I must be able to smile on cue. And watch the news with an impersonal eye."

Wolfe's archaeological enterprise is first and foremost an attempt to remember, to counter what he describes as the "cultural strip-mining" in which a "performance is stripped of [a] context" that is always "very intense, emotional, complicated, violent as well as joyful." And just as *Noise/Funk* represents a recontextualization of 'da Beat, so does *Jelly's Last Jam* (1992) restage the birth of jazz. It calls up the spirit of Jelly Roll Morton to examine the role he played in the production of early jazz. Knowing that it is "a lie" to relive one's "past with none of the pain," it splits him into two figures, Old and Young Jelly, in order to stage his inner ambivalence about his racial identity, his desire both to fashion himself the inventor of jazz and deny his African heritage. Yet *Jelly's Last Jam* finally demonstrates the folly and arrogance of trying to lay claim to an art form that issues from and expresses less the emotions of a solitary individual than the sufferings, strivings and joys of an entire people. It reaches its climax when Jelly accepts the pain that reverberates "inside every note" and realizes that his friends, lovers and enemies—the history of his entire community—represent the real substance of his art. "We," sing the entire ensemble, "are the feeling in your song."

Wolfe's dramatizations of the complex and varied histories of African-Americans give the lie both to the many whitewashed versions of America and to myths of racial and cultural purity. For his pieces insistently demonstrate, as he puts it, that "the Melting Pot is a lie. It's all these divergent ingredients colliding with one another that create a dynamic culture." Just as the vibrancy and power of jazz is in part a function of its hybrid and collective nature, so is the vitality of America in part the result of its inability to reconcile its contradictions. In a nation in which "we're all mutts," it is imperative to know one's own history and its complex and often painful interrelationship with other people's histories. This knowledge alone becomes an antidote to "cultural denial" and a way of taking responsbility. For only by confronting the past can one hope to transform the oppression and violence that have defined this nation's identity: "Americans are so frightened of dealing with the true history of this country because everybody is indicted, either from guilt or rage or responsibility or fear."

August 12, 1998—George C. Wolfe's office, The Joseph Papp Public Theater/
New York Shakespeare Festival, New York City

DS: How did you get interested in theatre?
GCW: I was born interested in theatre and I really can't explain it because I'm from a part of Kentucky that's really not the cultural center of the universe. But from the time I was born I was always fascinated with crafting realities. A cousin of mine told me recently that when we would all play, instead of playing along, I would tell people lines that they had to say as we were playing. So it reveals not only the control freak in me, but also that I was very into sculpting realities and using other people to sculpt them. Also I went to this great school where there were lots of plays during the course of the year. And then I came to New York when I was thirteen and saw commercial Broadway theatre and I went, "Oh, you can make a living doing this." That formed a shape for me. Then I went to some high school theatre thing at Miami University of Ohio when my brother was away getting a doctorate. There were these little blocks that kept getting moved into place, so that by the time I finished high school, it was completely and totally clear to me that I was going to be working in the theatre. In college I started out as an actor and a designer, and then I became an actor and a director, and then my last year in college I started to write. So it's been the writing and directing, although since I've been at the Public it's been less writing and more other stuff.

So your interest in writing goes back to when you were a little kid.
I would write plays when I was six, seven and I would hide them, literally. I think the writing thing was the hardest thing to admit I wanted to do. It was easier to admit that I wanted to do theatre, but somehow it took courage to say that I wanted to write.

Why do you think so?
I'm not sure, I think because the writing felt private, whereas performing or directing are public dynamics. So it was like sharing something about myself in the writing. I had to use directing to trick myself into

becoming a writer, because I said, "I can't find anything exciting to direct, so let me start writing." I could never just say I wanted to be a writer. I had to trip, you know, do that little round-the-way walk around the corner and down the street and into the alley and then enter the house. I was not interested in going in the front door.

Do you still find that writing is more private for you than directing?
It's a different me that writes. It's a very calm, it's a very focused me, a very isolated me, a very centered me. And the person that's interested in creating theatre is the public side of me, the extroverted side of me, the one who likes to go into a room and play with other people. I think the writing side of me is deeper and the directing side, the creating theatre side is smarter, in some respects.

So then, part of directing your own work is dealing with the other you.
I remember when I was working on *Jelly's Last Jam* on Broadway, and we were in previews and there was a lot that needed to be fixed, and as is the case in commercial theatre, it's incredibly brutal, but in previews it's especially brutal. Everybody's looking for someone to sacrifice to the gods of potential failure. I was very much in charge of the situation, receiving all these challenges and assaults. At one point it became very clear to me that my director brain could not fix what needed to be fixed, my writer brain was going to have to fix it. I sort of "clicked in" to the writer brain which has to be vulnerable and completely available, as opposed to the director brain which has to be smart and completely alert. I was still in charge, but people who had never messed with me during the whole experience, or people who had messed with me but hadn't been able to penetrate me, certain ones instantly knew that my director force-field was down. I stayed like that for an incredibly painful week, to see the piece and experience it in a different way if I was going to fix it successfully. It was like being vulnerable in the middle of napalm falling all around you. After about a week I slipped back into my director dragon mode and was able to kill off whatever gunk had built up around me and around the show while I was in my sensitive mode. It sounds sort of schizophrenic, but, I mean, it completely and totally is.

In one interview you talk about seeing *Hello, Dolly!* with Pearl Bailey and how exciting that was. Also, I know you have a degree in musical theatre. When I read that I thought that it explains certain things about your writing.
I think almost every play I've ever created has had music in it. Because music and laughter are the two things that create instant trust in an audience. You can make an audience laugh, or the sound of music, the

sound of rhythm, makes them instantly surrender. Whereas in a dramatic play, a straight play, you have to talk for a good ten minutes before you win people's trust, because we're trained naturally to dissect the lies of language, whereas we're trained instantly to surrender to laughter and music. So, the director side of me—I love manipulating an audience, taking them down one alley where they're just laughing along, but then I love pulling the rug out from underneath them and throwing in a truth. And they go, "My God, I wasn't ready for that, but I've already swallowed it so I guess I have to keep swallowing it." I love that more than anything else in the theatre, when you violate wildly an audience's expectations. Laughter and music are just two things I choose to use as much as I can to achieve that result. I'm also just fascinated by heightened expressions of communication which can articulate in extraordinary ways the human spirit soaring, which dance can do, and song can do, which becomes mythic, and in some strange Aristotelian principle becomes a manifestation of spectacle. But it's the spectacle of the human heart, as opposed to the spectacle of a helicopter taking off or a chandelier crashing.

So music can penetrate, and I love it that theatre is such a whore, and I love those moments when in the middle of this hybrid art form an artistic expression of purity takes place because then I think it makes both the harshness of the mutt and the beauty of the pureness exist in relation to each other. Like, say, opera is profoundly not interesting to me because it's all sung, so that after a while nothing matters. People die for opera, I'm just not one of those people. I love the collision, the tension between the frailty, the vulgarity, the harshness, the lyricism of the human voice, all of its forms from speech to chant to moan to song. Certain emotions just lift and you surrender to them instantly if it's sung. And rhythm is probably the thing that I obey more than music. As a director and as a writer, once I understand a theme's rhythm, once I understand a character's rhythm, then I know instantly what to do with them. I need to understand that more than anything else, because then I can connect to it on a completely intuitive level. My brain is there, my emotions are there, my heart is there. So I have the skills to think and craft these things out, but I much prefer this unconscious understanding, and rhythm is one of the easiest ways I can click into and understand that.

One thing that fascinates me about musical theatre is how seductive it is.
Completely and totally.

That's precisely what you're describing. An erotic component comes through—in rhythm, melody or just bodies moving on stage.

And you will surrender. A really good musical just grabs you and takes you where it wants you to go: "Come over here, now stand still, now watch this." It has to do that, otherwise you won't believe it, you'll pull back and start to judge it. Like a really great party should never let you out for air, because then you gain a perspective, but when you're inside the party and you're eating and drinking and people are dancing, you surrender a certain kind of control.

What you're describing is exactly what Jelly's strategies are as a musician, as a man: to be the seducer, to arrange everything. It seems to me that so many of the great musicals are precisely about pleasure, about seduction.
Exactly.

So many are backstage musicals, they're about musical theatre itself, about the power of music.
And they're also pieces that are very specifically about America, and America is about the collision of rhythms and about who owns history. It was the most fascinating thing, when I was directing *The Tempest*, the piece became about who owns history. In the first scene, Prospero tells Miranda for the first time in her life, her history, their history. In the second scene, she defies him, because now she owns her own history. When I first realized that it was so startling. To control Ariel, Prospero tells her her history. He tries to do it with Caliban, but Caliban has his own history, so Caliban tells him back, "You have your version of your history, this is my version of your history." So that became the crux of their adversarial relationship. Much like what Jelly and the Chimney Man are about. Jelly's going to tell his version of history, and the Chimney Man's going to say, "No, this is my version of history!" It's who owns your history. Growing up in a segregated town, and going to a black private school, I was told my history very early on. As a sort of Bible. As a weapon, not just a series of facts, but as a means of survival and empowerment. So if you know your history, it will empower you to go into this potentially hostile world and survive in a whole other way. So almost every single work I've been draw to, or worked on, or created is about fully claiming your history.

To me your act of claiming seems to be an archaeological project. Your work is so much about going back to the past and understanding it. Both *Bring in 'da Noise* and *Colored Museum* begin in middle passage.
Exactly. Because if a black person is lucky, they can trace it back to that. I saw a photo of my great-great-grandmother who came over from Africa, and I can't tell you what that did to me, what that settled inside

of me. And learning about Africans going to Brazil did the exact same thing. In Brazil, because of Catholicism and the politics of the way the Portuguese abused slaves as opposed to the way the Puritans abused slaves, Africanisms are allowed to live in a much more overt way. Whereas in the United States the Africanisms became subliminal, and choose to live in various other ways, either in language, rhythm, food. I view Brazil and the United States as reflections of one another, as a kind of cultural picture that complete one another. And that was extraordinarily important to find out the tangibles of my family, to talk to as many people, and fill in as many blanks. That was deeply important to me, I could now attach an intellectual reasoning to the hunger, "I must know this, tell me this, tell me this, tell me this." So the fact that it's in my work is just an extension of something I've been actively searching for all my adult life. History as a means of empowerment, going back to *The Tempest*.

As you're talking about this, I see that it's not only an archaeological process, but a question of taking control.
Precisely.

Letting it live, and making a new kind of history.
Everybody in America is a mutt. It's like some Gothic novel, the mutt is always searching for purity. How the bastard can be claimed, can no longer live in the cottage but move into the mansion because he's really the child of the lord. And Americans love to create romance. White Americans do it about Europe, you know, and black people create this fantasy Africa that never existed. Extraordinary Africas did exist, but not this fantasy Africa that black Americans walk around with. The Americas are their own sort of bizarre creation. If you search for purity and you're not pure, you're either going to function from a place of delusion or inadequacy. Whereas if you go searching for your own complexity, it's going to be a much more fulfilling solution. So to me that's been the goal: to try as a human being not to choose this quality over that quality, but to try to embrace all of them. That's so much what *The Colored Museum* was all about, "I'm not what I was ten years ago or ten minutes ago, I'm all of that and then some."

When I first came to New York, people were very confused by various projects that I was writing. Because here I was this black writer writing in all these different forms, and most of the plays that were being done for black audiences were these socioeconomic, realistic, "Last Mama-on-the-Couch" plays. Which was one of the reasons I went after that. My imagination does not work that way. It doesn't fit inside of four walls, it just doesn't, and it never will. So I wrote *The Colored Museum* not just as a person of color, but as a form of liberation, so that after I wrote that play, I said, "Now I can write any play." It's why it experiments with form as much as it does, why it collides images, to become some sort of treatise in which I can say, "As a person who creates theatre, I'm going to function completely by my own rules. I will not be placed in a category, I will not be forced to write 'Mama, I'm cryin' 'cause I got so much pain.'" That was my way of freeing myself, of standing naked in the middle of Times Square going, "This is it."

So it's about dramatizing contradictions, not a question of either/or, but both/and.
And I got trashed for it! I got trashed by a lot of black people for it because they didn't see the flip side, they only saw the side that nobody's supposed to talk about. At the time it was painful, but then you realize that it's just part of the essential intellectual or psychological or emotional baby that you need to lose in order to go to the next level.

On the one hand, your work is clearly a break from the realistic tradition of writers like August Wilson, but on the other hand, it seems to me there are clear antecedents for your work, for example the Black Arts movement.
I don't think August is that realistic. I think his plays have been packaged in a realistic form in productions, but I think he experiments with form all the time. I think they've just been put in boxes that look like reality, but they aren't reality.

That was exactly my impression when I interviewed him ten years ago for the first volume.
I don't know a black writer whose writing isn't heavily informed and defined by either jazz or the blues or vaudeville. Vaudeville and minstrel show is a huge form for me—it's bottomless to me in terms of its structure, what it does. So some plays of August's are jazz, some are ragtime, because there are secrets in those rhythms, they aren't just music.

And both *Jelly's Last Jam* and *Bring in 'da Noise* are so consciously dealing with those forms, histories, rituals, stereotypes.
I remember when I first started working on *Jelly* I would listen to all his music, and I'd find myself drawn to certain songs, and the song would give me a moment or a story or a something in the piece, and then when we started working, if we would slow the song down then suddenly all this emotion . . . Even the song, "Lovin' is a Lowdown Blues," which Susan Birkenhead wrote this sort of wonderfully erotic, dirty lyric for, the tempo is fast. Slowed down it's the sexiest, darkest thing you'd ever

want to see. It's in the music and nothing got changed with the melody, it's just in the phrasing of the musician playing it that day, because jazz and the blues are so intensely personally interpreted that they can't help but reveal the human emotions. Even though the notes were written down, the musician would bend and twist the notes to put himself or herself in the music. So when you go to the music, you can't help but get a piece of the person who played it.

At the same time, you're getting the sense of an entire community.
That's precisely the thrust of *Jelly's Last Jam*. Intellectually and ego-wise, I understand why you claim you invented jazz. You did not invent jazz. A people, a circumstance, invented jazz. You are clearly a brilliant messenger of the form, but you're not allowed to say that, in my opinion. I showed an early version of the script to Joe Papp, and it was the first act, and it was very different. Anita, Jelly's girlfriend, was his adversary who was forcing him to go on this journey. At the end of act one, this character called the Chimney Man appeared and blew black dust in Jelly's face. That was his only appearance. Joe had read the script, and he'd write these little comments. Then he came and said, "Now that Chimney character, there's something interesting there." I was like, "Yeah, yeah," because it was a meeting with two of the producers, so he was showing off a little bit, but about two or three months later it became very clear to me that the Chimney Man was going to become the other important character. I was developing it, and I was talking to Joe one day and I said, "Joe, you know the thing you said about that Chimney character, well he has become my other character." And he said, "Do you want to know why?" And I went, "Okay, why, Joe?" And he said, "Because you hadn't found your voice in the piece, you hadn't found somebody to say the things you wanted to say about the character. And that's what the Chimney Man became." He was completely and totally right. Once I could find that voice I was free to live inside the piece in a completely different way. I was still in the process of fusing history and theatricality, but I hadn't found a way to make that battle live inside the piece.

Because the Chimney Man is also the emcee who calls up Jelly's spirit.
And also in many respects he's representative of the Trickster figure who in the pantheon ultimately does not have a tremendous amount of power, but is completely and totally available to the people. He's not the president, he's the councilman. The Trickster's in folklore all over the world, because it's the people without power who can touch him, who can reach him.

So he, too, is the voice of the collective.

As a protector and a deity as well, because I took the figure of Barón Sam Dee from Haitian voodoo, and combined him with the physical silhouettes of the chimney sweeps from New Orleans in Jelly's time. The Barón Sam Dee character from Haiti has a top hat and a cutaway and a cigar, the ashes from it are the sperm that he's repopulating the Earth with. So it's taking the form of this chimney sweep and combining it with this Haitian god and putting them together.

I'm really interested in Jelly's function as a ghost. I saw it on Broadway, but when I was reading it, I couldn't help thinking about New Orleans. The fact that no city is as haunted as New Orleans, and I think that *Jelly's Last Jam* is very much about that haunted past.

Because in New Orleans they acknowledge the dead. Why show up at a place where they aren't gonna throw you a party? That's why I think there are so many ghosts there, because they go to a place where somebody's going to receive them. Not these hard, nonbelieving, urban places. Who believes anything up here? You can see there was something before you and that you're part of that continuum. Large, impersonal, urban landscapes make you—in the little boxes that you live in—believe that it is about you.

So he brings a sense of the past, of history, with him and he's also a voice of a people. I hadn't really thought about the ghost as the expression of a collectivity, but I see now that's also how it functions.

I believe that my ancestors are around me all the time, it's a fully evolved belief system. I had my house burned, I guess about two years ago, and I was sleeping in my bed, and the beams had completely burned over my head all night. The smoke stayed trapped between the ceiling and the floor. The beams were completely burned. No fire ever dropped down on me. It is a miracle that I am alive today. My grandmother's picture was over the bed the whole time. She had been in a fire, with burns over two-thirds of her body, and so nobody on the planet can convince me she was not protecting me, because there's no logical reason why those beams did not fall down on me or the smoke did not suffocate me. This was all night. I woke up at 8:30 the next morning. So I completely and totally believe that the people who came before me are with me all the time.

So history for you is not the least bit abstract. It's here around us, in us.

Exactly, and the more information, the more lines that get filled in—at one point I found out about a great uncle on my father's side who was a labor organizer in the hills in Kentucky and a great orator who could give great speeches and rouse up the crowd. And one night—he was about twenty-four or twenty-five—like four in the morning, these men knocked on his door and said the sheriff wanted to see him outside, and he walked out and was shot, assassinated. They never found out who killed him. If my being is like this brick wall that's fallen down, that's like a brick, a ruin, you don't know exactly how that piece of the column fits in. And then you hear that story and—boom!—you know exactly how that piece fits in. And so you are built by that, you come closer to completing yourself every time you hear one of these stories. And because that has happened to me, I'm always addressing some relationship to history, because I think that's the most interesting thing you can know about yourself: how you got to this point, and who got you there.

How do you write a play? How do you start?
It's different things. Now there's this realistic play that's building in my body, and I'm going, Oh my God, does it really have to be realistic? People sitting around in chairs and talking? I'm trying to understand it, to me it's like characters are in the room next door to me, and the door is closed. I hear the dialogue going on, but I don't know what they're saying yet. This is where the isolation comes in, because you've got to isolate yourself from other people's rhythms, from popular culture rhythms—I can't listen to music or read when I'm writing—so that I can move my overt sense of self out of the way and listen. What's so complicated about directing is you have to have an extraordinary sense of yourself, because what you're doing is sculpting space and people in relationship to that reality. You can bully people, or you can be charming, but you have to be acutely aware of yourself, your relationship to other people all the time. When you write, you let yourself go, it's not about you at all, so I'm trying to get clicked into the discipline of letting that all go, so I can hear what's going on in the next room. I can hear it, but I can't hear it. The hearing comes from surrendering to it. Also, the plays living inside my head are getting more personal. I'm older, I've lived through periods of my life, so I can see them. Up to this point I was trapped inside of them. I sort of celebrated them and mourned them, too.

That's one reason why Jelly is a ghost.
Exactly.

The play is an act of mourning.
Completely and totally. At one point, in theory, all artists have to replace ambition with grace, and I think that, subjectively speaking,

that was an impossible thing for him to do, because in his life he never got what he deserved, ever. So long after that period when the grace should have entered, he was still holding on to that idea, "One day I will get my parade, I will get my due. It will happen in this life."

So part of it is about his own losses . . .
. . . that have never been processed. He just kept on borrowing confidence from the next day and going forward. What happens when you get to that day and there is no next day, you get to the end? All the loss happens in one day, and I think that's what happened to him. That's what happens in the piece, all the loss he never experienced he's forced to confront in one day. Which he does, so ultimately he can be free of it and not have the weight of that dragging him down to Hell. If you can't let it go, it drags you down, if you release it, you lift. Hell's not about sin, Hell's about carrying too much pain with you once you're no longer alive.

You don't have to get rid of it, but you have to deal with it.
While you're alive. Culturally, too, those who don't remember the past are condemned to repeat it. Also, the wonderful James Baldwin quote, "People are trapped in history and history is trapped in them."

As you're describing your process of writing, you sound like a kind of medium, hearing otherworldly conversations and transcribing them.
I also think as a child you store so much stuff. Adults will say things you just don't understand. Realities will happen that you have no idea, so you just store it somewhere. All this information, about people, about things that you see—you know it's interesting, so you just put it away for a while. And as you get older a lot of these things that you hear are things that you heard, and you didn't know what they were. And those things just start talking to you, you start remembering things, or hearing things, or your grandparents say things. I've written things that characters have said who possess a wisdom that I just don't have. I'm sure it's a wisdom I heard my grandmother say. I'm fascinated by things that you know before you understand them. I don't mean to make it sound so mystical, but . . .

And I'm encouraging you by asking about ghosts.
That's not a leap for me.

I was a bit surprised to see John Lahr describe you as a folklorist. Do you think of yourself in those terms?
Not specifically.

There are folkloristic elements in *Spunk*.

That's Zora's stuff. That language is just like taking a shower in some-thing luxurious, it's so extraordinary. I think that's more my Southern-ness, because the way Southerners use language, everybody in my hometown speaks in run-on sentences, and they will repeat things twice. So, because I stuttered when I was little, I still do sometimes, I think I listened to people's rhythms, and was acutely aware of my own. It was so much that my brain was working faster than my tongue could. So it's more the Southern thing. I also have an intense passion for folk art. It's the thing I love about early blues. There's this song "Black Snake" that I tried to use in *Spunk*. It's like, "Oh, oh, blacksnakecom-erunaroundmydoor," it's got all these words and they really don't fit in the form that the blues has taken, but whoever wrote it decided he was going to fit all those word in there. That's what folk art does: you bend the form, just to fit your agenda or your limitations or your skills. I have this figure I bought in Sicily where the lower body is extremely short, and then the torso, head and arms are large, almost life-sized. So, I thought, Either that person only had a small piece of wood, or he was very good at making torsos and not lower bodies. But that person's skill and limitations are both on display in this piece of art. So, it's the imper-fections of the human spirit, and the reaching of the human spirit, that are embedded so intensely in folk art. I think that should be the case in all art. I just love that dynamic that in its imperfection is such extraor-dinary beauty and reach and fragility and damage and heroics.

I was interested to hear you talk about theatre at the beginning of this interview as a strange hybrid, a mutt, which is precisely the word you have used to describe Americans. Which suggests to me certain things about your idea of theatre and how central it is to being an American. How do you see them as working together?

That's why I love the musical theatre form. Even though most of the time I don't think it accesses the potential of the form. They usually end up accessing some sort of dumb, giddy joy, or now we're going through this period of the dark, dull epic. If it's dark and dull, it's gotta be art. No, it's just dark and dull. It's sort of what I love about Shakespeare. Sometimes it's in exquisite verse, sometimes it's in the bawdiest, cheap-est vaudeville language that he could possibly come up with, and the tension between the two is the brilliance, not just the beautiful poetic language, but the tension between the two, going back to the folk art thing. That's what I love: the tension between now I'm singing, now I'm speaking, now I'm dancing. And how they collide with each other. All of the art forms that I can find myself so easily inside of, going back to Greek theatre, have those heightened components. It's the smallness of the human figure reaching for something godlike, mythic and pure. And not achieving it, reaching for it. That's where the power lives.

Which is precisely how America is imagined, we have this country with this nightmare history, and yet America was founded as a utopian nation, and we're still reaching for that.
You couldn't have jazz without one of the parents being the nightmare. It would not have happened. That to me is what's extraordinary about that, that the violation has given birth culturally to not only some ugly, crass children, but some exquisitely beautiful children who have transformed the world. And yet those beautiful children very probably would not have been born of beautiful parents. That's what's amazing about this country: we took somethin' from nuthin' and made it somethin'. As simple as that phrase is, that's that.

But you're also talking about the magic of theatre. Making something from nothing.
Exactly, "The magic of . . ." It is a metaphor for theatre, it is a metaphor for creativity, for black American culture—which is a world culture, as opposed to being an American culture. So it's all of this. It's just fascinating, the crafting of the broken parts into an object that's playful and mocking and ridiculous and exquisite at the same time.

As producer, how do you feel about all of the very serious problems that theatre has been confronting? How do we keep theatre alive in this country?
I don't know. One has to count on the fact that there will always be clueless, passionate people who, for whatever childhood mistake, are drawn to wanting to release their creativity in this art form. I don't know, I think as technology becomes more and more sophisticated, and more and more available . . . when you separate theatre from community you're placing it in a very dangerous, precarious state. Because theatre can only exist within a community, and Broadway has absolutely nothing to do with community. Occasionally a project can come into that landscape, say *Angels in America*, and it can bring with it a sense of community based on the people that it attracts, but the commercial landscape has nothing to do with community whatsoever. That's just where you go to play. And community keeps on becoming more and more endangered in this country. So, in addition to reactionary, right-wing people, and to funding decreasing, what's scariest to me is the dissolution of community. So much of what we've tried to create here at The Public, through various outreaches, is a connection with various communities, so that people feel some sort of ownership about this building.

That's always been the mission of this theatre.

That's the name of the place, The Public. The challenge is to figure out how to solidify that as the age changes, as people are less and less interested in visiting landscapes that are not their own—people are really only interested in seeing themselves. I think that's one of the advantages that Joe once had. People felt a cultural and social obligation to enter into other people's worlds. There's still a population that feels that way, but it's a shrinking minority.

I've noticed that theatre tends to survive and to be most exciting on the cultural margins, as an expression for people who do not have access to other media.

Exactly, the thing which one counts on is that there is something intrinsic to the human condition, because we're a pack animal that loves being in the middle of a clump of people. Our power is in being a part of the pack, so I think there's just a genetic need that the human animal has to periodically find itself in the middle of a clump of people. One of the places you can still do that is the theatre.

You're talking about the difference between what goes on in this theatre and the commercial Broadway stage. How do you feel then about moving *Bring in 'da Noise* uptown? Does that mean the community was lost?

Yes, if you don't go out to those communities and drop Hansel and Gretel bread crumbs all the way from the Bronx to the Ambassador Theatre. We've also done that in every city around the country. Three to four months before it goes on tour, Donna Walker-Kuhne, who heads the community affairs department here, goes out and creates community outreach in every single city that *Noise/Funk* is going to. So, by the time the show lands in their city, those people feel ownership of the show. We've found corporations who are willing to give money for a thing called "Bring in the Kids," where they pledge to buy ten tickets, twenty tickets, a hundred tickets so that these kids can come to see the show free. So that if you're going into that landscape and community doesn't exist, then you've got to do your fieldwork and create a structure whereby theatre can exist there. Otherwise it just wouldn't happen. And the theatregoing experience wouldn't be the same. That all these people who only share airspace in New York City are sitting in the same room. You get extraordinarily young kids, you get the old people, you get the fabulous New Yorkers who come to see it. They're all in one room. They're part of a collective experience. In almost any other scenario, they wouldn't deal with each other at all. I think there's a certain tension in the air that gets released through the show, so it's urban cultural therapy, in some fascinating way. We're all arriving at the same rhythm, watching a show that's about nothing but rhythm from the second it begins to the second it ends.

When I went to see it shortly after it opened on Broadway, I really felt something working itself out in that theatre.
Also, rhythmically what it does, because it assaults, then it caresses, it invites you in and then it slaps, and it keeps on varying so that the rhythm that is inside of you is forced to surrender. You can't pull back, you've got to go on the journey. That to me is what's craftsmanlike and intellectually fascinating about that show.

Although I think *Jelly's Last Jam* works in a similar way.
What's different is, it's like *Jelly* moves into a house and it knocks down all the walls, but it doesn't really rearrange the house. It rearranges all the furniture, but it acknowledges the form, because it's taking a black musical form and redefining it, completely and totally by its own rules. *Bring in 'da Noise*, from the beginning of the show, knocks down the walls and says, "Okay, I'm in charge, follow us." That's what I like about *Jelly*, it was a musical, but the story that it told and the imagery that it told was completely and totally different. The phrase I use all the time is cultural strip-mining, which is what I think Broadway musicals have done with black rhythms. They mine it for the ore, but they take out all the dirt and the stuff which allowed the ore to grow.

The context.
Exactly. The context and the history and the texture. So you get the juice, but none of the grit. You get the gravy but you don't get any of the grime, and then you're not getting the human thing. You're getting something else, but it don't got anything to do with being human.

Do you want to say anything else about your plans for the future? I realize you wear a lot of different hats.
I guess my big human goal is to try to write more consistently. I have a couple of new plays I've been trying to work on, but it's been very difficult in relationship to being a producer. I'm a very disciplined person, but I have to have another level of discipline in order to deal with that. I sometimes wonder whether I'll stop directing, sooner rather than later. I'm an artist, I do it, I think it is artful or artistic, but I don't consider directing an art, I think it's a craft. Which means I love it and I love being in a room making theatre, crafting theatre as a director, but I'm not sure how fulfilling it is to the soul. I think it's fulfilling to a bunch of other aspects of myself, but I don't think it's very fulfilling to

my soul. The child in me likes it and the smart person who likes to solve problems likes it and the person who likes to be a part of a community, all those aspects of me are completely in love with it. It used to nourish me, but it doesn't nourish me anymore. This producing thing is interesting. I sort of get it now, but I don't know what it is. It's taken a while.

This is your fourth year here?
I don't know what the hell it is, maybe my fifth year. I feel like I was born in this building. I think I've been doing it long enough that I understand the craft of the job. At first it was just passion. Then I tried to do it with passion and skill. Now I understand the craft, which is the most basic level. So now I know how to make it function on its most basic level, then I can add in passion or skill or flourish anytime I need it. So, fundamentally, I don't kill myself, which I came very close to. It's fascinating. The thing that I like most about the job is that I love talking to artists. My least favorite people to talk to are directors, they're just impossible people. I have no idea, I think something's coming and it could be writing or it could be film. Since 1986, film people have been dancing with me, but I think ultimately I'm too unruly a partner for them, because I like doing things my way. I really don't know. It's an interesting time. I'm very glad I can go dabble in the commercial work, but I'm also just as glad that I don't have to live there. I could live there, but I'm glad I don't have to. You do find your own life, but I can't see doing a Broadway show, then another Broadway show, then another Broadway show. But I love playing there sometimes. And I love the war zone of it, the ego challenge of it, I love to go exercise those muscles and then get out. Right now I'm here, I don't know what's next. There will be a next, I just don't know when that next is coming.

David Savran has published widely on American theatre, film and popular culture. His journalistic work includes a previous book of interviews, *In Their Own Words: Contemporary American Playwrights*, also published by TCG. His most recent works of cultural theory are *Communists, Cowboys and Queers: The Politics of Masculinity in the Work of Arthur Miller and Tennessee Williams* and *Taking It Like a Man: White Masculinity, Masochism and Contemporary American Culture*. He is Professor of English at Brown University.

Related TCG Books:

Jon Robin Baitz

A Fair Country; The Substance of Fire and Other Plays; Three Hotels: Plays and Monologues

Philip Kan Gotanda

Ballad of Yachiyo

Tony Kushner

Angels in America, Part One: Millenium Approaches; Angels in America, Part Two: Perestroika; A Bright Room Called Day; A Dybbuk and Other Tales of the Supernatural (adapted from S. Ansky); *The Illusion* (freely adapted from Pierre Corneille); *Thinking About the Longstanding Problems of Virtue and Happiness: Essays, a Play (Slavs!), Two Poems and a Prayer*

Suzan-Lori Parks

The America Play and Other Works; Venus

José Rivera

Marisol and Other Plays

Nicky Silver

Etiquette and Vitriol (The Food Chain and Other Plays); Raised in Captivity

Paula Vogel

The Baltimore Waltz and Other Plays; The Mammary Plays (How I Learned to Drive and *The Mineola Twins)*

George C. Wolfe

Jelly's Last Jam (lyrics by Susan Birkenhead); *Spunk: Three Tales by Zora Neale Hurston*

Related TCG Books (continued):

Between Worlds: Contemporary Asian-American Plays, Misha Berson, Editor; includes work by Philip Kan Gotanda

Coming to Terms: American Plays & the Vietnam War; includes work by Terrence McNally *(out of print)*

Moon Marked and Touched by Sun: Plays by African-American Women, Sydné Mahone, Editor; includes work by Suzan-Lori Parks, Ntozake Shange and Anna Deavere Smith

On New Ground: Contemporary Hispanic-American Plays, M. Elizabeth Osborn, Editor; includes work by José Rivera

Out from Under: Texts by Women Performance Artists, Lenora Champagne, Editor; includes work by Holly Hughes

The Way We Live Now: American Plays and the AIDS Crisis, M. Elizabeth Osborn, Editor; includes work by Terrence McNally and Tony Kushner